EVALUATING COUPLES

A Handbook for Practitioners

By the same author

Family evaluation (with Eric Strauss)
Family resources: The Hidden Partner in Family Therapy (Editor)

A Norton Professional Book

EVALUATING COUPLES

A Handbook for Practitioners

Mark A. Karpel, Ph.D.

W. W. NORTON & COMPANY
New York • London

Composition by Bytheway Typesetting Services, Inc.

Manufacturing by Haddon Craftsmen, Inc.

Library of Congress Cataloging-in-Publication Data

Karpel , Mark A .
Evaluating couples : a handbook for practitioners / Mark A.
Karpel .
    p . cm .
    " A Norton professional book . "
    Includes bibliographical references.
    ISBN 0-393-70180-8
    1 . Family assessment . 2. Marital psychotherapy 3. Interviewing
in psychiatry . I. Title .
    [DNLM: 1 . Marital Therapy . WM 55 K18e 1994]
RC488.53.K37 1994
616.89 ' 156--dc20
DNLM/DLC
for Library of Congress   94-32970
                                                              CIP

W.W. Norton & Company, Inc., 500 Fifth Avenue, New York, NY 10110
W.W. Norton & Company, Ltd., 10 Coptic Street, London WC1A 1PU

2 3 4 5 6 7 8 9 0

For Denise

CONTENTS

ACKNOWLEDGMENTS

I AM DEEPLY INDEBTED to two individuals in particular for their generous support on this project. My wife, Denise Gelinas, provided abundant encouragement, editorial feedback, and clinical expertise. I am grateful for her understanding when I was working on the book and for her excellent company when I wasn't. Eric Strauss provided invaluable support and encouragement, as a sounding-board, editor, and friend. Eric read much of the manuscript in draft form and was always available with a seasoned and sensible opinion when I "lost the forest for the trees." Harold Raush helped in a similar way at one critical point; Joel Feinman provided feedback on several chapters. Several individuals helped with the book's final section by reviewing chapters in their areas of expertise and, in some cases, agreeing to be interviewed on the subject as well: Michelle Bograd, Lewis Breitner, Lewis Cohen, JoAnn Krestan, Joseph LoPiccolo, Susan McDaniel, Richard Meth, Eric Strauss, and Stephen Treat. The following individuals provided concrete assistance, moral support, or intelligent advice: Ann

Bakis, Ellen Berman, Eva Brown, Betty Carter, Hap Dunne, Mark Haffey, Joan Kagan, Ron Sabatelli, Suzanne Slater, Edward Tronick, and Lenore Walker. Susan Barrows Munro was responsive but never intrusive as an editor; Regina Dahlgren Ardini provided detailed copyediting and served as a gracious go-between on technical matters. Finally, my thanks to my children, Madeleine and Marshall, for their patience and their threats to "blockade the study" if I try to write another book soon.

INTRODUCTION

THIS IS A BOOK FOR practitioners. Its focus is on "what to do and how to do it" in work with couples. It is written in response to a peculiar anomaly in clinical practice, namely that although most therapists do treat couples, and couple therapy is professed to be hard work, very few therapists receive formal training for it. Besides therapists who specialize in couple therapy, those who work with couples include family therapists, many individual therapists, and sex therapists. Clinical work with couples is a routine part of divorce mediation, pastoral counseling, psychotherapy with children and adolescents, foster and adoptive placement, custody evaluations, and crisis intervention. It is a useful component of treatment for alcoholism and other substance abuse, depression, anxiety disorders, trauma, and serious medical illness.

Couple therapy has a (deserved) reputation among mental health professionals for being fairly difficult, particularly because the clinician can quickly wind up "in the soup"—losing focus and clinical distance, being caught in problematic triangulation, and experiencing debilitating countertransference. However, in spite of the risks and rigors of couple therapy and its widespread usage, it is relatively rare for professionals to receive any formal training in work with couples. This book is written, then, for any clinician who meets regularly with couples for whatever reason in his or her daily practice (or who wants to, but has been deterred by the daunting reputation of couple's work).

The book focuses on evaluation for two reasons. A careful, thorough evaluation of the couple can greatly minimize the potential problems and obstacles that arise later in couple therapy. In addition, evaluating couples may prove extremely valuable, both to clinicians and clients, in a variety of other clinical contexts in which *the primary complaint does not involve difficulties in a couple's relationship* and when *couple therapy is not recommended* following the evaluation.

The book provides a format for evaluating couples: for assessing the problems *and* resources they present, for deciding whether treatment is indicated (and, if so, for whom and what kind), for creating alliances with both partners, and for "setting the trajectory" of treatment—that is, choosing goals, methods, and conditions of treatment that will avoid potential obstacles and maximize the likelihood of successful outcomes. The book gives specific recommendations on every aspect of the evaluation, from the initial telephone call to the therapist's summary delivered to the couple at its conclusion.

When the evaluation does lead to couple therapy, it helps the clinician to "start out right"—to take advantage of opportunities and to side-step potential risks inherent in the opening phase of treatment. This is particularly helpful in couple therapy, where the definition of the problem may be contested between the partners and their goals and agendas for treatment may conflict. Choices regarding treatment are potentially complicated, as are the tasks of the therapist, who must try to express sympathy for both partners' experiences, accommodate to their sensitivities and represent both of their interests. These factors introduce a level of ethical and pragmatic complexity that is often greater than that found at the start of individual treatment.

Even when the evaluation is not followed by a recommendation for couple therapy, it serves to

- identify more promising recommendations
- facilitate the couple's acceptance of these recommendations
- help the therapist understand the primary relational context for a particular problem
- in some cases, secure a valuable ally for treatment

The goal of the evaluation is to help couples better understand the nature of their difficulties and make more informed decisions regarding possible treatment. It can serve either as a careful "first step" in couple therapy or as a distinct clinical procedure unrelated to couple therapy.

Evaluating Couples is designed for practitioners who devote a majority of their professional time to treating couples and for those who do not but who want to sharpen their skills in this area. It is also designed to help students who are learning about counseling and psychotherapy, especially those who plan to conduct couple therapy, sex therapy, or family therapy. It will help them to "start off right" and to have a framework for evaluating couples in the context of other forms of treatment.

While the primary purpose of this book is to provide a detailed description of the pragmatics of evaluating couples, I also hope to provide a counterweight to certain oversights, or imbalances, in the literature on couple relationships. Both conceptual material and recommendations for the conduct of the evaluation will stress the importance of *fairness* and *trustworthiness* (the ethical dimension of close relationships), as well as *sexuality* and *gender* as organizing forces in couple relationships. I want to encourage readers to look for and, if possible, to promote resources, or strengths, in couple relationships. Finally, I try to move away from idealized models and assumptions and to encourage readers to think instead about "good-enough" (Winnicott, 1960) couple relationships as well as the criteria of a good-enough couple evaluation.

One of the tasks for the therapist who evaluates couples is to orient clients to the structure of the evaluation. This is my opportunity to orient the reader to the structure of this book, which parallels that of the evaluation. Part I provides a summary of basic assumptions about couple relationships — about the forces that organize and shape them and the gratifications and challenges they provide. Part I also examines the characteristics of couple relationships at a conceptual level before moving to guidelines for evaluation.

Chapter 1 examines the influence of attachment, attraction, and expectations in shaping interactional patterns, strengths, and difficulties in the relationship. Chapter 2 focuses on the "givens" of culture, gender, and the life cycle. Chapter 3 explores a number of organizing forces that present unavoidable challenges for couples, including commitment, autonomy and attachment, fairness and trust, sexuality, communication, the "unconscious matrix" of the relationship, its wider relational context, and vitality.

Part II covers the pragmatics of conducting the evaluation, and case examples are used to illustrate specific aspects of the evaluation. Chapter 4 introduces the format, which is elaborated in subsequent chapters. Chapter 5 presents guidelines for arranging the evaluation. Chapters 6 and 7 describe, respectively, the conduct of the initial couple session and the subsequent individual sessions with each partner. Both chapters move sequentially through these sessions. Chapter 6 describes opening the session, exploring the presenting problem, using "probe" questions, assessing resources, inquiring about the history of the relationship and previous treatment, and concluding the session. Chapter 7 suggests advantages, disadvantages, and specific clinical indicators for holding individual sessions with each partner as well as ground rules for the conduct of these meetings.

Chapter 8 moves back to conceptual material since, at this point in the evaluation, the therapist needs to develop a formulation of the couple's problems. This chapter utilizes questions for the therapist to consider in developing a formulation and, in this sense, a "conceptual checklist" of factors that commonly contribute to couples' difficulties. Chapter 9 presents basic considerations in deciding on treatment recommendations, as well as a number of common recommendations with clinical indications, contraindications, and guidelines for each. Chapter 10 offers suggestions for designing the therapist's response to the couple at the conclusion of the evaluation, while Chapter 11 describes the conduct of the final couple session in which this response is shared and discussed.

Chapter 12 discusses advantages and modifications involved in evaluating couples in other clinical contexts; Chapter 13 describes other formats for evaluating couples. Chapter 14 concludes Part II by providing criteria for a good-enough couple evaluation.

The next six chapters comprise Part III and focus on problems and patterns commonly encountered in clinical work with couples but which may or may not be the couple's primary complaint; they include, respectively, sexual difficulties, domestic violence, alcoholism, depression, extramarital involvements, and serious illness. Each chapter provides basic information, guidelines for assessment, considerations for treatment recommendations, and references for further reading for therapists and, in most cases, for clients as well.

A few clarifications are in order involving the use of language. Should we speak of "couple relationships" or "marriage"? "Couple therapy" or "marital therapy"? I've chosen the former in both cases in recognition of the fact that not all couple relationships are legally sanctioned. Many partners in stable, committed couple relationships choose not to marry for a variety of reasons. Homosexual couples, at the time of this writing, cannot marry legally in most states even if they choose to. Furthermore, while the fact of legal marriage may influence the evolution of the relationship in some ways, it does not create, as it were, a "different animal." The forces that organize couple relationships operate independently of legal sanction. For these reasons, I use the terms "couple relationship" and "couple therapy" rather than "marriage" and "marital therapy." Similarly, I use the terms "partner" rather than "spouse" and "couple evaluation" rather than "marital evaluation."

This choice still leaves a minor semantic question: Is it "couple therapy," "couples therapy," or "couple's therapy"? There is no uniform standard in this area; however, there is consistency in our usage of "family" (rather than "families") therapy and "individual" (rather than "individuals") therapy. With these usages in mind, I've chosen to refer to "couple relationships," "couple therapy," and "couple evaluation."

Finally, a distinction is made throughout the book between "couple therapy" and "couple sessions." The latter refers to the actual membership of a particular session; the former to an orientation to treatment with conceptual, practical and ethical underpinnings, which may well (and often does) involve conjoint sessions but needn't necessarily do so. As the terms are used here, "couple therapy" might utilize either conjoint or separate sessions with the partners or both; "couple sessions" always involve both partners in the session.

The book presents a picture of what one practitioner does in his work with couples. It draws on no one school or approach to therapy and does not represent a survey of existing formats. Chapter 13 examines other formats for evaluating couples based on available written accounts. This includes some discussion of paper-and-pencil "instruments" which are used by some clinicians to evaluate couples, but this is not a major focus of this volume. I rarely use these instruments in my own work; my impression is that the same is true for most practicing clinicians. Chapter 13 includes references to other sources that describe a wide range of instruments for evaluating couples. My preference is to direct the reader to those who are most familiar with these methods and to limit myself to what I know best: the process of evaluating couples through clinical interviewing.

While I present my own theoretical biases in Chapters 1, 2, 3, and 8, the recommendations for conducting evaluations throughout the book are somewhat "generic" or atheoretical. This is because the constraints of this clinical procedure—couple evaluation—impose a certain uniformity of practice. As in other forms of treatment, one finds that experienced practitioners with very different theoretical orientations often arrive at many similar conclusions about priorities, ground rules, and useful interventions. Much of the text here, derived from nearly 20 years of experience treating couples, is a combination of common sense and sound clinical principles. My hope is that *Evaluating Couples* will be useful to therapists who have varying theoretical orientations. The format for evaluation creates a structure or "container" which the therapist can "fill" with those questions and procedures he or she considers most important. My hope is that the book will contribute to readers' efforts to master the tasks of evaluating couples, to deliver more competent clinical services, and to feel more confident in this particular clinical domain.

EVALUATING COUPLES

A Handbook for Practitioners

I

COUPLES

THE CENTRAL FOCUS of this book is the process of evaluating couples—"what to do and how to do it." However, it makes little sense to launch into a discussion of "how" to evaluate without first introducing "what" is being evaluated. The following three chapters summarize my assumptions about the nature of couple relationships—about the forces that organize and shape them, about the gratifications they provide and the challenges they pose, and about what, after all, these relationships mean to us.

Imagine two individuals, each standing on a small raft, being carried along by the current of a river. Imagine that they form a connection by locking arms on each other's shoulders or by each placing one foot on the other's raft. Now each is balancing on his or her own raft and balancing across rafts with one another. The rafts cannot occupy the exact same spot so they are subject to slight differences in perturbation. One goes over a small rock; the other skirts a branch. The individuals try to maintain the connection, to take the dips and jolts in tandem.

1

Imagine further that each has to balance with others—parents, children, siblings, jobs, etc. Each partner carries the others on his or her shoulders, as if part of a delicately poised acrobatic act. Some of those they carry may get off; others may climb on. Either way, these changes briefly destabilize the shifting structure and call for new efforts to rebalance.

The metaphor suggests something of the emotional experience of being in a couple relationship. No one can stop the river or get off the raft. They can choose to travel *connected* or not. Travelling connected adds to both partners' individual stability, creating a more stable structure, but at the same time it requires a more strenuous effort at balance since each person has to balance not only his or her own acrobatic partners but those of the other as well. In addition, each is subject not only to the dips and jolts of his or her own raft but also to those of the other. The connection may save you at one moment from falling in when you hit a spot of turbulence; a moment later, you may be dumped by the currents your partner has encountered.

The image suggests the inexorable flow, the interdependence, the intricacy of balance, and the greater stability as well as greater vulnerability of each partner by virtue of this connection. If these trade-offs of stability were the only considerations, there would probably be a lot fewer people travelling down the river in tandem. But humans have a deep need for connection, beginning with the infant's inborn need for attachment (Ainsworth, Blehar, Waters, & Wall, 1978; Bowlby, 1969) and arcing across the life cycle. The hope, and often the reality, is that it is both comforting and enjoyable to have a partner in the journey downstream.

The raft metaphor also suggests something of the constraints within which couple relationships evolve. These relationships are influenced and shaped by certain inescapable organizing forces. The outcomes are not predestined but the constraints are never erased. When two people play racquetball, an infinite number of different sequences and outcomes are possible. However, the distances between floor, walls, and ceiling, the physical properties of the ball and the rackets, and the fixed givens of velocity and trajectory, muscle contraction, and caloric output are never suspended. They shape and constrain the game.

In couple relationships, these forces are artifacts of the chemistry of attachment between humans, the interpenetration of unconscious relational structures, the jostling of need against need, the evolution of relational systems over time, the confluence of family legacies, and the influence of cultural norms and expectations. Theory-building for couples and family systems involves an effort to identify these organizing forces. They "play out" in very different ways, depending on the idiosyncracies of the individuals involved, but their influence is un-avoidable.

These organizing forces constrain and direct interactional patterns between partners and present challenges with which they must grap-ple. The challenges are analogous to developmental tasks in the life cycle of individuals and families. The better the couple's resolution of each of these challenges, the more resilient and satisfying the relation-ship is likely to be. In other words, successful resolutions function as *resources* in the relationship. Good resolutions contribute to more successful, coordinated coping and to the longevity and vitality of the relationship; poor resolutions contribute to dissatisfaction, chronic conflict, alienation, separation, and divorce.

The forces that shape couple relationships begin with the universal human need for attachment, the experience of attraction, and the ex-pectations the partners bring to the relationship (along with the disap-pointments these expectations engender). The relationship is shaped by certain "facts of life," including the cultural milieu in which it is embedded, the fact of gender (along with cultural constructions of gender), and the inexorable passage of time. Lastly, the relationship is organized by a number of unavoidable challenges, including commit-ment, the dialectic of attachment and autonomy, fairness and trust, sexuality, communication, the "unconscious matrix" of the relation-ship, its wider relational context, and the importance of vitality.

In the following three chapters, each of these factors is addressed, along with the challenges they pose for couples and problematic pat-terns commonly associated with them. The discussion concludes by considering the characteristics of a good-enough—that is, a realisti-cally healthy—couple relationship.

~ 1 ~

THE ARC OF ATTACHMENT

Attachment

THE MOST OBVIOUS FACTS are the most easily overlooked and the most obvious fact about couple relationships is that they involve powerful emotional attachments between the partners. These attachments may bewilder the individuals involved and they may be as much a source of grief as of gratification, but they are a central fact—if not *the* central fact—of these relationships. Their power and tenacity seem to echo the earlier attachment between an infant and its mother (or other primary care-giver).

There are striking similarities between these two types of relationships. In both, the two individuals experience a powerful need to touch one another, to hold, and to be held. In both, nearness to the other enhances a feeling of safety while separation can lead to feelings of anxiety and fear. In both, there is a private language of gestures, nicknames, and shared jokes; there is play and the experience of joy. Both relationships provide comfort and soothing as well as excitement and

5

stimulation and, in both, the loss of the other leads to sadness and grief.*

These similarities are implicitly recognized in popular culture. For example, the vast majority of popular songs are either about the pain of longing for and losing a beloved person or the joy of having and holding the other. They can be seen, as Hendrix (1988) points out, in the behavior and language of lovers in the privacy of their relationship—the cooing and petting, the delight in each other's bodies, the holding and "molding," and the use of diminutive nicknames (including the nearly universal term, "baby").

These similarities are not coincidental. There is widespread agreement that both types of relationships express the same organizing principle of human development—attachment. The study of attachment over the last two decades has transformed our understanding of infant development (Ainsworth et al., 1978; Bowlby, 1969, 1973, 1980; Stern, 1985; Tronick, 1989), adolescence and adulthood (Main, Kaplan, & Cassidy, 1985), couple and family relationships (Diamond & Doane, 1990; Doane, Hill, & Diamond, 1991; Hazan & Shaver, 1987; Wynne, 1984) and psychological trauma (van der Kolk, 1987). Attachment theory derives from observations and studies of human infants and their primary care-givers as well as from research studies and naturalistic observation of nonhuman primates, other mammals, and some birds.

This tendency to form close enduring attachments is seen as a universal principle of human life; it is evident in the relationship between the newborn and his or her primary care-giver, in enduring couple relationships between adults (which may last until death), and in the relationship of the now-adult care-giver with his or her own children. The newborn's tendency to depend on, and maintain proximity to, a primary care-giver serves a vital biological function; it is essential for the infant's survival, given its relative helplessness for months—even years—after birth. The relationship is also essential for the infant to regulate internal states of distress (Tronick, 1989) and to develop a coherent sense of self (Stern, 1985). Needs for attachment are not considered to be derivative of needs for food, but rather as distinct from them and equally important for survival.

> Nor is the urgent desire for comfort and support in adversity regarded as childish. . . . Instead the capacity to make intimate emotional bonds with other individuals, sometimes in the careseeking role and

---

*This description is admittedly based on the ideal of such relationships. The fact that these characteristics are not always present has important implications for both human development and couple relationships.

sometimes in the caregiving one, is regarded as a principal feature of effective personality functioning and mental health (Bowlby, 1988, p. 121).

This earliest attachment relationship provides "a secure base" (Bowlby, 1988), which is essential for psychological health. Bowlby suggests that attachment is maintained by means of a control system in the central nervous systems of both newborn and care-giver that is "analogous to the physiological control systems that maintain . . . blood pressure and body temperature within set limits" (1988, p. 123). When contact is interrupted the newborn emits a distress cry, which triggers protective behavior from the care-giver. Research on nonhuman primates indicates that both the infant's distress call and the maternal response to the call are mediated by endogenous opioids in the brain (van der Kolk, 1987). This control system serves to maintain proximity between the infant and its attachment figure within certain limits of distance and accessibility. For example, in Rhesus monkeys less than six weeks old exploration rarely extends beyond a two-foot radius of the mother which is, as Bowlby (1969) points out, close enough for her to be able to reach out and pull the infant back to her at any time. As development proceeds the infant is increasingly able to tolerate separation from the mother and to explore its environment. He or she must, however, be able to safely return to her when separation becomes distressing, especially in response to fear, pain, and fatigue.

When the offspring feels secure, he or she will move away from the mother to explore the environment. When alarmed, anxious or unwell, he or she will feel an urge for proximity with the mother. This pattern of exploration from a secure base is characteristic of primate and mammalian development. The developing human infant uses different capacities and stratagems as they become available in the service of attachment. Clinging and the separation cry (Bowlby, 1973) serve to restore proximity to the care-giver immediately after birth. Later, gazing (Stern, 1985; Tronick, 1989), smiling (Izard, 1982), gesturing, and babbling will serve the same ends, as will speaking and locomoting at one to two years.

As Bowlby (1980) indicates, attachment relationships are inseparable from an intense emotional life.

Many of the most intense emotions arise during the formation, the maintenance, the disruption and the renewal of attachment relationships. The formation of a bond is described as falling in love, maintaining a bond as loving someone, and losing a partner as grieving over someone. Similarly, threat of loss arouses anxiety and actual loss gives rise to sorrow; while each of these situations is likely to

arouse anger. The unchallenged maintenance of a bond is experienced as a source of security and the renewal of a bond as a source
of joy. . . . the psychology and psychopathology of emotion is . . . in
large part the psychology and psychopathology of affectional bonds.
(p. 40)

Disruption of this relationship, as noted by van der Kolk (1987), is
devastating.

> In . . . monkeys, social isolation for various periods during the first
> year of life produces grossly abnormal social and sexual behavior.
> Isolated monkeys do not produce offspring, and artificially insemi-
> nated females will mutilate or kill their babies. Young monkeys who
> are separated from their mothers become socially withdrawn and
> unpredictably aggressive. They also develop self-destructive and self
> stimulating behaviors such as huddling, self-clasping, self-sucking,
> and biting (Harlow & Harlow, 1971; Sackett, 1965; Sackett, Griffin,
> Pratt et al., 1967; Sackett, 1972). (cited in van der Kolk, p. 35)

Spitz (1945, 1965) and others have also demonstrated the catastrophic
effects of early separation from the primary care-giver in humans.

Human and nonhuman primate infants develop attachment to a
specific care-giver; other care-givers are not readily accepted as substi-
tutes. Very young infants are able to discriminate between their primary care-giver and others. For example, DeCasper and Fifer (1980)
demonstrated that neonates can discriminate their mother's voice
from another woman's voice reading the same material. Bowlby (1988)
notes that within days of birth infants can distinguish their mothers
by smell and by the way in which they are held by her. Separation from
the primary care-giver elicits anxiety and distress; reunion provides
comfort and security.

Significantly, for the infant to experience the absence of its particular care-giver and the need for reunion, there must be some form of
internal representation of the self and the care-giver. Bowlby (1988)
refers to these as "working models"; Stern (1985) prefers the term "RIGs"
(Representations of Interactions that have been Generalized). These
internal representations correspond to those inferred by many clinicians (Dicks, 1967; Fairbairn, 1952; Hendrix, 1988; Kantor, 1980;
Scharff & Scharff, 1991; Winnicott, 1958, 1965, 1971); they play an
important role in organizing interaction in couple relationships, a
topic that will be discussed later in this chapter and in Chapter 3.

Ainsworth et al. (1978) postulated three common patterns of attachment. In the pattern of *secure attachment*, the infant or child is confident that the care-giver will be available, responsive, and helpful if he

or she is in need. This allows the child to feel safe enough to be able to explore the environment. The pattern is fostered by a care-giver who is readily available, sensitive to the child's signals, and responsive when he or she seeks protection or comfort. A second pattern is referred to as *anxious resistant attachment*. This describes the child who is uncertain about whether the care-giver will be available and responsive if needed. In light of this insecurity, the child is especially prone to separation anxiety and tends to be clingy and afraid to explore the environment. This pattern is fostered by a care-giver who is only erratically available and responsive, and by separations and "threats of separations used as a means of control" (Bowlby, 1988, p. 124). The third pattern is referred to as *anxious avoidant attachment*, and describes the child who has learned from prior experience that care will not be given if it is sought and that he or she may be forcefully rejected. The child ceases to look for caretaking and tries to become emotionally self-sufficient. This pattern is fostered by a care-giver who repeatedly rejects the child when care is sought.

A variety of studies demonstrate that these attachment patterns tend to *endure* over time and that they can *generalize* to relationships other than those between the child and the original care-giver. Patterns of attachment observed between mother and child at 12 months of age are highly predictive of interactional patterns between them when the child is 2½ years (Matas, Arend, & Sroufe, 1978) and at age 6 (Main & Cassidy, 1988; Wartner, 1986). The type of attachment observed at 12 months was also found to predict how the child would behave in a nursery group, with mother absent, at age 4½ years (Sroufe, 1983). While the persistance of these patterns is initially a reflection of actual experiences in the relationship, it is assumed that over time a pattern becomes increasingly a property of the child so that "he tends to impose it, or some derivative of it, upon new relationships such as with a teacher, a foster-mother, or a therapist" (Bowlby, 1988, p. 127). This is assumed to take place via the development of internal representations of the self and the care-giver.

While prospective studies have not yet traced these patterns into adult couple relationships, it seems inevitable that they will be found to be highly influential in organizing patterns of attachment there as well. Certainly, the dividend of security—or lack thereof—would seem to be closely related to an individual's capacity for trust in close relationships later in life. This is precisely the reason for summarizing the assumptions and research associated with attachment theory in this context. *The couple relationship inherits the legacy of attachment*, that is, not only the *universal inborn need* for attachment (which is transferred from original care-giver to adult partner) but also the partners' *particular experiences* in their respective relationships with their original care-givers, for better or for worse. It is one part of the arc of attachment that spans the human life cycle.

This brings us back to the similarities noted at the beginning of this chapter between the earliest attachment relationship and the attachments formed in adult couple relationships. The transfer of attachment needs to the adult partner contributes to the tenacity of these relationships.* As Scharff and Scharff note, this "lends . . . a poignancy that few other relationships approach" (1991, p. 12). But beyond mutual needs for attachment, the couple relationship also inherits the vicissitudes of early attachment experiences for each partner; this can be not only a source of poignancy but of great difficulty when these early experiences have not been "good-enough." Difficulties in early attachments can lead to an inability to trust, to unmet and therefore excessive needs for attachment, to internal representations that distort perceptions of the partner, and to unconscious defenses that preclude vulnerability and intimacy. When these are the legacies of early attachment, the challenge of finding satisfaction in a couple relationship is greatly complicated for the partners.

The Mysteries of Attraction

A couple's relationship usually begins with *attraction*—with an emotional pull of some kind toward a particular person—however murky its bases may be to the participants. This sets off the emotional forces of the relationship, beginning a developmental process that is only partially under the conscious control of the two individuals. Couple therapists often feel that they can see the origins of a couple's current dilemma in the stories of their initial attraction to one another: the woman who hoped she would "learn to love" her partner after they

---

*Observers of children abused by their care-givers (Green, 1980) and primate researchers (Harlow & Harlow, 1971; Seay, Alexander, & Harlow, 1964) have noted an especially suggestive finding in this context, namely, that abuse by care-givers *intensifies* attachment seeking. Harlow and Harlow conducted experiments in which infant monkeys received a particularly noxious stimulus when they clung to their mechanical "surrogate mothers." In keeping with the inborn instinct to seek contact with the primary care-giver when alarmed or in distress, they clung all the more tenaciously to the "mother." Without being reductionistic in an area of multiple causal factors and great complexity, this finding may be partially implicated in the tendency of partners to remain in highly unsatisfying and even physically abusive relationships as adults.

were married and who never did; the man who was instantly and powerfully drawn to a woman as unpredictable and volatile as his mother had been; the partners in a lukewarm but well-established relationship who married because of pressures from friends and family only to find themselves, several years later, bored with each other and both having multiple affairs.

The power of attachment as an organizing force in human life drives the process of attraction but it does not illuminate why adults become attracted to certain individuals and not to others. Most laymen view this as an unremarkable matter. They assume that they know why they are attracted to their partners: because of looks, shared interests, or a common ethnic or cultural heritage. They say: "She was pretty," "He was easy to talk to," or "We seemed to like the same things." These and other factors, such as status and wealth, are admittedly important to varying degrees. However, therapists—who have the advantage of seeing, over and over, how these attractions play out over time—know that the process is much more complicated.

Two common scenarios suggest that there is greater complexity to the chemistry of attraction. The first is expressed in the popular truism that "opposites attract." But why? A possible answer lies in the shrewd observation that people sometimes marry not who they want to *be with* but who they want to *be*. A quiet, somewhat passive man is drawn to a fiery and ambitious woman. A fearful and self-deprecating woman finds herself attracted to a man who appears to be self-confident and bold. It is as though the individual recognizes and seeks out his or her missing half. Significantly, if the person needs to "erase" these qualities in herself because of difficulties in early attachment relationships, she may later reject or persecute the partner for having the very qualities that first attracted her—a pattern familiar to most couple therapists.

A second scenario is equally familiar and even more compelling. An individual is repeatedly attracted to a particular kind of partner; the ensuing relationships are almost identically painful and disappointing. The *repetition* of the pattern and its predictable outcome (regardless of seemingly striking differences between the objects of attraction at more superficial levels) indicate that something other than random selection is involved. The fact that the individual has *no conscious awareness* of these deeper similarities or of choosing these unhappy outcomes indicates that the pattern involves unconscious processes.

There have been many attempts to describe these unconscious forces of attraction (Dicks, 1967; Fairbairn, 1952; Framo, 1981; Hendrix, 1988; Ravich, 1974; Sager, 1976; Scharff & Scharff, 1991). A common belief is that particular characteristics of the original care-giver and of the child's early relationship with him or her may be internalized by the child and remain dormant, ready to be reactivated in an adult intimate relationship. These "traces" are most likely implicated in the phenomenon of "love at first sight"—the sense of instant attraction to and almost *recognition* of the other as someone who "just feels right." Attraction expresses both the nonspecific inborn need for attachment and, more specifically, the unconscious recognition of something about the partner and the feeling of relating to him or her that in some way resembles the characteristics of the individual's intimate relationships with early care-givers.

This is further complicated by the fact that attraction is a bilateral process. There are two individuals, both of whom are responding to their own unconscious representations. Theorists have suggested that there is often a specific fit between the unconscious representations of the partners in a couple relationship. These "unconscious complementarities" (Dicks, 1967) shape interactional patterns between them. They can be the source of much difficulty in couple relationships, as will be discussed in Chapter 3.

In terms of attraction, I suspect that, in many good-enough couple relationships, the partners manage to unconsciously select a *benign version* of the parental traits that were problematic for them. For example, a man with a domineering and intrusive mother may be attracted to a forceful woman who is able to respect his boundaries, thus securing a fit with unconscious representations without having to compulsively reenact difficulties of the original relationship.

Regardless of how the partners meet or the sources of their original attraction, the evolution of the relationship will be partially shaped by what they expect from it and by the experience of disappointment, which is the inevitable counterpart of expectation.

Expectation and Disappointment

In fairy tales, the princess kisses a frog and he turns into Prince Charming; in everyday life, the scenario is rather different. She marries someone whom she *expects* to be Prince Charming and he turns into a frog; he *expects* that marrying her will rescue him from being a frog and turn him into a prince but it doesn't and he blames her. The partners' expectations of what the relationship will be like constitute early organizing forces in the evolution of that relationship.

What do people expect from couple relationships? There are some common, if not universal, expectations that people bring to relationships: to be cared for and cared about; to be special to someone; to be supported, respected, and treated fairly; to share responsibility for making the relationship work; for their partner to be reliably invested in the relationship, and to be able to count on this investment, especially in times of personal difficulty; for their partner to be relatively accessible for physical, nonsexual contact, including touching, kissing, and holding; and an active and, in most cases, monogamous sexual relationship. These expectations are, for the most part, quite conscious, so much so that they are formally expressed in many marriage vows. But if couple relationships were simply a matter of conscious expectations, there would be more happy couples and fewer couple therapists.

As discussed earlier, intimate relationships between adults reactivate needs and longings from infancy and early childhood. When early attachments have been "good enough," this adds intensity to the couple's connection and deepens the gratifications of the relationship. When early attachments have not been good enough, these longings may be exaggerated by virtue of having been unmet and may contribute to exaggerated and unrealistic expectations.

The woman whose husband is temporarily less available because of illness may feel totally rejected and abandoned as she unconsciously reexperiences the abandonment she suffered with a depressed and unavailable parent. She may desperately need and expect her husband to magically make these feelings go away, to validate her as lovable and good, and to make the pain of a lifetime disappear, all while he is bedridden and in physical pain. We might be tempted to ask, rationally, "Can't she see that he is just sick and not rejecting her?" But it is the irrational, overwhelming feeling of loss and isolation that is fueling her reaction. Couple therapists see these exaggerated reactions and expectations daily in their offices. They are the nuts-and-bolts of couple therapy.

Add to this the importance of "unconscious complementarity" (Dicks, 1967) and Bowen's observation (1978) that people pick partners at roughly the same level of differentiation as one another (i.e., of having had roughly similar *degrees* of disturbance of early attachment relationships) and the stage is set for *two* individuals to bring exaggerated and unrealistic expectations to their relationship, to be unable to fulfill these impossible expectations for one another, and for a variety of complicated and confusing impasses to result. Also remember that conscious and unconscious expectations may be in conflict not only *between* but *within* the individuals involved. These clashing and exaggerated expectations are fundamentally implicated in the problems that many, if not most, couples bring to treatment.

The very fact that expectations exist — whether the straightforward, conscious expectation that a partner will be stable and faithful or the unconscious expectation that he or she will undo the damage done by early relational failures—sets the stage for what is perhaps the most universal emotion in couple therapy cases—*disappointment*. How the partners deal with this disappointment will be a critical factor in the success of the relationship. They may respond with chronic conflict and power struggles, loss of love, extramarital involvements, and depression or somatic symptomatology.

The challenge is for both individuals to have *realistic expectations* of what their partner and the relationship can provide for them, to recognize and be able to tolerate the fact that their partner will also have expectations, and to be able to manage inevitable disappointments in a way that preserves trustworthiness and vitality. These factors, and the positive early attachments that almost always make them possible, constitute valuable resources within satisfying, long-term relationships. This challenge is complicated by problematic early attachments that fuel impossible expectations, hobble the ability to temporarily serve the interests of the other's expectations, and impair the ability to accept and overcome disappointment.

⌒ 2 ⌒

FACTS OF LIFE:
CULTURE, GENDER,
AND TIME

T HE COUPLE RELATIONSHIP does not exist in a vacuum. It is embedded in time and place and in the biological fact of gender. These
facts shape and constrain the evolution of the relationship. The couple
lives in a particular culture in a particular time (for the purposes of
this volume, this largely means late 20th century Western societies).
The partners cannot escape biological differences between men and
women and the cultural constructions of gender which that them. (In
homosexual relationships the influence of gender operates differently
but is not eliminated.) Finally, the relationship exists in time, and
its evolution is further shaped by the cogwheeling of individual and
relational life cycles.

15

Cultural Expectations

The most significant social forces impinging on couples in late 20th century America—and other Western industrial countries—represent the continuity of traditional patterns, expectations, and attitudes as well as more recent changes that have challenged and transformed those traditions. For example, for the most part, individuals can choose their romantic partners rather than having the relationship arranged for them by family members or others. Couple relationships are assumed to be based on love rather than economic or political arrangements between families or clans. This increases the expectations of happiness and fulfillment, which both partners bring to the relationship; it also sets the stage for outcomes—such as a partner's decision to divorce for reasons of boredom or loss of love—that would be unthinkable in more traditional cultures.

Traditional assumptions about the nature of marital relationships endure but they have eroded over the last several decades. Spouses generally expect to be sexually available to one another and that the relationship will be sexually monogamous—in spite of the fact that 37% of husbands and 29% of wives report having had extramarital affairs (Reinisch, 1990). The expectation of longevity also endures; presumably most people hope that their relationships will be long-lasting but, in recognition of the fact that one in two marriages end in divorce (Weiss, 1979), more and more couples are excising the traditional marriage vow to remain together "'til death do us part."

These statistics reflect what is probably the single most influential change in the cultural context of couple relationships over the last several decades: the growing emphasis on *individual* development and fulfillment as a dynamic counterweight to the traditional emphasis on marital and family togetherness. These forces—the needs, welfare, and entitlement of the individual and those of the marriage and family—have always been at least potentially in conflict. Historically, the weight of most social institutions was lopsidedly on the side of the integrity of the family unit, regardless of the cost to the welfare of particular individuals. Especially since the 1960s there has been a growing emphasis on the value of individual self-actualization and satisfaction in life. This confusing clash of values has been painful to large numbers of individuals who find themselves unsure of which choices to make and which values to uphold.

The most dramatic (but not the only) expression of this shift in values has been the feminist movement which has, over the last 20 years, had a striking impact on a wide range of American institutions, especially marriage and the family. Coupled with the dramatic increase of women in the work force—in 58% of two-parent families with children, both parents now work (Hochschild, 1989)—these changes have dislocated the assumptions that were easily taken for granted 40 or 50 years ago. Solutions to conflicting interests that reflexively favor men—husband's career comes first; a woman's place is in the home—are becoming less automatic. This increases ambiguity and conflict, both of which are stressful to families, but it holds out the possibility that solutions from a wider "menu" of choices, negotiated between equals, will contribute to more enduring and satisfying relationships.

Another recent cultural change that affects couple relationships involves the saturation of readily available material on intimacy and marriage, from self-help books to magazine articles to TV talk shows. This is something of a mixed blessing. The wider dissemination of information about couple relationships can help normalize difficulties and provide guidelines and tools for dealing with them. Certainly some couples who would have needed to seek treatment in the past are now finding solutions through these media.

However, many articles and books promulgate highly idealized visions—and therefore unrealistic expectations—of what couple relationships should be like and what they can deliver. These unrealistic expectations contribute to dissatisfaction and conflict for some couples; if a self-help book written by a married couple describes their relationship as characterized by "life-long passion," "maximum self-actualization," and "higher spirituality," then why isn't the reader's? And isn't it really the partner's fault, after all, for being so uptight, materialistic, self-involved, or traditional?

One possible benefit of this wealth of marital analysis may be to pull the culture as a whole toward what have traditionally been seen as women's values—connection, intimacy, and talk about relationships—and thus to correct somewhat for traditional male socialization which has made it difficult for couples to discuss or resolve problems in relationships.

The Influence of Gender

Nothing could be more obvious than the simple fact that a heterosexual couple relationship involves two different genders, but until recently the significance of this fact has been largely overlooked in most conceptual analyses of couple relationships. A number of feminist theorists and therapists (including, among others, Bepko & Krestan [1985], Goldner [1985, 1989], Goodrich, Rampage, Ellman, & Halstead [1988], Hare-Mustin [1978], Lerner [1985, 1989], Luepnitz [1988], McGoldrick,

Anderson, & Walsh [1989a], and Walters, Carter, Papp, & Silverstein [1988]) have focused their attention on the influence of gender in couple relationships and family life, and proposed that it is a central organizing principle in these systems.

While many theories assume that both partners enter the couple relationship with equal power, these relationships are in fact, as Walsh and Scheinkman (1989) point out, "already 'rule-governed' by larger systems, especially by the family of origin and culture, which co-influence socialization processes in human development" (p. 19). This is true in modern couple relationships as well as in more traditional ones. As Walsh (1989) suggests, even when the partners do not make explicit traditional gender bargains, there may be "out-of-awareness relationship rules" that organize interaction (p. 282).

The organizing influence of gender in couple relationships is most evident in four areas: differences in socialization, differences in legal and economic status and power, differences involving childbirth and parenting, and differences in sexuality. While gender differences are a source of misunderstanding and frustration in couple relationships (Tannen, 1990) and a threat to fairness and trustworthiness, they are also a central aspect of the attraction between men and women, a complex of welcome and stimulating differences.

It is important to note that the *consequences* of marriage and divorce are very different for females than for males. Women have historically given up more than men to be married—their name and occupation, for example—and have been expected to adjust to the life of the man (Goodrich et al., 1988). Married women become more symptomatic and prone to stress than do men, exhibiting poorer health, lower self-esteem, more depression, and greater marital dissatisfaction (McGoldrick, 1989). Married men are "physically healthier and achieve greater job success than single men, while the opposite is true for women" (McGoldrick, 1988, cited in Walsh, 1989, p. 271). Women also do the vast majority of household chores—typically between 74% and 92% of housework and childcare tasks—and this is no less true when both partners work (Berheide, 1984, cited in McGoldrick, 1989; Walsh, 1989).

The different implications of marriage for men and women are starkly evident in statistics concerning domestic violence. Avis (1992) points out that "in North America, 95% of marital violence is perpetrated by men (husbands or ex-husbands) against wives. . . . In terms of physical injury, violence against women by their husbands or partners occurs more often in Canada and the U.S. than all incidents of car accidents, muggings, and rape combined" (pp. 226–227). The diverging fortunes of men and women continue after divorce. While men experience a 42% average rise in their standard of living after divorce, women experience an average 73% decline (Weitzman, 1985). Ninety percent of custodial single parents are women (O'Rand & Henretta, 1982).

In terms of socialization, McGoldrick states, "There has always been a 'his' and 'hers' version of human development, although until recently only the former was described in the literature" (1989, p. 202). The fact is that men and women are raised very differently from one another. From infancy on, they receive different types of responses from adults and different messages about the types of characteristics to which, as men and women, they should aspire. McGoldrick asserts that "parents tend to encourage more physical activity in boys and more dependence in girls . . . , that parents talk and look more at girls and engage in more rough play with boys" (1989, p. 213). Tannen (1990) notes that "gender differences in ways of talking have been described by researchers observing children as young as three" (p. 44).

Boys are, in general, socialized to be more aggressive and more competitive. Independence is encouraged along with implicit permission to focus on their own needs. They are discouraged from showing emotion (with the possible exception of anger); feelings of fear, weakness, and dependency are especially discouraged. Girls are generally encouraged to focus more on relationships, to be more concerned with the needs and feelings of others. A wider range of emotional expression is encouraged; drive and high achievement, much less so. Boys are steered toward action and competition; girls, toward talking and relationship.

These messages about what men and women should be like lead, in a sense, to the creation of two different cultures, making all heterosexual couple relationships essentially "mixed marriages." The same trials and misunderstandings that attend mixed ethnic, religious, and racial relationships (McGoldrick, Pearce, & Giordano, 1982) exist in heterosexual couple relationships as well. Tannen (1990) has documented the pernicious effects of this cultural difference on communication in couple relationships, while others have spoken to its impact in other areas, such as decision-making. Walsh (1989) believes that

> [m]en are socialized to argue their positions as forcefully and convincingly as they can, with the aim of meeting their needs as fully as possible. Since women are raised to put the needs of others before their own, they tend to defer and accommodate. . . . The male rule for good negotiation is to make the strongest case and push for one's own position. For women, rules for good negotiation start with consideration of the other's position and compromise to take the other's

needs into account. As one wife [stated]: "Since I never play by his rules and he never plays by my rules, things always end up his way." (p. 280)

Over time, this pattern can contribute to feelings of powerlessness in the woman and to alienation in the relationship.

Historically, cultural messages about the roles, responsibilities, and rights of men and women have largely resolved conflicts of interest in favor of men, generating and reinforcing "default" solutions that are advantageous to men. A classic example is the assumption that it is the woman's duty to follow the man's job, regardless of how this affects her interests. A corollary insists that, if both partners work, the man's job comes first when decisions have to be made affecting the relationship or family. Women have been expected to accept secondary roles, such as caretaker and supporter, rather than primary ones and to submerge their own ambitions, facilitating those of their husbands or children instead.

While gender socialization has been more unfair and more injurious to women, it has, as Zilbergeld (1992) suggests, created hardships for men as well.

> Males are . . . forced to suppress huge parts of themselves, the softer and vulnerable aspects. . . . While this is usually heard as a complaint from women, there is little recognition of how men suffer because of it. They are the ones who aren't able to get hugged or comforted, who can't physically or verbally express the love they feel for male friends they may have known for half a lifetime, who can't find release and relief through tears, who can't openly admit fear and despair. (p. 9)

Men are taught to feel that they must be breadwinners. If they are unemployed or struggling financially or if their wives make more than they do, they may suffer a sense of personal failure that is not likely to be experienced in the same way by a woman.

The formalities of dating provide a simple example of the different burdens imposed by these gender expectations. Women have been expected to wait patiently for men to "ask them out," being censured as unwomanly if they wanted to take some initiative themselves. Men have had the burden of *having* to be the one to ask. Most men can remember the adolescent anguish of having to "make the first move" but being terrified of rejection, of being expected to look smooth and self-confident while feeling awkward, uncertain, and inadequate. These differences carry over into sexual patterns as the relationship progresses. Women were traditionally expected to let men take the lead sexually and were censured for displaying too much sexual appetite and initiative. Men were expected to be "sexual experts," to initiate sex, to always be ready to "perform," and to be responsible for their partners' pleasure—to "give her" an orgasm.

The issue of gender is even more complicated for men and women today because of the impact of the women's movement over the past 20 years. The challenge to centuries of male and female socialization has created opportunities for both sexes to redefine their views of what men and women can be and how they can relate to one another. It has also, however, caused confusion and, in some cases, anguish as traditional definitions undergo transformation. For women, the expectation that they will be mothers and homemakers has been complicated by the newer expectation that they will work and pursue professional ambitions, all of this *without* societal changes—corporate day-care, flex-time, family leave—which could support these demands. At the same time, full-time home-making has become vaguely stigmatized, squeezing women between clashing and largely irreconcilable expectations. Similar clashes can be seen in the area of sexuality. Women are now more likely to feel expected to be avid and accomplished sexually while their male partners may be threatened by this behavior and the stigma of "promiscuity" has not vanished.

> Men have also been caught in a clash of cultural values as traditional expectations undergo transformation. Virtually everything men were trained to do and everything they think, want, and are has come under scrutiny and attack. A man who has followed the precepts taught by his parents, the mass media, teachers, coaches and other authorities is now in the very strange position of hearing that everything he learned was wrong. (Zilbergeld, 1992, p. 10)

Men are expected to be more emotional and vulnerable, less driven, and less willing to sacrifice marriage and family to professional ambition, but they may turn women off if they are seen as weak or "wimpy," or if they do not live up to traditional standards of status and success. The effect of these changes is that many couples are now coping not only with differences in gender socialization but with confusion over gender roles as well.

When we look at gender socialization, it is as though a deck of cards—each representing one quality or characteristic of human life—has been shuffled and different cards dealt to men and to women, without their being able to have any say in which cards they received, let alone which cards were in the deck in the first place. Both genders have suffered from the rigidity of the hands dealt and from the lack of freedom to reshuffle the deck in ways that best suit their individuality and their idiosyncratic relationships. However, it is clear that women have suffered more, because the cards dealt to them often represent qualities that are *devalued* in the culture at large, because of the prevalence of "default" solutions that favor men's interests, and because of institutional structures that serve to enforce second-class citizenship for women.

Economic, political, and legal structures reinforce the differences described above. In the workplace women make, on the average, 64 cents for the dollar that a man earns for the same job (McGoldrick, 1989) and are less likely to be promoted, regardless of qualifications. Economic discrimination has both resulted from and contributed to political underrepresentation, which has limited women's political power. There are some areas in which societal structures work against the interests of men as well, although they are nowhere near as pervasive as those that put women at a disadvantage. Perhaps the clearest example is the fact that, in most states, unless parents are legally married, the biological father has no legal rights of parenthood in relation to his children. Furthermore, while 100 years ago there was a widespread legal bias toward granting custody of children to fathers in a divorce, this has since been reversed, with the "default" solution now favoring the mother. It is not surprising that these areas of discrimination against men should involve childrearing since these responsibilities have been so prominently left to women.

How does all of this affect what goes on in a particular couple relationship? Goldner (1989) suggests that family therapists typically assume a disjunction between what goes on inside the home and what goes on outside it: "[F]amily therapists do not deny the fact that women are politically and economically one-down; they simply hold onto their conviction that, in the privacy of their own homes, men and women are equals" (p. 51). She points out that this is especially incongruous in a field that prides itself on its ecological perspective.

Inequities between men and women in the larger culture do make their way into the "haven" of the home, to varying degrees and in varying ways. The more complicated question involves whether and in what ways patterns of discrimination against women in the larger male-dominated society are *replicated* or *reinforced* in the intimate system of the couple relationship. My own sense is that these patterns necessarily impinge on couples and coevolve with a number of other important factors, such as socialization and patterns in the families of origin, unconscious factors in the relationship, relative force of personality, and commitment to fairness and equality.

In some relationships men deliberately take advantage of cultural and institutional discrimination against women by exploiting the woman's greater financial insecurity and feeling free to be abusive or indifferent to her needs, knowing that she will not feel safe enough to leave. In other cases men unwittingly exploit women's cultural disadvantages. They don't intend to exploit; they simply don't see it as exploitation. In either case, these patterns erode closeness and trust. In other relationships, there may be a clear commitment by both partners to interact in ways that are fair. The partners have appreciable, but not total, control over the ways in which male privilege enters into the fabric of trust in their relationship.

The challenge for couples is to try to integrate gender differences in ways that are acceptable to both partners. This involves an effort to create and preserve a relationship that respects gender differences without devaluing either one, and in which there is an ongoing effort to balance fairness *as the couple defines it* and not by fixed external criteria. The central elements of such efforts are: *respect* for both genders and *sympathy* for the particular difficulties and dilemmas that accompany each, a *commitment to fairness* in the relationship, and a willingness to cocreate structures that are *responsive* to the idiosyncratic needs, abilities, and entitlements of both partners. Goldner (1989) is right to point out that the couple's relationship is not automatically an oasis of fairness in a desert of male privilege. However, to varying degrees for different couples, it can be such an oasis, based on the efforts of both partners to mobilize empathy, respect, and fairness as countervailing forces to the divisive effects of legal, economic, and political discrimination against women in the wider society.

The Life Cycle: Stability and Change

Couple relationships are embedded in a temporal context, as well as cultural and physical ones. Our understanding of the effects of time on relational systems has been enhanced by a recognition of the importance of the life cycle for individuals, couples, and families. The life cycle framework attempts to describe the *predictability of change*. Erik Erikson's framework (1959) for understanding how individuals change over the course of their lives included assumptions that are now widely accepted: transitions between stages in the life cycle are marked by *increased stress* and *disruption* and there are *inevitable developmental tasks* associated with each new stage. A further assumption is that the more successfully an individual resolves the developmental tasks of one stage, the easier the challenges of successive stages will be.

When researchers and clinicians recognized that families, as well as individuals, experienced life cycle changes, they began to spell out the tasks and stresses associated with these stages. Carter and McGoldrick (1989a) provided critical mass by presenting these concepts to an audience of family therapists.* Underlying assumptions for the family life cycle are similar to those for an individual. It is assumed that there are predictable and unavoidable stages through which all families move. These stages are precipitated by life events which demand change and adjustment on the parts of all family members.

Carter and McGoldrick's (1989b) framework, based on intact middle class American families, suggests the following six stages of the family life cycle:

1. leaving home: single young adults
2. the joining of families through marriage: the new couple
3. families with young children
4. families with adolescents
5. launching children and moving on
6. families in later life

They also propose stage frameworks for variations in the family life cycle, for example, for divorced and remarried families. (See also Ahrons & Rodgers, 1987.)

One of the complexities the family life cycle adds to the relative simplicity of the individual life cycle, and one with real significance for couples, involves the joining of individuals and families who are experiencing *different stages* of the life cycle at the same time. For example, a divorced mother of two teenagers and a divorced father of one teenager conceive a child and decide to marry. They will experience the stresses of three stages simultaneously—forming a committed relationship, having a new baby, and parenting adolescents. This pile-up of stresses and conflicting demands can seriously tax the coping resources of the healthiest individuals, and it will constitute a significant organizing force in the evolution of this marriage.

---

*While schemas have also been proposed for the life cycle of couple relationships (Abrams, 1977; Blanck & Blanck, 1968; Campbell, 1980; Gans, 1975/1976; Haffey, 1986; Katz, 1978; Levant, 1982; and Tomashiro, 1978), they have most often been organized around the arrival and effects of children and have not attained the same widespread visibility as have those for individuals and families.

Carter and McGoldrick's (1989b) discussion of "horizontal" and "vertical" stressors is a helpful addition to the life cycle framework. Horizontal stressors are those associated with the family's development over time. They include predictable stresses as well as unpredictable events, such as illness or serious injury, job loss, or the death of a child, which can disrupt the life cycle. Vertical stressors involve "patterns of relating and functioning that are transmitted down the generations in a family" and include "all the family attitudes, taboos, expectations, labels, and loaded issues with which we grow up" (p. 8). They assert that

> the degree of anxiety engendered by the stress on the vertical and horizontal axes *at the point where they converge* [italics added] is the key determinant of how well the family will manage its transitions through life. . . . Although all normative change is to some degree stressful, we have observed that when the horizontal (normative) stress intersects with a vertical (transgenerational) stress, there is a quantum leap in the anxiety engendered. (pp. 8–9)

This formulation highlights a convergence of organizing forces, namely, "unfinished business" from family-of-origin intersects with predictable and unpredictable stressors.

By recognizing that *all* individuals, couples, and families undergo predictable stages of development, with increased disorganization and stress at transition points, the life cycle framework is inherently normalizing. It serves as a brake on the tendency among clinicians to focus only on pathology. Behavior and symptomatology that may appear extreme out of context can be appreciated as more normative when understood as an acute reaction to stresses associated with life cycle transitions. These frameworks also help by turning our attention to how couples *cope* with stressors, a focus that emphasizes resources and resourcefulness.

Stress is conceptualized as "a state which arises from an actual or perceived imbalance between demands (e.g., challenge, threat) and capability (e.g., resources, coping)" (McCubbin & Patterson, 1983a, p. 10). Hill (1958) has proposed a cogent theoretical framework for the processes involved when couples or families cope with stress. Known as the ABCX Model, it was later elaborated by other researchers (McCubbin, Boss, Wilson, & Lester, 1980; McCubbin, Cauble, & Patterson, 1982; McCubbin & Patterson, 1981, 1982, 1983a, 1983b). Within this framework, a stressor is seen as "a life event impacting on the [couple] which produces, or has the potential to produce, change"

(McCubbin & Patterson, 1983a, p. 7). Examples include a serious illness or accident, the death of a loved one, or the loss of a job. Positive changes, such as a promotion for one partner or the arrival of the first child, also have the potential to disrupt the couple's relational system and therefore to produce stress. Hill's ABCX Model is defined as follows: "A (the stressor event)—interacting with B (the family's crisis meeting resources)—interacting with C (the definition the family makes of the event)—produces X (the crisis . . .)" (1958, p. 141). This schema draws our attention to two significant factors in this interplay—the couple's resources or coping abilities and the couple's definition of the stressor.*

The definition of the stressor involves the *meaning* the couple makes of it. Is it experienced as a meaningless tragedy, an insurmountable setback, a challenge to be met, an opportunity for growth? Events can have highly idiosyncratic meanings. This was brought home to me one night when I tuned in to the middle of a television program in which a man was discussing the accidental death of his young son in a drug-related shoot-out. I assumed that this was a program on drugs and violence. It wasn't; it was a program on the My Lai massacre during the Vietnam war. The man was an American soldier who had taken part in that massacre. He described having knowingly shot and killed a young boy at that time. He was convinced that his son's death was a punishment for what he had done.

McCubbin and Patterson (1983a) point out that "because family crises evolve and are resolved over a period of time, families seldom are dealing with a single stressor. Rather, . . . they experience a pile-up of demands" (p. 14). Whether couples are coping with predictable or unpredictable stressors, the ABCX Model offers a useful framework for conceptualizing the most important factors involved and the relationships between them.

The transitions of the life cycle are, in a sense, part of a larger dialectic in couple relationships—the dialectic of stability and change. Most people have a deep need for stability; this is one aspect of safety. They like the rituals and routines of their lives; they settle (if they can) in homes and neighborhoods and enjoy the continuity of activities that endure over time (Little League games, church or synagogue, get-togethers on the block, summer outings in the park or at the lake). Change is forced on people by inherent developmental processes: Young lovers become parents, become middle-aged, become old. But

---

*Resources will be discussed in detail in later chapters (specifically, Chapters 6 and 8).

even apart from life's unavoidable changes, most become bored with the "same old routine" and seek change.

Every couple manages this dialectic differently, with different ways of maintaining stability and introducing change. The challenge this poses for couples today is greater than in the past because the life span has increased and because individuality and personal development are more strongly sanctioned now than they were 50 or 100 years ago. Michael Ventura (1988) suggests that

> [w]hen two people "get involved," each usually has a clear (if usually nonverbal) idea of what he or she needs for the next stage of his or her growth. Virtually every serious relationship or marriage is a partially conscious means by which this "next state" is achieved, is grown. Crisis time comes when one or both of them have pretty much exhausted this more-or-less intended stage of growth in the other and are trying to figure out if they can accompany each other through another significant stage. We are living in a society in which there are few things more rare than two people accompanying each other through more than one significant run of growth. (p. 330)

Walsh (1989) echoes this point:

> It has been said that adults today need at least three marriages: for youth, one based on romance and passion; for childrearing, one based on shared responsibility; and later in life, one strong in companion-ship and mutual caretaking. (p. 283)

If partners are going to "grow up" together, they must be able to tolerate change in one another and therefore in their relationship.

The challenge for couples is to create a relational structure that fosters individual development while maintaining a lively connection between them. This is especially difficult because individuals grow at different rates, at different times, and in different directions. Couples must be able to tolerate periods of disaffection from one another when the streams of their individual development simply cannot converge; for example, she is ready and aching for children while he is putting all his energy into professional advancement, or he is full of discontent at midlife while she is feeling relief that the children are older and enjoy-ing the stability of their family life. This challenge is even greater when there are complex overlappings of different stages of the life cycle. Nevertheless, the challenge for all couples remains the same: to integrate stability and growth while allowing the relationship to change as the needs of the partners change over time and preserving relational continuity and vitality.

Finally, when this meshing seems impossible to accomplish, when connection can be preserved only at the price of individual growth and satisfaction, the decision to end the relationship is not necessarily a negative one. Couples must wrestle with the complicated and painful questions posed by this choice, especially when there are children, but they should be able to do so with the understanding that in some cases divorce may be the healthiest and most constructive decision.

~ 3 ~

RELATIONAL CHALLENGES

A TTACHMENT, ATTRACTION, and expectations, together with the facts of culture, gender, and time, set the stage for the relationship's evolution. Once it begins, its development is shaped by other organizing forces and by the challenges they pose for the partners.

Commitment

Once a relationship begins, the question of *commitment* inevitably arises. Relationships do not stand still; they must evolve. Commitment helps shape the direction of this evolution; for partners to experience any sense of psychological safety and stability there must be some degree of commitment. The extent of the commitment may vary. For one couple, it may be "'til death do us part"; for another, "for as long as we are both happy in this relationship." The commitment may or may not be to a monogamous relationship. But whatever the

29

variation, both partners will know that they have defined some type of relationship, as well as some if not all of the terms of that relationship.

Couples typically make a series of graded commitments to one another. In the most traditional form, this progresses from a commitment to go out on one date, to a commitment to "dating," to exclusive dating, to engagement, marriage, householding, and often, children. Without commitment, there is no real safety or stability in the relationship. It would be like living in a home and not knowing from one day to the next whether you will be living there or elsewhere. Like all forms of ambiguity, this one is stressful, especially because it involves what should be a "secure base" for the individual. Commitment plays an especially important role in the preservation of the relationship when stress and conflict are high and gratifications are low. At these times, commitment is the clamp that can hold a damaged relationship together until stress is reduced and emotional repairs made.

The most common pathological pattern related to this particular challenge involves couples in which one or both partners cannot decide whether to be a couple. These partners *cannot define* the relationship; they cannot choose one way or the other. When one partner is unable to commit, the couple's interactions are organized by a pattern of distance and pursuit. The distancing partner does not say "No" to the relationship, at least not a definitive "No" that would end it once and for all. In fact, if the pursuer stops pursuing, the distancer may begin to pursue, to entice the pursuer just enough to reactivate his or her pursuit, reconstituting the old pattern.

For other couples, it is not one but both partners who have difficulty defining the relationship as either "On" or "Off." There may be a seesaw pattern of distance and pursuit, with one distancing when the other pursues and then both partners reversing roles. Only rarely are both eager for closeness at the same time. The relationship may be characterized by intense conflict and frustration for both partners, leading them to feel hopeless about it but unable to give it up.

The inability to commit is usually related to painful experiences in earlier attachments which have led the partners to fear being close. They are constrained by the twin fears of being swallowed up in a close relationship and being abandoned and cast out (Karpel, 1976). Individuals who have not had these early difficulties will find it easier to make a choice and stick with it, recognizing that a relationship either is or is not "good-enough" for them. The challenge for both partners is to be able to define the relationship in a way that feels comfortable to both of them and to live with it on these terms until a time comes when they may need to change this definition.

"I" and "We": Autonomy and Attachment

Most partners in close relationships experience a constant oscillation between the phenomenological states of "I" and "We." In the state of "I," I experience myself as separate and independent from you; I see you as a separate person. I have my own opinions, my own feelings, my own thoughts, and I am well aware that they may differ from yours. In the state of "We," I experience myself as part of something larger than myself but still very private and special. I belong to the relationship, and I experience almost everything—people, places, movies, even feelings—as part of a shared experience. *We* are happy. *We* are special. *We* have a secret. *We* see others in the same way. *We* are grumpy or uneasy, silly or pleasurably sated.

In the state of "I," I see you as a part of *my* life; in the state of "We," I see myself as a part of *our* life (not our *lives*). In the state of "I," there is a boundary *between* us; in the state of "We," there is a boundary *around* us. In the state of "I," I must explain what I mean to you as I would to anyone else; in the state of "We," no explanations are needed for I know that you already know what I mean.

Partners in a healthy couple relationship move in and out of these states throughout their hour-to-hour, day-to-day existence. This smooth shifting between the states of "I" and "We" may go unrecognized by the partners but it represents a significant developmental accomplishment. The couple's interactional patterns (and felt experience) of autonomy and attachment are shaped in part by their experiences in early attachment relationships. Early patterns of attachment persist and generalize to relationships other than those with original care-givers. Secure attachment makes it easier for children to explore away from the care-giver and to return and experience gratification in closeness. Difficulties in early attachments may lead either to fear of separation and clinging or to self-sufficiency and the avoidance of dependency and closeness (Ainsworth et al., 1978).

These complications mirror the twin difficulties that characterize adult relationships as well. The partners may form a relationship characterized by a very strong "We" and very little "I." These "fused," "undifferentiated" (Bowen, 1978), or "symbiotic" (Searles, 1965, 1973) relationships are organized by both partners' fears of separation and loss and are characterized by at least some of the following features. Difference and disagreement generate anxiety and are therefore avoided whenever possible; there is relational pressure for the partners to think alike and feel alike on almost everything. Separation is also extremely anxiety-provoking and is therefore minimized or avoided—they feel safe only with each other. The partners pour much of their energy into efforts to maintain the relationship, which results in stunting their individual development. These relationships are further complicated by the fact that this rigid and anxious attachment may feel necessary but distressing to one or both partners. They may feel suffocated, or "swallowed up" by the other, raising fears associated with the loss of self in the undifferentiated "We."

The parallel danger is that the partners will form a relationship characterized by a strong "I" and a weak "We." In these "disengaged" (Minuchin, 1974) relationships, the partners' experience of themselves as separate individuals rarely shifts into the state of "We." They lead separate lives and the relationship often has a devitalized quality. The partners may have their strongest attachments outside the relation-ship—with parents, siblings, children, close friends, or with the pa-trons of a local bar—or they may be isolated socially with no strong attachments. Here, anxieties associated with intimacy shape the pat-terns of avoidance within the relationship.

For many couples, there is a fierce struggle over the terms of "I" and "We" in the relationship. These struggles are a hallmark of couple conflict and are usually referred to as distance-pursuit cycles. One partner pulls for greater closeness while the other resists and main-tains a more separate "I." In some cases, the pattern is straightforward. The partners seem to have made an error in choosing one another; their needs for closeness and separateness are quite different. In many more cases, however, the pattern expresses a more complicated struc-ture.

Both partners may have strong anxiety associated with *both* "I" and "We." They may polarize in such a way that one partner becomes the "pursuer" in the relationship and the other the "distancer," but this overt pattern masks their deeper ambivalence. In these relationships, if the pursuer stops pursuing, the distancer typically begins pursuing or entices the former pursuer back into the game. The distancer is made anxious by closeness but is equally anxious about abandonment; the same is true for the pursuer. Their uneasy pattern of distance and pursuit is a symptomatic interactional compromise which results from both partners' unresolved anxieties about attachment that they have submerged and displaced into the current relationship.

The challenge for couples is to develop relational "rules" that suit reasonably well both partners' idiosyncratic needs for attachment and autonomy. In a "good enough" relationship, these rules will foster both partners' individual development as well as a satisfying connection. This does not imply a perfect meshing of their needs at any given moment, but rather requires flexibility for shifting from one state to the other in response to their partner's needs. This flexibility is enhanced when both partners have low levels of anxiety associated with both closeness and separation, and fostered by patterns of fairness and trust—since each knows that the other will do the same in return.

Fairness and Trust: The Ethics of Intimacy

The most basic expectations for intimate relationships are for safety and caring. We expect to be safe *with* our partners, facing a world of people who do not know us and are indifferent, even hostile, to our welfare. We certainly expect to be safe *from* our partners, from physical and emotional injury at their hands. But we expect more than merely the absence of injury. We expect caring and concern and concrete efforts to protect our welfare. The relationship, at least in theory, should be a "secure base" (Bowlby, 1988) for both partners. This sense of safety is impossible without fairness and trust.

Maintaining fairness is one of the most important challenges for couples. Fairness is not the same as equality and it does not rely on perfectly balanced quid-pro-quo exchanges between partners. An "anatomy" of fairness begins with the recognition that there are multiple interests in close relationships that interact in unique ways. In couple relationships and in couple therapy, there are at least three sets of interests ("interests" being used to indicate the welfare or well-being of an individual or a relationship): those of partner A, those of partner B, and those of the relationship.* Each person has his or her own individual interests; these may be related, unrelated or in conflict. When two individuals "join their fortunes" by committing to a relationship in which they love and care about each other, the potential competition that exists in less intimate relationships becomes subtly but significantly altered. Intimacy blurs the boundaries between altruism and self-interest. It transforms the usual equation of competing interests so that, *in couple relationships, a "victory" in a power struggle is almost always a pyrrhic victory.* If one partner can succeed in getting his or her way by overpowering the other, either verbally, through belittling or shaming, through physical intimidation, or by playing on the other's weakness, the effects on the relationship are ultimately harmful. If they can resolve differences without such tactics, the interests of both parties and of the relationship as a whole are preserved.

*When the couple has children, there are other important interests to consider. The discussion that follows, however, focuses only on these three factors in order to highlight the dynamics of fairness and trust.

When one wins, both lose. When no one wins, both win. This "rule of relationship" can be momentarily bent and in some cases violated for long periods of time, but it cannot be broken indefinitely without serious damage to the relationship.

At the risk of oversimplification, there are three main ways in which people can try to protect themselves, to be safe, in an intimate relationship: power, withdrawal, and trustworthiness. Some individuals try to reduce their vulnerability through power—by intimidating or overpowering their partners. Others seek safety through emotional withdrawal; they are so lacerated by the wear-and-tear of intimacy, or so defeated by their partner's inflexibility, that they retreat into what Guerin and his associates call the "island of invulnerability" (1987). The last and by far the most effective way to be safe involves collaborating to create a trustworthy relationship.

In a trustworthy relationship, each partner has reason to expect that his or her needs and wishes will be seriously considered by the other because he or she extends the same serious consideration to the other. The partners create a "generous economy" for the relationship, one in which each is more inclined to do things to please the other because he or she knows that the other will do the same and because this makes life together sweeter and more enjoyable. Conflicts are resolved, as much as possible, by discussion and by some form of compromise, a willingness to "give in" now and then in the expectation that the partner will do the same.

For these reasons, there is a subtle *convergence* of interests in the alchemy of intimate relationships. It is in both partners' interests to "lose" some of the time in order to preserve trustworthiness and generosity in the relationship. (This does not mean that the partners' interests *always* converge. Her wish to have children may threaten his life-long dreams of financial security, leisure, and travel. His wish to accept an appealing job may require her to sacrifice her own career ambitions. The interplay of the partners' converging and diverging interests creates an important subtext in couple therapy which is sometimes belatedly recognized by the therapist.)

Having considered the complexity of converging and diverging interests in close relationships, we can examine the components of fairness. Contextual theory and therapy (Boszormenyi-Nagy & Spark, 1973; Boszormenyi-Nagy & Ulrich, 1981; Boszormenyi-Nagy & Krasner, 1986), which focus specifically on the *ethical dimension* of relationships, provide a language which is well-suited to this task. The vocabulary of this language includes: entitlement, obligation, claim, and acknowledgement.

Contextual therapists assume that in every close relationship there is a constant oscillating balance of entitlement and obligation between the parties. Both terms refer to *relational debts*. I am *entitled* to something from you; I am *obligated* to you. I owe you something or am owed something by you. This oscillating balance, or "ledger of accounts," applies to matters both large and small. If one parent has gotten up for midnight bottle feedings with a newborn several nights in a row, he or she may feel entitled to let the other parent take the next few; hopefully, if they assess fairness in similar ways, the other will recognize this entitlement and feel obliged, out of fairness, to take over. At a more profound level, if one partner—let's say the husband—is seriously injured, the wife will probably recognize his entitlement to greater help from her in areas he used to handle by himself.

"Claim" refers to an individual's entitlement. The wife who is exhausted from the multiple midnight feedings expresses a claim when she says, "Honey, I just did four nights of these in a row. Would you take over for a few nights and let me catch up on sleep?" If the husband recognizes the fairness of the claim, he will feel obligated to comply and do so. In another couple, the woman's claim might be represented by her saying, "I worked and put up with the stress of your going to medical school. Now I feel it's my turn. I want your support while I go back to school for a graduate degree." Or a man might say, "Listen, I agreed to let your father live with us during his last few years. Now my mom is sick and we need to do the same for her."

"Acknowledgement" involves admitting the validity, or fairness, of the other partner's claim. It requires listening sympathetically; it is made easier when residual trust (see below) enables the listener to give the partner "the benefit of the doubt"—to assume that there must be some validity to his or her claim and to be willing to admit or accept that. The withholding of acknowledgement is a cardinal feature of the chronic conflicts that many couples present in treatment.

Fairness does not involve a perfect meeting of each other's claims. There are many situations in which this is simply impossible. The claims may collide, as when both feel entitled to extra support and care-taking after especially harrowing days at work. (Contextual therapists refer to this as a "colliding entitlement.") Or the partners may assess entitlement in ways which give different weights to various factors. Or one of them may have difficulty seeing the legitimacy of the other's claim because of personal factors, such as high stress levels or powerful family legacies. Even when both partners are able to sympathetically consider one another's claims and when they weigh them similarly, events which are external to the relationship may abruptly alter the balance of fairness, as in the example of injury or a serious illness.

Instead, fairness consists of *an ongoing effort by both partners to consider the legitimacy of each other's claims* and a willingness to try to find solutions in which neither partner feels permanently short-changed. The recipe for this balance of give-and-take requires that each person put forward his or her own claims to entitlement and *listen sympathetically* to the claims of the other. From this dialogue, the partners try to find solutions that maintain the *overall* fairness of give-and-take in the relationship over time. This requires *respect, reliability*, and *repair* (see Chapters 6 and 8). Even with the best of intentions, fairness and trust will inevitably be compromised in long-term relationships. For this reason, repair is a critical element in *restoring* fairness when damage has occurred. This facilitates *forgiveness*, an interactional process by which injury to the trust-base of a relationship is repaired. What is essential is that each partner know that the other is committed to finding solutions that *preserve* fairness for both of them.

Fairness, respect, reliability, and repair make it possible for individuals to *trust* (and for trust to be justified or merited). Trust develops as a psychological and relational consequence of being treated in a trustworthy manner. Partners come to the relationship with varying capacities for trust based on their previous experiences in close relationships—in early attachment relationships and in adolescent and adult love relationships. Beyond their individual capacities for trust, however, the development of trust in any particular relationship depends on the *trustworthiness*, that is, the actions, of the partner. Is the partner dependable? Reliable? Fair? Does he or she keep his or her word? Trust may not be everything in a relationship but, without it, there can be little else. In an untrustworthy relationship, generosity withers, passion becomes contaminated, affection is exhausted, and vitality is snuffed out.

The most common pathological patterns associated with fairness include relationships characterized by chronic disrespect and those in which one or both partners behave in ways that are fundamentally unreliable. They also involve couples who cannot negotiate conflicts because important components of the dialogue of give-and-take are missing. Partners may feel uncertain of their entitlement and therefore have difficulty presenting claims. This does not necessarily mean that they will graciously accept imbalanced give-and-take. They may burn with resentment and even withdraw emotionally or retaliate in some way but still be unable to stand up for themselves in a straightforward and assertive way.

Even more common are individuals who are perfectly capable of presenting their claims clearly but who seem either unable or unwilling to listen sympathetically to the claims of their partner. When one partner consistently rejects the other's claims, this usually elicits an even more strident assertion of those claims (or else a frustrated and increasingly defeated disengagement) and a matching "deafness" to the views of the other. This is the malignant recipe for the "dialogue of the deaf" which so many couple therapists see in their offices on a regular basis.

Partners may give themselves permission to violate norms of respect, reliability, and fairness in particular circumstances, such as during times of stress or when criticized by the partner. Finally, they may be unable or unwilling to repair damage when it is done. This is common when apology equals humiliation for an individual or when he or she is so convinced of his or her rightness that apology is unthinkable.

The challenge for couples is to establish and preserve patterns of mutual respect, reliability, and fairness over the life of the relationship—and it is no small challenge. Both partners must be able to respect themselves in order to be respectful of their partners. They must be able to present their claims of entitlement, to listen sympathetically to the partner presenting his or her claims, and to acknowledge those that they can see are legitimate. They must be able to tolerate "giving in" in some areas so that they can justifiably gain in others. They must have some capacity for trust and be able to act in ways that are essentially trustworthy. They must be able to repair, when their actions have intentionally or inadvertently injured their partners, and to forgive when forgiveness is merited. Lastly, they must try to preserve these patterns in the face of multiple claims on their energy and attention and multiple stresses and crises across the life cycle.

Sexuality: The Pleasure Bond

There is a strong and reciprocal connection between a couple's sexual relationship and their satisfaction with their relationship as a whole. As Zilbergeld (1992) suggests,

> What goes on in the relationship can result in frequent, loving, exciting, and highly satisfying sex. It can also result in infrequent, boring, or nonexistent sex. Relationship dynamics can cause sex problems, help maintain already existing problems, and make problems difficult or impossible to resolve. On the other hand, good sex can make a relationship more harmonious and satisfying and help resolve nonsexual difficulties, whereas dissatisfying or dysfunctional sex can cause or worsen problems in the rest of the relationship. (p. 12)

Longings for sexual satisfaction are central to most couple relationships; they derive from physiological needs, cultural expectations, and needs for attachment, intimacy, and passionate vitality in a relationship. The power of these longings makes the quality of a couple's sexual relationship and the quality of their relationship as a whole inseparable.

There is a unique feeling of connection that comes from the intimacy of being sexual partners, as suggested by the phrase, "the pleasure bond" (Masters & Johnson, 1975). This bond develops from knowing the other person's body and his or her sexual needs and responses and being known in the same way, from the sense of accessibility to the other and allowing oneself to be accessible, and from shared moments of passion, playfulness, vulnerability, and satisfaction. Adding sexuality to a relationship activates powerful emotional and unconscious forces in both partners. This can, as the Scharffs (1991) suggest, "lend . . . a poignancy that few other relationships approach" (p. 12). However, there may also be a darker side to this intensification of emotional forces. Walker (1984) points out, in her research on domestic violence, that physical abuse rarely begins until sexual intimacy takes place.

A mutually satisfying sexual relationship requires the integration of biological differences and gender (in heterosexual relationships) and idiosyncratic individual differences. The starkest biological difference involves the fact that for a man, sex *can* mean only the ejaculation of semen; for a woman, it may mean nine months of pregnancy, the physical labor and risks of delivery, and a lifetime as a mother, or the experience and consequences of abortion. This inescapable fact organizes many of the patterns that dominate sexual politics.

There are other sexual differences between men and women that can complicate a couple's sexual relationship. Women are more likely to require additional stimulation beyond that provided by intercourse for orgasm (Kaplan, 1974). Men, with external genitalia, are unable to "fake" arousal or orgasm, increasing the potential for performance anxiety. Other common differences may be related to either socialization or innate biological differences or both. Men's sexual desire appears to be somewhat less connected to their feelings toward their partners than women's. Men are more likely to want frequent, genital- and orgasm-focused sex, with less emphasis on foreplay and emotional closeness. Women are more likely to connect sexual satisfaction with closeness and satisfaction with the relationship as a whole. This leads to a common conflict in couple relationships in which the man feels that if they were having more frequent sex he would be more generous and loving, while the woman feels that if he were more generous and loving she would be more interested in sex. These differences may contribute to conflicts and misunderstandings which undermine closeness, trust, and satisfaction in the relationship as a whole.

It is more difficult (but not impossible*) to establish a satisfying sexual relationship if one partner has a diagnosable sexual dysfunction. Masters and Johnson (1970) estimate that 50% of all American couples suffer from some type of sexual dysfunction. In a survey of happily married couples, Frank, Anderson, and Rubinstein (1978) note that 40% of the men report erectile or ejaculatory dysfunction and 63% of the women report arousal or orgasmic dysfunction.

Even where no diagnosable dysfunction exists, there may be what Lief (1991) refers to as "sexual difficulties." These include significant differences in the partners' sexual preferences involving: frequency, setting, time of day or night, time devoted to foreplay, repertoire of sexual activities included in an encounter, coital positions, timing of penetration, afterplay, degree of passion and affection expressed, acceptability of fantasy, or involvement with other sexual partners. These differences are part of every individual's idiosyncratic "sexual script" (Rosen & Leiblum, 1988), which defines the kinds of partners and the kinds of activities required for sexual excitement and satisfaction. Rosen and Leiblum (1992) point out that "[t]he sexual scripts of partners in a relationship may vary considerably, and this lack of congruence frequently paves the way for the development of a sexual dysfunction or desire disorder" (p. 244). (See Chapter 15 for further discussion of sexual scripts and sexual dysfunctions.) Ideally, there is enough overlap in the partners' scripts that a mutually satisfying sexual relationship can be worked out.

A wide range of obstacles can complicate a couple's sexual relationship, including: sexual ignorance and common sexual myths (Zilbergeld, 1992), a history of sexual abuse, early difficulties with attachment contributing to fears and defenses associated with intimacy, difficulty communicating sexual needs—"turn-ons" and "turn-offs"—and thus a failure to secure each partner's necessary conditions (Zilbergeld) for sexual excitement, diagnosed and undiagnosed medical problems, difficulties in the overall relationship (especially anger, fear,

---

*Surveys and clinical reports by sex therapists include frequent examples of couples who report satisfaction with their sexual relationship in spite of diagnosable sexual dysfunctions. Typically, they are not especially distressed by the particular difficulties and develop sexual patterns that accommodate to them: He may have erectile problems but she enjoys oral stimulation as well; she may be unable to achieve orgasm with intercourse but they use intercourse to bring him to orgasm followed by manual or vibrator stimulation for her.

alienation, and mistrust), and systemic functions served by sexual symptoms (LoPiccolo & Daiss, 1988; Zilbergeld).

The most common pathological patterns associated with sexuality involve partners who are locked in a power struggle, which spreads to their sexual relationship and can become focused on virtually any aspect of it. Over time, this contributes to growing dissatisfaction with the sexual relationship, decreased desire, and sexual avoidance. A couple's sexual relationship may also suffer from excessive and prolonged stress, from one partner "falling out of love" with the other, from severe physical or psychological problems experienced by one partner, and from intimidation and coercion. Difficulties may stem more directly from diagnosable sexual dysfunctions, the sexual difficulties described above, sexual ignorance, and difficulty communicating about idiosyncratic sexual turn-ons and turn-offs.

The challenge for couples is to maintain an active sexual relationship that is satisfying enough to both partners. Zilbergeld (1992) cites sex therapist Carol Ellison's definition of "good sex": "You're having good sex if you feel good about yourself, good about your partner, and good about what you're doing. If later, after you've had time for reflection, you still feel good about yourself, your partner, and what you did, you know you've had good sex" (p. 62). In order for this to be possible, the partners need to be able to maintain a good-enough overall relationship so that other problems do not invade and contaminate their sexual relationship, communicate verbally and nonverbally about turn-ons and turn-offs, be oriented toward pleasure rather than performance, and appreciate and accept sexual differences (Zilbergeld).

Communication and its Discontents

Communication may well be the most overrated aspect of couple relationships. It's not that it's unimportant, but it has been discussed and analyzed out of proportion to its influence as one of many organizing forces in these relationships. If we were to compare the number of references to communication in marital theory and therapy over the last 25 years, and the relative influence of these references, with those for sexuality or gender or the life cycle, this disproportionate emphasis would be obvious.

This has also led many theorists and therapists to assume that most, if not all, difficulties experienced by couples are the result of *deficits in communicational skills* and that skill training in communication will therefore remedy them. There are legitimate differences of opinion on this score. My own feeling is that relatively few couples who present for treatment are suffering primarily from communicational deficits. More often, their difficulties stem from more complicated underlying forces, including unconscious fears and defenses related to intimacy, legacies and loyalties involving family of origin, and differences in gender socialization. Nevertheless, communication is certainly an organizing force in couple relationships even if it is not the central one.

Communication serves three types of important functions in couple relationships: emotional, practical, and ethical. Communication is an important medium for emotional connection between the partners. It is one means for achieving a sense of intimacy and closeness. The importance of self-disclosure and talk about feelings has been widely, and rightly, emphasized in the literature on communication. We should remember, however, that even couples who do little "processing" of their feelings about the relationship may have other verbal and nonverbal means of feeling close, such as private jokes and pet names, shared values, gossip, and the sheer familiarity of the other's characteristic ways of speaking and well-known concerns ("There he goes again; he's off on the Democrats").

Communication is also important as a practical function: in "steering" the relationship, in facilitating shared coping with the chores and challenges of shared lives. Should they buy a new house or stay where they are? Should she look for a different job? What changes will they need to make in order to care for her father in their home? Trying to arrive at such decisions without communication would be virtually impossible. This is especially complicated because decisions must preserve fairness by taking the entitlements and obligations of both partners—or when there are children, all family members—into account.

This is the third function of communication—to maintain the balance of fairness in the relationship. Without communication, it would be virtually impossible for couples to renegotiate their characteristic patterns of give-and-take. For example, a couple who originally agreed that the woman would be responsible for all housework later decides that for financial reasons she will take a job outside the home. The original contract, however, is never changed, so that she is now working full-time but still doing all the housework. For her to express her unhappiness about this arrangement, for her partner to acknowledge its unfairness, and for the two of them to renegotiate the original contract, they must be able to communicate about it.

It is easy for communication to go awry for couples and there is no shortage of culprits when it does. Men and women are talking across a gulf created by their different styles of communication. Tannen (1990) has observed that "women speak and hear a language of connection and intimacy, while men speak and hear a language of status and independence," making communication between men and women resemble "cross-cultural communication" (p. 42). The partners must struggle with other forms of cross-cultural communication when they come from different ethnic groups, as demonstrated by McGoldrick, Pearce, and Giordano (1982). In one sense, all couple relationships involve cross-cultural communication because of differences in communicational styles between different families of origin, even within the same ethnic groups. One family's patterns of communication may be boisterous, crude, and uninhibited; the other's, secretive and reserved.

Communication is especially difficult for couples because intimacy involves vulnerability. When emotional vulnerability is problematic because of difficulties in either the current or prior relationships, communication becomes more guarded, indirect, confusing, and unsatisfying. Unconscious expectations and disappointments, ambivalence, projection, and defense can derail what might otherwise be fairly simple communicational exchanges. When couples are frustrated and stuck, their communication sequences tend to fall into uniform and predictable patterns. (See Bach & Wyden, 1968; Stuart, 1980; and Watzlawick, Beavin, & Jackson, 1967 for detailed descriptions of these patterns.)

However, a few points about communication that are less often emphasized should be kept in mind. First, for most couples the problem in communication is not speaking, but *listening*. Some individuals do have difficulty expressing their feelings and needs on issues of importance to them, especially when their sense of entitlement and self-confidence are low. More often, however, the partners are able to present their views adequately—even forcefully—to one another but have tremendous difficulty *hearing* what the other is actually saying. This contributes to the repetitive and endless interchanges that are so common in couple therapy. Each wants to be *heard* by the other but feels attacked. In defending him- or herself, he or she shuts out the other's message, thus reinforcing the other's sense of being unheard. Each feels that he or she is—and needs to be—"right." (A friend of mine asks "Would you rather be right or married?") These interchanges are often referred to as a "dialogue of the deaf" or "the blame game."

Second, what is *not said* can be just as important and helpful as what *is said*. A good-enough relationship depends not only on the partners' being able to say what needs to be said but also on their being willing and able to *refrain* from saying something hurtful or destructive, which highlights the importance of "editing" (E. Strauss, personal communication) in couple relationships and during couple therapy. The therapist's suggestions about judicious editing in the partners' communication are one ingredient of effective couple therapy.

Third, communication involves more than just verbal interchange, even if we include the speaker's body language and intonation. *Action* constitutes a language all its own in couple relationships. It can serve all of the functions described above. The husband who has heard his wife complain about his sarcasm for years but has never responded suddenly realizes how deeply it is affecting her when she begins sobbing one day. He does not verbally acknowledge the pain he has inflicted but he is careful to control this behavior in the future. His actions say that she has finally gotten through to him, even if he cannot say so in words. This may or may not be enough to restore trust, but communication has been made via action. As another example, a woman pleads with her husband to stop staying out late drinking with friends, but he makes no response and does not change his behavior. His *inaction* speaks volumes.

The partners' private physical language reinforces the intimacy of their relationship to one another; an example would be touching each other in familiar and private ways, such as when he kisses the bridge of her nose. Physical gestures may do more to foster positive attachment than would an hour of verbal communication in a therapist's office. For many couples who have difficulty verbalizing, the language of action is an important means of communication. Communication skills have their limits, and couple therapists should be aware of them. Better communication skills will not necessarily create passion where there is none; they will not necessarily bridge fundamental differences in the partners' dreams in life and their visions of an ideal relationship, nor will they solve conflicts based on the clash of irreconcilable individual interests.

There are several common pathological patterns involving communication. The first, and perhaps most common, involves couples who are locked in a "dialogue of the deaf." Both partners feel unheard; they experience frustration and disappointment in trying to "get through" to the other. Both feel attacked and misunderstood. These repetitive conflicts take a toll on feelings of warmth and connection and lead to weariness and alienation. For other couples, one partner may be unable to stand up for his or her own interests while the other is all too ready to do so. This leads to an imbalance of give-and-take, which leaves one partner chronically short-changed. For still other couples, neither partner can express needs or complaints or disagreements with the other. They expect or wish the other to "read their minds," to know without their speaking what they want or don't want. This can lead to frustration and disappointment as well as tension and alienation from one another. When these forces build to a certain point, there may be an eruption of anger or acting-out (such as an affair or a move to separation) or the outbreak of symptomatology.

The challenge for couples is to cocreate patterns of communication—talking, listening, editing, and acting—that allow them to feel connected to one another, to coordinate coping with the stresses and demands of life together, and to maintain a sense of fairness of give-and-take in the relationship.

The Wider Relational Context

The couple relationship is embedded in a wider relational context of family, friends, neighbors, coworkers, and others. These outside relationships constitute potential resources as well as potential threats to their relationship. Family, friends, and others can provide safety and stability, a sense of belonging, and concrete and emotional support in times of stress. They can dilute the pressure to have all needs met within the couple relationship. However, they may also impinge on the couple's privacy, limit their ability to take control over their lives, foster conflict, and damage trust within the relationship. In structural language, the couple's ability to manage these relationships involves boundaries and triangles. In contextual terms, it involves the effort to balance multiple legacies and loyalties. The most problematic relationships are usually those that are most intimate and intense. These typically involve children—either from the current or previous relationships—and members of the partners' families of origin.

For most couples, the arrival of the first child—and subsequent children—constitutes the most profound transformation that will affect their relationship. The partners are faced with a host of new functional chores and responsibilities, a loss of freedom, and the physical (and often sexual) changes that accompany and follow pregnancy and delivery. Both parents must be ready to accept the enormous psychological responsibility of caring for a largely helpless human being. The twosome must become a threesome (and then some). The arrival of the child introduces inevitable triangular dynamics and the need to rebalance emotional availability, entitlement, and obligation. Both partners must cope with less attention from each other as more of their attention becomes focused on the child.

The most common pathological pattern associated with this challenge involves a lasting alliance between mother and child, with father in the peripheral role of "outsider." In the early stages after delivery, this is a natural and harmless development. However, failure by the parents to reestablish closeness will create greater difficulty in other areas of their relationship in later stages of family life. Other pathological patterns include an ongoing struggle between the parents for the primary loyalty of the child and, in some cases, the neglect or abuse of the child.

The challenge for the couple is to provide a good-enough developmental context for the child—that is, one that includes love, an ability to respond to the emotional needs of the child, and competent supervision of his or her physical needs and safety—while maintaining or restoring a loving connection between each other. It involves the effort to integrate the child into a loving system and to continue to balance the now more complicated equations of entitlement and obligation.

The most common pathological patterns associated with the wider relational context involve couples for whom the boundaries around the marriage are too weak and, conversely, those for whom they are too strong. In the former category are couples in which one partner is still deeply dependent on one or both parents; the intensity of this tie undermines the connection between the partners. In contextual terms, the issue is one of attempting to balance the claims of different relationships, which is no easy matter. The greater the degree of emotional maturity and individuation of the partners, the more able they will be to make choices that preserve the trustworthiness of their multiple relationships, including the couple relationship. The partners' abilities to negotiate fairly with each other will be limited if they are unable to define and to defend their own rights vis-a-vis their parents and siblings. Similarly, the higher the trust-base in the relationship, the more able the partners will be to tolerate disappointment when other choices are made.

While excessively weak boundaries represent one problematic pattern, excessively strong or rigid boundaries represent another. These couples are so emotionally fused with each other that there are no significant relationships outside of theirs. They are socially isolated and most likely distant from their families of origin. The complexity of balance has been "solved" by simply eliminating one half of the equation. It is certainly possible that for some couples this represents an optimal adaptation. For many, however, it introduces serious problems. Both partners lose out on the richness and vitality that comes from other relationships in life. This arrangement also strains the couple relationship; since no needs can be met outside the relationship, all needs must be met within it which is often exhausting and disappointing.

The challenge for couples is to develop boundaries that are firm but flexible (Minuchin, 1974), that preserve the integrity and uniqueness of the couple relationship while fostering satisfying relationships with family and friends. Both partners engage in an ongoing effort to balance what they owe to their partners and to others (as well as to themselves) so that no one is seriously and permanently "short-changed."

Vitality

I remember talking with a client once who requested psychotherapy because of feelings of depression and dissatisfaction with his work and family life. The expression "to have a hoot" came up, meaning a flat-out, hilarious, and wonderful experience. I remember the terrible sadness with which he said, "My wife and I never have a hoot."

It's more difficult to define this aspect of relationships than most others, but it's no less and may be even more important. Vitality—I can think of no better word for this quality—is essentially what most of us look for in a couple relationship. We hope for a relationship that is lively, stimulating, fun, enriching. It may be hard to identify what makes this richness possible but it's easy to distinguish between a relationship in which there is vitality and liveliness and one that is devitalized, alienated, and "on automatic pilot."

It certainly has something to do with whether or not *positive feeling* and *closeness* have endured in the relationship. Do the partners continue to feel love, affection, and appreciation for one another? It seems related to some form of *intensity* between them. This might be the intensity of their mutual love, playfulness, sexual connection, intellectual relationship, or shared passions such as gardening or wilderness hiking. In all of these examples, there is something that provides an excitement—a spark of liveliness—that they share. There is some kind of "juice" or "pizzazz." The relationship may be stormy—in fact, the presence of strong conflict is itself an indicator of some form of vitality. The partners might wish it could be expressed more easily in other ways but we are unlikely to mistake theirs for a devitalized relationship, a relationship, as it were, without a pulse.

As the vignette concerning "a hoot" implies, a relationship with vitality also suggests the experience of fun, of "bright moments," of enjoyment. This implies some degree of *spontaneity*, the opposite of the "automatic" behavior that characterizes lifeless relationships, where the partners have well-worn ways of relating to each other. The peck on the cheek, for example, and the pro-forma "Goodnight, dear," may at one time have reflected feelings of love and lust but are now enacted "on automatic pilot" to keep life running smoothly, if uneventfully.

In relationships with vitality, one senses that an awareness of the *specificity* of the partner has been preserved. Instead of relating to each other as a kind of "generic" husband or wife, one senses that each partner knows exactly who the other is, with all of his or her peculiarities, and "gets off" on at least some of them. One woman once said to me about her very creative and intellectual husband, "I love his head like a jungle." The phrase captured perfectly the richness of this very creative man's mind and showed me how well she knew him.

Vitality confers resilience. The strength of the connection makes the relationship less vulnerable to threats from within and from outside it. It functions as a relational resource, facilitating joint coping and therefore making it more likely that the relationship will endure. A long-term relationship with vitality depends on the emotional maturity of the partners, their efforts at maintaining and improving the relationship, and some degree of good fortune. Emotionally immature partners can manage a vital relationship in the initial honeymoon period (this hardly takes much managing since it is the nearly automatic result of initial attraction) but will have great difficulty preserving this vitality as time passes and commitment deepens.

The most common pathological pattern involving vitality is the relationship in which the partners interact in an automatic way, in which there is little passion, intensity, or spontaneity between them and little sense that they know and appreciate the idiosyncrasy of the other. The challenge for couples is to preserve this quality of vitality beyond the honeymoon phase of the relationship, to preserve passion, connection, and spontaneity, and to hopefully at least occasionally "have a hoot."

The Unconscious Matrix of the Relationship

In the discussion of attraction and expectations in couple relationships in Chapter 1, I noted the common scenario in which individuals repetitively select partners with whom they proceed to play out familiar and frustrating relational patterns. Examples include the woman who repeatedly chooses men who abuse or neglect her or the man who always picks women who pursue him for more closeness, triggering his fears of intimacy and his subsequent withdrawal. The *persistence* of these patterns and the unerring accuracy of the *selection* of a *particular type of person*, made *without the conscious awareness* of the individual, suggest the operation of unconscious forces in couple relationships.

Every couple (and most couple therapy) has to reckon with the unconscious; it is impossible to avoid. Partners typically are ignorant of this and woefully unprepared for it. They assume that they can consciously set the terms and directions for their relationship and then simply follow them. The most common scenario seen by couple therapists is that of the partners' "best laid plans" going awry, of their being overwhelmed by intense emotional reactivity, which they experience as virtually uncontrollable. The couple who swore to love and honor one another—and meant it—find themselves sulking, nagging, criticizing, and hurling insults at each other. The spouses who loved to do everything together now find themselves irritated by how their partner talks or walks or by his habit of humming or her inability to resist sweets. The wife who was drawn to her husband's quiet and polite manner finds herself angry at his lack of assertiveness in bed.

In the context of family therapy, Lynn Hoffman has referred to "the thing in the bushes": "Descriptions of the creature that family therapists are out to get have been notoriously unsatisfactory. Clinicians know that there is something rustling about in the bushes, but nobody has done a good job of finding it and explaining what it is" (1981, p. 176). If we rule out more straightforward couple cases—in which treatment progresses well and is quickly terminated with good results—and limit ourselves to those cases that most frustrate and bewilder couple therapists, "the thing in the bushes" usually involves unconscious forces *within* each partner that have come to be played out *between* them.

More specifically, it involves unconscious images or representations derived from early attachment relationships and now projected onto the partner in the adult couple relationship. In certain situations, these forces can be activated by individuals whom the person may not even know, as in the experience of instant attraction to a stranger or the adoration of a well-known media figure (and its darker expression in "celebrity stalking"). Most of the time, however, these unconscious forces are activated in close relationships of some *duration* that involve *intimacy* and *sexuality*. These are the relationships that can trigger feelings of ecstatic union, jealous possessiveness, desperate longing, the urgent need to "fix" the other, rage, vindictiveness, and despair.

When the individual's early attachment relationships have been good-enough, the *gratifications* of attachment will be foremost in directing the forces of attraction. As the Scharffs (1991) suggest, this lends poignancy and intensity to the couple's connection and deepens the gratifications of emotional and sexual intimacy. When early relationships have not been good-enough, these longings are likely to be *intensified*, by virtue of having been unmet, and to be accompanied by *fears* and *defenses* which have developed to cope with a range of negative feeling-states (such as frustration, rage, shame and guilt, fear of abandonment, grief, and despair) and which interfere with the natural development of the individual's capacity for intimacy. However, because these feeling-states are so distressing, they are likely to be repressed by the individual so that he or she has little conscious awareness of them, but instead expresses them unconsciously in the give-and-take of close relationship.

The vicissitudes of these early attachments shape the "relational profile" of each partner—his or her characteristic ways of forming close emotional attachments with another person. The fit between the partners' relational profiles forms the "unconscious matrix" of the relationship and organizes interactional patterns between them.

These early difficulties appear to be the source of the repetitive and frustrating relational patterns alluded to earlier. In Framo's words, "current family and marital difficulties largely stem from attempts to master earlier conflicts from the original family; these conflicts are being lived anachronistically through the spouse and children" (1981, p. 134) and "insoluble intrapsychic conflicts [are] acted out, replicated, mastered or defended against with the current intimates" (p. 137). Terminology used by theorists to describe these processes vary; they have been referred to as: "internalized object relationships" (Dicks, 1967; Fairbairn, 1952; Scharff & Scharff, 1991; Winnicott, 1958, 1965, 1971), "RIGs"—"Representations of Interactions that have been Generalized" (Stern, 1985), "marriage contracts" (Sager, 1981), "relational need templates" (Boszormenyi-Nagy & Spark, 1973), "critical images" (Kantor, 1980), "signature premises" (Sheinberg, 1988), and "imagoes" (Hendrix, 1988), among other terms. All of these terms suggest an unconscious image or representation of some aspect of the early problematic relationship.

Theorists largely agree on *how* these images influence the adult couple relationship. In essence, they are assumed to play a role in attraction and selection of a partner, in distorting the individual's perceptions of the partner, and in "inducing" (Laing, 1969)—or unconsciously eliciting—certain kinds of feelings and interpersonal behaviors from the partner. It is also assumed that, to varying degrees, what is projected onto the partner "fits" his or her own unconscious representations in a complementary fashion. The individual is attracted to someone who will "fit the part" of one or more of these unconscious images. It is as if an internal "director" has picked a partner to fill a role in a critically important unconscious drama of some kind. The image will typically represent some aspect of the other (the care-giver) in the original attachment relationship *as experienced by the person* or some aspect of the self in that relationship *as experienced by the person*.

In terms of the other, the individual is attracted to someone whom he or she unconsciously recognizes as similar to the original care-giver. Hendrix (1988) suggests that this will be a combination of the positive and negative qualities of the problematic parent. My own experience suggests that, when early relationships have been frustrating, the most irresistible person is the one who superficially seems to represent the *antithesis* of the frustrating parent but who is in actuality *deeply similar* to that parent, especially in those ways that were most problematic for the individual involved. For example, a woman might assume that in choosing an artistic and bohemian boyfriend she has found the opposite of her father—a hard-driving, critical CEO—but later discovers that her new husband is no less narcissistic and no less critical of her "failure" to recognize the "rightness" of his ways. I also suspect that in many satisfying relationships, the partners have managed to choose a "benign" version of the qualities in a parent that were problematic for them.

In terms of the self, the individual selects someone whom he or she unconsciously recognizes as fitting a disowned aspect of the him- or herself. For example, the person projects onto the other an image of his or her negative or devalued self, the particulars of which depend on specific difficulties encountered in the original attachment relationship. It might involve the image of someone who is "retarded," completely incompetent (a "stumbler," as one client remembered being called), selfish, or always sulking and miserable. Whatever the particulars, the image is fraught with feelings of shame and worthlessness. The individual gains relief from the pain associated with this image of him- or herself by unconsciously projecting it onto the partner and then repeatedly criticizing or "helping" or rejecting the now-devalued partner.

Projected images typically serve defensive or protective psychological functions. For example, a man with strong but denied sexual insecurities may unconsciously choose a wife who is only minimally interested in sex. At a conscious level, he may feel frustrated and complain about her disinterest while unconsciously he is relieved since it protects him from feelings of sexual inadequacy. If the woman becomes less inhibited and more aware of her own sexual appetite, the man will most likely not be pleased but will instead find himself avoiding her sexual advances, criticizing her, starting fights when sex is likely, or developing symptomatology of his own, either sexually or in some other area.

Perceptual distortion of the partner has been noted in virtually all accounts of couple therapy. For example, a man "sees" or experiences his partner as if she were the relational embodiment of the original care-giver—depressed and unavailable, or angry and punitive, or seductive but dangerous, or invasive and overcontrolling; he responds to the partner very much as he did to the care-giver. Alternatively, he "sees" the partner as the walking embodiment of that part of himself which is most troubling to him—his weakness and dependency or his inadequacy; he responds to the partner as he would—and as he did—to that part of himself, typically with persecution and rejection.

The distortion is accompanied by affective, cognitive, behavioral, and (often undetected) somatic patterns. That is, there are characteristic feeling-states, thoughts, interpersonal behaviors, and even body sensations which accompany it. The individual may, for example, *feel* a familiar futility, accompanied by *thoughts* that he or she will never feel okay. These feelings are accompanied by the slumped or collapsed *body posture* and *relational withdrawal* that observers of infant-mother interactions have identified when the mother does not respond to the infant's communicational signals (Tronick, 1989). Or, a different person may feel a panicky sense of being "cast out" by the other along with terrifying thoughts of never being able to feel safe again. These experiences are accompanied by rapid breathing and heartbeat and by a desperate need to physically or emotionally reconnect with the other.

These patterns often have a particular and very noticeable quality in couple sessions. They are marked by the intensity of the individual's reaction and by its apparent misfit with the context of the observed interaction. For example, the woman seems, in the therapist's eyes, to calmly and reasonably ask that the man try to call her when he is going to be extremely late coming home from work. The man becomes infuriated and, with an edge of panic in his response, explodes about her always "checking up on me." The intensity of the reaction is striking and the phrase "checking up on me" seems to come out of nowhere. It stands out from the rest of the interaction and serves as a tip-off that this has special meaning for the man and that difficulties from earlier relationships may be distorting interactions in this one. Object relations theorists (Dicks, 1967; Fairbairn, 1952; Scharff & Scharff, 1991; Winnicott, 1965, 1971) refer to this process as "projective identification." (See Scharff & Scharff [1991] for a cogent and well-organized discussion of projective identification in the context of couple relationships.)

The partner in these processes is not merely a passive, inert recipient of these distortions but is, to varying degrees, emotionally affected by (or unconsciously introjecting) them, so that he or she comes to actually *feel* and *act* consistently with the image. For example, a normally easygoing woman may find herself feeling and even acting like a raging, sadistic oppressor, or like someone paralyzed by anxiety and disorganization.*

One common pattern enacted in the unconscious matrix of couple relationships involves a repetitive unconscious effort to repair the wounds of early difficulties and their effects on the individual's sense of his or her own "goodness" or lovableness. The individual has the life-long feeling that something is "missing" or "wrong" and this lack of resolution is painful and oppressive. *The inability to have these needs satisfied* is so painful and so central to the individual's well-being that it dominates his or her emotional and relational life, especially in a couple relationship.

The individual is unconsciously primed to find someone who can fix this wound, who can make him or her feel whole and loved and good. The characteristics of that person will not be random. They will in some way resemble those of the person, usually a parent, with whom the original difficulties occurred. A man with a harsh, critical parent repeatedly finds himself attracted to harsh, critical partners. A woman whose mother had been depressed and emotionally inaccessible finds herself trying desperately to elicit warmth and loving involvement from a similarly depressed, withdrawn husband—trying to "bring him to life." In doing so, she is propelled by the fear of abandonment that she experienced as a child and is unconsciously acting out her early recognition that unless she can bring her mother to life she will be alone and deprived.

These repetitious patterns appear to represent unconscious efforts at mastery, attempts to resolve the most pressing and painful emotional wound in the individual's life. The problem, of course, is that this effort takes place through a proxy, typically the current partner, thereby conflating two different relationships and almost certainly adding to the confusion and complication of the current relationship.

The partner—that is, the "target" of the projection—is even more likely to play out his or her part if the distortion complements his or her own unconscious images. For example, let's return to the woman discussed earlier who reenacts with her depressed husband her earlier experiences with her depressed and unavailable mother. The husband's early difficulties involve an intrusive and highly controlling mother. This image is now projected onto his wife. Her desperate attempts to bring him to life unconsciously reactivate the feelings of vulnerability,

---

*Psychotherapists know how powerful these distortions—or transferences— are in the context of treatment; they can not only distort the client's perception of who the therapist actually is but affect the feelings and, unless he or she is aware of them, the actions of the therapist as well.

helplessness, inadequacy, and resentment he originally experienced as a child with his mother. Naturally, he resists these efforts and retreats further into an angry, self-protective isolation.

This relational knot is compounded by the *misunderstandings* generated by the unconscious material. The wife feels resentful and misunderstood because her husband fights her efforts to be helpful to him. The husband feels angry and misunderstood because of the pressure he feels from her to "pull himself up by his boot-straps" when this feels impossible. Both partners' unconscious relational needs have undermined the hopes of generous love and support they each brought to the marriage.

In these situations, the partners' complementary unconscious images are acted out between them in a repetitive interactional loop that is unsatisfying but irresistible. The loop is always characterized by intense reactivity—that is, a sort of chain reaction of intense and highly predictable emotional responses that short-circuit detachment, reflection, and flexibility. Typically, there is an elegant interlocking between each partner's vulnerabilities and defenses. For example, when he feels vulnerable, his typical defense is to withdraw emotionally, which triggers her sense of vulnerability, activating her defense which is to cling and desperately seek reassurance, which increases his sense of vulnerability, and so on. There is no way that their conscious expectations for the relationship can be met given these highly reactive interactional patterns.

The pathological expressions of this aspect of relationship involve, as described above, "contaminations" and distortions in the current relationship fueled by unconscious images derived from unsatisfactory experiences in early attachment relationships. There is confusion between "then and there" and "here and now." Needs for attachment may be greatly intensified and impossible to satisfy in an adult relationship, or anxieties and fears associated with attachment may lead to defenses that make pleasurable intimacy all but impossible. The projection of internal images onto the partner leads to confusion and misunderstanding as the recipients of these projections feel themselves to be suffocated by the needs of the other, unfairly blamed, criticized, and devalued or, alternatively, impossibly idealized and bound to disappoint. Their interactions come to be dominated by repetitive sequences characterized by intense reactivity, sequences that reactive the painful and distressing affects of early attachment difficulties and that undermine conscious intentions in the current relationship.

The challenge for couples is to be able to separate then-and-there from here-and-now, to be able to see beyond the most extreme and destructive projections in order to see at least some of the reality of the actual partner. This means trying to separate what is going on *within* the self from what is going on *within* the partner and *between* the two of them. No couple can be entirely successful in this challenge. The nature of the unconscious material involved and the blurring of inter-personal boundaries, which is, at least to some extent, inevitable in couple relationships, make it unlikely that all projections can be iden-tified.

Probably the greatest resource for partners facing this challenge is having had good-enough early attachment relationships, a resource which cannot, unfortunately, be generated post-hoc in any form of therapy. When early relationships have not been good-enough, individ-ual psychotherapy or couple therapy may help the individuals become more aware of their distortions and of those of their partners. Distin-guishing then from now, and within from between involves an effort to differentiate oneself from past and present relational contexts (Bowen, 1978), to contain distressing affect instead of simply discharging it at one's partner and to listen sympathetically to the partner's description of his or her own experience instead of insisting deafly on one's own. It requires an ability to look at one's own possible contributions to rela-tional difficulties as well as an effort to meet the distortions of the partner with, ideally, both love and some confidence and firmness about the ways in which they do not fit one's own experience, feelings, and behavior. It is a subtle but immensely important process that occurs for some couples through some form of therapy and for others through the accretion of years, or even decades, of "life lessons" in the relationship; for still others, it never occurs because the power of the distortions finally overwhelms the resources that might have cor-rected them.

A Good-Enough Couple Relationship

It's important in discussing couple relationships, especially when self-identified experts are doing the discussing, to be *realistic*. Referring to "systematizers," or theorists, Kierkegaard suggested that "most system-atizers are like a man who builds an enormous castle and lives in a shack beside it" (1938, p. 156). Couples' difficulties sometimes involves idealized and unattainable expectations for an intimate relationship. If the therapist shares these unrealistic expectations, it will be much harder to help them. We need a realistic model of couple relationships, not an idealized and unattainable one. I can think of no better expres-sion of the contrast between the two than an ad and a comment I remember from the early 1970s. The movie *Love Story* had been released and was being advertised with the wildly idealized statement, "Love is never having to say you're sorry." John Lennon was interviewed some months later and said that love was having to say you're sorry over and over and over again. I've always liked the mordant realism of that sentiment.

A good-enough couple relationship is one that meets both partners' "narratives," or images of the relationship they want, on *enough* major points to allow for a feeling of relative contentment. The partners are able to *define the relationship* in a way that feels comfortable to each of them and then to live with this definition until a time comes when they may need to change it. The relationship provides a mixture of attachment and automony—of "I" and "We"—that suits the personal needs and styles of both partners.

Satisfying couple relationships are characterized by the feeling of being "at home" with one another *most* of the time, by some degree of closeness, fun, passion, and shared understanding, and by an overall contentment with the relationship, a sense that it feels "right," that one is glad to be involved with *this* person. However, not even good couple relationships meet all the needs and expectations of the partners nor will the experience of contentment and satisfaction be unending and uninterrupted.

Even in satisfying relationships, people have to accept some limitations and disappointments. A partner doesn't share her partner's deep love of hunting or opera or tag sale hopping and shows not the slightest inclination to join him in these activities. Or he is generous and loving but not nearly as passionate sexually as she might wish. Or the sexual relationship is lively and fulfilling but she is so driven in relation to her work that it's hard for her to relax with him. Or he can relax with her but he doesn't really know how to respond when she talks about politics or ideas that interest her.

In a good-enough relationship, both partners recognize that no one person could possibly meet all of their needs; they can accept particular limitations without damaging their appreciation of the goodness, or rightness, of the relationship for them. Even here, realism is in order. This does not mean that the partners are never frustrated by these limits. It means that, over time, they are able either to cooperatively change what is intolerable or to accept what is frustrating or disappointing but tolerable. In the process, they come to terms with what is and is not available to them in the relationship. In other words, they come to have more *realistic expectations* of what their partners can provide for them and to recognize and tolerate the fact that their partners also have expectations of them.

Even this hard-won contentment can be interrupted by a variety of internal and external factors: a serious illness, a death in the family, the loss of a job, or simply a syncopation or miscoordination in the timing with which both partners move through their individual life cycles. In most good couple relationships, the partners move through cycles of closeness and greater distance, periods when the satisfying "We" dominates the mood of the relationship and periods when they are—or one is—more preoccupied with personal life issues. Periods of contentment can be disrupted by events that unbalance the fairness of give-and-take in the relationship; it requires action or dialogue or, in some cases, simply time to restore a new balance of fairness.

Partners develop their own idiosyncratic patterns that serve to maintain fairness and to repair damage to the trustworthiness of the relationship. They can tolerate "giving in" in some areas so that they can justifiably gain in others. They have some capacity for trust and can act in a way that is basically trustworthy. They try to repair when their actions have intentionally or inadvertently injured their partner and to forgive when forgiveness is merited. They try to respect gender differences without devaluing either side.

They develop their own patterns of communication—talking, listening, editing, and acting—which allow them to feel connected, to coordinate coping with the stresses and demands of life, and to maintain a sense of fairness in the relationship. They try to maintain boundaries that are firm but flexible, that preserve the privacy and integrity of their relationship while fostering satisfying connections with family and friends. They try to balance their obligations to those they care about so that no one is seriously and permanently short-changed.

The good-enough relationship is not problem-free. The partners do not exist in a timeless sense of spiritual communion, oneness, and deep loving. They may experience irritation, boredom, hurt feelings, doubts, exasperation, superiority, rage, guilt, and fear. They may find themselves overwhelmed by challenges stemming from external stresses or from interactional patterns that they cannot control. They may seek professional help from a minister or therapist. But they preserve the relationship because they *choose* to be in it, because they are able to rediscover what makes it *worth it* for them, because its gratifications outweigh its trials. They understand that the relationship is their joint creation, their private world unknown in many ways to the outside world. They appreciate that it is the relational equivalent of the home they make for themselves; it shelters them and helps them to grow and to try to become more themselves. They know that, in the river of time, it is with this person and on this raft that they choose to travel.

━ II ━

THE EVALUATION

T HE FOLLOWING CHAPTERS move from the conceptual to the practical. An initial chapter outlines the overall features of the evaluation format; subsequent chapters concentrate on specific phases or
aspects of conducting the evaluation, including:

- arranging the evaluation
- conducting the initial couple session
- conducting the individual sessions with each partner
- developing a formulation
- considering treatment recommendations
- designing the therapist's response to the couple
- conducting the final session

Each chapter examines clinical considerations and offers guidelines and practical suggestions for these tasks within the evaluation; these considerations and recommendations are illustrated whenever possible with case examples.

The three concluding chapters round out this practical focus on the evaluation. Chapter 12 suggests modifications of the evaluation format for a variety of clinical contexts which do not involve a request or referral for couple therapy. Chapter 13 examines other formats for evaluating couples, and Chapter 14 summarizes the criteria for a good-enough couple evaluation.

4

THE FORMAT OF
THE EVALUATION

Description of the Evaluation Format

THE FORMAT FOR EVALUATING couples has several basic features:

1. conceptualizing evaluation as a distinct clinical procedure that precedes and is differentiated from couple therapy
2. meeting jointly and separately with both partners during the course of the evaluation
3. presenting a summary of the therapist's impressions and recommendations at the end of the evaluation
4. recommending that the couple postpone any major changes in their relationship until the conclusion of the evaluation

Couple Evaluation as a Distinct Clinical Procedure

When a couple calls requesting couple therapy, instead of immediately complying with this request, the therapist offers to conduct an evaluation. The evaluation is *time-limited* and takes place *prior to* any treatment that may be recommended. The therapist *serves as a consultant* to the couple, conducts the evaluation and, at *its conclusion*, provides a response to what they have shared—a summary of observations, impressions, and recommendations. When couple therapy is recommended, the evaluation serves as the first step in that process. When it is not, the evaluation provides detailed information that adds depth and credibility to other recommendations, thereby hopefully facilitating their acceptance by the couple. The therapist's task is to help the couple better understand the nature of their difficulties and to make more informed decisions regarding possible treatment.

This aspect of the evaluation is designed to minimize the risks of clients and therapist moving precipitously in what may be an unhelpful or even destructive direction for treatment. The evaluation gives the therapist time to try to understand the nature of the couple's difficulties and the approaches that are most likely to be helpful for them. It also gives ambivalent, fearful, and resistant clients an opportunity to initially make a more limited—as opposed to an open-ended—commitment.

Couple and Individual Sessions

The therapist meets initially with both partners together. This is the simplest and most straightforward means of assessing a couple relationship and it minimizes risks associated with meeting with each partner individually. Both partners start out on the same footing. In this initial couple session, the therapist

- works to build balanced alliances with both partners
- gathers information about the facts of the couple's life together (in order to understand the practical and relational contexts in which problems are embedded)
- explores the presenting problem in detail
- assesses individual and relational resources
- investigates the evolution of the relationship over time
- examines overall features of the couple's relationship (such as patterns of intimacy and fairness)
- explores both individual's goals and agendas for the evaluation

This is followed by separate individual sessions with each partner. In these sessions, the therapist

- works to strengthen individual alliances with each partner
- gathers individual and family history as well as a history of earlier couple relationships
- explores each individual's feelings about his or her partner as well as his or her level of commitment to the relationship
- tries to understand each partner as an individual, including his or her identity, values, and worldview, and his or her social and work life outside the relationship

Following this, the therapist again meets with the couple at which point he or she presents a summary of observations, impressions, and formulations and includes recommendations for treatment and/or other forms of intervention.

When the evaluation takes this form, the number of actual sessions may vary. Some therapists will conduct the complete evaluation in one sitting, although this will very likely require at least 2 to $2\frac{1}{2}$ hours. Others will conduct the first three parts—the initial couple session and both individual sessions—in one sitting and follow up with a final couple session at another time. Still others may wish to conduct four separate sessions. (To simplify discussion, each of the four parts of the evaluation will be referred to as a "session" in the chapters which follow, whether they are held at the same time or on different occasions.) The number of sessions will be determined by the personal preferences of the therapist and a variety of logistical factors. Therapists who are relatively unfamiliar with couple evaluation should allow three to four hours if they plan to conduct all four sessions together. This should include time between the inquiry and feedback/summary portions of the evaluation to weigh and consider the information and impressions gathered before generating recommendations for treatment. The evaluation can be expanded when complexity or idiosyncratic factors call for it. This is especially likely when the therapist feels the need to assess other family members, such as children or parents living in the home. (In the case of one couple I evaluated, both partners spoke in the initial session at such remarkable length and both were so clearly disinclined to be interrupted that I indicated the evaluation might take twelve sessions. The couple readily agreed; it actually took six.)

Not only the number of sessions but also their sequence may vary. As suggested above, the most straightforward and least risky way to open the evaluation is for the therapist to meet simultaneously with both partners. However, therapists should feel free to adapt to special circumstances. One partner may initially refuse to participate, leading the other to ask for an initial individual session. If the therapist agrees, and if the discussion with the attending spouse paves the way for the other partner to attend the next session, the initial order of sessions will have been reversed. This is somewhat less desirable but should not be rejected out of hand by the therapist. In some cases, it may be necessary because of time constraints or advisable because of idiosyncratic factors to dispense with the individual sessions. In these cases, the therapist will either forego most of the agendas for the individual sessions or pursue them as best as possible in couple sessions. (See Chapter 7 for a discussion of advantages and potential disadvantages of individual sessions in the evaluation.)

The Therapist's Response at the End of the Evaluation

At the end of the evaluation the therapist presents a summary of his or her observations, impressions, and recommendations. Some therapists may wish to share aspects of their thinking with the couple as the evaluation proceeds. In many cases, this will do no harm and possibly some good since it may heighten the collaborative nature of the process. However, there may be significant detriments to disclosing your thoughts too soon. These are discussed later in this chapter.

The Therapist's Suggestion to Defer Major Decisions

The therapist typically suggests that the couple make no major changes in their relationship until the end of the evaluation. The point here is to try to slow down a "runaway" process and to enable couples to make decisions based on a better understanding of their relationship. Many couples are relieved when this suggestion is made, especially when emotions are both intense and ambivalent. This is usually most helpful with couples who are in crisis and considering separation or divorce. An affair may have been recently discovered or disclosed and one partner may be planning to leave. Or the couple may have been anguishing over a decision to separate for some time. The move to consult a therapist, prompted by one or both partners finding their impasse increasingly untenable, may be accompanied by an impulse to "do something" by separating. Especially when children are involved, there is likely to be little harm and considerable benefit from the recommendation that such changes await the end of the evaluation. The same principle holds in reverse. Couples who are already separated and considering getting back together can also benefit from the suggestion that they wait until completing the evaluation. As always, there are exceptions.

A woman who recently discovered her husband's extramarital affair is angry and deeply hurt. She is willing to begin couple therapy but insists that her husband move out of the home. She makes clear that this represents her way of sending a powerful message to him about how badly he has hurt her and is a means of salvaging self-esteem. There is no compelling reason for the therapist to oppose this. If the husband is willing to comply, then the therapist can as well, especially because this represents an act of self-respect on the part of the wife.

A husband and wife who have been unable to contain their verbally abusive arguments agree that, for their children's sake, it would be better for them to live apart until they can hopefully find a way to argue more constructively. The therapist can easily endorse this plan.

Encouraging postponement of major changes until after the end of the evaluation is useful but not critical to the evaluation. If both partners choose to disregard this advice, it may introduce somewhat greater instability into the evaluation but is unlikely to sabotage it. The therapist can reiterate his or her concerns but accept the arrangement and continue. One byproduct of this exchange is that the couple will be assuming greater responsibility for the course and outcome of the evaluation.

Advantages of the Evaluation Format

Framing the Evaluation: A Map Through the Maze

The evaluation format creates a "frame," which most clients find reassuring. The structure provides a sense that at least someone knows what he or she is doing and is going about it in an orderly way. This can be extremely helpful to individuals who may be under great stress, emotionally reactive, and confused by their current situation. They may feel that they are in chaotic or unfamiliar terrain. When the therapist communicates that he or she knows this terrain, has been around it before, and has some clear ideas about how to profitably explore it, this sense of expertise and structure often contributes to a palpable sense of relief in the clients.

The orderliness implied in the structured format of the evaluation can help clients regain at least a temporary sense of control over their situation, a foothold in an otherwise unfamiliar environment. In this sense, the therapist offers "a map through the maze." This temporary stabilization is strengthened by the suggestion that the couple postpone any major relational changes until the evaluation is completed.

Buying Time

As already mentioned, the therapist tells the couple that he or she will provide a summary of impressions and recommendations at the end of the evaluation; their questions are welcome but, unless there is an immediate crisis, attempts to answer them should be deferred until the evaluation is completed. This gives the therapist time: time to get to know the partners, time to understand what has contributed to their problems and what maintains them, and time to think about how to present his or her impressions so that they are most likely to be helpful to these particular individuals.

Building Credibility

The therapist's recommendations, whatever they are, should be *convincing*. The couple should find the assessment credible and compelling. The therapist needs to "capture the imagination" (E. Strauss, personal communication), to persuade that the perceptions are informed and the conclusions reasonably accurate. The evaluation format provides the detailed information required to support these observations and recommendations in a plausible and convincing way. In a family context, for example, it's one thing to assert that two brothers' fighting is a "systems" problem and "probably related" to the parents' separation one year earlier; it's another to point out that the fighting increased significantly within weeks of the separation, that both boys admit to being furious at their father but afraid to confront him directly, and that their sister remarked, "Since they can't very well beat up on Dad, they just have to beat up on each other."

Evaluation as a Two-way Street

Evaluation is always a two-way street; the clients are also evaluating the therapist. Clients want to know that the therapist they choose is *sympathetic to their interests* and *competent* if not *expert* at the enterprise at hand. The evaluation format allows the therapist to demonstrate trustworthiness and effectiveness as well as whatever particular strengths he or she brings to the task at hand. In particular, the evaluation format itself suggests carefulness, thoroughness, and a willingness to serve as a disinterested consultant.

Drawing in Resistant Partners

Couples very often present with one partner reluctant to be involved. This partner is likely to be more reluctant if he or she thinks treatment involves an open-ended, undefined, and possibly long-term commitment. These individuals are often reassured by the time-limited nature of the evaluation. They will probably find it easier to commit to one to four sessions, knowing that they will get a clear presentation of the assessment by the end of that time, than to sign on for "couple therapy."

Heightening Receptivity to the Therapist's Recommendations

Time works for the evaluation in yet another way. Simply put, the structure of the evaluation builds suspense. During its course, the therapist takes in a great deal of information before summarizing his or her impressions and recommendations to the clients. Very few couples can resist a natural curiosity, after having waited through one to three sessions, for this summary which, when finally delivered, has echoes both of the ancient mythic oracles (Papp, 1980) and a physician offering a diagnosis after thorough testing on a possibly serious illness. This is one of several ways in which the evaluation format utilizes drama to heighten clients' receptivity to the therapist's summary. Here the therapist uses the structure of the evaluation itself and the clients' natural curiosity. This does not mean that clients will automatically *accept* the therapist's observations and recommendations, merely that they are significantly more likely to *hear* them.

Avoiding Unproductive Treatment

The evaluation format reduces the likelihood that clients and therapist will become involved in unproductive sessions. For example, a woman wants to pursue couple therapy; her husband, who is highly critical of his wife and their relationship, is noncommittal to the point of being unwilling to describe any changes he would want, unable to say he wishes to work on improving the marriage, and adamant that he has no interest in changing these feelings. This represents a point of personal conviction for the therapist. Some therapists (the author included) would feel that in many such cases couples are best served by the therapist's recommending against treatment, since the necessary prerequisites are almost certainly not present in both partners. The therapist's guiding principle should always be: *When in doubt, test,* meaning that if any doubt exists in the therapist's mind, he or she should *try* to conduct treatment rather than assuming that no progress can be made.

Setting the Trajectory of Treatment

Sometimes it happens that couples present for treatment in a straightforward manner. The problems are fairly obvious, the requests are compatible, the direction is clear-cut, and the outcome is often successful. But this is more of an exception than a norm. Frequently, couples present in much more complicated ways, with problematic requests or conditions, troublesome outside relationships, burdensome arrangements, and self-defeating convictions; for example:

- The woman who has brought her unexpressive mate unsuccessfully to three previous therapists may wish the new one to tackle the same task—to "make him talk."
- The man having one or more affairs may ask to help his wife and himself without being willing to give up any of them.
- The husband who is troubled by his wife's disinterest in him may, from fear of losing her, insist on couple sessions; if her "disinterest" is part of a profound depression, however, initial couple sessions in which she quite literally has nothing to say to him may be far from productive.

One of the greatest advantages of the evaluation format is that it increases the chances that the therapist will *see* the difficulties posed by these conditions or requests and be able to avoid them in favor of more hopeful directions.

This chapter has presented the broad outlines of a format for evaluating couples. Subsequent chapters fill in the details. They present guidelines and specific recommendations for every phase of the evaluation beginning, in the next chapter, with the process of arranging it.

⌐ 5 ⌐

ARRANGING THE EVALUATION

O NE OF THE CORE assumptions of this book is that careful attention to the process of evaluation, at the start of a couple therapy
case, can help the therapist avoid potential obstacles and mistakes
later in treatment. The same holds true within the evaluation itself.
The process of arranging the evaluation is an opportunity to "start out
on the right foot." The care that you put into this process can prevent
problems and misunderstandings in the evaluation and increase the
likelihood of a successful outcome.

Couple evaluations can be arranged in any number of ways, depending on the type of treatment requested and the context in which services are delivered. In order to highlight basic considerations and
guidelines, the following discussion assumes the most common and
straightforward scenario: the initial telephone conversation between a
client requesting couple therapy and a therapist making the arrangements to meet with the couple him- or herself. This situation involves
an inherent *congruence* between the request for treatment and the

format of evaluation as well as the clearest *continuity* between the person arranging the evaluation and the person conducting it. Other situations, such as when the clinician who evaluates the couple is not the person who takes the initial call or when callers may have different requests for treatment, are discussed later in this chapter. Modifications in the format that are called for when the couple evaluation occurs in other clinical contexts are discussed in Chapter 12.

The main agenda for the initial telephone conversation is:

1. Gather enough information to be able to judge whether a couple evaluation is appropriate.
2. Make a positive connection with the caller.
3. Explain the structure and rationale for the evaluation.
4. Schedule the initial couple session.

In the handling of this call, it is important to remember that treatment begins *before* the first session.

Treatment Begins Before the First Session

Therapists, especially novices, may think that what takes place before the actual first session is relatively incidental, like an informal rehearsal before an important performance, as though what goes on there "doesn't really count." Experienced therapists know better. Treatment begins before the first session, before actually meeting the clients. For the therapist, the initial telephone call represents an opportunity to begin the processes that will dominate the actual sessions: joining, gathering information and impressions, and clarifying the purposes and structure of the evaluation. For clients, the call represents the first step in a process of *testing*, of trying to answer the (usually unspoken) questions, that for them dominate the evaluation: Will we like this person? Will we feel safe with her? Can we trust her? Does she know what she is doing? Will she help us feel good about ourselves or make us feel ashamed? Will she be able to help us? How the therapist conducts this conversation "counts" as much as anything that takes place in subsequent sessions.

What messages does the therapist convey about herself during these brief and relatively simple discussions? Does she seem to be gracious and understanding of the client's constraints, or is she hurried, impatient, peremptory, and condescending? Does she come across as sympathetic and competent? How quickly does she return their call? How accessible is she, in terms of scheduling? Does she seem reasonably clear about how to proceed or is she halting and uncertain? Does she explain clearly the structure and rationale for the evaluation, or is she obscure, inarticulate, or confusing?

One final caveat: Treatment may begin before the first session but this is not an invitation to begin interpreting and intervening on the initial telephone call. Remember that you know precious little about the clients at this point. If you try to reframe the caller's views on central issues or to offer suggestions about how to handle certain matters, you run the risk of "shooting from the hip," without either enough information or enough trust from the clients. For this reason, try to avoid initiating such interventions yourself; if the caller directly solicits advice or reactions and you are uncertain about how to respond, defer attempts to do so until you have more information about the couple. You can explain this to the caller and express the hope that you will be able to respond more specifically by the end of the evaluation. This explanation makes sense. It is usually readily accepted by clients and, if anything, suggests a thoughtful and responsible professional.

Gathering Basic Information

The initial telephone call represents a "mini-evaluation" (Karpel & Strauss, 1983). You want to gather enough information to be able to make sensible decisions about whether to schedule the evaluation, who should attend, and any other special considerations that might be involved. These calls usually take about 10 or 15 minutes.

I ask for ages of all family and household members. I ask for a brief description of the presenting problem: "Could you tell me a bit about what led you to call me at this point?" I want to know whether both are employed and what kind of work they do. How did they get my name? Have they been involved in couple therapy in the past? Is either partner currently or recently involved in any other psychological treatment? This information begins to orient me to their relational context and to the reasons for their seeking treatment at this point in time. Is the couple married? Do they have children? Are they unmarried but living together? Are they separated? Is this a stepfamily sharing custody with other parents?

Often, if there are special circumstances involved, you will get some indication of this during the initial call. For example, a woman calls saying that she does not know whether or not her husband will agree to attend. Or she and her partner see this contact as "a last resort," meaning that if they do not see progress in treatment at this point they plan to separate. As one caller delicately put it, "Either it's you or I'm out of here."

_One woman called requesting treatment and mentioned paren-
thetically that, for several years, she had noticed "funny ways"
in her husband which he refused to explain to her. These included
insisting that they not share the same dishes or cups and always
washing his clothes separately from hers. She added that he was a
Vietnam veteran; she wondered if this was somehow related to his
exposure to and preoccupation with Agent Orange. These details suggest a series of questions or hypotheses: Was the husband preoccupied
with his health prior to exposure to Agent Orange or only subsequently—if it actually occurred? Is the husband suffering from an
undiagnosed obsessive compulsive disorder? Is he afraid of infecting
her in some way and does this indicate the possibility of an extramarital involvement and a sexually transmitted disease? Finally, is this
comment part of an effort on the wife's part to predispose the therapist
to seeing her husband as the "sick one" in the relationship?_

_A married woman asked if it would be alright for her mother
to pay for the evaluation. It turned out that mother and daughter have a joint checking account, and the daughter's finances were
almost entirely separate from her husband's. This raises questions
about triangles, generational boundaries, and the degree of maturity
of the spouses._

Details such as these, and the feelings and hunches they elicit, can give you a head-start in generating and testing hypotheses with a particular couple.

Presenting the Evaluation Format

Once I've ascertained that the case is appropriate for a couple evaluation, I explain the structure and rationale of the evaluation format in the following way.

Let me tell you a little about how I work. What I always do in these situations is to set up an evaluation or consultation. I would meet with the two of you together for the first session. I would probably then meet with each of you individually one time, try to speak—

with your permission—to any other therapists recently or currently
involved with either of you, and then get back together with both of
you. At that time, I'll try to say as much as I can about what I think
is going on and what directions I think might be most helpful to you.
This might involve continuing with couple sessions but it might not.
It's hard to know beforehand what will be most helpful; that's the
main reason for the evaluation. It also gives you a chance to get some
idea of who I am and, if we decide to continue, whether you'd be
comfortable working with me.

We jointly decide whether the evaluation will be conducted in one
long appointment or over the course of two or more sessions. We
discuss fees and, when appropriate, insurance coverage. If the client
has no significant objections to this proposal, I schedule the first session and give directions to my office.

Discussing the Unexpected

A good rule of thumb for these telephone calls is to alert clients as
soon as possible to any aspect of treatment they might not expect to
encounter. For example, if the caller's descriptions suggest that the
couple's children are significantly affected by their problems, let the
caller know that you will expect to meet with the children during
the course of the evaluation. The same is true for any other possibly
unexpected aspects of treatment: possible inclusion of other family
members, use of videotaping, use of outside consultants (e.g., medical
evaluation in a sex therapy case or psychiatric evaluation for possible
medication), the necessity of gathering detailed sexual histories when
a sexual problem is prominent, or talking with therapists currently
or recently involved with the clients. This allows clients to prepare
themselves for these potentially more threatening aspects of the evaluation and facilitates a smoother transition through its stages.

Tracing the Referral Route

During the initial telephone call you can begin to trace the referral
route that has led the couple to you. You want to understand why
these individuals are seeking treatment now, how they have come to
contact you in particular, and what all of this means to them. This
information may impose constraints on the evaluation and it may
have prognostic implications for treatment. You can gather some of

this information during the initial telephone call and add to it later in the initial couple session.

Who referred the couple to you? Was it a friend of theirs who had a positive experience with you as a therapist in the past, one partner's individual therapist, or another professional who has worked with them? This information may be revealing in its own right as when, for example, couples are referred by an attorney in divorce proceedings. (Many couple therapists assume that couples who are referred in this manner have a lower prognosis for successful treatment, "successful" here meaning reconstituting a positive intimate relationship.) More important is understanding how they feel about this person and the implications this holds for the evaluation. For example, if the couple has been referred by a close friend who feels very positively about her treatment with you, this is probably an asset since it increases both your credibility and their hope for success. The picture becomes more complicated if the couple is split in their feelings about the referral source.

Joanne and Bob were referred to me by Joanne's best friend, who had recently left her husband of 15 years. In Bob's eyes, this woman was a bad influence who had been "meddling" and encouraging his wife toward greater independence from him. Joanne was prepared to feel positively about me because of her friend's positive experience in treatment. However, I knew that I would have to convey to both of them that I did not believe the friend's solution— leaving her husband—was automatically the right solution for everyone and that I would try my best to represent both of their interests without preconceptions.

In some cases, clients may come to you with more specific impressions of your work; these impressions can help you understand their goals for the evaluation. These agendas are suggested by comments such as: "We heard that you 'call a spade a spade.' We've seen two therapists who we felt just held our hands. We want to either make things better or end this and get on with our lives." Another couple might have a very different agenda: "She said that you really work hard to help people save their marriages."

An Anomaly: A Couple Evaluation But an Individual Caller

One last feature of the initial telephone call that bears mentioning is the fact that although arrangements are being made to evaluate a *cou-*

ple, you will almost always speak with only one *individual*. Except in rare cases when both partners make clear that they want to participate in this conversation or when you happen to connect with both on the telephone at the same time, one partner assumes or is delegated the responsibility to call and make the appointment. What are the implications of this discrepancy, if any, for the evaluation itself?

It's certainly worth considering *who* is calling and what significance this may have. Usually, it is the more motivated partner who calls; typically this is the partner who is most discontent with the current terms of the relationship. Sometimes, however, the caller is engaged in an act of atonement or a demonstration of commitment. For example, a husband has resisted couple therapy for some time but, when his wife threatens to leave, he agrees to make the call in order to prove his sincerity to her. In talking with only one partner, you are receiving an inevitably biased picture of the couple's current difficulties. For this reason, while you absorb all the information shared on the phone, you take it "with a grain of salt," knowing that when you meet with both partners you will most likely see another side to the caller's descriptions.

Does it affect the evaluation in any significant way that it is arranged not by the couple but by an individual? In the vast majority of cases the answer is "No." Obviously, one partner has to explain to the other what you've said about the purposes and structure of the evaluation and there is always room here for misunderstanding or deliberate misrepresentation. However, if you follow the suggestion made earlier, that you be extremely conservative with interpretations and advice, there is little risk of controversy.

Furthermore, in my experience it is quite rare for callers to "dump" on their partners in these calls. Interestingly, the intense criticism and blame that often characterize couple sessions, along with the jockeying to be seen as "the good one" by the therapist, are strikingly absent from these initial calls. It is as if, no matter how intense the conflict, a membrane of togetherness still surrounds the couple before this third party is added to the equation. The partners' loyalty to the relationship is still stronger than any connection to you; at this point you are merely the voice of a stranger on the telephone.

Special Circumstances

The process of arranging the evaluation is not always this straightforward. The following common scenarios call for somewhat more complicated decision making about whether and how to evaluate a case and who should attend.

When the Caller Requests
Individual Treatment

If a caller requests individual treatment and presents issues that do not appear related to a couple relationship, you should respect the client's wishes for an initial individual session. In these cases, the caller is emotionally focused on him- or herself—his panic attacks, her depression, his conflicts with his boss, her fears about new professional responsibilities. If the caller is in a committed couple relationship, you can mention over the telephone that you may want to meet with the partner after the initial individual session. This allows you to join with the client on his or her initial request but makes it easier to ask to meet with the partner later if this seems indicated, either to help you understand the client and his or her problems or to assess the couple's relationship. It is almost always easier to convince clients that a particular direction might be more helpful after having met them in person, relieved anxiety, and communicated a sympathetic understanding of the problems with which they are most concerned.

If the caller does describe relational difficulties but asks for an individual session, you should be aware of certain risks and test a bit more aggressively whether the caller is willing to attend a first session with his or her partner. Risks include the partner feeling left out and assuming that you are now on the caller's side or the caller using the individual session to gain advantage over the partner, trying to secure a special ally in the therapist. (Be especially cautious with this request if the caller seems to be overtly *trying* to create an alliance against the partner.) However, in many situations, these requests are reasonable and essentially harmless. They may reflect the genuine confusion of the client, a vague but persistent sense of vulnerability associated with couple sessions, or an uncertain sense of whether he or she is entitled to ask for the partner's help.

If the couple relationship seems to be a major focus of the caller's concern, suggest that you meet initially with both partners. This will enable you to evaluate the relationship, assess the relational context of symptomatology, secure a richer understanding of the individual, identify a possible resource for treatment, and in some cases identify a partner who may also be in need of services. The advantages of evaluating the couple when a caller requests individual treatment are more fully discussed in Chapter 12.

If the caller agrees, simply schedule an initial couple session. If more attention needs to be paid to specific symptomatology, a subsequent individual session can be used for this purpose. At the end of the evaluation, you may recommend couple treatment, individual therapy, some combination of the two, or something else altogether, depending on what you have learned during the evaluation.

However, the potential risks of an initial individual session must be weighed against the risks of alienating the caller by pressing for a couple session. If the caller is reluctant to schedule an initial couple session, you can adopt the fall-back position described above, agreeing to meet individually at first but letting the caller know that you may ask to meet with the partner sometime after the initial session. Finally, if the caller has described relational difficulties but is firmly against the partner coming in under any circumstances, you can accept the request but with qualifications. Alert the caller to the possibility that, after one or two sessions, you might conclude that you cannot be of help unless the partner is included. As long as you are clear that you may ask the partner to attend a subsequent session and as long as you balance your alliances with both parties, little is lost by acceding to the request to meet with one partner individually at first.

Usually these clients feel a strong need to secure help for themselves individually. Agreeing to meet with them on these terms expresses the conviction that this is a legitimate desire. Unless the material they present suggests that you *cannot* help them in this way or that, by doing so, you will be hurting or neglecting someone else who is vulnerable, you should be willing to meet with them on these terms. This balances respect for the client's wishes with a responsibility to be alert to potential dangers and to advise the client based on personal convictions and professional experience. If the caller is unwilling to meet with his or her partner because of information that is secret, agree to meet with the caller individually and to serve as a consultant about which direction for treatment might prove most helpful. (Detailed guidelines for managing secrets during the course of the evaluation are presented in Chapter 7.)

When the Caller Requests Family Therapy

When an individual describes a problem that involves a child or children, assuming that you are comfortable evaluating and treating families, you can accept this definition of the problem and schedule a family evaluation. If either the telephone conversation or the initial family session leads you to suspect significant couple difficulties, you can then ask to meet with the parents separately from the children. This session can begin with a focus on the presenting problem and hopefully lead into exploration of the couple's relationship. The pragmatics of these shifts of focus are discussed in Chapter 12.

When the Caller is Undecided
About the Format of Treatment

Sometimes a caller is undecided about whether he or she wishes to pursue individual or couple therapy. The caller describes both personal and relational problems but appears uncertain about what type of treatment she wants. Her indecision may be related to ambivalence over how committed she is to her partner or she may be fearful of upsetting him with her dissatisfactions and hoping that she can solve things on her own. These cases are particularly appropriate for the couple evaluation format. Respond to the caller's ambivalence by recommending the standard evaluation procedure. This defers the immediate question about the modality of treatment, which may appeal to the caller's uncertainty about how to proceed. It allows both the therapist and the couple to look at the whole picture and it provides the couple with input from an outsider with relevant professional experience before decisions regarding treatment are made. If she is reluctant to schedule a couple evaluation, agree to meet her individually, with the same caveats described earlier.

When Not to Schedule
a Couple Evaluation

You should not schedule the full four-part couple evaluation if the caller and/or his or her partner appear to be in an acute and potentially dangerous crisis. When there are indications of psychosis and/or a possible suicide attempt, you simply cannot afford the time necessary for a thorough couple evaluation — nor are the partners likely to be able to shift their focus from the intensity of the crisis to a leisurely investigation of their relationship. In these cases, *always evaluate the crisis first.* You will still want to meet with both partners. If one partner is symptomatic, the other may be able to provide valuable information which the symptomatic partner either cannot or will not provide him- or herself. This partner may also be able to serve as an ally in managing and resolving the crisis. You will be able to assess the couple's relationship but, in these cases, this is a secondary concern.

Do *not* schedule a couple evaluation if the caller describes a pattern of domestic violence. You may offer to meet individually with the caller or to refer her to emergency services, protective services, or a women's shelter. (Guidelines for responding to crises are discussed in Chapter 9; responding to domestic violence is discussed in Chapter 16.)

When the Therapist Does Not Take the Telephone Call

Sometimes, the arrangements for the evaluation may be made by someone other than the therapist. This is a common practice in many organizations such as mental health centers, training centers, and HMOs. This break in clinical continuity can be problematic, especially if the person arranging the evaluation does not understand its structure and leads the couple to incorrect expectations regarding the evaluation.

Ideally, intake workers should know how to determine which cases call for which evaluation formats and how to explain this to the caller. However, the realities of organizational life make this ideal scenario far from universal. There may be multiple therapists with different procedures for intake. There may be organizational policies and mandates that complicate this process such as relatively untrained secretarial staff arranging intakes or, in an HMO, for example, the expectation that mental health staff will automatically accept a physician's referral (i.e., for an individual evaluation) regardless of how they might wish to structure the assessment.

Intake procedures and staff training which are informed by the considerations described in this chapter can eliminate many of these difficulties. Where they cannot be so informed, the damage is rarely major. In most cases, the worst that will happen is that a therapist will meet initially with an individual and use this session to schedule a couple's evaluation (if he or she feels that this is indicated). This is a less than ideal way to begin the evaluation and it runs some risk of antagonizing the other partner, but these difficulties are rarely insurmountable.

When to Include Children

Some couples request family therapy for what are clearly problems between the parents. Conversely, callers may request couple therapy when there are significant problems either involving or affecting children. You should meet with children if you think they are significantly involved in and negatively affected by the adults' relationship. One caller might describe intense arguments, with a child attempting to mediate or with children lining up as allies for each parent. Another may describe conflicts over one partner's children from a prior relationship. In one case I treated, the couple's presenting problem involved the wife's emotional (and possibly physical) relationship with a male neighbor. The teenaged and adult children had organized themselves into a kind of detective squad, trying to spy on their mother and to gather information from other neighbors.

You also want children to attend the evaluation if you hear about behaviors or statements that concern you, for example: "He gets very angry and won't go to school in the morning," "He said he wishes he were dead sometimes," "She doesn't see any of her friends anymore." These are signs that the child may be having serious difficulties which, whether they are related to couple problems or not, need to be carefully evaluated in their own right. You should also be alert to significant breaches in boundaries, as when a mother reports, "My 12-year-old daughter knows that I'm thinking about leaving my husband but he doesn't know." These statements suggest that the child is enmeshed in the couple's difficulties and this enmeshment will almost always create stress and tax individual development.

When these "red flags" go up, let the caller know that you will probably want to meet with the child or children during the evaluation. Be sure to point out that such sessions will be separate from those in which details of the couple's relationship are discussed. These sessions can be presented as a standard part of the evaluation or as an expression of normal concern given what the caller has described. If the caller agrees, you will then be able to evaluate not only the couple but also the family. This will enable you to gain a fuller picture of the overall family situation, to closely evaluate a child who may be in need of services, and to have greater credibility if you recommend family therapy or some other form of treatment addressing the child's difficulties. Whether therapists should *always* meet with children as part of a couple evaluation is a matter of personal conviction. My own feeling is that this is not always necessary.

In some cases, you may wish to defer discussion about meeting with children until the first couple session, for example, if you anticipate that this will be threatening or unnecessarily worrisome for the caller, or if you wish to have more convincing data before making such a recommendation. Again, many potentially difficult transactions are more easily conducted in person, after some degree of trust has been established, than they are with the therapist as a disembodied stranger on the telephone. In other cases, the caller may express enough anxiety of his or her own that this proposal will be comfortably if not gratefully accepted.

If the initial telephone call has gone well, you will have gathered basic information, including the referral route, made a reasonably positive connection with the caller, explained the evaluation format, discussed unexpected aspects of the evaluation, and scheduled the first couple session.

~ 6 ~

CONDUCTING THE
INITIAL COUPLE SESSION

T HE THERAPIST'S AGENDA for the first session involves forming alliances with both partners and beginning to gather information
and impressions that will help him or her generate recommendations
for treatment. Sometimes the second task can serve the interests of
the first, that is, the process of information gathering can serve as a
vehicle for the therapist's efforts to join with both partners. Sometimes
these tasks clash. As a stranger to the clients, the therapist cannot
anticipate their reactions to all questions; certain questions may trigger feelings of defensiveness or shame which may threaten the alliances the therapist is trying to build. Each partner also has an agenda,
part of which may dovetail with the therapist's; their agendas may also
clash with each other's. Part of the challenge of the first session lies in
the therapist's effort to integrate and balance these sometimes converging and sometimes colliding considerations.

Opening the Session

Most often, this will be your first meeting with the couple. In some cases, you may have already met with one or both partners, for example, when the couple session follows an initial family session or an individual session with one partner. This chapter presumes that you have not met previously. (Modifications of this format in other clinical contexts are discussed in Chapter 12.)

The opening of the first session is always characterized by a certain intensity of feeling, whether this is expressed or not. The clients may be feeling apprehensive and ambivalent about seeking treatment. They may feel shame, guilt, frustration, intense anger, and even panic at the prospect of revealing their problems to a stranger. Feelings of discouragement may coexist with some degree of hope. There may be a sense of failure, a diminishment of self-esteem, and some degree of defensiveness. (You may also feel some nervousness, wondering what these individuals will be like, how they will feel about you, and whether you will be able to help them.) While your first formal task is to gather identifying information, the more important initial task is to put the clients at ease and begin forming alliances.

Easing Into the Meeting

If the session is to be productive, you need to anticipate the distressing feelings that the partners may experience at this point. This does not mean explicitly discussing them, although if they bring them up a passing comment that normalizes these feelings can help them feel more comfortable. Try to interact with the couple in a way that will reduce any feelings they may have of shame, uncertainty, defensiveness, and failure and that will increase feelings of safety, comfort, reassurance, and self-esteem. You want to convey, by how you interact with them, that their willingness to seek outside help indicates to you that they are not resourceless but resourceful. You do not see them as "one-down," but recognize that virtually all couples have periods when they feel "stuck" and that talking with an "outsider" at these times is not only not shameful but, in your estimation, healthy and enterprising.

You want to convey that you are there to serve *their* interests and not your own. In other words, you are mature enough to be able to focus on their concerns. You don't need to feel superior to them, to show off in order to win their esteem, or to share your own problems. Try to contain your own feelings so that you do not "leak" irritability or anxiety or confusion; try to respond sensitively to their feelings and agendas.

You want to dissipate any sense of shame and failure associated with seeking treatment and to generate the atmosphere of a constructive and collaborative effort conducted by equals: therapist and clients all "in the same boat," all facing the challenges of human and relational life. In these ways, you convey a stance of respectfulness, trustworthiness, and professionalism.

Gathering Identifying Data

Gathering identifying data serves a convenient delaying function; it allows all three participants to ease into the session without immediately facing the exploration of potentially painful or vulnerable areas. It provides a neutral, nonthreatening task on which to focus. By moving back and forth between the partners, directing questions to both partners, you demonstrate equal interest in and respect for both and begin building balanced alliances.

You want to supplement the information you have already obtained either over the telephone or through the admission procedures of the agency or clinic. Be sure you have the clients' home address(es) and home and work telephone numbers. Depending on the context in which services are delivered, financial data relating to treatment may also need to be obtained and procedures regarding fees and insurance discussed.

Following are sample questions for gathering relationship data:

- What are the ages of both partners?
- How long have they been together?
- If they are married, for how long? Did they live together before they married?
- If they are unmarried, do they live together? If so, for how long?
- Have there been previous marriages—or other serious relationships—for either partner? If so, what are the dates for marriage, separation, and divorce?
- If a previous marriage ended with the death of the spouse, when did this happen and what was the cause of death?
- Have there ever been any separations? If so, when and for how long? Are they currently separated?

Ask about children: Are there children from this relationship or any previous one for either partner? If so, what are their names and ages? If there are especially noteworthy facts about children—such as a serious medical disorder or disability—one partner will usually mention them at the start.

Find out about employment:

- Does either partner work in the home (as a homemaker or as part of their job or business) or do both have jobs outside it?
- What is the nature of their work?
- For those working outside the home, what are the hours?
- How long have they been in their jobs? If only for a short period of time, what did they do before this?
- Are they self-employed (in which case they may be working many extra hours and weekends)?
- How much does each partner contribute financially to the household? (This may influence power and entitlement in the relationship.)

Inquire about other household members (grandparents, relatives, boarders, etc.) as well as individuals who live nearby or are significantly involved with the couple. These individuals may prove critical to an understanding of the couple's problems and, in some cases, to the treatment itself.

This information can be organized by means of a genogram, which makes a wealth of information immediately visually accessible. Some therapists encourage clients to make their own genograms beforehand and to bring them to the initial session. Others will construct the genogram together with the couple, on a large pad, for example, that all three can see. I simply create a very informal genogram in my own notes to organize the information. This does the job adequately and requires very little time.*

Move back and forth between the partners as you gather identifying data. This reinforces the collaborative nature of the evaluation and prevents either partner from feeling (or being) left out. It also dispels gender-related concerns that the couple may bring into the evaluation—that, for example, the therapist will direct all questions about children only to the woman, implying that parenthood is her sole province, or that he or she will direct the initial questions to the male, suggesting that the therapist sees him as the "head of the household."

Gathering identifying data also allows you to "kibitz," to chat infor-

---

*For more information about the creation and uses of genograms, see McGoldrick & Gerson, 1985.

mally or to make comments intended to dispel tension and increase the couple's sense of safety and respect. If they comment on their infant's sleep disruptions or minor illnesses and if you also have children, you might make a light comment indicating an appreciation of what it's like to live with these tribulations of family life. You may join with them in relation to some aspect of coupleship, such as conflicting work schedules or living too far from (or too near to) one partner's family of origin. You may simply comment on some aspect of the momentarily shared environment, such as the rain or cold or humidity that tried all of you that day, the lack of nearby parking spaces, or the ambiguous sign on an office suite down the hall. The common denominator is that these lighter, more conversational comments convey, without your having to deliver a speech, that all of you inhabit the same universe, are subject to the same constraints of human life, and can begin the evaluation as equals, with mutual respect and goodwill.

Building Alliances

Building alliances is the emotional imperative of the first session. Unless you establish good-enough relationships with both partners in the first session, there may be no subsequent ones, and the most skillful information gathering will have been for nothing. Alliances are built by demonstrating to both parties that you are *trustworthy* and *competent* as a therapist. In other words, you are sympathetic to their interests and effective, if not expert, at the enterprise at hand.

Trustworthiness. Approach the couple with an attitude of *sympathetic understanding*: You want to understand what they are experiencing, how they feel, and how they think about the relationship; you want them to see that you can, to some degree, "put yourself in their shoes." In the practice of individual therapy, this is relatively straightforward, but in working with couples and families it is more complicated. How do you sympathize with a wife's complaint concerning her husband's neglect or disrespectful treatment if the husband adamantly denies that this is the case and expresses outrage at her "turning the tables" since in his view she is constantly demeaning to him?

The traditional approach in training therapists to handle such conflicts is: "Don't take sides"—a warning that blithely overlooks the most difficult aspect of this dilemma. Clients need and deserve a therapist who will try to be on their side, and for this reason the principle of multidirectional partiality, or multilaterality, derived from contextual theory and therapy (Boszormenyi-Nagy & Krasner, 1986; Boszormenyi-

Nagy & Ulrich, 1981; Boszormenyi-Nagy & Spark, 1973), provides a more useful frame for alliance-building.

Simply put, it encourages the therapist to *take both sides*, by extending sympathy to each partner in turn. In the example above, you would make clear to the wife that you understand how neglected she feels while indicating that you also understand how demeaned the husband feels. Appreciating the *ethical dimension* of relationships, in which all parties are seen as having entitlements and obligations which derive from the constant "give-and-take" of close relating, the therapist sides with both partners' claims of entitlement while retaining the freedom to hold each of them accountable at some point for how they treat their partner.

Competence. Building alliances also involves the ability to convey professional competence or expertise. This is a difficult area to discuss, since "competence" means different things to different clients and can be conveyed by therapists working in very different styles and approaches to treatment. Most clients wish for a therapist who is wise, caring, and virtually omniscient, just as all children wish for parents with the same qualities. (The emotional echoes of early attachment relationships are never really absent from therapy.) However, while they may wish for a Perfect Parent in the therapist, most clients can tolerate and accept a less perfect human equivalent.

Clients want to be sure that the person to whom they entrust themselves is not only well-meaning but also professionally skilled and knowledgeable. You should be able to convey that you have a reasonably *good understanding* of individuals and relationships. A therapist who spouts "systems" language but seems to have no comprehension of what people actually feel may engender as much uneasiness in couples as does the therapist who indicates a deep understanding of internal states but little appreciation of what it's like to be in a relationship with another person.

You should also convey a sense that you *know how to assess* couples, that you "know the territory" and how to explore it. You should be able to convey a sense of *conviction* in what you say. There may be times when you deliberately choose to qualify a hunch or even communicate your confusion about a certain area; however, unless you convey in your overall demeanor that you consider what you are saying to be worth listening to, it is unlikely that they will. The response you share at the end of the evaluation provides a good deal of information to clients about your expertise — but remember that clients are forming impressions about your competence throughout the course of the evaluation.

The Presenting Problem

Couples seek treatment because one or both parties are distressed by something they consider to be problematic. Usually this involves some aspect of the relationship: too much conflict, not enough passion, an inability to resolve a particularly important issue. In some cases, the problem is presented as "belonging" to one partner: her inability to show affection, his lack of interest in sex. The therapist tries to understand the forces that contribute to and maintain these problems.

Common Presenting Problems

Every relationship is unique and yet the problems couples present are often remarkably similar. The organizing forces discussed in previous chapters constrain the variety of problematic patterns which typically evolve in these relationships. Some of the most common presenting problems are described below. These are not formulations of couples' difficulties, that is, attempts to analyze the underlying forces which create and maintain difficulties. They are, instead, descriptions of the kinds of complaints couples present when they explain why they are seeking treatment. As with all conceptual efforts, the categories described here may overlap to varying degrees for different couples. The two most common complaints in my clinical experience with couples and, I suspect, in those of other practitioners, involve repetitive unresolved conflict and lost love.

Unresolved Conflict. Repetitive unresolved conflict probably constitutes the most common problem that brings couples into treatment. For some couples, there is no single emotionally charged issue; instead the partners fight about "anything and everything." It may be that their inability to resolve one major issue has led to disappointment, bitterness, and mistrust, which contaminate all other issues, or that one or both partners' fears of intimacy propel them into repetitive conflicts. There may be active and intense arguing or a chilly resigned distance or cycles of one followed by the other.

For other couples, there is one emotionally charged and polarized issue. It may involve an area that does not easily lend itself to compromise, such as where to live or whether or not to have children. It may involve the kind of life they live together—one organized by materialistic pleasures or idealistic commitment, ambition for wealth and status, or a low-key enjoyment of life's simpler pleasures. It may involve the terms of the couple's physical and sexual relationship—when they will be physically close, how they signal desire for physical contact, and what they do when they are together sexually. It may involve an impasse over what one or both partners experience as a past injury or betrayal by the other.

In virtually all cases of unresolved conflict, both partners feel *unheard*, which is why, when therapists make efforts to enhance communication, it is more often *listening* than speaking that poses the greatest challenge to the partners. Typically, one or both feel either controlled or deprived by the other. In terms of formulation, unresolved conflicts may involve skill deficits in conflict resolution, clashing—and possibly incompatible—expectations for the relationship, colliding entitlements, and one or both partners' fears associated with intimacy.

Lost Love. In these cases, one partner has "fallen out of love" and begun to distance emotionally from the other. Usually this goes beyond ongoing distance-pursuit struggles, which many theorists and clinicians have described (although lost love may represent an exacerbation of preexisting cycles of distance and pursuit). For these couples, the degree of distancing is more extreme, suggesting the possible dissolution of the relationship.

The couple may actually be separated, one partner having felt the need to live apart. One partner may be romantically involved outside the relationship. Outside relationships may be romantic and sexual or they may be nonsexual, characterized instead by frequent intimate conversations in which the individuals provide emotional support for one another (a scenario captured by the well-worn line, "My wife doesn't understand me").

The disenchantment may be "out in the open," with one partner saying quite explicitly that she no longer feels love for the other, or it may be unspoken but felt, as when one partner complains that the other is no longer affectionate or thoughtful or sexual with him. The disenchanted partner may justify his or her loss of feeling or may express regret but an inability to change it. The disenchanted partner is often highly ambivalent, especially when the relationship has been long-lasting and is embedded in a comfortable family life.

The alienated partner may never have been "in love" with the other or may be reacting to changes as they have grown older and further apart. The distance may be a result of the partners' inability to resolve significant conflicts. The distancing partner may have been driven away by difficulties associated with some aspect of the other partner's relational profile, for example, persistent remoteness, unsatisfiable demands, relentless criticism, or physical or emotional abuse.

Three other presenting problems, while less common than the two already discussed, are nevertheless well-represented in the caseloads of couple therapists. The first involves conflicts over intimacy; the second, a lack of passion and intimacy; and the third, a mutual inability to define the relationship.

Conflicts Over Intimacy. In this very common scenario, couples present with some complaint relating to intimacy. They may complain about chronic and intense arguing, which interferes with closeness, or about one partner who is identified as being uncomfortable with intimacy. There may have been a falling off of sexual relations or you may observe a see-saw pattern in which, whenever one partner seeks to be close, the other is in some way unavailable (variously described as cold, angry, busy, or involved with other things). The common denominator in these patterns is always a constriction of tenderness, mutual comfort, and love. Often, both partners have had painful experiences in earlier relationships which make intimacy threatening and anxiety-laden. This leads to the development of unwritten "rules" in the relationship that significantly curtail the experience of intimacy. Whatever the surface fluctuations, these underlying rules preclude situations in which one person offers warmth, affection, and love and the other accepts it. They present for treatment when one or both partners' tolerance for the frustrations of this pattern is exceeded.

Devitalized Relationships. In these relationships, the partners are often on very good terms. They are supportive of one another and manage the affairs of their shared existence smoothly. They rarely argue; they exhibit little of the intense emotional reactivity so common in most couples who request treatment. The problem is that they experience little intimacy or passion in the relationship. Carol Anderson and Diane Holder (1988) have referred to this type of relationship as "the marriage without weather," a phrase that captures the absence of vitality in the relationship. These couples often say that they live "like roommates" or "like brother and sister." One woman said that she and her husband were like "polite strangers" with one another. Usually both partners experience some degree of dissatisfaction with the relationship, although one may be more dissatisfied, or dissatisfied sooner, than the other.

Some couples present because of a recently disclosed extramarital affair, because one partner is bored or dissatisfied with the relationship, or because both partners are dissatisfied. They present for evaluation wondering if anything can be done to make the relationship more passionate and exciting. Other couples present when one or both partners have begun to express their dissatisfaction through some type of symptomatology.

Inability to Define the Relationship. These couples call the relationship itself into question but have enormous difficulty making a decision about whether to stay in or to get out of it. Some degree of ambivalence is almost always present when couples are deeply dissatisfied with their relationships; for these couples, ambivalence is both more intense and more chronic. There may have been multiple separations followed by reconciliations.

One couple I saw briefly had completed divorce proceedings three times over the course of a 27-year relationship; they contacted me one month before their fourth postdivorce waiting period was due to expire. They said that they loved each other and wanted to stay together but were afraid that this reconciliation, like all the others, would not succeed.

In other cases, there may be no actual move toward divorce or even separation but the relationship may have shifted into a "twilight zone." Usually this takes one of two forms, which might be described as unilateral or bilateral ambivalence. In the former case, one partner may be unable to either leave or emotionally engage in the relationship, while the other wants the relationship but tries to accommodate the constant shifts of the first partner's ambivalence. In the latter case, neither partner can decide whether they are "in" the relationship or "out" and they oscillate back and forth between the two.

These patterns express the powerful ambivalence felt by at least one, if not both, of the partners. You should be aware that the decision to seek treatment may represent, at least in part, an effort to *perpetuate* the lack of definition in the relationship—that is, to "do something" that promises resolution without requiring it. In situations of maximum ambivalence, this becomes in effect a desperate delaying tactic with the therapist, like the couple, unable to influence matters toward a decision.

The following patterns are seen occasionally among couples seeking treatment.

Difficulties with Third Parties. These couples ask for help because they have been unable to resolve difficulties with one or more third parties. However, unlike couples who are locked in intense conflict over third parties, these couples present in agreement rather than conflict. They share a similar viewpoint about their difficulties but have been unable to solve them.

Ed and Denise, both in their mid-50s, describe being "at our wits' end" in dealing with Ed's 90-year-old mother who lives with them. The mother requires a great deal of physical help and is described as being quite critical, especially of Denise; she pointedly ignores Denise when the three of them are together. Ed avoids contact with his mother, relieved to "pass her off" to Denise, who resents and "stews" about her mistreatment by her mother-in-law. The situation has led to some conflict between the spouses. However, they call for treatment soon after the problem becomes evident and are therefore able to present this as a shared problem, with little blame or hard feeling between them.

Acute Crises. These couples present for treatment because a recent event or set of events has destabilized their relationship. This might involve the disclosure or discovery of an affair, an injury or serious illness for one partner, or a child who imposes new strains and alters the balance of entitlement in the relationship. A variant of this pattern involves the development of serious psychiatric symptomatology in one partner.

Karen and Ray, both in their 40s, call for an appointment when Karen discovers that Ray has had a brief sexual relationship with a woman in their town. Ray works as a night guard; Karen cleans offices. They have two grown daughters. Theirs has been a traditional and largely satisfying relationship for over 20 years until, three years earlier, Karen was diagnosed with a serious medical disorder. The illness is chronic; it has required surgery, ongoing medication, and a significant weight gain. Karen reports that Ray "saved my life," visiting her daily for three weeks at a hospital two hours away from their hometown and often making return trips on the same day to bring the children. He bathed and fed her through the worst period of the illness. However, their sexual relationship ended after Karen's surgery. Ray has continued to love Karen and to desire her sexually. Karen, however, has felt self-conscious about her weight gain and scarring from the surgery and has avoided sexual contact. They were unable to discuss these changes and, after three years, Ray became sexually involved with another woman. Karen's accidental discovery of this relationship confirmed her own sense of being damaged by surgery and her illness.

Sexual Difficulties. When couples are in conflict or alienated from one another, their sexual relationship may suffer. Couples for whom this is the case may mention their sexual difficulties at the outset of the evaluation or they may not, often waiting to see if they feel safe enough with the therapist before raising these concerns. Some couples present with sexual difficulty as the primary or one of the central aspects of their dissatisfaction.

Premarital Counseling. Requests for premarital counseling were once a rarity but are becoming more common. These partners usually request treatment because one or both of them are concerned with some problematic aspect of the relationship which they hope can be resolved before it causes more difficulty.

Opening Discussion of the Presenting Problem

A good rule of thumb is to open discussion of the presenting problem not later than five or at most ten minutes after the initial couple session begins. This is enough time for everyone to get more comfortable but makes clear that you are prepared to "get down to business." When you have finished gathering identifying data, signal the shift to discussion of the presenting problem with a clear, direct question such as, "Could you tell me about what brought you here today?"

Direct this question to the *couple* rather than to one particular partner, letting them decide who will speak first. Directing this question specifically to one partner may contribute to erroneous and unfortunate inferences: They may assume that you see that partner as more intelligent or better able to explain their situation. They may interpret it as a sign that you blame this partner, especially when there has been socially stigmatized behavior such as alcoholism or an affair. As always, there may be exceptions. For example, if a husband is attending "under protest" and is clearly highly resistant, it probably makes sense to direct this opening question to his wife first. This avoids starting off with an immediate power struggle. The husband's resentment over what he considers inaccuracies in his wife's description may be enough to catapult him into active participation.

At this point, the couple begins to shape the direction of the session. The exploration of the presenting problem differs markedly from case to case; there may be disagreements in perspective, nuances of feeling, unexpected revelations (the wife who has been complaining of boredom in the marriage reveals that her mother committed suicide at roughly her present age and that she is herself seriously suicidal), and surprising developments (a husband bolts from the room when his wife mentions his visits to his ex-wife) during the interview.

Regardless of idiosyncratic differences, the exploration of the presenting problem constitutes a *gradual unfolding* of the story of the relationship—or at least one important aspect of it. The first one or two descriptive sentences are increasingly elaborated as the therapist asks specific questions, moving back and forth between the partners, and as they express more of their experiences, thoughts, and feelings. At its most satisfying for the therapist, the exploration of the presenting problem becomes like a puzzle or a fascinating story, as all three parties become caught up in the feelings and the force of the narrative.

Exploring the Presenting Problem

The exploration of the presenting problem is designed to illuminate its *meaningful context*—that is, the relational context in which the problem has meaning. In the course of this exploration, different aspects of the presenting problem will be investigated. These fall roughly into three categories:

1. the *definition* of the problem and its *meaning* for both partners (and in some cases for significant others in their wider relational context)
2. the temporal or *historical context* of the problem—when it first began, how its course has varied over time, previous problems, etc.
3. the *consequences* of the problem—how it has affected the couple's relationship as well as each individual

The following questions are designed to help you clarify the definition or meaning of the problem. These questions are not intended to be asked explicitly, but to guide your impressions about these areas by listening to the partners' general discussion of the presenting problem and by being aware of nonverbal behavior, affective states, and jarring or unexpected phrases and reactions. In particular cases you may want to inquire about certain aspects directly.

How Does the Couple Define and "Locate" the Problem and How Do They Understand its Causes? The definition of the problem is crucial to possible solutions. If a couple presents with a sexual problem, is it defined as "his selfishness," "her impossible and controlling demands," or "our difficulty meeting each other's needs sexually"? For a couple complaining of unresolved conflict, is the problem defined as "his unwillingness to talk to me," "her needing to know every single thing I think during the day," or "a pattern of arguing that we can't seem to stop"?

Do they think of this as a problem "in" one partner, for example, depression, alcoholism, extreme dependency, or jealousy? Is it seen as a problem between them, for example, constant fighting, a sexual mismatch, mutual lack of passion? Or do they see it as involving others, such as children, members of one or the other's family of origin, a neighbor, a minister, or a therapist? Do the partners agree with one another? And, when you hear more about the situation, do you see it similarly or differently?

The partners' views of the nature and causes of the presenting problem may be highly polarized since they so powerfully involve patterns of criticism and blame. They may illuminate broader aspects of their individual narratives and of shared narratives in the relationship. Finally, it's important to inquire about how they understand the causes of the presenting problem because *there is a good chance they may be right.*

Who Takes Responsibility for the Problem? A well-worn cliche asserts that while victory has a thousand fathers, defeat is always an orphan. The same can be said of relational difficulties. Even when they agree on the definition of the presenting problem (and especially when they do not), partners are likely to disagree on who is responsible for the problem. Precisely because so much conflict for couples involves the partners' difficulties recognizing and admitting their own responsibility for relational problems, this may have diagnostic and prognostic significance. When partners *can* accept responsibility for some aspect of the presenting problem, it is often a good prognostic sign. However, as always, there are exceptions. One partner may berate herself for a problem which, to you, clearly implicates the other. For example, the wife may blame herself for "stupidity" and "clumsiness" when her husband has a tirade; you, on the other hand, may immediately notice how demeaning this man is not only with his wife but also with you or others. Or one partner may quite openly blame himself for the problem but with such blithe nonchalance that positive expectations for treatment should be guarded. In general, however, the partners' ability to accept some measure of responsibility for relational problems constitutes a potential resource for treatment.

How Do Significant Others Define and Locate the Problem? This question is intended to expand your view of the couple to the wider relational context within which the couple's relationship is embedded and to the possible existence of problematic triangles and alliances. In some cases, one or both partners will introduce these third parties at the outset; in others, the person's importance only gradually becomes clear as the evaluation, or even treatment, proceeds. You may want to ask directly about important outside relationships and how they think these other individuals view the couple's difficulties. Usually, the most important "players" are members of one or both partners' families of origin. In some cases (especially those involving remarriage), they may be older children from previous relationships. Third parties might also include close friends, clergy, current or previous therapists, or other professionals.

The following questions examine the *temporal context* of the problem. You will want to ask these directly.

When Did the Problem Start? This suggests the relative chronicity of the problem. Is this a difficulty that has only recently developed or has it existed for years, perhaps even since the beginning of the relationship? Is it a problem that has occurred on and off over time? As with all these temporal questions, do both partners agree in their answers?

What Changes, If Any, Were Taking Place When or Soon Before the Problem Developed? This question helps you identify precipitants. One or both partners may be aware of a major precipitant, such as the death of a parent, loss of a job, or diagnosis of a serious medical problem, or they may be unaware of any connection between particular life changes and the problems they are experiencing. In the latter case, one potential benefit of the evaluation is that it helps them become aware of these precipitants and their effects, thereby gaining perspective and understanding in relation to their current problems. Information about possible precipitants to the presenting problem lends itself to the therapist's formulation of why this problem has developed and why it persists.

Joan and Larry requested couple therapy in response to Joan's emotional withdrawal from Larry over a period of several months. Joan didn't understand why she felt differently toward Larry and neither of them were sure when it had started. Questioning revealed that Joan's withdrawal began soon after they witnessed their dog being shot and killed accidentally by a hunter while they were walking together in the woods. The shot "blew him apart" and almost hit Joan. At a concrete level, this meant that Joan no longer felt safe walking in the woods which eliminated an important form of emotional contact for this couple. The loss of the dog also seemed to reactivate Joan's grief over the death of a beloved younger brother when she was a teenager. Finally, Joan could not overlook the fact that Larry enjoyed hunting and, even though she knew the dog's death was not his fault, she found herself blaming him by association.

Have the Partners Experienced Similar Problems In the Past, Either In this Relationship or In a Previous One? This also suggests the relative chronicity of problems. For example, a couple is currently separated after a major explosive argument. Is this the first time this has occurred in an otherwise stable long-term relationship or is it the seventh repetition of a pattern that predates their marriage? One or both partners may have had similar problems in previous relationships as well. For example, the husband whose wife complains about his intense workaholic patterns and emotional unavailability turns out to have lost his first wife and an earlier fiancee over similar complaints. The wife who complains about her husband's drinking has had two previous husbands and several boyfriends with similar addictive and irresponsible patterns. This suggests important aspects of the partners' "relational profiles." Repetitive problematic patterns across multiple relationships should raise the therapist's level of suspicion that the couple's difficulties are strongly influenced by problematic relational profiles derived from early attachments and their convergence in the "unconscious matrix" of the relationship.

How Has the Problem's Course Varied (If at All) Over Time? How has the problem evolved over time? Has it steadily worsened? Have there been cycles of improvement and deterioration? Have things actually improved to the point that both partners are now able to agree on working together to try to eliminate the problem? Is the problem unchanged but is one or both partners less willing to tolerate it now? Fluctuations may help identify factors that exacerbate the problem and/or relieve it.

Why Do They Seek Treatment Now? Except in acute crises, the problems that motivate couples to seek treatment have usually existed for some period of time, in many cases, for months or years. Why do they seek treatment *now*? The answer may be fairly obvious, as when the departure of the last remaining child at home prods the couple into examining their devitalized relationship. This question may reveal important and less visible aspects of the presenting problem.

Belinda and Mark had great difficulty responding to this question. Mark indicated that Belinda had insisted they come for treatment. Belinda, however, was extremely vague and confusing on this matter while she was able to be quite clear about her dissatisfactions in the relationship. In her individual session, she revealed that she was emotionally, but not yet sexually, involved with another man who had recently indicated to her that she would have to choose between her husband and himself. His ultimatum had motivated her to seek treatment.

What Steps Have They Taken to Address the Problem, and with What Result? This question works on several levels. First, it tells you something about the couple's resources. You may be surprised at the creativity or dedication that the partners have already brought to the problem. The question is inherently respectful and indicates that you want to appreciate their strengths as well as their limitations. The answer may indicate something about the couple's judgment or common sense and it provides further information about their values and worldview. There is one final reason for asking what steps the couple has taken to try to address the problem: bluntly put, to avoid looking stupid. If, after two or three hours spent evaluating a couple, you recommend something they have already tried for six months without success, their impressions of your expertise may not be favorable.

Asking about the *results* of previous efforts to improve the problem can suggest promising directions for treatment and add credibility to your recommendations. For example, when the couple has taken steps that did improve things but were discontinued for some reason, you may want to recommend a resumption or modification of these steps. In other cases, where the steps taken clearly backfired or resulted in little change, you can use this experience to bolster the credibility and attractiveness of alternative approaches.

Two final questions tap into the *consequences* of the problem. These can also be asked directly.

How Has the Problem Changed Their Lives? This question is directed at the formulation of the problem. Symptoms may serve functions — particularly protective functions of some kind — for individuals or for relational systems. The *consequences* of a symptom or problem, therefore, may reveal a good deal about its possible function.

44-year-old Steve marries 23-year-old Maureen. This is the third marriage for him, the first for her. Their presenting problem involves her loss of sexual desire soon after the wedding. They have constant arguments over this; Steve is harshly critical of Maureen. Although he presents himself as confident and worldly, he reveals that he had sexual difficulties in both of his prior marriages, involving early ejaculation and, at times, difficulty maintaining erections. He has been preoccupied and deeply ashamed of these difficulties in the past. His new wife was incestuously abused as a child but seems to have recovered well from this and has generally had a positive orientation to sex. Whatever psychological factors may or may not be operating for her, it is noteworthy that Steve is no longer consumed with shame and anxiety about his own sexuality. Instead, he feels, if anything, self-righteous at his sexual deprivation and psychologically focused on her sexual difficulties rather than his own.

What Do They Expect Would Happen if the Problem Disappeared? This is the Milan group's "hypothetical" question (Selvini et al., 1980). It represents another way of trying to ascertain possible functions served by the presenting problem. Instead of looking directly at the consequences of the problem, in effect it "erases" them by encouraging both partners to imagine that the problem disappears. Their responses may surface hidden consequences of the problem, suggesting its possible function for one partner, the couple, or a wider relational system in which they are embedded.

Guidelines for Exploring the Presenting Problem

Strive for Specificity. Couples will usually describe their problems with language that is familiar to you. However you can not assume that you understand what this language means to them. When one couple complains of excessive fighting, they may mean that they are yelling and swearing at one another, with plates and threats flying. Another couple using the same phrase may be indicating that, while their exchanges are still unfailingly polite, they have become chilly and brusque. And of course, one partner may mean something quite different from the other. In order to understand *what they mean* and *what it means to them*, you must inquire carefully and specifically.

A second reason for inquiring into the specifics of problems is suggested by the cliche that "God is in the details." Your ability to identify the patterns and forces that maintain the presenting problem is greatly enhanced by your understanding of the particulars of the problem.

William and Mary presented multiple couple and family problems. Primary among them was Mary's obsessive-compulsive disorder. She needed to wash her hands over 100 times a day, went through elaborate cleaning rituals in order to use shared household appliances, and could not tolerate physical contact with William or their daughters.

A detailed inquiry revealed that these symptoms had begun soon after William gave up his high-paying career to become a Lutheran minister, a change which meant a significant decrease in the family's standard of living. Mary resented this deeply but did not feel she could oppose it. Detailed questioning revealed something of even greater significance, namely, that when she spent several days away from the parsonage (which she referred to as "my prison"), Mary's obsessive-compulsive symptoms were "80% improved."

These details, together with others, revealed during the exploration of the presenting problem, allowed me to formulate the problem in my own mind as a symmetrical power struggle, with both partners largely disowning responsibility for their present difficulties. William could hardly be held responsible for his career change since, as he pointed out, he had "been called" to the ministry. Nor could Mary be faulted for her withdrawal from William and her daughters since this was an aspect of her disorder, no more a matter of her choice than William's calling. It is noteworthy that, later in treatment, when William agreed to give up his position as a parish minister and to take a more remunerative and less socially demanding position, Mary reported with amazement that she had been healed by Jesus; she remained largely free of symptoms afterward.

Balance Inquiries Between Partners. Both partners should be active participants in the exploration of the presenting problem. This is sometimes more difficult to achieve than you might think it would be. One partner, feeling mistreated by the other and having anticipated this discussion for some time, may be especially pent-up and eager to "make a case." The other may be withdrawn and monosyllabic, either out of guilt, resentment, embarrassment, or sheer exhaustion. If one partner needs to present all of his or her feelings and perceptions largely without interruption, the other is relegated to the role of passive nonparticipant and the process of the session becomes skewed. The second partner may become discouraged or resentful and begin to feel that you are siding with the one who is holding the floor. In addition, you may appear ineffectual if it is clear that you wish to move to the other but are unable to do so.

To avoid these difficulties, balance your inquiry by moving back and forth between the partners. Follow one person's statement by turn-ing to the other and asking for reactions. Use a transition to a different aspect of the problem to shift to the other partner. You may need to politely interrupt the speaker; this can be softened by indicating that you'll come back for an elaboration of what he was saying after first getting a response from the other. If need be, you can comment on your function as an "editor" (E. Strauss, personal communication) in sessions, that is, someone who keeps track of the goals and the prog-ress of the session and who tries to ensure that the latter is serving the former. Rarely is this a major problem. As indicated earlier, couples expect you to lead; once you make clear that you expect *both* partners to participate in this discussion, most couples will readily cooperate.

Accept Their Definition of the Problem. One potential benefit of the evaluation involves your ability to reframe the presenting problem, that is, to offer the couple a more helpful way of understanding their difficulties, one which deemphasizes blame, promotes resources, or induces greater flexibility for solutions. However, it is important that you *not* challenge the partners' definition(s) of the problem at this early point in the evaluation.

Beginning therapists may feel that they can, and should, "help" cli-ents by challenging their definitions of the problem, for example by suggesting that an individually focused symptom is really a systems problem. This is usually countertherapeutic as well as disrespectful when it takes place at the very start of the evaluation; this type of reframe will be much more helpful at the end of the evaluation. By allowing yourself to explore the presenting problem *within* the frame(s) that the couple initially presents, you are demonstrating re-spect (and clinical judgement). You are more likely to be successful in changing their beliefs and feelings about the problem after you have fully assessed the relationship, gotten some sense of each partner's worldview, values, anxieties, and defenses, and, most importantly, gathered enough supporting evidence to make your own views plausi-ble and compelling.

One codicil to this rule involves couples in which one partner's definition of the problem is patently demeaning to the other partner. In these cases, you should make efforts to not be seen as uncritically accepting or endorsing these views and attempt to reframe them as soon as possible.

Prioritize Multiple Problems. When asked why they have sought treatment, some couples will present not one but a veritable catalogue of difficulties. You can easily become overwhelmed by the sheer number of areas they identify as problematic and by their lightning shifts from one problem to another as you try vainly to explore one, *any* one, of them. In these situations it is useful to encourage (and, if need be, to insist) that they prioritize these problems, indicating which they consider most serious or destructive or urgent. In some cases, this blizzard of difficulties serves to perpetuate a relational impasse, to protect one or both partners from changes that seem threatening; these couples will resist the clarification and organization of problems. If this happens, suggest that, in your experience, when couples are unable to prioritize problems the likelihood of a positive outcome is diminished.

In part, this is a diagnostic matter; more importantly, it is a pragmatic one. If you are to be of any help to these couples, you must be able to target problems that can respond to treatment. To do this, you must be able to prioritize them so that goals can be identified. You also have to maintain your own emotional balance and mental clarity; if you are overwhelmed and disorganized, you will be of little help to your clients.

Probe Questions

Evaluating couples is anything but a standardized procedure. Even couples who present with very similar problems can be markedly different from one another in their individual and relational idiosyncrasies, the specifics of their separate and joint histories, their stances toward their problems and toward therapy, and the chemistry between both partners and the therapist. For this reason, initial sessions will inevitably pursue highly idiosyncratic directions. It is especially helpful therefore to include at least a few routine questions to ask most, if not all, couples.

These questions provide a way to explore several aspects of the couple's overall relationship, including fairness, sexuality, resources, each partner's capacity for self-focus, and the history of the relationship. Some therapists will use these questions in all cases, making them an invariable part of the evaluation. Others may use them more selectively, choosing those that seem especially germane to a case, or keeping them in reserve for clients who have difficulty being specific about their problems or whose answers are unusually terse, circumstantial, and tangential. Most practicing therapists have a few such favorite questions; I recommend the following.

What Attracted You to [Your Partner]? This question works on several levels. It sheds light on each partner's relational profile and on the fit between them; it suggests something about the level of maturity, attachment needs, expectations, and self-image of each partner; and it encourages even bitterly embattled partners to evoke a happier and more satisfying time in their relationship, thus hopefully surfacing potential relational resources.

One woman answered, "He seemed like he wouldn't bleed all over me." She described her father as "tense, melancholy, and wound up." He would impulsively hit her when she was growing up and then beg for her forgiveness. She chose a man who seemed solid and in control of himself. As is often the case, this was less true than it appeared. He had experienced intense depression and anxiety in graduate school and he had felt that he was "going crazy." For years afterward he felt "fragile psychologically," but projected a public persona of confidence and control. When this couple presented for treatment, the wife complained that he treated her like "the crazy one" all the time despite his own periods of rage and extreme threats.

When You Remember Your Wedding and Honeymoon, What Stands Out in Your Memory? This question taps into levels of commitment during the formation of the relationship and the influence of patterns in the families of origin, but its utility goes beyond this. It can provide a condensed version of themes and problems in the relationship, as well as feelings both partners have about it, in a way that is similar to the use of dreams in treatment. In my experience, when both partners have positive memories associated with this event, their prognosis in couple therapy is higher. With unmarried couples living together, you can ask about their memories of moving in together.

Marie and Ted provided a number of responses to this question. Their relationship had been characterized for over 20 years by Marie's intense ambivalence and dissatisfaction, her sense of being neglected by her husband, his sense of being unable to please her, and their long-term sexual difficulties. She remembered feeling "like I was on a train that I couldn't stop" at the wedding rehearsal, feeling "trapped" and "out of control." She was so badly sunburned on their honeymoon that they could not have sex. Both partners remembered the same particular detail about their wedding reception, but in a different way: When they walked down a flight of steps into the reception after their wedding, Marie slipped and fell down one or two steps. For Ted, this is a somewhat comical, light memory; he remembers feeling that he wasn't sure what to do. Marie was humiliated by this *and remembers with pain and anger that her new husband did nothing to help her, but stood by while a staff person stepped forward to help her up.*

___*Beth, with a long history of psychosomatic complaints, which eventually overwhelmed and alienated her husband, commented, "I couldn't believe I didn't have a headache that day," suggesting the prominence of physical suffering in her life.*

___*One couple's answers to this question were especially vivid and positive. Sam, who had difficulty with intimacy and commitment in his previous and, to some degree, in this current relationship, said, "I felt as alive as I ever had. Seeing her walking down the aisle, there was a welling-up in me." Julie said, "Walking down the aisle, I felt absolutely wonderful, unrushed, and ethereal." Their answers spoke volumes about the resources in their relationship.*

How Has Your Relationship Changed Over Time? Responses to this question may help you get a sense of the history and evolution of the relationship. This supplements information shared while discussing the history of the presenting problem. Their answers may suggest possible formulations for current problems and deepen your understanding of their overall relationship. They may identify important turning points in the history of the relationship. Consider these common and varied responses: "We were very happy for about five years until our daughter was born. Then all hell broke loose," "Nothing ever changes. It's been up-and-down from the start," "We've just gradually grown apart. At this point, I feel like I barely know him," "We had a horrible first three years together; then I left. We were apart for about six months. Since then, things have been much better and at least now he's agreed to come in to see someone." Note the similarities and differences in the responses to this question.

What Have You Had to Give Up or Give In On for This Relationship? This question highlights the fairness of give-and-take in the relationship—the degree to which each partner has been willing or required to sacrifice for the other and the degree to which such sacrifices have been fairly balanced. More than most probe questions, this one may have an immediate therapeutic impact. Most couples are surprised when it is asked. Usually at least one partner has never considered the question before and often both are surprised by the answers it generates.

Bev and Dan had been living together for six months. Bev worked a 50-hour week; Dan did carpentry work when he got it. They lived in the house that Bev owned. Bev's income was three times that of Dan's. Their presenting problem involved Bev's complaint that Dan would stay out drinking with his friends until 3:00 or 4:00 AM without calling her. When asked what they each had to give up or give in on, Bev said, "My own self-esteem and being able to do any of the things together which I'd like to do." Dan said, "I don't get to go out as much at night as I want to." (At this point, he averaged three to four nights out each week.) These answers underscore the unfairness of give and take in this relationship.

What's It Like to be Married to You? This question was developed by Harry Dunne, Jr., Ph.D., a family therapist working in Connecticut (Dunne, 1991). It goes to the heart of couple therapy. Often what is accomplished by the end of successful couple therapy is that both partners can now answer this question in a way that is congruent with their partner's experience. Answers to this question suggest something about the partners' abilities to see their own contribution to shared problems, to empathize with their partner's side of the relationship, and to accept faults and imperfections in themselves.

One husband, who presented himself as a "simple Joe," who didn't understand or have much interest in psychology or therapy, gave a particularly insightful answer to this question. "I'm tough to live with. I'm a perfectionist and I have mood swings, so it's hard. But I'm devoted to Anne, faithful, and I love her. I'm also secure. I'll always be there for her." This response helped me appreciate resources in this man and in their relationship.

What is the Best Part of Your Relationship? This question surfaces relational resources by identifying areas of bonding, vitality, and mutual satisfaction between the partners. The areas they describe are those in which "something is going right" in the relationship. This provides balance to the inevitable problematic focus of the evaluation. It also reveals something important about the relationship when one (or both) partner is unable to answer this question in a convincing way.

Jerry and Roberta complained of chronic conflict, particularly in relation to Jerry's drinking and what he felt was her nagging and criticism. However, their answers to this question revealed signif-

icant resources of trust and attachment. Roberta said, "I can talk to him more easily than to anyone else. Outside of this problem, I feel like we really understand each other." Jerry said, "Humor—sex—and I feel like I can say anything to her."

How Has Your Sexual Relationship Changed Over Time? This question is essential for couples who present with sexual difficulties; with other couples it is a valuable but potentially challenging question. Its value lies in the deep connections between sexuality, intimacy, love, passion, and vulnerability. What happens (and what doesn't happen) in bed in a couple's relationship may illuminate far more of the real emotional truths of that relationship than what happens when they argue at dinner. The answers to this question can provide a "fever chart" for the vicissitudes of intimacy in the relationship. Similarities and differences in their views of these changes are especially significant.

Unless I sense specific contraindications, I use this question with all couples I evaluate and only rarely find couples seriously troubled by it. They can and do exercise control in this context by deciding how vague or how specific they wish to be. This gives you further cues about how far to pursue the inquiry. However, some couples who do not present with sexual difficulties will feel embarrassed, exposed and, in some cases, angry at what they may see as a violation of their privacy in this question. For couples who seem acutely uncomfortable in the first session, this question might be omitted. This is one of many judgment calls that need to be made on a case-by-case basis.

What Are Your Goals for this Evaluation? This question will help you understand what these individuals want from the evaluation and from possible treatment. Questions about goals illuminate similarities and differences between the partners in what they want from the therapist and from the relationship and they guide your efforts to match and utilize their agendas for the evaluation.

In addition, questions about goals serve notice that both partners are responsible players in the evaluation—responsible for knowing what they want from it and to some extent for what they get from it. Clients who say that they want to "be happy" should be asked to be more specific. Does this mean fewer arguments? More open expression of affection? Greater efforts by their partner to notice how things are going between them and to try to improve closeness? Using questions about goals to indicate the importance of personal responsibility (in the evaluation, in treatment if it should follow, and in the relationship itself) is especially important when one partner is being "dragged" to the evaluation by the other and may be adopting an irresponsible relational stance.

Quite often, one partner will answer this question in a way that says in essence, "I want to figure out how to make this relationship work." The partner's answer amounts to, "I want to figure out whether or not we're really right for each other." The differences in their answers highlight a discrepancy in their level of commitment to the relationship which may not have been detected earlier in the session.

The following case illustrates one couple's responses to many of the probe questions described above.

Gloria and Jeff, a couple in their mid-30s, requested treatment following Jeff's disclosure of a brief affair. They have been married for 10 years and have three children. Jeff says, believably, that the affair is ended and both want to save the marriage. He is described as a "workaholic" and a "tennis fanatic" who plays four or five times a week. Gloria works part-time and does the vast majority of child care. Jeff's family history includes an emotionally unavailable father and the death of his mother when he was 12 years old. He has always placed a premium on "independence" and has avoided intimacy. Gloria's family history involves a distant and critical father who was never challenged by his children and for whose approval several sisters competed. He also happened to be a "tennis fanatic."

When asked what attracted them to each other, she replied, "He's just like my father! He's handsome, exciting, a tennis nut, and he's never around." He cited her beauty and added, "She took a real interest in me. Did a lot for me and with me." He explained that she would cook for him and do his laundry. These answers illustrate the interlocking of her efforts to get approval from an unavailable man and his need for a somewhat maternal figure to take care of him. It is not surprising that this couple evolved a relationship organized around his needs and his emotional vetoes.

When asked to remember their wedding, Gloria said, "He wouldn't tell anyone about it." Jeff's first memory was the same: "Her disappointment with my denying it was happening." These answers deepen the impression of his discomfort with intimacy and commitment.

Asked what each had to give up or give in on for the relationship, Gloria responded, "Professional advancement, my own needs (you know, time away from the children either for work or for relaxation),

and my ideal of what family life should be (meaning close relationships with an involved father)." Jeff answered that he had not been
able to play tennis as much as he would like. Their answers reveal
how imbalanced the fairness of give-and-take has been between
them, a pattern for which both acknowledge some responsibility.

Finally, when asked about goals for treatment, Jeff stated emphati-
cally that he wants to save the marriage and "to prove to her that he
can be closer, a better husband and father." Gloria wanted to be sure
that the affair would not repeated and to find out whether or not he
could change. She added that if she didn't see changes in six months,
she'd pursue divorce. Their answers to this question are especially
significant. Gloria indicates a seemingly greater ability now than in
the past to set a "bottom line" in the relationship. If she is able to
maintain it, the relationship is less likely to fall into the same one-
sided patterns of the past. Jeff's answer, which seemed quite sincere,
suggested commitment and motivation to make sacrifices and changes
in order to save the relationship. This constitutes a significant resource for treatment. Together, their answers lend themselves to a
concrete process of testing—both his flexibility and determination
and her ability to insist on a more balanced relationship; this creates
a specific and positive focus for treatment.

Previous Treatment

It is important to inquire about previous experiences the clients have
had in couple therapy or in other forms of treatment. Ask about the presenting problems at that time, the nature and length of treatment, their
feelings about the therapist and how he or she worked, and their assessment of its benefits. Their answers will illuminate the chronicity of current problems and the ways in which they have handled them in the
past, how well they have used treatment and, most importantly, *what
methods and stances you might want to either avoid or emulate.* An
extremely reserved couple may have been turned off by a previous therapist who moved immediately to some form of experiential enactment. A
couple with "new age" values may have felt uncomfortable with a therapist's reliance on paper-and-pencil marital inventories.

*One couple said of their former therapist, "He just listened,"
signalling their desire for a therapist who would be more active
in guiding their interactions and in making suggestions that might
improve their relationship.*

*Another couple summarized their view of the previous thera-
pist by saying that her attitude was "Just jump." This conveyed
their feeling that she had asked the impossible of them; it indicated
that the current therapist would need to "test the waters" cautiously
and incrementally in making specific suggestions.*

They may describe positive responses to a previous therapist whom
they can no longer see, either because he or she has left the area or
because of changes in insurance coverage. These responses are also
useful guides for the current therapist. "She was very goal-oriented. We
never felt like we were just sitting around chatting." "He was very
active and he was blunt. Actually, we found this much more helpful
than if he had sat back and not said much." These responses are like
compass points, steering the new therapist toward directions that are
more likely to be helpful with these particular clients.

Finally, questions about previous treatment have prognostic value.
When a couple reports that they received some benefit from previous
treatment, this is generally a positive prognostic indicator. It might
simply mean that they are uncomfortable saying anything negative
about anybody, or that they need to believe something positive happened in order to cling to an unsatisfying but safe relationship. More
often than not, however, a positive report about previous treatment
suggests that there were some resources within the relationship that
at least one therapist was able to engage and mobilize in therapy.

Negative responses about the benefits of previous treatment are *not*
necessarily poor prognostic indicators. The lack of progress may have
more to do with the limitations of the therapist than those of the
couple—even a skilled therapist may fail to connect with a particular
couple. Resources may be currently available for treatment which
were previously unavailable; for example, one partner may be more
clear about the importance of the relationship or more ready to admit
his or her contribution to problems. However, reports of multiple failures in previous couple therapy should alert you to the possibility of
poor prognosis *without* closing your mind on the subject.

Personal and Relational Resources

Both therapists and clients are predisposed to focus on pathology. The
couple comes in because one or both partners have defined something
as "wrong" or problematic; they hope that therapy will help "fix" it.
Most psychological and systemic theories have a highly developed vo-

cabulary for pathology and a meager one for strengths or resources. However, if therapists look only at pathology, weakness, and deficit, they are doing their clients and themselves a disservice. If a couple can be helped to *recognize* their own resources, they may be empowered to use them in the service of their goals. If they can be helped to *promote* resources, this can strengthen the relationship, facilitate coping, and increase satisfaction for both partners. And if the therapist can *utilize* available resources in treatment, there is significantly more leverage for positive change. Therapists need to ask themselves, "What do they have going for them?"

Resources are like love; we can recognize their importance but still find them difficult to define. I think of resources as *individual and systemic characteristics of relationships that promote coping and survival, limit destructive patterns, and enrich daily life* (Karpel, 1986). The couple's resources help them cope with predictable and unpredictable stressors and contain the damage they produce. Resources can limit destructive patterns generated from within the relationship as well. An example would be relational "rules," which forbid disrespect, cruelty, and humiliation, or one partner's self-respect, which enables him or her to refuse to tolerate the other's increasingly uncontrollable drinking. Finally, resources contribute to the rewards of being part of a couple; they make it possible for individuals to experience satisfaction, security, and vitality in their relationships and in their lives.

The couple's relationship is a reservoir of potential and actual resources for both partners; likewise, both partners are reservoirs of potential and actual resources for the relationship. In treatment, resources provide a foothold for interventions and change. Understanding resources in couple relationships begins with the distinction between personal or individual resources and relational or systemic resources.

Personal Resources

Personal resources involve characteristics of individuals. The most important for a "good-enough" couple relationship are self-respect and protectiveness. Other personal resources include affection, commitment, tolerance, self-focus, humor, and hope.

Self-respect refers to an individual's sense of having value or worth and deserving to be treated in accordance with that value. Self-respect is involved in almost everything that goes right in close relationships. It is the basis of one's ability to treat others—partners, for example— with respect. When self-respect is lacking, individuals are more likely to try to gain security through interpersonally destructive maneuvers such as overcontrol, manipulation, extreme dependency, distancing, or attacking another's vulnerabilities. Self-respect makes it easier for a partner to resist the destructive pull of the other partner's weaknesses and destructive patterns, as when a wife refuses to be physically or emotionally abused by her husband. If there is such a thing as "finished business" (to turn a therapeutic cliche on its head), self-respect is at its core.

Protectiveness is the impulse or desire to protect those we care about. It can be expressed in a variety of ways. A woman "sticks up for" her partner when he is criticized socially. A man takes on an onerous task to spare his partner who is exhausted and overwhelmed. Protectiveness can be expressed pathologically, as when it leads to secrecy and triangulation; however, wherever it exists, protectiveness is a potential resource that can be utilized, promoted, and redirected in treatment.

Genuine *affection* in a relationship—actually liking each other—is a powerful resource. Affection makes things easier; it is inherently motivating. It makes one *want* to treat the other well—to be kind, thoughtful, generous, and close. Affection makes it easier to be tolerant and patient and, when conflicts arise, to "do the right thing."

Commitment is not necessarily the same as affection, although affection naturally inclines us toward commitment. Commitment involves a determination to make a relationship work, to stay with it, and to honor one's obligations and promises. As noted earlier, commitment works like a clamp, holding a damaged relationship together while emotional repairs are made.

Being in a long-term relationship can feel at times like Chinese water torture, even in the most satisfying relationships. Areas of sensitivity, disagreement, and conflict may be rubbed raw as proximity and longevity push the partners together. Intimacy assures that each partner will experience the other up close, skin-close, over a long period of time. The experience of having the partner "under your skin" is both the reward and the price of intimacy. For this reason, *tolerance* is a powerful resource in close relationships. Tolerance involves an ability to accept differences, to contain negative feelings (rather than dump them on the partner), and to be nonreactive. Tolerance for each other's idiosyncrasies, for differences, and for the other partner's loyalties to others can go a long way toward making life in close relationships livable.

Guerin et al. (1987) use the term *self-focus* to describe "the ability to see one's own part in an emotional process" (p. 129). Self-focus contrasts with patterns of blame and accusation which are so common in couple relationships and for this reason it is immensely important in couple therapy. Self-focus makes it more likely that the partners will be able to acknowledge each other's claims, which facilitates trust-building and conflict resolution.

Humor is one of the most underrated resources in relationships. Humor "greases the wheels" of interaction. It can make potentially threatening interactions go more smoothly. It disarms, or encourages individuals to relax defenses. Humor encourages perspective and non-reactivity. It has been identified as a valuable resource in coping with serious illness and in promoting health (Cousins, 1979). Humor can decrease the "toxicity" of painful feelings such as shame and can be used in therapy to interrupt and reframe highly charged emotional impasses.

Hope implies a belief in possibilities and a personal involvement in a particular outcome. As Jules Henry (1965) noted, without hope, no other resources are mobilized.

Relational Resources

Relational resources, as suggested earlier, are characteristics of rela-tional systems. They involve the (usually unwritten) rules of the sys-tem, rules which limit destructiveness and encourage behaviors that make living together easier and richer.

Respect at the relational level corresponds to self-respect at the per-sonal level. Relational rules foster interactions between the partners that communicate that the other is valued and that his or her experi-ence, feelings, and contributions are seen as important and legitimate; it is communicated in words, gestures, and actions. Disrespect is a corrosive force in relationships. It erodes the self-respect of the part-ners, poisons interactions between them, encourages more powerful defenses, and thwarts coordinated problem-solving and coping. Over the course of countless interactions between the partners, invisible limits evolve which regulate the expression of respect and limit the expression of disrespect. These rules can be strengthened, maintained, threatened, eroded, and repaired by the actions and reactions of the partners.

Reliability refers to the ways and degrees to which the partners can depend on one another. Do they keep their word? Do they do what they say they will? This applies to both small (who gets up to give a bottle to the baby at 2 AM) and large (honesty and fidelity) matters. Reliability is essential for the partners' sense of safety in the relation-ship.

Reciprocity involves the fairness of give-and-take in the relation-ship. These relational rules encourage both partners to fulfill obligations, to recognize entitlement, and to repay sacrifice. Reciprocity increases trust; it allows us to feel "well held" and it increases our motivation to be responsible to the other. As the therapist, you must remember that it is not *your* definition of fairness that matters, but the partners'. Your task in couple therapy is to help the partners negotiate terms that feel fair to both of them, not to impose your personal definitions of what those terms should be.

Repair involves rules that govern behavior when other rules are broken. When one partner has been disrespectful to the other or unfair or unreliable, are there relational norms that encourage acknowledgement and repair of this violation of relational rules? Rules concerning repair can take many different forms. One couple remarked that they "never went to bed angry." Arguments had to be repaired, *even if they could not be resolved*, by bedtime. When harm has been done, repair can interrupt or prevent escalating cycles of accusation, defensiveness, and withdrawal. Repair facilitates *forgiveness*. The inability to repair is a significant component in most couple cases that involves chronic conflict.

Trust allows us to feel safe and secure in a relationship. Without it, self-disclosure, vulnerability, spontaneity, and vitality are inconceivable. Without it, communication is futile, commitment is uncertain, and intimacy is elusive. It is the foundation upon which any satisfying and stable relationship is built. Trust is impossible without *trustworthiness*, which refers to the overall level of merited trust in a relationship (Boszormenyi-Nagy & Krasner, 1986; Boszormenyi-Nagy & Ulrich, 1981). Trustworthiness involves an ongoing effort to try to be reliable and fair. Trust refers to the individual's capacity to believe and rely on his or her partner; trustworthiness refers to whether or not (or more accurately, to what degree) such trust is merited. Merited trust is based on past actions and predicts future ones. It is based not on what a person says he or she will do but on what he or she actually does.

Residual trust (Boszormenyi-Nagy, 1987) refers to those aspects of trust that remain intact even when the overall trustworthiness of the relationship has been damaged. For example, imagine that you are sitting with a couple who are angry, mistrustful, and stuck. The husband says, "If I had known you really wanted to go, I would have been more willing to at least consider it." You turn to the wife and ask if she *believes* what the husband has just said. Now imagine two different possibilities. In one case, she says, "No. I don't believe a word he says. He wouldn't know the truth if it fell on him." In a different case, she answers, "Yes. I know he wouldn't make it up. If he says it, it's true." The latter is an expression of residual trust, and the task of working with the second couple will probably be considerably easier than working with the first.

Finally, relational rigidity—the inability to alter interactional patterns—is a hallmark of many couples who present for treatment. For this reason, *flexibility* is a highly desirable trait in couple relationships and in couple therapy.

The effort to identify resources continues throughout the evaluation and, if couple therapy is recommended, over the course of treatment as well.

Wrapping Up

If the entire evaluation is being conducted in one sitting, at this point you can simply segue into the first individual session. However, if the individual sessions are to be scheduled for a later date, you need to help the couple close down the process the three of you have opened up. People need closure. When, at the end of a piece of music, we hear the first half of a plagal cadence—the "Ah-" of "Amen"—we wait suspended for the closure of the final chord; when it is sounded, we settle back with satisfaction. As someone said once in reference to children and the books that are written for them, they may not need a happy ending so much as a satisfying one.

If the first session has gone well, the couple will have opened themselves up to an unusual degree to a complete stranger. They may be feeling vulnerable, exposed, or "raw." Precisely because you do *not* wrap up the initial session with an extensive closing statement, you should make efforts to provide closure in some other way. This might involve an acknowledgement of their honesty and effort in the meeting, a sympathetic remark about the stresses they have described, or a reference to particular areas you hope to pursue further in subsequent meetings. It may simply involve a comment that recognizes that this has been difficult and a shift to a more neutral, conversational topic before ending. However it is done, you want to draw the first session to a close in a way that conveys sympathetic understanding and a generally positive attitude about the evaluation.

If the individual sessions are to occur at a later date, arrangements can be made at this time. If you have not done so already, you may need to discuss the structure of what will follow, financial matters, and material—such as legal limitations on professional confidentiality and privilege—which is necessary for the clients to provide informed consent for treatment.

If the individual sessions are conducted in the same sitting as the initial couple session, hold off on wrapping up until the end of the individual sessions. At that time, it is helpful to reconvene both partners for a very brief closing, to respond to their needs for closure, and to schedule the second and final meeting. Whether they immediately follow the initial session or are scheduled for a later date, the individual sessions become the therapist's next area of concern.

ᚖ 7 ᚖ

CONDUCTING THE INDIVIDUAL SESSIONS

T HE INITIAL COUPLE SESSION is indispensable for evaluating couples; the individual sessions are discretionary. Whether or not therapists hold individual sessions with both partners will depend on their theoretical orientation, general pragmatic considerations, and specific considerations related to particular cases. Therapists whose conceptual base is influenced by psychoanalytic theories or those who emphasize family of origin are generally more likely to want to meet with the partners individually than are more systems-oriented therapists. Probably the most common pragmatic consideration in this decision involves the constraints of the treatment setting. When treatment must be brief because of limitations related to managed care, insurance coverage, or institutional policy, therapists will be more reluctant to devote the extra time required for the individual portion of the couple evaluation. Beyond these considerations lies a landscape of trade-offs.

This chapter will examine the advantages and disadvantages of separate individual sessions and propose guidelines for conducting them.

Advantages of Individual Sessions

The individual sessions serve three main purposes:

1. They help the therapist build alliances with each partner.
2. They may provide a clearer impression of the partners' feelings
   about each other and about the relationship.
3. They can be used to gather family and relational history as
   well as to assess any individual symptomatology, and to better
   understand each partner as separate individuals in their own
   lives.

Building Alliances

The individual sessions provide an opportunity to build alliances with
each partner, often more easily than might be possible with both of
them present. The triangle formed in the couple session strains the
therapist's alliances with each individual in two major ways. First,
because the partners may disagree strongly on certain issues and feel
injured by one another, your sympathy to one may threaten and antag-
onize the other. This will not normally destroy an alliance with the
other partner but it may strain it.

Second, the individual sessions free each partner from the impact of
the other partner's presence. They will not be put on the spot, either
directly or indirectly, by having to respond to the other partner's complaints and accusations. This can greatly reduce defensiveness. The
therapist's comments and questions can not be "contaminated" by
the partner's interjecting his or her complaints or criticisms before the
other can respond; as an example, note the following scenario. You ask
the man, as neutrally as possible, about his hours of work. Before he
can respond, the woman interjects, "Yeah, tell him. Tell him about
how you promised five years ago that you'd stop working weekends
and you haven't been home more than two weekends since." This
common occurrence taints your neutral question with a strong dose of
anger and blame, and interferes with your attempt to build alliances
based on respect and sympathy. You can, and should, be able to intervene in couple sessions to minimize these interjections. However, this
requires effort, it does not guarantee success, and it is just as likely to
alienate the other partner.

In the individual sessions, no such interference can occur. You can give the client your undivided attention. You can adjust to the individual's needs and vulnerabilities, his or her pace, use of language, and style of interaction without having to be aware of and adjust to the partner's. On issues that severely polarize the couple, you can show somewhat more sympathy than might be possible in the presence of the other. In the individual sessions, you are freed from having to consider the partner's potential reactions to every comment you may make. For all these reasons, the individual sessions can enhance your efforts to build alliances with both partners during the course of the evaluation. These alliances create a fund of credibility and goodwill which you may need to draw on at the conclusion of the evaluation when you share impressions and recommendations with the couple.

Assessing Feelings and Commitment

The individual sessions allow you to further explore each partner's experience of the relationship. You can follow up on areas of ambiguity from the initial couple session or invite the individual in a more general way to help you understand how he or she feels about the partner. Partners who express relatively minor dissatisfactions in the initial couple session may reveal more profound discontent in the individual session. These sessions are especially important in forming the most accurate picture possible of each person's feelings about and commitment to the other.

Marcia calls, requesting marital therapy for herself and her husband, Roger. Both are in their mid-30s. They have been married for 10 years. There are no children. Over the telephone, Marcia says that she and Roger don't communicate well and that she is dissatisfied with the relationship. She adds that Roger does not feel that there are serious problems.

In the first couple session, both partners impress as very reserved individuals. Marcia has difficulty being assertive. There is a note of frustration in her description of their relationship. Roger impresses as a quintessential Yankee, a thoughtful man who keeps his thoughts to himself, prides himself on his independence and capacity for hard work, and is acutely uncomfortable to find himself for the first time in the office of a psychotherapist.

In the couple session, Marcia says that she feels "it is time to start working on the relationship," that they don't communicate well, and that she cannot do it by herself. She says that neither of them can express angry feelings and that "this gets in the way of good feelings." Roger says that he "doesn't know what she's looking for" but he admits that when tension develops, both of them get quiet. One important issue involves their having moved to this area from their home state for his work. Marcia has been unhappy here and has longed to return home for almost 10 years. Roger has reassured her but not taken action to find another job. The couple session leaves the impression of a relatively good relationship in which the partners have difficulty disagreeing and expressing anger. Marcia is clearly more dissatisfied with the status quo but her dissatisfaction does not seem particularly acute. Roger is wary of therapy and reluctant to express his feelings but willing to participate in therapy.

In her individual session, Marcia reveals far more of her discontent. She says that she was relieved after the couple session because "it didn't blow him away." She goes on to say that she feels she is "about to explode"; she is "furious" over the nearly 10 years they have spent away from their home state. At one point she says, "Everything he does drives me crazy." She has persistent thoughts about leaving Roger and makes clear that she is ambivalent even about proceeding with couple therapy but that she wants to try.

The discrepancy between Marcia's presentation in the couple session and later in the individual one may not be startling but it is significant. It allowed me to understand that her discontent was significantly greater than she had acknowledged in the couple session. Marcia felt, probably with justification, that if she had expressed to Roger in the first session how negative her feelings were, he would have been overwhelmed and most likely would not return for subsequent sessions. It also seemed that she simply could not bring herself at that point to express these feelings openly in his presence. Besides helping me form a truer picture of the relationship, this helped me assess each partner's tolerance for the work that therapy would require. It allowed me to appreciate that the length of the fuse on her explosive feelings was considerably shorter than it had appeared to be in the couple session.

Because she did not actually plan to leave Roger and because no secrets were revealed, I was free to use the information obtained without having to press for disclosure and discussion of it. It did not change the focus of couple therapy but made it less likely that sessions would presume her patience and possibly lead to her abruptly opting out of both the marriage and the therapy.

This case illustrates how the individual sessions can help the therapist understand the partners' real feelings about each another; this needn't always involve negative feelings. Sometimes when one partner seems frustrated or ambivalent in the couple session, a direct inquiry in the individual session will elicit an unambiguous response such as, "Oh no. Ed drives me crazy sometimes and I wish to hell he'd stand up to his parents but I love him and I really want to make this work." Answers such as these also help to more accurately assess the individual's motivation and tolerance for the time and energy required by couple therapy.

Gathering History and Assessing the Individual

The individual sessions constitute condensed individual evaluations with a special emphasis on what each partner brings to the relationship. Inquire about the individual's family of origin as well as previous couple relationships; try to get some feel for who this person is as an individual and how this impinges on the partner. Note that these are not in-depth psychiatric assessments; instead of thoroughly surveying the details of a new territory, you are trying to establish some prominent landmarks and essential features, knowing that more detailed mapping may follow later.

Family of Origin. Information about family of origin can be recorded in the form of a rough genogram. It provides information on two levels: historical and current. It also illuminates the individual's earliest attachments and thus about the crucible in which his or her relational profile was shaped. These relationships provide the "trust base," whether precarious or solid, that the individual brings to all other relationships. They influence conscious and unconscious attraction between the partners and problematic patterns that may develop in the relationship. At the second level, you learn about the influence of the families of origin *currently* in the couple's relationship. Are these partners having difficulty consolidating their own relationship because of intense pressures from one or both families? Are the partners overly close to or cut off from them? Do family members function as resources for the couple?

After getting names and ages for all members of the individual's family, as well as marital status, occupation, and number of children (both in the original family and in those formed by siblings), inquire about early relationships with parents or parent-substitutes. Be careful to ask about relationships with each parent separately rather than allowing them to be lumped together into an undifferentiated unit. Typical questions are:

- Tell me a little about your father.
- What kind of person is/was he?
- What kind of father is/was he?
- How did you feel about him when you were little?
- What were things like between you and him?
- When you think about your father when you were small, is there a particular scene or picture that comes to mind?

The last question derives from the truism that "one picture is worth a thousand words"; sometimes these emblematic scenes convey more emotional information than the client's description of the parent. It may help clients who have difficulty finding words to describe the parent and who can more easily report an image that comes to mind. When the father is still living, you might ask, "What are things like between you and him now?" The same questions are asked about the mother.

When the individual was raised by adults other than his or her parents, try to identify the primary attachment figure(s) and conduct the same inquiry. Even when children are raised by parents, there may be strong affective ties to others, such as grandparents, other relatives, neighbors, or the parents of a close friend. You want to understand the resources and difficulties the individual may have experienced in these relationships.

Sibling Relationships. If the individual has siblings, you should get some idea about past and present relationships with them. Ask about family roles. Many clients will understand this term; others can be helped by a brief illustration of common roles—"the little mother," "the rebel," "the hero," "the black sheep." Inquiring about their childhood nicknames provides another way to explore this. One client reported being called "Stumbler" by his father; another was referred to as "Grizelda," a homely and ill-tempered witch in a popular cartoon strip.

Relationships with siblings can be especially important in light of transferential patterns that can develop in couple therapy. Just as individual psychotherapy elicits transference reactions to the therapist based on early relational patterns with parents, couple therapy can elicit what might be thought of as "triangular transference" related to experiences with parents *and* siblings. One or both partners may find themselves feeling "left out" or "pushed aside" in the therapy and may become intensely competitive in response to these feelings. One client may urgently endeavor to get the therapist to help her partner, while another has a sense of gloating at what she sees as her advantage over the other partner in sessions. Each of these feelings may replicate problematic triangular relationships with parents and siblings. For these couples, sibling-related transference probably operates outside of therapy as well; the couple may present with intense conflicts involving third parties other than the therapist. Finally, sibling-related transference can operate directly between client and therapist when the therapist reminds the client strongly of a particular sibling.

Childhood and Adolescence. Try to get a general sense of the individual's experience during childhood and adolescence. Questions about family of origin fill in a portion but not all of this. What kind of child was she? What was her mood like? Was she outgoing, shy, moody, depressed, fearful? What was she like socially? Did she have a group of friends, one best friend, or was she more of a loner? Where did she feel safe? Was there anything she loved to do? What was her school experience like? How did she spend time after school? Were there especially important experiences, such as an illness or death in the family, a serious illness or injury to the child herself, an experience of molestation, a disruptive family move, or a drastic change in the family's finances?

Previous Relationships. Ask about prior couple relationships that the individual considers important, including but not limited to marriages. Try to get a feeling for how the partners related to one another and ask whether the individual sees any patterns in the earlier relationship that are similar to patterns in the current couple relationship. Has the husband whose wife complains of his remoteness already been left by two previous women for the same reasons? Has the woman who protests her boyfriend's unavailability due to work been in other relationships with men who were unavailable?

This information is crucial for your effort to understand the individual's relational profile—his or her characteristic ways of forming close emotional attachments with another person. The existence of similar problematic patterns in previous relationships is one indicator that the individual's relational profile may be an important factor in the couple's current problems. Information about previous relationships can also help you appreciate how the individual came to be in the current one. For example, it might become clear that the individual was deeply in love with someone who ended an earlier relationship and so he or she began the current relationship "on the rebound."

Identity, Work, Social Relationships, Aspirations. Try to understand the client *as an individual,* apart from the partner. Who is this person in his own right? How does he see himself? How does he wish to *be* seen, and how *not* to be seen? How does he feel about his work life? Does he have other close relationships, such as friends or siblings? Does he have goals or aspirations in life? His answers can have significant bearing on the couple's relationship; note the following examples.

A man in his 60s who prides himself on his youth and vigor becomes alienated from his wife whom he sees as "having a retirement mentality."

A woman in her 20s has no close relationships apart from her husband and her mother whom she sees daily. She has little self-confidence and no clear notion of what she wants in life. She has been content to be her mother's confidante. When her mother and stepfather move to a different state, she becomes even more dependent on her husband and develops panic attacks which further intensify her dependency. The husband feels suffocated and overwhelmed; the wife feels abandoned by both her mother and her husband.

A man in his 40s who has been intensely identified with his upwardly mobile career and sees himself as "a real go-getter" is suddenly laid off and unable to find comparable employment. He finds work in a different field at a lower salary and with no real chances for advancement. He becomes depressed and bitter and markedly increases his drinking.

How these individuals see themselves and what they want out of life has tremendous bearing on what goes on in their primary couple relationships. To focus only on what goes on between the partners and to overlook these defining aspects of each individual is to deprive yourself of information that may help you understand the couple's difficulties and how to relate to them in the evaluation and, possibly, later in treatment. Often, these questions needn't be asked directly because the information is conveyed "between the lines"—in how the clients dress and speak (about themselves as well as others), in offhand comments they make, and in their responses to other questions. When this is not the case and you are having difficulty "sizing up" the individual, these questions can be asked directly; the individual can be invited to talk about his dreams or goals in life, his feelings about work, and his friendships and other social relationships.

Individual Symptomatology. When the couple's presenting problems include individual symptomatology of some kind, such as depression, obsessive compulsive disorder, panic attacks, or posttraumatic stress disorder, the therapist must be sure to assess this area thoroughly. This assessment may be conducted in the initial session, with both partners present, but you may want to inquire about symptoms in more detail in the individual sessions. Furthermore, if symptomatology is not central to the couple's major complaint and did not initially seem of crisis proportions, most of the initial couple session may have been devoted to exploring the couple's relationship. In these cases, part of the individual sessions can be used to provide a more detailed picture of individual symptoms. This inquiry can be made of *both* partners since they may have different perceptions and hunches about them.

In addition, some clients may present a truer picture of their symptoms in a separate session with the therapist than they will with their partners present. For example, a man who is experiencing depression for the first time in his life and who blames himself for "giving in to these feelings," may have concealed from his partner how seriously depressed, and even suicidal, he feels. Whenever clients describe depression, the therapist must assess for severity of symptoms and potential lethality. (See Chapter 18 for recommendations on assessment in these cases.)

"Worst Feeling": An Individual Probe Question. One probe question that I have found helpful for assessing *individuals* involves asking the individual to describe the worst feeling he or she has ever had. I make sure that the client does not assume the question to be confined to this current relationship but instead to the entirety of his or her life. Sometimes the answer is unremarkable, as when someone refers to the death of a parent or another close relative. Other times, however, the answer can illuminate the central emotional impasse of the couple's relationship. It functions as a kind of Geiger counter for relational pain, guiding the therapist to individual experiences which may have led to emotional vulnerability and consequent defenses, and which can make intimacy with the partner both compelling and dangerous.

In one couple, Tom was extremely sensitive to any sign of distance on his wife's part. He adopted a resentful, deprived stance and criticized her constantly for "pulling away" from him. His wife became more and more angry and alienated from him. When asked about the "worst feeling" he had ever had, he recalled his mother's sudden death when he was 10 years old. He remembered feeling "left by the side of the road," the precise emotional experience that he both feared and precipitated in relation to his wife. Experiences like these are often critical ingredients in the relational profiles that form the unconscious matrix of the relationship.

Davina described an abusive former lover and feeling "helpless at the hands of a madman." She wondered why she had stayed in that relationship for so long. This was not the only abusive relationship she had experienced and, although her current relationship was far better, here too there were moments of mutual violence. Significantly, she was raised by her mother and a stepfather until their separation when she was 9 years old. She has some memories of this man's violence toward her mother and has been told that he was "alcoholic, paranoid, and a complete lunatic." "Helpless at the hands of a madman" aptly describes the relational scene she continues to reenact with almost all of her partners.

Potential Disadvantages of Individual Sessions

Time and Cost

The most obvious disadvantages of holding separate individual sessions involve the logistics of time and money. The sessions require an additional time commitment on the part of the therapist and the clients. This may mean an additional hour or more added onto the initial couple session and held in the same sitting, or separate individual appointments for each partner. In the latter case, the need to schedule two additional hours may be inconvenient for clients and for the therapist and will delay the completion of the evaluation. The extra sessions will be costing someone (presumably but not necessarily the clients) more money. One question, then, is: Do the advantages of the individual sessions outweigh these practical disadvantages? My own feeling is that in the majority of cases they do.

Unbalancing Alliances

You may worry that individual sessions will unbalance your efforts to form balanced alliances with both partners. It is possible that, by meeting with each partner individually, you will be so swayed by one partner's views that balanced siding becomes extremely difficult. However, this scenario has less to do with individual sessions than it does with the unavoidable challenge of maintaining balanced alliances, which is part of the art and skill of treating couples.

An attitude of sympathetic understanding toward both partners should be maintained, and this balance preserved in the face of "special pleading" by the partners. Clients may be somewhat freer in separate sessions to present a more detailed and convincing picture of their poor treatment by the partner but this does not introduce a new element into the clinical equation. In both cases, you must consider what each partner expresses while feeling ethically responsible to both of them and assuming that there will usually be valid points in both partners' complaints.

In other cases, *you* may not feel that your siding has been compromised in any way by the individual sessions but it may *appear* that way to one or both partners. This is more likely to occur when one partner embellishes on how terrifically he or she got along with you. While this may happen, it rarely becomes a serious problem. Partners are usually cognizant of one another's characteristic ploys and able to take these "she-likes-me-better-than-you" messages with a large grain of salt. Furthermore, if you have demonstrated balanced siding in the initial couple session, the partners will usually give you the benefit of the doubt unless or until this appears unwarranted. For these reasons, concern over the dangers of individual sessions, for your effort to balance alliances, is largely unwarranted. This is not the case, however, when one partner shares secret information in their separate session and tries to secure a pledge of secrecy from you.

Complications Related to Secrets

Meeting separately with the partners increases the likelihood that one or both partners will reveal information of which the other partner is unaware. The introduction of secrets into the evaluation (especially when the client requests that *you* keep the secret) may create serious complications which, in some cases, can sabotage the evaluation and injure one partner or the relationship itself. Many therapists forego the individual sessions for this reason, fearing the complications that secrets can introduce and not wanting to invite them. My own feeling is that the advantages of the individual sessions clearly outweigh the disadvantages posed by the greater likelihood of secrets being shared. This is especially true given that the clinical management of secrets is rarely complicated. In most cases, the potential threats that secrets pose to the evaluation can be easily neutralized by following a straightforward set of guidelines. Managing secrets in the evaluation is covered later in this chapter.

Idiosyncratic Factors

There may be idiosyncratic situations in which the difficulties created by the individual sessions outweigh their advantages. The following case illustrates one such situation.

Carol and John had been married for 1½ years; they had no children. Carol's depression was one among several problems they presented. In the initial couple session, John related that another problem involved his extreme uneasiness when Carol had to have a medical examination of any kind. In the past, he felt this uneasiness when Carol had gynecological exams, routine medical check-ups, and chiropractic sessions. With reluctance, he admitted to a persistent fear that the professional would make sexual overtures to Carol and that she would respond. He knew that there was no rational basis for his reactions but simply could not help feeling acutely anxious in these circumstances. His reactions may have been related to difficulties in the couple's sexual relationship which seemed to be related to Carol's depression and to John's life-long sexual insecurities.

When asked if he anticipated having similar feelings about Carol's individual session with me, John's "No" was far from convincing, delivered as it was with manifest uneasiness and a lack of conviction. I felt that to insist on individual sessions before trust could be established between us would be to start out on the wrong foot. Given John's misgivings, the advantages of the individual session simply did not outweigh these threats to the evaluation and possible later treatment. I let the couple know that I often meet with both partners individually but that this was not essential for the evaluation and that, if they wished, one or both could "sit in on" the other's individual session. John chose to sit in with Carol which she indicated was fine with her; Carol chose not to sit in on John's session. The evaluation was completed and the couple made significant progress in treatment.

Specific Clinical Indicators

The separate individual sessions are especially likely to be helpful when one or more of the following factors are prominent in the couple being evaluated.

Ambiguity About Commitment and Feelings Toward the Partner

Separate individual sessions are more desirable if you sense that you are not getting the whole picture in the couple session. This usually involves a sense that one partner's feelings and level of commitment to the relationship may be quite different from those expressed in the couple session. As indicated earlier, one advantage of the individual sessions is that they allow you to more accurately assess feelings about and commitment to the relationship.

Extreme Discomfort in the Couple Session

Separate sessions may be particularly indicated when you recognize acute discomfort in one or both partners. You may notice marked feelings of embarrassment and shame either in relation to particular material or more generally. There is no guarantee that a client who is extremely uncomfortable in the couple session will be more comfortable in the individual session, but this is often the case, especially when he or she feels shame related to material which has not been thoroughly discussed with the partner (such as experiences of childhood physical, sexual, and psychological abuse; rape, battering, or a family history of alcoholism).

These clients may be fearful that in the couple session, they will not be able to control the parameters of discussion. They may fear having painful experiences reevoked and being catapulted into a state of shameful exposure with the partner and this stranger—the therapist—in the very first session. This is even more likely if they assume, correctly or not, that their partners will be either inadvertently or deliberately insensitive to these feelings. In these cases, it may help to meet separately with the individual. Here, you can try to explore these areas carefully and sensitively without having to worry about the needs or interjections of the other partner. In addition, the client's level of trust may be higher following the initial couple session.

One exception to this rule involves clients who will probably be *more* anxious in the individual sessions, those who might say, in effect, "Marriage counseling is one thing but to see a shrink by yourself, that means you're crazy." These clients will not be reassured by the move to an individual session. In some cases, this can be dealt with by reassuring the client about the purposes of the individual session in a low-key manner. In others, you might decide to forego the individual session.

Extreme Conflict in the Couple Session

Another circumstance in which individual sessions are likely to be especially helpful involves couples whose conflict is so intense in the initial couple session as to seriously interfere with the purposes of the evaluation. When the conflict is so great that virtually every statement is challenged by the other partner and these challenges lead to protracted arguments, the utility of the couple session will be greatly reduced. The intensity of conflict may also lead to one or both partners feeling so angry that they disengage emotionally, break off discussion, turn away from the other and, in some cases, even walk out of the session. In this case, you should try to contain this conflict in the couple session as much as is possible.

In other cases, conflict may be less severe but no less problematic. The partners can sit in a room together and converse with one another; however, they may be extremely guarded. Both fear that whatever they say in the session will be subsequently used against them by the partner. When the partners' self-protective concerns are this high and the level of trust is this low, you may learn more from the partners individually.

Ground Rules

Balancing the Individual Sessions

If you choose to hold individual sessions, be certain to meet individually with *both* partners. In some cases, you may feel that you really only need to meet with one partner. For example, when one partner is verbal and self-disclosing in the couple session and the other reticent and evasive, you may feel that you know enough about the more open partner but want to learn more about the quieter one. Or one partner's individual symptomatology may be so puzzling or serious (for example, when there are indications of suicidal lethality) that you recognize the need to conduct a thorough mental status exam and obtain individual and family psychiatric history. In cases like these, even when you feel that individual sessions with both partners are unnecessary for purposes of assessment, it is a pragmatic error to meet with only one of them. It would unbalance your efforts to build alliances with both partners, weaken the implicit relational frame of the evaluation, and lend itself to a variety of problematic interpretations by the clients.

Because couples' conflicts are so often organized as struggles over who is right or wrong, good or bad, sick or healthy, the ambiguity created when you meet with only one individual may well be perceived within these terms. This can lead to a number of problematic assumptions. One or both parties may assume that you favor one partner and have decided that this individual will be a more reliable informant, either more able or more willing to give you "the real story" about the relationship. Or they may assume that you have identified the individual with whom are meeting separately as the "sick" one or the one who is more to blame for their problems. For these reasons, meeting individually with only one partner should be avoided.

Meeting individually with both partners is a simple way to neutralize the possible threats to the evaluation posed by the assumptions described above. The sessions need not be exactly the same length. You can always use the time that is not needed for extensive inquiry to build your alliance with that individual. When the couple and individual sessions are conducted in the same sitting, the block of time can be more flexibly allocated in keeping with the needs of the particular case—for example, one hour for the couple session, 20 minutes with one partner individually, 30 minutes with the other and five or ten minutes to wrap up and schedule the next session.

Sequencing the Individual Sessions

The decision to meet separately with both partners raises two pragmatic issues: which partner to meet with first and whether this really matters. The sequence of sessions is rarely important. When the individual and couple sessions are held in the same sitting, the couple can decide for themselves who will meet first. They may hesitate and seem uncertain as to how to proceed. Most couples will not have had prior experience with couple evaluation so they will look to you for cues about how to proceed. You can inform them that the sequence is unimportant and let them choose who will meet first. Usually, the decision is easily made and has a "flip-of-the-coin" feeling to it. When the individual sessions are held on a subsequent date, the same principle applies—the sequence is generally unimportant. In these cases, the decision can be made logistically (based on the participants' schedules) or emotionally (when one partner has a more urgent need to meet sooner). Again, let them know that you consider the sequence unimportant and allow them to decide on it.

One possible exception to this principle involves cases in which you sense that secrets may play an important part in the couple's difficulties. In these cases, if you sense that one partner is a "secret-holder" and the other is unaware, there is some advantage to meeting first with the secret-holder. If the individual agrees to discuss the information without conditions (see the following discussion on managing secrets), there is some advantage to hearing it sooner rather than later. A greater awareness of the couple's *real* circumstances will help you understand the meaning of their current situation. However, signals about secrets in couple sessions are highly ambiguous and you can never be sure that you have read them correctly. Furthermore, there is no guarantee that the secret-holder will share the information with you. Given these uncertainties, this exception to the rule that sequencing of the individual sessions is unimportant is a highly conditional one, and no harm will be done if you meet with the partners in a different order.

Handling Communication Related to the Individual Sessions

Clients may ask whether you will discuss material from their individual session with the other partner. They may ask about what the partner said, either in general or in relation to a particular issue. They may inquire as to whether it's okay for them to ask the partner about his or her session. This can become confusing and complicated unless you follow sensible guidelines about such communications. For example, one partner asks what his partner said about a specific issue in her individual session. He later relays your answer, filtered through his own feelings about the issue, to her. You then have to account to the wounded or angry or puzzled partner for what he said you said. Unless there are compelling reasons, you are best off avoiding these complications.

Emphasize that you will not report on either individual session to the other partner but that they are perfectly free to discuss anything and everything about their individual sessions with one another. This minimizes the potential for triangulation. The partners are in an intimate relationship with one another; communication between them should be as open as they wish. Nothing about the evaluation goes against this healthy standard of open communication *within* the relationship. In addition, you should refuse to serve as a go-between in relation to the individual sessions. It may be appropriate and helpful for a therapist to try to "translate" for the other what one partner means in couple therapy; it is neither appropriate nor helpful for the therapist to be used as a go-between during the evaluation.

"Previewing" the Therapist's Response

The structure of the evaluation builds suspense, which serves to heighten the clients' receptivity to the therapist's response at its conclusion. However, this is not without potential drawbacks. One or both partners may ask, usually near the conclusion of their individual session, for a preview of your observations and recommendations. Sometimes the question is posed quite seriously, even urgently; more often, it is presented with a light or humorous touch: "So, what do you think? We're a real mess, huh?" or "Do you think you can help us?" or "So, should we pack it in or what?"

It can be difficult to resist the pressure of these inquiries. Whether urgent or humorous, there is an implicit feeling that it would be rude or insensitive not to respond, especially given the stakes involved and the client's patience up to that point. The problem is that to offer such a preview poses a threat to your effort to maintain balanced alliances. If you told the couple at the beginning of the evaluation that you would discuss conclusions with both partners together at its completion, then you should hold to this structure. To do differently lends itself to the same problematic interpretations discussed earlier in this chapter.

For these reasons, even when the request for a preview of your conclusions is delivered with urgency, you should politely decline to do so. You may briefly remind the client of the original understanding about the response and stress the importance of keeping to this plan, or you may underscore the usefulness of having both partners present to react to all aspects of it. There may, however, be some innocuous aspect of your impressions that can be shared without giving that partner prior access to the most important elements of the conclusions. The tone in which these comments are delivered should always be sympathetic and low-key, *never* offending or judgmental.

Managing Secrets

Holding separate sessions with each partner increases the risk that one or both will reveal information that they do not want shared with their partner. Secrets can create ethical and practical dilemmas which complicate and undermine the evaluation—and possible later treatment—unless they are handled with care. The clinical management of secrets begins with the recognition that, once secrets are shared, there is no way for you to interact with the clients without taking an ethical position. If you agree not to disclose the information, you are taking the position that the secret-holder is entitled to keep the information secret and that you will collaborate with this effort. If you refuse to keep the information confidential, you are taking the position that the unaware partner is entitled to know it. There is simply no way of proceeding *without* taking such positions so it behooves you to think through your convictions regarding secrets.

My position starts with a distinction between *secrecy* and *privacy*. I assume that in close relationships, some information can be reasonably considered private while other information is more clearly secret. The distinction hinges on the *relevance* of the information for the unaware. If the information has little direct relevance, it can be considered private, rather than secret. For example, a husband's knowledge that his older brother was born out of wedlock or that his sister became pregnant as a teenager most likely has little real relevance for his wife. He might *choose* to disclose these facts but he would probably not feel that he *owed* it to her to do so. If, on the other had, the husband is sexually involved with his wife's sister, this is highly relevant for his wife and would be seen as secret rather than private.

These examples point out two troubling but unavoidable aspects of managing secrets in clinical practice. First, distinctions between secrecy and privacy are not always so easily made. Is an affair that ended eight months ago secret or private? Are a husband's homosexual experiences before he met his wife secret or private? The difficulty of making these decisions does not allow you to duck them. You must decide whether or not you feel that the unaware is entitled to this information and whether you endanger your professional trustworthiness with that partner by agreeing not to disclose it. Second, when confidential information is shared with you, decisions about its relevance for the unaware are unavoidably being made by yourself and the secret-holder and not by the individual who is unaware. This is less than ideal but unavoidable.

A second consideration in managing secrets involves their relevance to the formulation of the case. When the secret is highly relevant to the formulation and you are not free to share it, your ability to communicate honestly and *meaningfully* about real problems is seriously compromised. For example, a wife who presents as distant with her husband but says she does not understand why, later reveals that she is having an affair with a neighbor; her husband feels negatively about this man without knowing why and chides himself for his "critical nature." There is simply no way to discuss the real issues in this case or set sensible directions for treatment without acknowledging this reality. And this is only one of the complications introduced into the evaluation—and possible treatment—when the therapist agrees to keep secrets. If you attempt to conduct therapy with this couple, you will be part of a hidden alliance with the wife, thereby contributing to the husband's mystification. In addition, you are vulnerable to the possibility of the husband discovering both the affair and your knowledge of it with the obvious danger to your therapeutic alliance with him. However, if you are ignorant of information which has significant bearing on the case, your understanding of the couple's problems is likely to be faulty and incomplete. This is the fundamental trade-off which must be considered in deciding on a policy toward secrets and in implementing this policy in specific cases.

Some therapists forego the individual sessions in an effort to avoid complications associated with secrets. As stated earlier, I feel that the advantages of individual sessions clearly outweigh potential disadvantages because managing secrets is rarely complicated if the therapist follows a straightforward set of guidelines. The best possible scenario involves the secret-holder sharing the information without any restrictions on the therapist's freedom to use it in the course of the evaluation. When this is not possible, the therapist faces several "next-best" options.

The simplest way to avoid the dangers posed by secrets is to let the clients know at the end of the first couple session that you do not keep confidential information *within* the couple's relationship. This is probably the preferred stance for beginning therapists because it is the simplest, the most straightforward, and the safest. With this stance, you are least likely to become entangled in hidden alliances or vulnerable to being seen as untrustworthy if disclosure occurs later. (If you do choose this option, be sure that the clients understand the distinction between your legal obligation to maintain confidentiality in relation to persons *outside* the relationship and your policy of not maintaining confidentiality *within* it.)

You can also explain how secrets interfere with your ability to be helpful and let them know that for that reason you choose not to hold confidential information in the evaluation. There are a number of ways in which this can be done. One therapist accomplished this by routinely telling clients, "I have the biggest mouth in town." Another communicated the same policy, with self-deprecatory finesse, by telling clients that he'd probably have difficulty remembering what they wanted him to keep quiet about so instead they should just assume that anything they told him was fair game.

You might want to elaborate by encouraging them, if they have any questions, to weigh the importance of the information for your ability to understand their situation fully. If the information is highly relevant, it is unrealistic to expect you to be helpful without it being disclosed. However, if disclosure is out of the question, the information should not be discussed with you privately. In these ways, you protect your own trustworthiness for both partners and make them responsible for the decision to withhold or disclose information.

Some therapists, myself included, choose not to make a blanket statement about secrets. The primary reason involves not wanting to discourage disclosure of secrets that may have significant bearing in a particular case. A lesser factor involves the risk of clients taking offense at this apparent assumption that they might be less than honest with one another. A related consideration involves the relative simplicity of managing secrets if and when they arise in the individual sessions.

The therapist's policy and position in these circumstances remain the same but they are communicated when the issue actually arises. This can take two forms—preventive or reparative. The former refers to cases in which you are able to *anticipate* disclosure of secrets; this happens far more often than one might think. Clients commonly preface disclosures with a question such as, "Do you tell him everything I tell you?" They become fidgety or uneasy. When this occurs, head off disclosure by explaining the dangers and complications posed by secrets in the evaluation and encouraging the client to weigh them. You hope that the client will disclose the information without conditions—that is, giving you the freedom to discuss the information in the partner's presence *if* you feel that this is necessary. In some cases, the information may not be important enough to necessitate disclosure; you can then proceed as you would with any other information shared during an individual session.

If you feel that disclosure to the partner *is* necessary and if the client agrees, you can offer to facilitate this in a way that minimizes potentially destructive outcomes. This might involve exploring the individual's fears and feelings as well as the risks and costs of disclosure versus nondisclosure. It might involve offering to participate in the disclosure in a couple session or respecting the client's wish to disclose to the partner in private.

If the client refuses to disclose the information unless you swear yourself to secrecy, decline to do so and proceed without it. This is less than ideal but preferable to colluding with the secret-holder and being powerless to use the information openly in the evaluation. No ground rules can cover every situation and the therapist must use common sense to adapt policies to particular situations. For example, you would be extremely reluctant to endorse private disclosure—that is, without your being present—of a highly charged secret to a partner with a history of violence or suicide attempts.

These considerations guide the management of secrets when the therapist is able to anticipate the client's disclosure, but that is not always possible. If the client discloses abruptly and if you feel that the information is not sufficiently relevant to the formulation and does not endanger your trustworthiness to both partners, you can, as in the scenario described earlier, proceed as you would with any other information shared. If you feel that you cannot do this, proceed as you would in the situation described above, the only difference being that this occurs *after* disclosure. Explain the dangers and complications of secrets, ask for permission to use the information openly if this is necessary, and offer to help make disclosure as nondestructive as possible. If the client agrees, you have extricated yourself from an entangling alliance and the integrity of the evaluation has been maintained.

The most difficult scenario occurs when you have been unable to anticipate disclosure, the information is highly relevant, and the client refuses to give permission under any circumstances for the secret to be shared openly with the partner. These cases, fortunately, are rare for they present few good options. Some therapists will agree to keep the information secret, hoping that it will become "digestible" by the couple at some point in the future. I do not recommend this for the reasons already described. Some therapists might unilaterally take responsibility for disclosing the secret to the unaware without the secret-holder's permission. I strongly discourage this option. If resources are insufficient to disclose the secret, they are probably insufficient to process it constructively. The therapist can refuse to participate in keeping secrets, and he or she should not take personal responsibility for what is or is not disclosed in that relationship.

Given the trade-offs involved and the uniformly undesirable options, I would recommend respectfully informing the secret-holder that regrettably you can not conduct the evaluation under these conditions. He or she is free to maintain secrecy but you cannot help them under these conditions. Let them know that regrettably, you need to terminate the evaluation. You might offer to help them think about other directions to pursue. Doing this is less than ideal; however, it preserves your trustworthiness for both clients, underscores the importance of open communication, upholds your need to use highly relevant information in an effort to help them, and maintains the integrity of the evaluation. Faced with the stark choices that exist when a secret-holder adamantly refuses to give permission to share already-disclosed information with the partner, my own convictions lead me to prefer this option to any others. This least desirable scenario is, fortunately, also the least common.*

Collateral Contacts

The therapist's communication with other professionals who either have treated or are currently treating one or both partners takes place apart from the scheduled sessions with the couple. Because these collateral contacts should be made before you finalize your formulation

---

*For a more detailed discussion of patterns involving secrets in relationships and the management of secrets in treatment, see Karpel, 1980, and Imber-Black, 1993.

and recommendations, the end of this chapter is as good a place as any to address them. Collateral contacts raise three issues: (1) whether to have them, (2) with whom to have them, (3) when to have them.

Some therapists choose not to communicate with other professionals from a conviction that such communications "break the frame" of safety and privacy that is necessary for successful treatment. My own feeling is that such contacts are highly desirable. I have never regretted contacting professionals who are currently or recently involved in a particular case. These discussions may deepen your understanding of one of the individuals, of the couple, or of their larger relational context. They also minimize the risk of misunderstandings and competition across professionals. When treatment follows evaluation, they reduce the danger of clients being caught in a crossfire of conflicting advice from different professionals.

With whom are such collateral contacts desirable? Each therapist will generate his or her own answers to this question, determining which contacts are of the highest priority and which are less important. In general, therapists should try to speak with all mental health professionals currently involved with one or both partners. This often means outpatient psychotherapists, specialists in treating substance abuse, leaders of particular groups (such as survivors of sexual abuse), staff on an inpatient psychiatric unit, or outpatient psychiatrists supervising psychotropic medication. It might involve social service personnel who are working with the couple as parents in the home or a probation officer for someone involved in the legal system. When there are significant medical problems, therapists should communicate with physicians who have examined or are treating the individual. This is especially true when complicated medical problems figure prominently in the couple's difficulties or in their daily life and when you are unsure as to whether you understand the ramifications and prognoses of the illness or injury. You may also wish to contact therapists who were involved with the couple in the recent past, or any previous therapist who provided couple therapy.

These contacts are only possible if clients give their legal permission for you to do so. This needn't involve a "two-way release" (one which gives permission to both professionals to convey impressions to the other) since at this point you are still in the process of *gathering* information. However, a two-way release is desirable, especially when there may well be ongoing contact between the partners and both professionals. It will allow you to share your impressions with the other professional when you are ready to do so. When the evaluation is followed by ongoing treatment, this open, two-way communication can coordinate treatment approaches.

If one or both partners decline to give their permission for such communication, the therapist is faced with a dilemma. Should you accept this limitation on your ability to explore all aspects of the case and proceed in spite of it, refuse to proceed (citing the contradiction between their asking for your help but denying you access to relevant information), or try to finesse the issue clinically? Most of the time, it's best to explore the feelings and reasons behind their reluctance and, if need be, to simply accept it for the time being. You can do this without further comment or by saying, in effect, "That's fine for now. If a time comes when I feel that this is problematic, I'll raise the issue with you again."

Often the client's reluctance represents little more than the need to keep a private personal sphere for him- or herself in individual treatment; occasionally it reflects his or her correct reading of the other therapist's preferences. It may involve secrets that have been revealed in individual therapy that he or she fears will be disclosed through this professional contact. However, your willingness to respect these limits does not endanger the evaluation in any way. It may limit your ability to fully understand them and may even preclude successful treatment but, if so, it is a choice they are making.

Does it matter *when* you contact other professionals? This is a matter of personal preference. Such contacts should be made before you organize your formulation and feedback to the couple. This allows your thinking and your response to be informed by the impressions and knowledge of the other professional(s). Beyond this, there are no strong indicators for when these calls should be made. The sooner you speak with other professionals, the more knowledgeable you will be about the couple when you meet with them. The later you do so, the most able you are to form your own first impressions of them. Different therapists have different preferences on these trade-offs. The question of when to speak to other professionals is much less important than the questions of whether and with whom to speak.

Wrapping Up

If the entire evaluation is being conducted in one sitting, you can follow the individual sessions by reconvening both partners to present your response. If the final couple session is to be held at a later date and if the initial couple session and both individual sessions were conducted in one sitting, you can reconvene the partners briefly to schedule the final session and to wrap up this one. Whenever the individual sessions are not immediately followed by the conclusion of the evaluation, you should be aware that the clients may not have much sense of closure at this point.

The same considerations that apply to closing the initial couple session apply to ending the individual sessions as well. Precisely because you do not provide closure in the form of a summary of observations and recommendations, you should bring the session to a close in a way that helps the couple make the transition from vulnerable self-disclosure to everyday life. As in the case of the couple session, this might involve a sympathetic remark about stresses they have described, a comment recognizing that this has been difficult and a shift to a more neutral, conversational topic, or an acknowledgement of their honesty and effort in the session. You want to bring the session to a close in a way that conveys sympathetic understanding and a generally positive attitude about the evaluation.

Having completed the "inquiry" portion of the evaluation, you are ready to pull together the impressions, observations, and hunches you have formed into a response that you can present to the couple. This begins with an effort to develop a formulation of the factors that may be contributing to and perpetuating their difficulties. This effort is the focus of the next chapter.

— 8 —

DEVELOPING A FORMULATION

THE LAST THREE CHAPTERS have focused on what the therapist *does* in the initial meetings of the evaluation. This chapter will examine how the therapist *thinks* about the material that has been presented. The formulation integrates the material that the partners have shared and the impressions that the therapist has formed. It addresses the probable causes of the presenting problems, that is, the relational patterns, individual personality factors, situational influences, and developmental processes that may be precipitating and maintaining these problems, and it suggests directions for treatment.

Formulation is a formal term for a hunch or a series of hunches. Throughout the evaluation, the therapist generates hunches based on information and impressions and then tests them via particular questions and further observation, revising, discarding, or strengthening them in the process. He is not required to be all-knowing; he tries to generate the best hunches possible about why a particular couple seems to be having their particular difficulties. If couple therapy is to follow, these hunches will be tested further over the course of treatment.

Formulation is a highly personal matter. Different therapists have differing theoretical frameworks and convictions about what is most important in human relationships. One therapist emphasizes deficient communication skills; another stresses lack of differentiation; a third focuses on colliding entitlements related to legacies derived from each partner's family of origin. A perusal of couple therapy literature indicates that, in spite of these individual differences, there is a great deal of overlap in different therapist's formulations about the difficulties couples present in treatment.

Rather than impose particular theoretical frameworks (although to some extent this is unavoidable), this chapter proposes a number of factors that might be implicated in the development and maintenance of a couple's problems and should therefore be considered when developing a formulation. The chapter also suggests how therapists can think about information and impressions gathered during the evaluation. Much of the material is presented in the form of questions, which are intended to focus the therapist's thinking and to progressively shape the formulation.

The Couple's Initial Presentation

How Does Each Partner Define Their Presenting Problem(s)?
How Do They Understand Its Causes?

Begin by thinking about the partners' definitions of the presenting problem and their hunches about what may be causing it. This represents an attitude of respect on your part and reduces the risk that you will move immediately to your own "pet theory" and overlook the couple's experience. Furthermore, they may be right; they may understand quite well what causes difficulty in their relationship and, if they do, they can steer you in the right direction. Also, regardless of their accuracy, their hunches may shed light on other aspects of the relationship and on the partners' values and vulnerabilities. Consider the degree of consensus in the partners' descriptions and hunches about the presenting problem. Greater consensus suggests—but does not always assure—a greater capacity to communicate and less polarization between the partners.

In some cases, the presenting problem and the formulation are one and the same. For example, difficulty coping with a serious injury to one partner may be both the presenting problem and an accurate formulation of the case when there seem to be no additional factors amplifying the stress. Amplifying factors might have included: idiosyncratic meanings of the injury to one or both partners, preexisting difficulties in attachment and intimacy in the relationship, or difficulties with communication and conflict-resolution which impede shared coping with these stresses.

When Did Problems Begin?
How Long Have They Experienced Them?

This question directs you to possible precipitants to their difficulties and thus to potentially important etiological factors.

Eve called after she had left her husband, Mike. The precipitant seemed to be an incident several months earlier in which Mike went on a week-long camping trip with some friends. Eve was left alone at home with their five-year-old daughter who was ill. She found herself feeling furious over being "trapped in the house" and was surprised by the intensity of her own reaction. Inquiry revealed that serious damage had been done to the trust-base of the relationship during her pregnancy five years earlier. Medical complications had required her to be bedridden throughout much of the pregnancy— literally "trapped in the house." She felt that, instead of trying to help her, Mike came home as little as possible. She was hurt and angry; the couple had argued about this but never resolved it. The precipitant to her leaving helped us to identify an "embedded" trust issue (Karpel, 1993) which had gone unresolved and fueled intense affect when the wife was again "trapped in the house" with their daughter five years later.

The couple's answers to this question may have prognostic implications. More recent problems may be easier to repair. Long-term problems may indicate greater damage done to the relationship (for example, more profound mistrust and greater emotional alienation) and one or both partners may be more entrenched in their positions in relation to the problem.

Why Are They Coming in for an Evaluation Now?

In some cases, this question overlaps perfectly with the preceding one. For example, in an acute crisis in which an affair has recently been disclosed, the precipitant and the reason for coming in now are identical. In other cases, the couple may describe a problem that they can identify as having begun years earlier. In these cases, their answers may surface details that are relevant to the formulation.

Peg and Richard requested treatment soon after Richard was offered an attractive job in another geographical area. The couple's relationship had cooled to an edgy, distant marriage of convenience over a period of several years. Peg enjoyed her own job and the area in which they currently lived. The job offer precipitated a crisis of commitment in a relationship with longstanding difficulties. No longer able to simply "coast" in the relationship, the partners were forced to assess how important it actually was to them. This produced stress but it also created an opportunity for them to more actively choose and shape their relationship and their individual lives.

How Has this Problem Changed Their Lives?

This question works on two levels. First, it provides detail about the stresses that their problems have imposed, the level of damage that has occurred in the relationship, and the seriousness of the problem. For example, a couple's living with one partner's father may lead only to increased arguments between the partners or it may contribute to an intensification of physical symptomatology in one partner, such as digestive problems, migraine headaches, or even increased fear of a heart attack. A couple's arguments may lead only to hard feelings or to permanent separate sleeping arrangements, the cancellation of a long-planned vacation, and the establishment of separate bank accounts.

On another level, this question can alert you to protective functions served by particular problems or symptoms. If a woman was planning to leave her marriage, but her husband's sudden onset of panic attacks made her feel that she cannot do so, this problem may serve the systemic function of slowing down precipitous change in the relationship. This scenario is discussed at greater length at the end of this chapter.

What Goals Does Each Partner Express for the Evaluation and for Possible Couple Therapy?

This question primarily informs decisions about directions and methods for treatment but it may also reveal aspects of the partners' feelings, values, and views of the relationship. Note the degree of consensus in the partners' descriptions of their individual goals for the evaluation and/or treatment; as mentioned previously, greater consensus suggests—but does not assure—better communication and less polarization between the partners. Differences may indicate significantly different "narratives" or visions of the relationship (which may be precisely what constitutes their problem) or important differences between the partners in their level of commitment to the relationship.

Rita and Alex, both in their mid-30s, have been married for 13 years. They called for an appointment one year after Rita discovered that Alex was involved in an extramarital relationship. The relationship had started three years before and was still continuing. Rita wanted Alex to give up the other relationship; he refused to do so. Rita would plead with him and become enraged with him but had not been able to give him an ultimatum about the relationship. One aspect of Rita's response to the question of goals was striking. Along with the hope that couple therapy would lead Alex to end the outside relationship and a request for support for herself, she said, "I need for someone else to empathize with him. Somebody has to take care of him if I'm going to be able to take care of myself." This comment underscored how powerful Rita's role as a care-giver was in relation to Alex. Not surprisingly, she had been involved in other relationships before this one in which she took care of troubled men. This contributed to her inability to set firm limits on Alex's outside relationship in spite of the pain it caused her.

Are There Any Unusual or Idiosyncratic Features of Their Initial Presentation? What Possibilities Do these Suggest?

Sometimes a comment or interaction or detail can reveal an important element of the couple's relationship or the presenting problem.

In the initial couple session Angela refused to answer a seemingly innocuous question about the names of her own and her husband's individual psychotherapists. Clients sometimes indicate an unwillingness to let the therapist who is evaluating them talk with their individual therapists, but I had never before had a client refuse to disclose the names of the therapists. This suggested the possibility that building trust would be especially difficult with this individual. I later learned that she had been severely and repeatedly abused by her stepfather and left unprotected by her mother; given this, she had very little reason to trust anyone. She was able to develop trust in subsequent couple therapy although I had to be much more careful than usual in my interactions with her. Significantly, her husband completely disregarded her preference for privacy on the issue of the therapists' names and unilaterally disclosed them himself. This precipitated an intense conflict before the first session was even concluded, and helped me appreciate the objective basis for her mistrust in this relationship.

How Do You Feel When You Are with Them? What Does this Suggest About Their Relationship and Their Present Difficulties?

How you feel while interacting with the couple may provide useful information about them. Positive feelings generally suggest resources of some kind in the couple's relationship. Negative feelings may help you experience first-hand some of what they experience in the relationship, for example, you may feel hopeless, confused, incompetent, or criticized. Your feelings in relation to one partner may shed light on what the other partner experiences—frustration, confusion, uneasiness, or outright fear. Precisely because these indicators are aspects of your internal experience, you must be especially careful to consider how they may reflect your own feelings, attitudes, and relationships and how these may color or distort perceptions of the couple.

Andrea and Sean described a history of unresolved conflicts which predated their marriage 10 years earlier. Andrea complained about Sean's rigidity and his intense anger at her, describing him as "like a bomb; you never know when it's going to go off." Sean complained about what he referred to as "the Wall," meaning the way in which Andrea would become withdrawn and inaccessible. I had heard descriptions such as these from many couples. With this couple, however, I was struck by how powerfully I felt what they were describing, even in the initial couple session. Sean made me nervous; something made me wonder if he might suddenly leap up and run from the room or even attack me physically. (Significantly, there had been no physical violence in this relationship.) Andrea answered my questions but seemed unusually opaque; I felt that I couldn't make emotional contact with her. Later, I learned that Andrea was living with a secret—an abortion—which was a source of intense shame and preoccupation for her. She said that she never met anyone without thinking of the abortion and of what they would think of her if they knew about it. Sean was hyperrational but filled with anger; his father deserted the family when Sean was less than one year old and *his alcoholic mother abandoned him when he was eleven. My own feelings in relation to this couple helped me appreciate how each partner felt in relation to the other.*

Facts

What is the Legal Status of the Relationship?
How Do the Partners Define It?
What is the Wider Relational Context?

Are they legally married? Are they unmarried but in what they consider to be a long-term committed relationship? Do they live together? Are they dating but living separately? Is this a homosexual couple? Is this a "bicoastal" marriage, with both partners spending a fair amount of time in different geographical areas, either for work or other reasons? Are they married but separated and considering divorce? If they are separated, has one or both already contacted a lawyer? Do they have children, either from this relationship or from earlier relationships? Do they live with or near members of one partner's family of origin or with any other individuals?

These differing structures and definitions alert the therapist to possibilities concerning particular stresses that the partners may experience and the nature of their commitments to the relationship. Couples in long-term but unmarried relationships may be struggling with issues of commitment to one another or with one or both partners' fears of intimacy. Couples who form stepfamilies must cope with a variety of stresses, including overlapping stages of the life cycle and difficulty balancing multiple loyalties. Equally important are the idiosyncratic meanings of these definitions and structures for the particular individuals involved. For example, do both partners in an unmarried relationship see this as a way of "testing things out" before making a more permanent commitment or does one partner experience it as a sign that she is not considered "good enough" for the other?

How Long Have They Been a Couple?

The longevity of the couple's relationship suggests possibilities concerning the challenges and issues they are facing. Couples in the early stages of a relationship are more likely to be dealing with the challenges of getting used to each other, establishing routines for living together and experiencing the clash between expectation and reality in the relationship. Couples in longer term relationships are somewhat more likely to be dealing with the strains of maintaining connection in the face of individual change and growth and with the challenge of preserving vitality in a "well-worn" relationship.

What Predictable and Unpredictable Stressors
Exist for this Couple?

Predictable stressors are those associated with the life cycle, such as marriage (or the formal start of a committed but unmarried relationship), the birth of children, children reaching adolescence and later leaving home, and the death of elderly parents. Unpredictable stressors include injury or serious illness, sudden unemployment, geographical moves, political instability, criminal victimization, violence, and sexual abuse. Stress taxes the resources of individuals and relationships by requiring that energy be devoted to coping. When stressors are overwhelming and resources insufficient, stress becomes crisis (Hill, 1958; McCubbin & Patterson, 1983) and in the extreme, it can be traumatic (van der Kolk, 1987).

Healthy individuals with good-enough relationships may request treatment when they are coping with stress. This is especially likely when efforts to cope lead to maladaptive responses that amplify difficulties in the couple's interaction. Furthermore, the idiosyncratic meanings of stressors for one or both partners may amplify the severity of the challenge for the couple. As suggested by Carter and McGoldrick (1980), the intersection of predictable and unpredictable stressors with unresolved difficulties from earlier life experiences and relationships can intensify maladaptive coping. These patterns may constitute a sufficient formulation of the couple's problems.

Hazel requested couple therapy saying, "Our marriage is falling apart." She had been married to Fred for 15 years; they had two children, ages 14 and 11. About two years before her call, Fred had sustained a serious back injury in an accident at work. The injury required several episodes of surgery; it created constant low-level pain and led to Fred being unemployed since the accident. The couple coped fairly well with the stresses imposed by this accident until, one year later, Hazel's sister died suddenly and unexpectedly from a perforated uterus caused by an IUD. The death was traumatic for Hazel and her family. Barely able to deal with her own grief, she now felt responsible for helping her mother and father cope with the devastating loss. At the same time, the family was beginning to experience some of the stresses that typically accompany a child's adoles-

cence. The partners were in frequent conflict with each other and with their older daughter. This overwhelming combination of predictable and unpredictable stresses transformed life in this family.

What is Their Financial Relationship?

As feminist family therapists have pointed out, money equals power. A couple's financial relationship may reflect and partially shape other aspects of their interaction. How much they each contribute to—and draw on—their shared finances may influence their sense of the overall fairness of the relationship and their respective senses of entitlement in it. Widely differing contributions to shared finances can be used to bolster power. The couple's financial relationship indicates something about their level of commitment to the relationship and about the balance of "I" versus "We." Are all finances shared in a common pool or do both partners keep their individual finances as separate as possible? Lastly, the couple's joint financial status may have significant bearing on their overall stress levels. According to Census Bureau figures ("Census," 1993), divorce rates for couples living below the poverty line are nearly double those for couples with higher incomes.

Are There Ethnic, Racial or Other Differences Between the Partners? What Role Do these Differences Seem to Play?

Partners in relationships that involve racial, ethnic, or religious differences may experience greater stresses related to these differences. This is especially likely to cause difficulty when these cultural differences are not recognized, when one partner more strongly identifies with his or her own culture, when there is little familiarity with each other's cultural group, and when there is less resolution of emotional issues in both families related to intermarriage prior to the couple's formalizing their relationship (McGoldrick & Preto, 1984). Pinderhughes (1991) notes that cultural differences can also be misused in the service of other agendas, such as to avoid accountability or intimacy or to win power struggles.

Robert and Claire have been married for 12 years. Robert is black; Claire, white. They live in a small town that has very few black families. Robert has complained for years about "the costs of living here as a black person," describing feelings of loneliness and saying, "I have never felt a part of this community." Claire has offered to spend more time with Robert's black friends in a nearby city but

Robert says, "She's just not comfortable with a lot of black people."
Claire feels that Robert won't let her try to help on this issue; Robert
feels that he has had to sacrifice his identity and his community for
the marriage. Their racial differences create challenges that would
not exist for a white couple living in that same town and that add to
existing stresses and strains in their lives.

Characteristics of the Individual Partners

In developing a formulation, you should consider not only the couple's
relationship but each of the two individuals as well. There is no limit
to the number of individual factors that might be considered here and
a case could be made for a large number of them. However, you are
evaluating a couple, not conducting two parallel in-depth psychiatric
interviews. The following four individual characteristics are, I feel,
most relevant to a couple evaluation:

- individual symptomatology
- relational profile
- stages or transitions in the life cycle
- the level of commitment to the couple's relationship

Is Symptomatology of Some Kind Being Experienced by One or Both Partners?

Individual symptomatology may stem from factors that are largely external to the relationship, such as biological processes, social stresses,
and traumatic events. However, such symptomatology may constitute
a powerful stressor in the relationship, calling for intense coping efforts, possibly creating conflict, and, in some cases, leading to exhaustion and the dissolution of the relationship. For these reasons, symptomatology secondary to external factors is still central to the case
formulation.

Alternatively, symptomatology may be caused or exacerbated by
relational patterns (as has been well-documented, for example, in the
case of depression [see Chapter 18]). Here, your formulation should
connect symptoms to the interactional patterns in the relationship
that induce or intensify them. Individual symptomatology may also
serve systemic or protective functions in the relationship. This scenario will be discussed in greater detail later in this chapter.

Certain types of symptomatology may reflect undiagnosed medical problems. For example, uncharacteristic violent episodes may indicate neurological damage; erectile difficulties may stem from vascular or endocrine disorders. It's hard to imagine a situation more tragic for clients and therapist than one in which the therapist fails to even consider a medical disorder when one is present. This may contribute to the exacerbation of the disorder, with serious and even lethal consequences, and to weeks or months wasted in "treatment" for the mistaken cause of the problem.

What is Known About the Relational Profile of Each Partner?

"Relational profile" refers to an individual's characteristic ways of forming close attachments. It includes conscious and unconscious needs, expectations, characteristic feeling-states, interactional roles, and repetitive patterns. The clearest indicators of the relational profile are historic patterns in intimate relationships, current patterns between the partners, and interactional patterns between the individual and the therapist.

Bruce described his history of close relationships by saying, "I've either been shit on or I've done the shitting." This self-description suggests that he is unable to imagine, let alone experience, relationships which are nonexploitative and nondestructive. It comes as no surprise that he consistently loses sexual desire for his partners after a period of weeks or months with them.

Penny, now in her fourth marriage, notes that all of her previous husbands and boyfriends had initially seemed active and forceful but became passive soon after the relationship began.

Lyn has been involved in several relationships, lasting between eight months and three years, before his current one with Terri. In each of these relationships, Lyn was initially attracted to the woman, but later found himself feeling critical of her in some area which made him end the relationship. He is currently disenchanted with Terri because he sees her as unexciting sexually. Lyn has never been in a relationship with a woman in which he sustained attraction and attachment over time.

Guy described his own relational profile with surprising candor and self-awareness: "I don't treat people that I'm close to well; I need someone to crack the whip."

It's easy to easy how these characteristic aspects of attachment would create difficulties in a couple relationship.

Relational profiles are shaped by the individual's history in early attachment relationships and in previous couple relationships. The fit of both partners' relational profiles, or lack thereof, may be the most important factor in the formulation of their current difficulties. This is especially true when one or both partners' difficulties with intimacy and attachment create unconscious complementarities that preclude intimacy and satisfaction in the relationship. These scenarios will be discussed later in this chapter.

Nancy and Doug complained of chronic conflict over a range of issues. Doug felt nagged by Nancy; Nancy complained that Doug agreed to do things she asked of him but never got around to it. She felt that she was expected to accommodate to Doug's way of doing things and to the time it took him to get things done. For Doug, this constituted a direct replay of his relationship with his mother, who always "had a list of things for me to do" and from whom he felt he received little genuine affection. For Nancy, this replayed relationships in her family of origin in which she was always expected to be understanding and to submissively put the needs of others before her own. This contributed to her "worst feeling," which she described as "being invisible."

What Stages or Transitions in the Life Cycle is Each Partner Currently Experiencing?

Transitions in the life cycle engender increased stress and disorganization for the individual involved. To varying degrees, they destabilize established relational roles and patterns and produce stress in the relationship or family. They can introduce overlapping stages of the life cycle within the relationship or family and with them conflicting needs and challenges. They may contribute to or exacerbate individual symptomatology. In some cases, an individual's extreme reaction to normative life cycle stresses may be the most significant aspect of the overall formulation of the case, especially when this is amplified by maladaptive responses by the individual or his or her partner and by idiosyncratic meanings of the particular transition for one or both partners.

Vivian and Kay have been in a relationship and living together for five years. Kay is 35 years old; Vivian is 47. Vivian had been married previously; Kay had not. Although Kay had some desire to have children (either via adoption or artificial insemination), they agreed, when their relationship began, that they would not. Vivian had raised two children of her own, one of whom had been killed at age 22 by a drunken driver. As Kay moved into her mid-30s, her desire for a child grew much stronger; she began to feel that if she couldn't raise a child, the emotional loss would be irreparable. The prospect of another 20 years of parenting dismayed Vivian who had already launched her own children. Her dismay was intensified by the pain associated with the death of her son. For this couple, a mismatch of life stages imposed enormous stresses that were intensified by Vivian's loss of her son.

How Committed to the Relationship Does Each Partner Appear to Be?

Are both partners strongly committed to the relationship? Are both ambivalent and erratic in their commitment? Is one less strongly committed than the other? These differing configurations of commitment indicate possible sources of strain in the relationship and have pragmatic implications for the partners' motivation for couple therapy. They do not, however, indicate whether or to what degree difficulties with commitment are sources of strain in the relationship or the result of prior difficulties in other areas. One partner's *recurrent* difficulties with commitment, observable in multiple previous relationships, may constitute an important element of the formulation; another partner's *loss* of a strong sense of commitment to a relationship may result from years of frustration or conflict or untrustworthiness in the partner.

The Relational Context of the Presenting Problem

Answers to the following questions will alert you to areas of particular difficulty for the couple. They may also indicate resources in the couple's relationship. Difficulties in these areas may cause, contribute to, or result from other problems in the overall relationship or "in" one — or both — partners.

What Attracted the Partners to One Another?
How Similar Are Their Expectations, or Narratives,
for the Kind of Relationship They Want?

The answers to these questions provide information about the relational profiles of each partner, indicating ways in which the "unconscious matrix" of the relationship may contribute to difficulties in the couple's daily interactions. They also suggest how *realistic* the partners' expectations for the relationship may have been, *how clear* they were—both to themselves and to the other—and how similar or dissimilar they were.

At the time of this writing, there is an increasing interest, in the family therapy field and elsewhere, in the role of stories or narrative in the lives of individuals, couples, and families (Hudson & O'Hanlon, 1991; White & Epston, 1990). As the writer Phyllis Rose notes in her examination of five Victorian marriages (1983), every individual creates a story of his or her own life, shaping that life into a narrative of a particular kind, and couples in satisfying relationships typically have a "shared narrative" for their relationship. In other words, they are "writing the same story."

In some couple relationships, the primary source of conflict involves a struggle over different narratives. He envisions a large and lively family; she is reluctantly willing to have one child but would prefer a "quiet" (i.e., childless) life in which they are free to indulge their own interests and desires. She wants a dual-career marriage with shared responsibilities for parenting and for the home; he wants a traditional marriage with husband as sole support and wife at home with children. She expects a relationship in which romance and intimacy are central and enduring; he hopes to settle into an arrangement in which she looks after his needs and gets hers met by the children and her women friends. For some couples, the differences between the partners' narratives are unbridgeable. In these cases, it's not that they need help developing communication skills or coping with maladaptive responses to stress; it is that they want fundamentally different things in life and both cannot get what they want from the same relationship.

Narrative differences may result from the partners' growing in different directions over time. One or both partners may have grown beyond the narrative that originally drew them together. This is especially likely given life expectancy in twentieth century Western societies and the emphasis on personal development and fulfillment in these societies. Outgrowing earlier narratives is especially likely when one partner becomes involved in a new social context that reorganizes the person's identity and worldview, such as a religious group or a corporate organization.

Narrative differences may have been present but perhaps unnoticed since the beginning of the relationship. For example, the partners may have married at a young age or in response to pressure from family members. Difficulties in the family of origin may have predisposed one or both to take the first opportunity to leave home without looking too carefully at their companion in flight. In some cases, such differences may have been noted but dismissed with the hope that they would prove to be insignificant.

Whether or not couples are able to bridge narrative differences depends on how much common ground exists between their visions of the relationship, how susceptible to compromise the differences are (whether to have children does not easily lend itself to compromise), how flexible the partners are, how well they are able to give and take fairly, and how strong the rewards of the relationship are to each partner, since a rewarding relationship makes compromise and sacrifice more worthwhile. The point to remember is that some couples who present for treatment are struggling with differences—in the kind of lives they want to lead and especially in the kind of primary relationship they want—that are essentially unbridgeable. As one female client elegantly expressed it, "I feel like I'm trying to change the color of his eyes."

In some cases, what appear to be narrative differences are really "red herrings" or secondary polarizations that obscure difficulties in the unconscious matrix of the relationship (see below). It may be difficult to differentiate between those couples who need to preserve a powerful if unsatisfying attachment and those who are simply mismatched. A trial of couple therapy may help to differentiate between these two scenarios.

How Does this Couple Balance Attachment and Autonomy in the Relationship?

The relationship may be characterized by strong attachment but very little autonomy, or there may be very little emotional attachment with both partners leading very separate individual lives. (Remember that attachment does not necessarily mean harmony and satisfaction. Couples in long-lasting conflictual relationships often have powerful unconscious attachments to one another; if anything, feelings of rage and hatred document the intensity of the emotional connection between the partners.)

There may be a struggle between them over the balance of attachment and autonomy, with one partner pursuing for greater closeness and the other distancing. Patterns in the balance of autonomy and attachment reflect both partners' relational profiles and the fit between them. The ability to move back and forth between "I" and "We" and to create a relationship that fosters both partners' individual development as well as their satisfying connection constitutes a resource and a good prognostic indicator for treatment.

Andrea and Peter have been living together for about one year. Their presenting complaint involves chronic conflict. They describe themselves as being "incredibly tuned in to each other," saying, "We can just about read each other's minds." They strongly believe in having no secrets from each other but they are often tormented by hearing one another's feelings, especially when these are negative in relation to each other or positive in relation to others. Both describe themselves as jealous; Andrea feels especially insecure if Peter spends time with a friend. Both feel guilty about wanting time alone. Peter considered changing jobs at one point for what seemed a more exciting career opportunity but Andrea felt so threatened by the thought of him in this work environment that he dropped the idea, but not without some resentment. This relationship is characterized by strong attachment which undermines both partner's separate individual development. Andrea seems the more insecure, but both partners contribute to a relational structure that makes any experience of separation difficult. These "rules of relating" may have met their needs (or their fears) when the relationship began but are now "cramping" and, to some extent, suffocating both of them.

To What Extent Are They Able to Communicate in the Service of Emotional, Functional, and Ethical Goals? How Successful Are They at Negotiating Differences and Resolving Conflicts?

Difficulty with communication is common in couples seeking treatment even if it is secondary to other etiological factors. What can you observe about this couple's patterns of communication? Do they seem to be able to discuss and resolve conflicts? Do they have ways of talking that allow them to feel close and connected to one another? Are they able to communicate when important decisions need to be made for the relationship or for the family? Can they talk with each other in a way that preserves a mutual sense of fairness and trustworthiness in the relationship? Can you identify particular problematic patterns of communication, such as criticism and disrespect, constant "side-tracking" which prevents closure, or the expectation of "mind-reading" rather than the clear expression of needs? These patterns may suggest goals for treatment. Problems with communication, like most other problems, may cause, contribute to, or result from other difficulties in the couple relationship.

How Do They Manage Gender Differences?

Gender differences can contribute to a couple's difficulties in several ways. Unrecognized gender differences may contribute to chronic conflicts in a way that is comparable to ethnic or racial differences. There may be an overt struggle between the partners concerning the gender roles they prefer for the relationship. Confusion over gender expectations is especially common given the enormous shifts in these expectations over the past 20 years (see Chapter 2). Couples who unquestioningly adopt traditional—or alternative—gender expectations that do not suit the idiosyncracies of their relationship may become locked into unsatisfying patterns. Finally, gender socialization (or the willingness to exploit it) may lead to persistent unfairness in the relationship which contributes to the "one-down" partner's gradual alienation and despair about the relationship.

Gender conflicts are especially likely to be implicated in patterns involving power, entitlement and fairness, roles and responsibilities, and parenting and sexuality. When evaluating particular couples, ask yourself whether they have uncritically adopted traditional—or alternative—gender roles. Do these appear to "work" for both partners? Have they been able to cocreate gender patterns that suit their idiosyncratic histories, personalities, and preferences? Do unresolved gender differences, conflict, or confusion over gender roles appear to be sources of stress and conflict in this relationship? Do gender differences appear to be amplified by other factors, such as extreme stress, difficulties with communication, or discomfort with intimacy or sexuality?

Betsy and Frank have been married for 15 years. Frank teaches at a local college. He is not a full-time employee but one of several staff who are hired on a course-by-course basis every semester. Betsy is a dean at the same college. Her salary is at least five times as large as Frank's. Her work requires several evenings a week in addition to normal daytime hours; she is frequently out of town for conferences or business meetings. In spite of these professional differences, Betsy is seen as primarily responsible for the care of their two children.

They have frequent protracted arguments over their work and home lives. Frank deeply resents the time Betsy gives to her job and the way in which he feels it limits what she has left to give him. It seems clear that he is ashamed of the discrepancy in their professional accomplishments although he denies this. He is unhappy about his professional status but instead of finding a way to change it, he focuses on the grievance he feels in relation to Betsy's career. Betsy feels caught in a no-win situation. Because of Frank's low income, she needs to generate more finances for the family, but she feels that Frank resents and punishes her for doing so. She feels guilty that she does not spend even more time with the children. She admits that she is reluctant to get home early because she anticipates angry confrontations with Frank when she gets there. In describing her goals for treatment, Betsy says, "I wish that he could see that if I'm a success, that doesn't mean that he's a failure."

Traditional gender expectations make it difficult for these partners to accept their differences and work out arrangements in their lives that best suit them. Betsy can't help feeling guilty for not spending more time with the children even though she is the primary breadwinner for the family. Frank cannot accept the fact that he is not the primary breadwinner without feeling like a failure as a man.

How Well Do They Maintain Fairness and Trustworthiness in the Relationship?

How do each of the partners experience the fairness of give-and-take in the relationship? Does each feel that the other makes an effort to be fair, to acknowledge entitlement, and to fulfill obligations? Does each see him- or herself as trying to be fair? Does there appear to be confusion in one or both partners about whether certain aspects of the relationship are fair or not? How do their impressions correspond to your own?

How would you describe the level of trust and trustworthiness in the relationship? Do the partners feel safe in the relationship or do they resort to power moves or emotional withdrawal? Have expectations of fairness and caring been so damaged that the partners give themselves license to be callous, disrespectful, or even abusive of each other? If trust has been damaged, what is the level of residual trust? How do unfairness and mistrust relate to the couple's presenting problems?

Donna and Bart have been married for 15 years. One year before Donna called requesting couple therapy, she received a telephone call from a man who told her that Bart and his wife were having an affair. Donna was completely incredulous and stunned when she mentioned this to Bart with puzzlement and he admitted that it was true. Bart agreed to end the outside relationship and, as far as Donna knew, he had done so. However, several months later, she found a letter from the woman to Bart; when confronted, he again confessed to ongoing (but he insisted, nonsexual) contact with the woman. By the time they came for the first session of the evaluation, Donna said that she had caught Bart being dishonest with her "about 10 or 15 times." At this point, Bart swore that he had terminated all contact with the woman. Donna was, understandably, furious and unable to believe that he was now telling her the truth. When asked about her "worst feeling," she stressed that it was not when she originally found out about the affair but when she discovered that, after swearing that it was over, Bart had deceived her again by continuing to see the woman and to lie to her about it. In this case, it was not only the original betrayal of fidelity but the ongoing deceptions and dishonesty that had eroded trust in the relationship. Donna said that she wanted to "get past my anger but I don't know how."

Do the partners' feelings of unfairness and mistrust appear to be related to specific actions, as in the example above, or do they seem more related to unrealistic expectations and the complexities of the unconscious matrix of the relationship? Do the partners' difficulties agreeing on the terms of trust appear to be amplifying or impeding the resolution of other problems? Finally, do issues of trust and fairness seem unrelated to the couples' problems? Relationships can be highly trustworthy but still unsuccessful if one or both partners also expect vitality and passion but seem unable to experience this with one another. When residual trust and mutual expectations of fairness exist, *to any degree*, in a couple's relationship, they constitute potential resources and positive prognostic indicators for treatment.

How Satisfying is Their Sexual Relationship? How Strong is the "Pleasure Bond"?

Sexual difficulties may be the primary irritant in an otherwise good-enough relationship, especially when there are diagnosable sexual dysfunctions, significant differences in "sexual scripts," or considerable sexual ignorance. Conversely, sexual difficulties may be symptomatic of other relational difficulties, such as conflict and mistrust, resentment, fear, and lack of vitality in the overall relationship. Lastly, sexual difficulties may result from individual symptomatology such as depression or posttraumatic stress disorder.

Leslie and Jim have been living together for four years. They are both in their late 20s. Their presenting complaint involves conflicts over the issues of marriage and children. Leslie wants both; Jim is more hesitant. He denies feeling ambivalent or fearful of these steps but insists that Leslie, who works as a waitress, should finish her college degree and establish a career before they take these steps. When asked about changes in their sexual relationship, they reveal that there has recently been a significant one. Although both were quite satisfied with the sexual relationship previously, Jim now finds that he cannot ejaculate on intercourse. The difficulty began when they began talking about having children and when Leslie began to be less consistent in using a diaphragm. In his individual session, Jim says that he does masturbate occasionally and that he has no difficulty ejaculating at these times. Jim's sexual symptom is obvious and eloquent. It suggests that he may be more ambivalent about fatherhood and/or greater commitment to this relationship than he realizes or admits.

How Does Their Wider Relational Context Affect Their Relationship?

Which larger relational systems—such as families of origin, religious groups, social groups at work, or close friendship networks—are important for the couple and how do they appear to impinge on their relationship? Do they support the couple's relationship? Do they contribute to stress and conflict? How do the partners create boundaries between their relationship and these larger systems? Do they agree or disagree about these boundaries? If there seems to be little or no wider relational context, this in itself may be important for the formulation. The partners may have recently moved to a new area, separating them from a support network of family and friends. The loss of this network will create stress and may overburden the capacity of the relationship to meet all of the partners' needs.

Kathy and Will had been living together for two years and were struggling with the question of whether to marry. They lived in a large house owned by Will's parents, who also lived there. This contributed to tensions and difficulties in the couple's relationship and to a certain measure of confusion as well. Kathy identified this confusion by asking at one point, "Are you living with them or are you living with me?"

Rita and Eileen had been living for two years in a household that also included Rita's former lover, Patricia, when they requested couple therapy. Rita and Patricia bought the house when they were lovers; when they ended their romantic relationship they continued to live as housemates. Eileen moved in with them several months after she and Rita began their relationship. Eileen was especially uncomfortable with this arrangement. She felt that Patricia was still interested in Rita romantically although both of them denied this. She also felt "like a fifth wheel" when Rita and Patricia had long talks late at night.

What Personal and Relational Resources Exist in this Relationship?

Although many of the questions discussed up to this point can alert the therapist to potential resources in the couple's relationship, resources are important enough to merit consideration in their own right.

In terms of personal resources, how strong is each partner's sense of self-respect? How willing are they to be appropriately protective of their partners and others with whom they are close? Do they seem to feel genuine affection for one another and to be committed to the relationship? How capable are they of tolerating differences, idiosyncrasies, and other relational attachments of their partners? How able are they to recognize and acknowledge their own contributions to relational difficulties? Are they able to bring humor to conflicts and stressful situations? Do they have hope—for themselves, for the relationship, and for life itself?

In terms of relational resources, how high is the level of trust and trustworthiness in the relationship? If trust has been seriously damaged, is there some degree of residual trust? Do the partners treat one another with respect? How reliable are they toward one another? Are there rules that encourage emotional repair when damage has occurred? How flexible do they appear to be?

To think about a couple only in terms of their problems or limitations contributes to a skewed and impoverished vision of their relationship which can further impoverish them and deprive treatment, if it should follow, of potential leverage for change.

One couple presented with a history of chronic conflict, explosive arguments, and impulsive separations dating back to the very beginning of the relationship, eight years ago. However, in the

first couple session, one said, "This is the longest and the best relation-
ship I've ever had and I don't want to lose it." The other nodded in
agreement. This helped me appreciate how valuable the relationship
was to each of them, in spite of their obvious difficulties, and became
a central feature of my formulation and my response to them at the
end of the evaluation.

Resources may be related to the presenting problem in one of three
ways (Karpel, 1986). They may exist in other areas of the relationship—or in its wider relational context—and be brought to bear on
the presenting problem; e.g. an individual's protectiveness toward his
partner could be mobilized in the service of greater tolerance toward
her human imperfections. Resources may exist as potential but inac-
tive alternatives to problematic patterns; e.g., a couple's ability to be
playful and humorous with one another may help them overcome
sexual inhibitions and shame. Or, resources may exist within the presenting problem itself; e.g., one partner's decision to stop tolerating
her partner's alcoholism—which precipitates the crisis that brings the
couple into treatment—may provide the spur needed for him to try to
become sober.

Do They Appear to Have Difficulty with Intimacy and Attachment? Are these Difficulties Implicated in the Problems They Present?

Intimacy can be a reward, a challenge, or both in a couple relationship.
It can mean different things to different people (which accounts for
some of the difficulty couples experience). Nevertheless, intimacy has
a common, everyday meaning which is straightforward and useful in
this discussion. The feelings and interactions of intimacy are best captured for me by the term "pillow talk." The image—two people, alone
together, in bed, talking—conveys most of the elements we typically
associate with intimacy: a sense of "We-ness," a closeness that for moments in time shuts out the rest of the world, a quiet togetherness,
shared private names and jokes, an easy cuddling, talking about one's
worries, joys, and fears.

For some couples, this is a natural and enjoyable experience that
provides a powerful relational bond. This is especially likely when the
partners' experiences in their early attachment relationships have been
good enough; the legacy of early attachment deepens the gratifications
of intimacy in the current relationship.

For other couples, there is an ongoing struggle over the terms of
intimacy, which may stem from a variety of factors. For example,

patterns of gender socialization complicate intimacy in couple relationships because men are trained to avoid the feelings that accompany it. However, difficulties with intimacy don't always follow gender lines. Regardless of gender, one partner may be markedly uncomfortable with intimacy and constantly avoid it. If the other partner wants intimacy, he or she will feel lonely, disappointed, and frustrated.

The partners' idealized visions of intimacy may clash. For example, one may need a mature, sensual, and passionate connection while the other prefers a more playful, child-like, or even regressed interaction. Some couples' flexibility and security enable them to resolve these difficulties; others can do so because the differences between their idealized visions are relatively minor. Still others may find it impossible to so; they may need to find a different partner who shares more of their vision of intimacy in order to feel "at ease."

When one or both partners have *not* experienced good-enough early attachment relationships—and when these difficulties have been compounded by painful experiences in previous couple relationships—intimacy and attachment are more likely to be complicated and problematic in the current relationship. Needs for attachment may be *intensified*, by virtue of having been unfulfilled, and accompanied by the early *fears* and *defenses* against negative feeling-states, such as frustration, rage, shame and guilt, grief, despair, and fear of abandonment. These defenses interfere with the natural development of the individual's capacity for intimacy and they shape his or her relational profile. In the current couple relationship, he or she may long for intimacy but *unconsciously avoid it*.

These couples are not simply coping with acute stressors in their lives or with maladaptive responses to those stressors; they are not simply having difficulty with particular aspects of being a couple, such as communication, sexuality, the wider relational context, or fairness and trust (although difficulties with intimacy and attachment are almost certain to create problems in one or more of these areas); and it is not simply that they have divergent narratives for their primary relationship and would be happy with a different partner who shared their narrative. Difficulties with intimacy may—and often do—masquerade as these kinds of problems but they have deeper and more complicated roots.

Difficulties in early attachment contribute to internal images, or representations, that the individual unconsciously projects onto others, including—and often most powerfully—the relational partner; he or she is unconsciously drawn to partners who fit these images in some way. These projections contribute to distortions in perceptions of the partner's motives and feelings (and may induce feelings that fit the distortion). The individual—let's assume a man—sees or experiences his partner as if she were the relational embodiment of the original caregiver and responds to the partner very much as he did to the caregiver. For example, a man with a harsh, critical parent may repeatedly find himself in relationships with stern, critical partners. Or, a woman whose parent had been depressed and emotionally inaccessible now finds herself trying desperately to elicit warmth and loving involvement from a similarly depressed, withdrawn husband.

Alternatively, the individual sees the partner as the walking embodiment of that part of him- or herself that was most troubling in the relationship with the original care-giver—weakness, dependency, or inadequacy—and responds to the partner as he or she did to that part of him- or herself, typically by persecuting and rejecting it. Furthermore, what is projected onto the partner often fits his or her own unconscious representations in a complementary fashion. The partners become, in a sense, "lightning rods" for each other's repressed and problematic internal representations.

For example, the woman discussed above reenacts with her depressed husband her earlier experiences with a depressed and unavailable mother. She is married to a man whose early difficulties involve an intrusive and highly controlling mother. This image is now projected onto her. Her desperate attempts to elicit warmth and loving involvement unconsciously reactivate the feelings of helplessness, inadequacy, and resentment he experienced as a child with his mother. Naturally, he resists these efforts and retreats further into an angry, self-protective isolation, which in turn heightens her anxiety and despair. This is compounded by the misunderstandings it generates. The wife feels resentful and misunderstood because her husband fights her efforts to help him. The husband feels angry and misunderstood because of her pressure when this simply feels impossible to him. The "transferential knots" (Napier, 1987) which result subvert the partners' conscious desires for satisfaction in the relationship.

In this way, the partners' individual difficulties with intimacy and attachment come to be played out unconsciously between them. Their complementary unconscious images contribute to repetitive interactional sequences which reactivate the painful affective experience of early attachment difficulties. These cycles of interaction are unsatisfying but irresistible. They generate feelings of deep yearning, jealous possessiveness, desperate longing, the urgent need to "fix" the other, rage, vindictiveness, and despair. They are characterized by intense reactivity—a chain reaction of predictable emotional responses which short-circuit detachment, reflection, and flexibility. The partners are trying to resolve the most pressing and painful emotional wounds in their lives; the problem is that this effort takes place through a proxy—the current partner—thereby conflating two different relationships and almost certainly adding to the confusion and complication of the current relationship.

One pattern often seen in these cases involves a mutual *unconscious* avoidance of intimacy. This is a particularly confusing relational pattern, especially for beginning therapists. The couple presents with some complaint relating to intimacy, for example, chronic and intense arguing, which interferes with closeness. They may identify one partner who is seen as uncomfortable with intimacy or describe a falling off of sexual relations. There may be a see-saw pattern in which whenever one partner seeks to be close, the other is in some way unavailable (variously described as cold, angry, busy, or indifferent).

Typically, there is an elegant interlocking between each partner's vulnerabilities and defenses. When he feels vulnerable (in his case, under attack), his typical defense is to withdraw emotionally, which triggers her vulnerability (a fear of abandonment) and activates her defense, which is to cling and desperately seek reassurance, which simply intensifies his sense of vulnerability, and so on. Their conscious expectations for the relationship—his for a wife who loves him and doesn't need to cling desperately to him, and hers for a loving, intimate partner—simply cannot be met given these highly reactive interactional patterns.

The common denominator is a constriction of tenderness, mutual comfort, and love. Whatever the surface fluctuations, the underlying rule seems to be that no situation can exist in which one person offers warmth, affection, and love and the other receives it. Novice therapists are often confused by these couples because they assume that both partners *want* intimacy and will welcome efforts to help them achieve it. However, when intimacy is problematic, it is often because it is deeply *threatening* to one or both partners. The therapist's—and the partners'—efforts to enhance intimacy *increase* the unconscious sense of dangerous vulnerability and contribute to unconscious attempts to obstruct or prevent it.

These couples may look as if they are simply disagreeing over the terms of intimacy; it may appear that the conflict is *between* them, when in fact it is actually *within* each of them. Their apparent conflict represents an unconsciously choreographed *cooperative effort* to avoid the pain and danger associated with intimacy. Couples for whom these patterns complicate intimacy and contribute to presenting problems can be differentiated from couples whose difficulties stem from a variety of less complex factors (simple differences, difficulty coping, or limited skills in negotiation) by the following: (1) a history of similar difficulties in prior relationships (relational profiles), (2) the ease with which the partners can seemingly reverse positions—that is, switch with each other to the opposite side of the issue over which they have been in conflict—which suggests that it is not the issue but the conflict itself that must be continued, and (3) the persistence with which efforts to enhance intimacy are subverted, opposed, or overwhelmed by both partners, which may result in a therapeutic impasse.

What Protective or Systemic Functions Might be Served by the Problems They Are Experiencing?

As indicated earlier, individual symptomatology may stem from factors that are external to the couple's relationship, such as biology or trauma. Symptomatology may be caused or exacerbated by relational patterns, and it may serve systemic or protective functions in the relationship. This constitutes the major theoretical contribution of family therapy: the recognition that symptoms can serve adaptive or protective functions not just for the individual, but for those with whom he or she is related emotionally.

One of the first couples I treated during my graduate training brought this point home for me. Stephen was a physician; Julie, a homemaker. Julie had been hospitalized psychiatrically for depression and anxiety. I was assigned to treat her. The couple presented what experienced therapists would recognize as a classic case of "overfunctioning" and "underfunctioning" partners. Julie saw herself and was seen by Stephen as a "mess." She experienced episodes of anxiety and depression as well as a variety of psychosomatic problems, most notably recurrent headaches. She was uncomfortable socially and avoided social gatherings when she could. She felt she couldn't do anything right.

Stephen appeared to be just the opposite—poised, confident, and outgoing. His stance toward her combined long-suffering condescension, altruistic encouragement, and exasperated contempt. It was as though he were always saying two different things to her: "You poor thing. I'll take care of you and help you along" and "What's wrong with you? Can't you get anything right!" Julie herself seemed to be saying: "I know I'm a mess. I never do anything right. You're so good to stay with me." Julie's brief hospitalization provided her with a set of new experiences outside the marital relationship and she used them well. Her individual and group therapy as well as the milieu of he unit provided situations in which people responded to her differently than did her husband. She began to feel better about herself and to grow more confident.

The results would not have surprised a more experienced couple or family therapist, but they were striking for me. Stephen, far from welcoming these changes, seemed irritable and depressed; he was either oblivious, dismissive, or skeptical about her positive changes. As we talked more, it became clear that Stephen was much less confident than he appeared to be. He had been a lonely child and still felt twinges of uneasiness in social interactions. He admitted that he was full of doubts about his abilities as a doctor, doubts that he discussed with no one.

I gradually understood that this somewhat insecure and socially awkward man had found a way to feel more confident and secure about himself by pairing himself with a woman who seemed even more insecure. By comparison, he felt like a paragon of mental health and social adjustment, and his role as the "healthy one" and "rescuer" prevented him from having to experience the weaker and more vulnerable sides of himself. At the same time, her social uneasiness provided an excuse for him to avoid social gatherings ("Oh, you know Julie. She's just not comfortable at these things") without having to acknowledge to himself or others his own social anxieties. Even more surprising was the fact that, as Julie's psychosomatic symptoms improved, Steven developed the identical (and atypical) headache symptoms of which Julie had earlier complained.

In this couple, Julie's individual symptomatology served to protect Stephen from having to acknowledge and grow beyond his own insecurities; it provided him with a shortcut to positive self-esteem at her expense. Her role as "the mess" may have been painful and degrading but it seemed to assure the continuing availability of a protector and care-taker, which she did not yet believe she could live without. Her symptoms not only supported the relationship as it was then constituted but were also reinforced by repeated interactions between them, which discouraged independence on her part and encouraged weakness and insecurity.

Hoffman (1980) has described this function of symptoms in the context of developmental processes in relational systems. In an exploration of "transformations" or change in families, she critiques the classical assumption in family therapy that systems are organized exclusively around the need to maintain homeostasis. She points out that they periodically outgrow plateaus of homeostasis and shift toward a new level of organization. Relational systems, she suggests, are characterized by contradictory tendencies, toward stability and change.

> Symptomatic displays could be thought of negatively as aborted transformations or positively as negotiations around the possibility of change. . . . [The symptom] represents a compromise between pressures for and against change. The symptom is only the most visible aspect of a connected flow of behaviors and acts as a primary irritant that both monitors the options for change, lest too rapid movement imperil someone in the family, but also keeps the necessity for change constantly alive. (p. 61)

Individual symptomatology does not always serve these kinds of protective functions. Individual problems may result from factors wholly external to the relationship. As Jacobson and Gurman (1986) suggest, the question for therapists

> is not whether individual symptoms serve interpersonal functions, but when do they do so? Posing the issue in this way allows for the possibility (indeed, in our view, the likelihood) that (a) some individual symptoms are routinely, or at least often, interpersonally functional; (b) some individual symptoms are never, or at least rarely, interpersonally functional; and (c) some individual symptoms are more variably interpersonally functional. (p. 8)

This position represents the most useful one for therapists who evaluate couples. It suggests that we maintain an open mind about whether individual symptomatology serves systemic functions in particular cases, that we explore this during the evaluation, and incorporate our best guesses into the formulation of the case.

A Final Note: Ambiguity and Certainty

The extent to which you feel that you understand the forces that cause and maintain a couple's problems will vary from case to case. Don't expect to be omniscient; even after a thorough evaluation and careful consideration, you may continue to feel that you do not understand important aspects of a couple's relationship. Fortunately, you are only one person in a triadic collaborative relationship. You are not responsible for handing the couple a "finished product" in which all questions are answered. There is nothing wrong with acknowledging puzzlement when this is what you are left with after the initial sessions. (In some cases, this may prompt subsequent disclosure of important information that had been withheld, allowing you to make sense of the couple for the first time.) Pointing out details that are striking to you may catalyze insights or new reactions from the couple even if you're not sure exactly what they mean. Your response can be helpful if it asks the right questions, even if it cannot answer them.

As you develop your formulation, you can begin to think about (1) which recommendations you feel will be most helpful to the couple and (2) how you want to present these conclusions and recommendations to them. The next chapter examines guidelines for choosing treatment recommendations along with considerations involved with specific common recommendations.

~ 9 ~

DECIDING ON TREATMENT RECOMMENDATIONS

THE THERAPIST'S FORMULATION, important as it is, leaves a host of questions unanswered. What form(s) of treatment seem most likely to foster positive change? What forms of treatment seem most — and least — likely to be acceptable to the clients? What are the most desirable goals of treatment? In what sequence should these goals be addressed?

Some therapists move automatically into traditional couple therapy — that is, sessions in which the therapist and the couple work together in a collaborative manner to achieve the goals of treatment. In some cases, this will be productive; in others, it will lead to much less desirable outcomes such as an intractable impasse, one or both partners dropping out of treatment, intensified conflict and hostility, or the kind of murky, confusing triangles in which the therapist feels hopelessly "in the soup." One of the greatest advantages of the evalua-

166

tion format is that it increases the odds that the therapist will be able to anticipate these outcomes and steer in directions that sidestep or avoid them. Deciding on treatment recommendations is central to this effort to "set the trajectory" of treatment; figure 1 presents a schematic overview of some of the questions and decisions the therapist will consider during this effort—all of which will be discussed in detail. This chapter begins with basic considerations in selecting treatment approaches, then moves to a more detailed examination of specific recommendations that therapists should consider before choosing a direction for treatment. Indications and contraindications for each of these recommendations will be discussed, along with idiosyncratic considerations related to each of them.

Basic Considerations

Alliances

The first consideration in deciding on any course of treatment involves the quality of alliances that you feel you have with each partner. These alliances reflect not only the partners' individual feelings about you but also about therapy and about the relationship itself. There must be at least some degree of need or distress on their parts, some hope for assistance, and some comfort and confidence in you.

The stronger the alliances, the more likely that the partners will trust and cooperate with your recommendations. If you have been unable to establish a positive alliance with one partner, couple therapy may be impractical regardless of the formulation of the couple's difficulties. Of course, alliances and motivation for treatment are not necessarily synonymous since alliances involve the particular person of the therapist. There are cases in which one or both partners have such negative or uncomfortable feelings in relation to a particular therapist that a referral to another clinician may make the most sense. Here, too, alliance considerations become the first determinant of treatment recommendations.

The "Location" and Definition of the Presenting Problem(s)

Treatment recommendations must be plausibly connected to the couple's presenting complaint. Ideally, the connection should be an obvious and straightforward one. For example, the couple's presenting problem involves repetitive arguments; the treatment recommendation is for couple therapy in which you hope to "track the process" of these

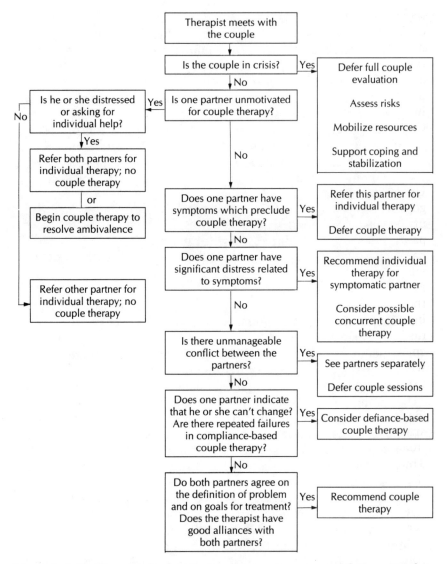

Figure 1. A decision tree for deciding on treatment recommendations. Readers should note that this figure cannot convey all of the complexities of this process; it should be used as a complement to the text.

arguments in sessions and together steer them in more productive directions. When treatment recommendations are less obviously connected to the presenting complaint, you must carefully explain the rationale for these recommendations, specifically emphasizing why and how you hope this form of treatment will effect the changes the partners desire. This is especially true when the presenting complaint involves what is seen as an individual problem. (See Recommending Couple Therapy in this chapter.)

The Clients' Goals for Treatment

Unless treatment recommendations are congruent with the clients' goals, the accuracy of the formulation is academic and its clinical utility nil. For example, a couple presents with concern over the wife's panic attacks. Your assessment may be that the attacks are related to a painfully triangulated relationship with her husband's family of origin, which has made her feel increasingly suffocated and powerless. However, recommending family sessions that include both partners and the husband's family when the clients are asking for help in eliminating the wife's terrifying symptoms of panic will almost certainly confuse and disappoint them. You would need to clarify how this apparently "individual" symptom could be connected to problems in the wider relational context and how this treatment approach could be expected to effect improvement in her symptoms.

Given what we have learned about the treatment of panic attacks (Barlow & Cerny, 1988; Wilson, 1986) and considering the intense anxiety they induce, you would be wise to include a component of treatment that is strongly directed to the symptomatic individual. This might involve regular charting of symptoms, an explanation of the causes and treatment of panic attacks, and strong support and optimism regarding progress. This combination of optimism and active intervention will most likely be reassuring for the symptom-bearer.

In most cases, in order to keep the goals and method of treatment congruent with the couple's priorities, you would emphasize the symptom-focused component of treatment first and allow discussion of problematic relational patterns to assume secondary importance. Treatment recommendations must be either congruent with or plausibly related to the clients' goals. When there are significant differences in the partners' goals, you should attempt to design treatment recommendations that do not validate one partner's viewpoint against the other's.

"Can't Change" Messages

Be alert for messages from one or both partners that indicate they feel they "can't change" their contribution to problematic relational patterns. These messages are different from messages indicating that they don't know how to change these patterns. In the latter case, the clients make clear that they are genuinely troubled by some aspect of their relationship and wish to change it. They may be somewhat ambivalent about change but they seem to be preponderantly invested in improvement. In the former case, they indicate that they are unable to change some problematic aspect of their relationship and you sense that they are preponderantly invested in the status quo.

Obviously, this can be a subtle distinction and there's plenty of room for ambiguity. But the distinction is important since it involves the degree of resistance you can expect during treatment. In general, you can assume that resistance is higher when there have been one or more failures of treatment that were organized on a "compliance" basis (Rohrbaugh, Tennen, Press, & White, 1981) — that is, treatment in which the therapist expects and wants the clients to comply with particular suggestions — and/or when the resistant partner seems to be relatively nonchalant or comfortable with the situation. "Can't change" messages are the clearest indication that a straightforward compliance-based approach to treatment is likely to be unproductive and that some form of defiance-based, or paradoxical, intervention may be more helpful.

Previous Treatment Experiences

Previous treatment experiences usually provide valuable lessons about treatment approaches that should be emulated or avoided. These lessons typically involve the theoretical frame and method of the previous therapist, as well as personal stylistic factors. For example, the couple who report feeling that their previous therapist's approach was "too mechanical, too behavioral, too much I'll-do-this-for-you-if-you-do-this-for-me" is sending an important signal to their current therapist. The signal becomes clearer when they communicate that they just don't think such a "superficial" approach will work for them and that they feel a need to "dig deeper" in order to understand the forces contributing to their difficulties. Alternatively, another couple complains that their former therapist "spent all this time asking about our childhoods and our parents. It really seemed like he was looking for real deep problems when we feel that we love each other and have a good relationship. All we need is a way to stop fighting about money all the time."

The lessons of previous treatment may also be positive ones, involving approaches to treatment or characteristics of a previous therapist that seemed helpful to the couple. For example, they may report having been helped several years earlier by a therapist who took a practical, short-term, problem-focused approach to treatment but who is no longer available (because of a geographical or institutional move, for example). A different couple may report how much they appreciated that their previous therapist seemed to share her thinking openly with them, making them feel that it really was a collaborative relationship with both sides actively and openly participating. These descriptions are "tip-offs" about ways of interacting with the couple that are likely to prove helpful, just as negative experiences in previous treatment constitute warnings or "red flags" about approaches that are less likely to be productive. Failures in other forms of treatment may make the couple more inclined to consider couple therapy.

The Sequencing of Treatment Goals

It is important to consider the sequence in which to address problems and goals of treatment. Even when the evaluation has gone well and therapeutic alliances are strong, cases can founder if the sequencing of goals is mishandled. The central consideration here involves timing or *readiness*. Issues should be tackled in treatment *when the partners seem ready to work constructively with them.*

The major danger is that the clients will attempt to resolve an issue before they are ready do to so. Usually, this means that there is either too much conflict, too little trust, or both. For example, there is no reason to expect that two partners who cannot discuss whether sweaters should go on the top or bottom shelf of a closet without an explosive, nasty argument should be able to resolve long-standing difficulties in their sexual relationship. They have to be able to *listen sympathetically* to each other before any real progress can be made in this sensitive area.

For this reason, many couple therapists will initially focus on the *process* of how the partners communicate with one another before trying to address serious *content* areas of disagreement. The partners must be able to declare a truce in their ongoing war before they can negotiate or converse like friends or even lovers. It is usually wise to begin treatment with less highly charged issues. The hope is that it will be somewhat easier to foster a meaningful and respectful dialogue in these areas and, in doing so, to *build trust and optimism* gradually as the dialogue progresses. The optimism and trust that develop in less difficult discussions provide resources for the effort to resolve more painful and highly charged areas of conflict later in treatment.

It is also possible for therapists to take *too long* getting to important areas of conflict. For example, if a primary complaint involves sexual issues that make the therapist uncomfortable, he may focus instead on areas of conflict that are less anxiety-provoking (to him). The couple may come to feel that the treatment is irrelevant to their most pressing problem. Therapists should be alert to this possibility but realize that it is a much less common problem than trying to address difficult issues before clients are ready.

Personal and Relational Resources

Personal and relational resources have prognostic implications. The presence of resources should increase your expectation that treatment will be a worthwhile enterprise; your assessment of them can suggest specific agendas and goals for treatment. Resources suggest something about the likely resilience of the relationship under the stresses of couple therapy. Relationships in which commitment, affection, and trust are reasonably intact are more likely to tolerate the challenges of treatment. Individuals who have reasonably good self-esteem and an ability to focus on their own contributions to problems in the relationship are more likely to tolerate your pointing out ways in which their behavior escalates conflicts or suggesting alternative ways of approaching disagreements.

Mid-course Corrections

This book began with the assumption that "starting out right" in couple treatment is desirable, that it is worthwhile to try to select a direction and a frame for treatment that complements the couple's needs and self-definition and that has the highest likelihood of success. However, even when you have done your best to "set the trajectory" of treatment, you may need to change directions, either because new information emerges or because testing a particular approach makes clear that it will not be successful. If you have established credibility, by demonstrating a reasonable understanding of their problems and connecting well with both partners, they will probably be able to accept a change of course if it should become necessary.

A mid-course correction might involve switching to individual sessions with one or both partners at some point. Another might involve moving directly to a particularly charged issue which you had originally planned to tackle much later in treatment but which now appears to be obstructing all other discussions; conversely, it might involve deciding to defer discussion of a particular problem which seems impervious to change at a certain point in treatment. You want your recommendations for treatment to have the highest likelihood of success but there are no guaranteed outcomes in therapy and you should be prepared for mid-course corrections as an inevitable possibility in treatment.

Couple Therapy

Couple therapy is the simplest and most straightforward treatment recommendation and probably the most common one. The underlying assumptions, goals, and methods utilized by different therapists will vary; the common denominator is that both partners continue to meet together with the therapist in an attempt to define or change some aspect of their relationship. This does not rule out the possibility of individual sessions with the partners or bringing other relatives into treatment at some point; however, couple sessions are expected to be the dominant format utilized in treatment.

Indications

The primary indication for couple therapy involves both partners' *motivation* for treatment. Without this, all other indications are insufficient. There also must be some degree of *consensus* on the definition of the problem and on goals for treatment. This needn't mean that both partners agree on every aspect of each other's agendas for treatment nor that they prioritize them in the same way; it does mean that there is general agreement on areas of change (e.g., less arguing, more closeness, better coparenting) or clear agreement on one major goal (improving their sexual relationship) or a willingness to discuss and consider each other's goals even if they initially differ. Flexibility increases the likelihood of successful treatment; the partners must be able to work together cooperatively.

Another indicator for couple therapy is the partners' definition of their problem as an *interactional* one, a problem *between* them. This is not the only situation in which a recommendation for couple therapy can be made, but it's an obvious one. The presence of personal and relational *resources* is also a good prognostic indicator for couple therapy. The partners' capacity for self-focus, their self-respect, and their caring for one another are also promising indicators, as are commitment to each other, trustworthiness, and vitality in the relationship.

Not all of these resources are necessary for treatment to be productive. Even when some of them are weak or seemingly nonexistent, couples can still benefit from treatment. When levels of self-respect and self-focus are low and emotional reactivity high, commitment to the relationship can help both partners tolerate the frustrations and difficulties of treatment. When reliability and repair are damaged or weak, residual trust can make discussion and trust-building possible. And even when commitment to the relationship is extremely low, the partners may benefit individually from the self-awareness gained through treatment and from the safety and holding it provides.

Contraindications

Poor Alliances with One or Both Partners. Whether this reflects their feelings about their relationship, therapy in general, or their particular therapist, inadequate alliances will generally subvert treatment. (Guidelines for responding to these situations are presented below under Considerations and Guidelines and in later sections of this chapter.)

The Partners' Inability to Agree on Goals for Treatment. When there is substantial disagreement about goals, there needs to be some degree of flexibility on both partners' sides concerning the focus of treatment. If they are adamantly opposed to each other's goals and unwilling to settle for anything less than a therapeutic contract organized around their own personal agendas, couple treatment is not likely to be helpful. You can proceed with couple therapy in spite of the conflict and hope that it diminishes or you can recommend a series of individual sessions with both partners in which to explore the potential for greater flexibility in one or both partners. Individual sessions may enable the partners to lower defenses and mobilize greater flexibility; however, they may simply defer recognition of an intractable impasse. Complete inflexibility may be associated either with a relationship that is at the verge of dissolution or with secrets, such as an affair.

Unmanageable Conflict Between the Partners. Intense conflict often occurs in couple therapy and any therapist who plans to work with couples must be able to tolerate it. However, there are some cases in which the conflict is so intense and unremitting that no real work can be done with both partners in the room together. In these cases, you can recommend separate sessions for each partner initially. The individual sessions are used to strengthen alliances with both partners, to encourage a greater degree of self-focus on their parts and, if possible, to see if either can make small changes in their interactional patterns (such as lessening criticism or initiating small acts of generosity and thoughtfulness) to reverse the cycle of attack and defense, resentment and withholding. If this progresses well, there will be a gradual reduction in the intensity of conflict and some increase in the level of trust in the relationship. These developments should make it possible, with the agreement of both partners, to begin couple sessions at some point and to continue the work of treatment in this format.

Characteristics of One Individual Make Couple Therapy Impossible. One partner may be so severely depressed as to be unable to concentrate on the partner's complaints, unable to mobilize the hope and energy necessary for change, and unable to respond to discussion with anything other than intense and paralyzing self-criticism. A husband's drinking may be so severe as to make his participation in evaluation sessions, and most likely any treatment to follow, erratic at best. In such cases, your initial recommendations for treatment should focus on these serious presenting problems. Couple therapy might be deferred until there is improvement in the individual's symptomatology, or it might prove altogether unnecessary. In some cases, joint sessions might be held concurrently with other forms of intervention. (See Recommending Treatment for One Partner later in this chapter.)

Domestic Violence. There is a growing consensus that to conduct couple therapy in the context of ongoing domestic violence is not only unlikely to be productive but also frankly dangerous. (See Chapter 14 for an extensive discussion of this issue.)

A History of Unsuccessful Couple Therapy. This is not a definitive contraindication for couple therapy but it should be taken into consideration when you weigh treatment recommendations. How many times have they been dissatisfied with couple therapy in the past? One negative experience in the past is a less compelling prognostic indicator than three or four. Are there any exceptions—instances in which they feel they derived benefit from couple treatment? If a couple identifies even one time when they feel that they were helped by couple therapy, this should encourage you to *test* the possibility of another positive experience in treatment.

Are there any new factors in the couple's situation that might introduce new resources for treatment? For example, the wife's discovery of her husband's affair breaks a long-standing pattern of emotional disengagement between the partners, triggering unprecedented sexual excitement and explicit conflict—signs of life in a previously lifeless and disengaged relationship. Or, a major setback—such as job loss—in the life of the partner who is "one-up" in the relationship unbalances their long-familiar complementary pattern of relating. In each of these situations, something new in the picture may enable couple therapy to be more productive than it was in the past.

Considerations and Guidelines

When the initial request is for couple therapy and when this is your treatment recommendation, the need for explanation and justification is minimal. However, you should try to say something about the goals, the methods, and, in some cases, the sequences that will most likely be involved in the couple sessions to follow. If the couple did not initially request couple therapy but instead presented what they considered to be an individual-focused problem or if there is conflict between the partners about whether or not the problem is individual or interactional, the recommendation of couple therapy is more complicated and needs to be presented more carefully.

You need to present a compelling rationale for *why* you feel that this is the treatment of choice. This might involve *reframing* the problem in interactional terms, hopefully revealing the systemic underpinnings of what may appear to be an individual problem, or you may rely on the credibility you have established during the evaluation and hope that the partners' trust will help them to accept the recommendation. If the partners disagree on whether their problems are individual or interactional, the recommendation of couple therapy will appear to be partisan, that is, congruent with one partner's view and contradicting the other's. This endangers balanced alliances and therefore requires corrective efforts.

When one partner is so ambivalent about the relationship that he or she is unwilling, or unable, to commit to couple therapy aimed at improving it, you have several options. If the reluctant partner is genuinely disturbed by the impasse in the relationship or motivated for help with his or her own dilemmas, you can recommend couple sessions aimed at further exploring the relational impasse. If both partners agree, these sessions can be used to explore how each partner came to be in his or her current situation and what he or she might do about it, rather than to actively try to "patch things up." In some cases, this may lead to little more than three parties sitting together with the impasse; in others, it may benefit one or both partners individually and help break the stalemate.

If the reluctant partner wants nothing to do with treatment — regardless of its format or goals — and the other partner is distressed and wants help, you should respond to the needs of that partner with a recommendation for individual sessions, either with yourself or with another therapist (on your referral). These sessions can be used to help the individual better understand the forces that maintain the current impasse in the relationship and to clarify what he or she might do about it. (This recommendation will be discussed in greater detail under Recommending Treatment for One Partner.)

Crisis Management

A couple presents for evaluation in which the husband complains of his wife's disinterest in him and their children. As the discussion proceeds, the therapist discovers that the wife is significantly depressed. She reports ongoing suicidal ideation and at least one recent incident which she is reticent to discuss but which might well have been a suicide attempt.

A therapist receives an urgent telephone call from a colleague, requesting that she evaluate a couple. The colleague has been treating the husband individually and is becoming increasingly concerned by his descriptions of escalating physical confrontations between him and his wife.

After a calm and seemingly uneventful initial couple session, a distraught woman calls the therapist reporting that in the discussion that followed the session she disclosed a previously secret affair to her husband. She says that he is now threatening to leave her and to initiate legal proceedings in which he will try to secure custody of their children.

Unlike many situations in which the optimal approach to treatment may be uncertain, cases that call for crisis management announce themselves in an unmistakable way. A crisis, after all, is a crisis. Typically the crisis is obvious in the first session if not on the telephone call or referral that precedes it. Sometimes, a case that presents routinely for the first session can be precipitated into crisis, either by the discussion and revelations of that session or by subsequent and perhaps unrelated events. Crises are characterized by intense affect and reactivity as well as destabilization of previous homeostatic processes. There may be an increased potential for emotional and physical injury.

In the context of couple evaluation, crises represent an extreme case of goal-sequencing since the therapist must help the couple manage the crisis—to prevent injury and to restabilize the individuals and the relationship—before any other goals or issues can be addressed. Recognizing that a particular case calls for crisis management does not answer more long-term questions regarding treatment recommendations since the therapist's mandate is to manage the immediate crisis. *Not* recognizing that a case calls for crisis management can have devastating consequences for clients and therapist alike.

Indications

Cases that call for crisis management can usually be identified by the heightened intensity of affect and reactivity. The partners feel themselves to be in extraordinary and extremely stressful circumstances and they communicate this with a sense of urgency, panic, and desperation. There is often an implicit, if not explicit, plea that the therapist "Do something!" to relieve this stress. This is not the only way crisis cases present. A therapist confronted with a husband who, in a quiet ruminative way, discusses the relative merits of killing himself or his wife or the man he suspects of being her lover, knows that he or she is faced with a potentially deadly crisis. *Any* case in which there are serious indications of the risk for suicide or interpersonal violence calls for crisis management.

Crises need not always be accompanied by such lethal threats. For example, a couple calls urgently requesting an appointment after the wife receives an ideal job offer in another part of the country. The partners have been dissatisfied with the marriage for years. The offer is time-limited and the couple must answer the questions it raises: Should the wife turn it down in order to stay in the marriage? Should the husband move to accompany his wife to the new job? Should they separate? The time limit on the job offer heightens the urgency of the decision. There may be no threat of suicide or violence but the situation is no less urgent to this couple; the therapist must recognize and respond to this urgency.

Contraindications

In crisis management, indications and contraindications for treatment are starkly simplified. If a couple seems to be in crisis, there are no contraindications for crisis management. There are, however, a number of important considerations and guidelines concerning the use of crisis management.

Considerations and Guidelines

Crisis management calls for

- a timely response
- careful assessment of risks
- utilization of all available resources

The goal is to help the clients cope effectively with the stresses they face in order to achieve good adaptation and greater stabilization.

The first consideration, timely response, is self-explanatory. The second consideration, careful assessment of risks, is a critical first step in managing crises. Presumably both you and the couple are already faced with a pile-up of stressful factors; the first priority of treatment is to prevent any additional emotional, relational, or physical injury and the further escalation of stresses that would accompany them. As a therapist who treats couples, you should be knowledgeable about assessing domestic violence, severity of depression, and the risks of lethality associated with suicidal ideation and impulses (see Chapters 16 and 18). You should know how to conduct a mental status exam to assess for a thought or mood disorder. If you are not knowledgeable in these areas, you must know where or to whom to refer such cases for immediate evaluation—and then follow up on the referral to be sure that contact with the new agency or practitioner has been made.

You should treat the crisis yourself if you have the necessary knowledge, and emotional resources, and time, or if you can supplement any areas of deficit by utilizing the resources of others. You should have some idea of the resources avialable and the steps to take to prevent destructive outcomes and to address specific presenting problems. These might include emergency services, psychiatric hospitalization, programs for domestic battering and shelters for battered women, and mobilization of extended family members. It is also important to know your legal responsibilities for managing these situations.

The theoretical and pragmatic basis for crisis management is *active coping* and *restabilization*. The immediate goal is to help the couple regain a sense of control over their situation and a sense of confidence that they can handle the challenges they face. Their active involvement serves to reinforce these feelings of confidence and control. The goals of preventing injury and fostering restabilization will most likely require specific suggestions. For example, a situation involving escalating threats of physical violence might call for a strong recommendation that the couple temporarily separate. A recommendation for emergency psychiatric hospitalization might be indicated where there is an acutely and perhaps lethally suicidal partner. However, whenever and to whatever degree it is possible, you should try to mobilize and include the partners in the process of coping with the crisis.

You should also try to mobilize resources to meet the challenges of the crisis. These might involve relational resources such as grandparents to look after children while the parents are absorbed in various aspects of coping, or friends who can be available to a depressed or distraught partner. They might involve community or professional resources such as emergency services, detox programs, support groups, day treatment programs, or professionals who can evaluate medical or psychiatric symptomatology. They might involve the personal and relational resources within the couple's relationship; they will certainly involve your resources (your empathy, acuity in terms of assessment, and practical experience with other similar situations).

Restabilization does not necessarily mean a return to the same relational patterns that existed before the crisis. When these patterns contributed to the development of the crisis, restabilization will hopefully bring changes to these areas. Crises represent potential opportunities as well as dangers. Any therapist who has had the experience of trying to treat a couple whose well-worn interactional patterns make them seemingly impervious to intervention will appreciate the often greater permeability of the relationship during a period of crisis. Precisely because the partners are feeling overwhelmed, out of control, and possibly in danger, the crisis can open a "window of opportunity" in which they are unusually receptive to outside influence concerning interactional patterns in the relationship.

The treatment recommendations discussed thus far are fairly straightforward. Beyond these recommendations are realms of potentially greater ambiguity, situations in which it is often more difficult to predict the optimal approach to treatment. Perhaps the clearest example of such a grey area is the question, in certain cases, of recommending couple therapy or individual psychotherapy, or some combination of the two. Similar ambiguities exist in cases that might also benefit from sex therapy or family therapy.

Clinical practitioners are constantly faced with these ambiguities and most develop their own biases and procedures for dealing with them. There is often less precision to these decisions than we may wish to acknowledge. In most cases, there are trade-offs, with advantages and disadvantages to each possible treatment recommendation. What follows are my own biases for making these decisions.

Defiance-Based Couple Therapy

In an article on the use of therapeutic paradox (Rohrbaugh et al., 1981), the authors distinguish between "compliance-based" paradoxical strategies — in which the therapist hopes that the client(s) will comply with his or her suggestion, and "defiance-based" paradoxical strategies — in which the therapist hopes that the client(s) will defy his or her suggestion. In the discussion that follows, the term "compliance-based intervention" refers to *any* intervention, paradoxical or not, in which the therapist expects the client(s) to comply with his or her suggestions. The term "defiance-based intervention" refers only to those interventions in which the therapist expects that the client(s) will resist or defy his or her suggestions and hopes that this defiance will move the individual or the relational system in a more positive direction. This type of approach is most often associated with what have been called paradoxical interventions and with strategic and systemic therapies. Haley (1963, 1976), Madanes (1981, 1984), Selvini Palazolli, Boscolo, Cecchin, & Prata (1978), Papp (1977, 1980), and Hoffman (1981) have all described variations on this strategy. Paradoxical interventions have also been identified in behavioral, Gestalt, and psychoanalytic approaches to treatment; in fact, Seltzer (1986) has identified 47 different terms used by various authors to refer to these techniques.

In couple therapy, a defiance-based approach might involve instructing the partners not to be intimate with one another and framing this suggestion with a warning that such efforts might produce unwelcome consequences of some kind. If the therapist guesses that the couple's avoidance of intimacy serves to protect each partner's strong attachments to their families of origin, he or she might suggest that they *not* become more intimate since this might endanger their relationships with their families, which would be tragic for both of them. The detailed content of the reframe would vary with different couples, based on the particulars of the case.

Defiance-based interventions derive from the same formulations as do compliance-based interventions but they "spin" the formulation by recommending that the partners *not* try to change some part of the presenting complaint. The shift to defiance-based interventions is dictated by the therapist's impression that more straightforward suggestions will meet a wall of resistance. Many therapists are uncomfortable with the use of these interventions; some feel that they are ethically dubious. Fisher, Anderson, and Jones (1981) suggest that some therapists may be ill-suited to carry off defiance-based interventions due to personality and stylistic factors. There are potential problems associated with defiance-based interventions (see Contraindications; Considerations and Guidelines below). However, there are, I believe, some couples with whom a compliance-based approach will lead to frustration for the therapist and a protracted impasse for the couple. Defiance-based intervention will probably not be used frequently by most couple therapists but they should be able to utilize it when it is clinically indicated.

Indications

The major therapeutic indicator for defiance-based interventions is resistance—*not* the common resistance present in virtually all couples who request treatment but resistance of an extreme and unusual degree. These are couples in which one or both of the partners are wedded to their relational impasse or distress. This resistance can be detected in one of several ways. The most obvious involve messages from the clients indicating that they *cannot* change in some way vitally related to the concerns presented in evaluation. For example, both partners complain bitterly about repeated angry arguments but reject every suggestion you make for finding alternatives to these conflicts. These "can't change" messages should alert you to the possible utility of a defiance-based approach, especially if they are communicated blithely, without discomfort of any kind.

A second indicator for defiance-based couple therapy is a history of repeated failures in compliance-based couple therapy. A final indicator is the therapist's awareness of his or her own hopelessness about a compliance-based approach being successful. If you find yourself feeling completely dispirited and discouraged at the thought of recommending a compliance-based approach, this may be a useful indicator that such an approach will meet with little success. This internal reading should *never* be the *sole* factor determining the choice of a defiance-based approach but it should alert you to the possibility that such an approach may be more productive.

Contraindications

Defiance-based approaches are contraindicated in cases that present with an acute crisis (Rohrbaugh et al., 1981). They also should not be utilized in cases involving serious depression and possible lethality; telling the couple that they either should not change or cannot change would simply be too risky. You want to shock or provoke in order to elicit resources that may be untapped in a client or a relationship, *not* engender real hopelessness and a sense of defeat. In these types of cases, you should assess the depth of the client's depression and possible lethality, take steps to prevent possible suicide attempts, and provide whatever treatment you feel will most rapidly and effectively alleviate the client's depression.

Defiance-based approaches are also contraindicated for couples in which one or both partners are likely to significantly misunderstand the paradoxical frame. This might include individuals with markedly paranoid features, a possible thought disorder, serious cognitive limitations or, in the case of foreign-speaking clients, a poor command of the language being used in treatment.

Considerations and Guidelines

One question that often arises concerning defiance-based approaches to treatment is whether compliance-based approaches should be tried first, especially if the therapist is uncertain as to which approach will be more helpful. My own feeling is that, unless a therapist feels confident that a defiance-based approach is required, there are advantages to starting out with a compliance-based approach. This type of approach is more explicitly collaborative and allows clients to experience more psychological "ownership" of progress in treatment. There is an inherent advantage to approaches that enlist the collaborative effort of all parties and enable clients to take responsibility for the changes they desire in their relationships.

However, when a therapist has discovered or strongly suspects that such approaches will only deepen the couple's impasse, a defiance-based approach is preferable to a stalemate or to no treatment at all. For these reasons, my own preference is to begin with compliance-based treatment (unless I am virtually certain that this will be unproductive) and to move to defiance-based treatment only if it becomes clear that the compliance framework is a dead end.

A second consideration involves how the prescription is presented. Rohrbaugh et al. (1981) distinguish between "soft" and "hard" restraining. "Soft" restraining implies that the client(s) probably shouldn't change. "For example, the therapist may tell the patient to 'go slow' or worry with the patient about the possible dangers of improvement (p. 454)." "Hard" restraining implies that the client(s) probably *cannot* change. Hard restraining, the authors suggest, is more likely to be helpful with the most resistant clients. Soft restraining could be used with less intensely resistant clients or as a probe to assess whether or not a more dramatic restraint is required.

Another consideration with defiance-based approaches concerns what is prescribed. Some authors have recommended a difference in the "target" of the therapist's prescription when one is working with a couple or family as opposed to an individual client. To put it simply, with an individual, the therapist prescribes the symptom; with a couple or family, the therapist prescribes the *relationship* between the *symptom* and the *system*. To use an example cited earlier, a therapist might encourage a couple to continue arguing about their patterns of intimacy, suggesting that to stop doing so might endanger each partner's relationship with a parent. Here the therapist prescribes not just the symptom—arguing over the terms of intimacy—but the relationship between the symptom and the wider relational system, which includes both partners and their relationships with their families of origin. This distinction is a useful one even if it is less neatly related to the nature of the client system than has been suggested. What does seem true is that prescribing the relationship between symptom and system suits a *relationally based formulation* whether the therapist is working with an individual, a couple, or a family.

The therapist should also consider the rationale that is used to justify the counter-intuitive suggestion that clients *not* try to "get better." When the *connection* between the symptom and the system is prescribed, the specific rationale is self-evident—in the previous example, greater intimacy should be avoided because it will pull the partners away from their families of origin. More generically, the therapist might also suggest that, because the underlying dynamics of the problem are so obscure, increasing the frequency of arguing might provide better opportunities to study it. Or, it might be suggested that an ability to "turn on" the problem might lead to a greater ability to "turn it off" later. Finally, it might be suggested that, since the problem is likely to occur anyway, it would be better for the partners to take control of the timing themselves by making it occur.

One final consideration involves cases in which one partner is strongly resistant but the other appears more cooperative. A variation on a defiance-based approach might be used, such as seeing the partners separately and using a defiance-based approach with one and a compliance-based approach with the other. (This type of approach is illustrated with a case example in Chapter 10.) Or, the therapist might try to work within a compliance-based frame with both partners together in spite of this difference, for example by accepting the individual's intransigence and focusing on how the partner chooses to respond to this. Whatever choice is made, recognizing this kind of resistance from one partner should prompt the therapist to consider the utility of defiance-based approaches to treatment.

Recommending Against Couple Therapy

There are some cases in which, at the conclusion of the evaluation, the therapist may tell the couple that he or she does *not* recommend couple therapy for them. It is a sensitive recommendation and should be used cautiously. This is not a defiance-based intervention in which the therapist will continue with the couple and hope that his or her unexpected pessimism spurs a significant change of some kind. Instead, it is the therapist's sincere recommendation that they not pursue couple therapy based on his or her assessment that it will be unproductive. If they accept this recommendation, they will most likely have no further sessions with the therapist (although they might agree on one or two follow-up sessions to help them digest this recommendation).

This represents an important point of personal conviction for a therapist. Will every couple be helped most by a trial of couple therapy regardless of all prognostic indicators? Or are there some couples who may be helped most by the therapist's sharing of his or her strong pessimism about the probable utility of couple therapy sessions? My own feeling is that there *are* couples who fit the latter description.

There are two treatment considerations important enough to raise at the outset of this discussion. The first is: When in doubt, test. In other words, if you have any sense that treatment might prove helpful, you should recommend a trial of couple therapy. If your pessimism is justified, there will probably be little lost by a few sessions, which may only reinforce the original appraisal; if it is not, there may be much to gain by offering a trial of couple therapy. The second treatment consideration is: *Always* try to anticipate the *effects* of such a recommendation on the couple in question. One would not present such a summary to a couple in which one partner were desperately focused on the relationship, severely depressed, and possibly suicidal.

When you recommend against couple therapy, you may or may not suggest a different form of treatment, such as individual psychotherapy for one partner; this will depend on the couple's presenting complaint(s), both individuals' motivation for change of the status quo, your own assessment of where the major problems or obstacles lie, and your reading of the resilience or fragility of both partners. Each of these considerations will be discussed at greater length below, under Considerations and Guidelines.

Indications

There are two types of situations in which you would be most likely to recommend against couple therapy. One involves couples in which one partner is totally noncommittal toward the relationship and toward treatment. These individuals are either unwilling to make changes or unable to commit to working together to improve things. Often, they are "willing" to attend further sessions, allowing themselves to be passively led along either by the partner or by the therapist, but a deep resistance underlies this apparent accommodation, a fundamental "No" under a superficial "Maybe" or "Yes." This situation requires you to make a judgement call. Should you recommend couple therapy in spite of this visceral resistance, or call attention to it and recommend against treatment because of it? Again, your motto should be: When in doubt, test. However, if you feel confident that the reluctant partner is *unable to commit* to the process of treatment, you may be more helpful to the couple by making this clear.

In these cases, it is best to tell both partners that you do not recommend couple therapy because the reluctant partner's stance indicates that this will be unproductive; there seem to be insufficient resources for couple treatment to yield positive results. Bear in mind that these reluctant partners are not necessarily indifferent or insensitive and, in some cases, they are anguished by their inability to commit to improving the relationship. In many cases, they have "fallen out of love" with their partner but not yet made the final decision to end the relationship.

Sometimes your feedback will shock one or both partners into a decision of some kind that moves them out of the impasse. The reluctant partner—let's suppose a man—may see that he needs to separate or, less commonly, faced with the real possibility of losing the relationship, may rediscover his motivation to maintain it. Other times, the other partner may see more clearly that she is fruitlessly waiting for a change in the partner that seems almost certain never to come. Your feedback may help her mobilize the personal resources necessary to end the relationship.

A second type of case in which you might recommend against couple therapy involves a chronic relational impasse. Typically, these relationships are characterized by long-term dissatisfaction. The partners may be severely polarized and unable to agree on the nature of the problem or goals for treatment. There may have been one or more treatment failures in the past. Trust may be low or essentially nonexistent. There are few visible resources and no real leverage for change. The couple presents with an impasse: They have been unable to either improve the relationship or bring it to an end and move on with their lives. Often they are explicitly asking whether they should keep trying or give up.

Because of the ethical questions and risks associated with this recommendation, the following case example is presented to illustrate some of these considerations.

A couple presents complaining of intractable arguments. Their question is, "Can we make it work or should we get a divorce?" Michael is 56 years old; Rose is 43. They have been married for 16 years. Rose has a 21-year-old daughter from a previous marriage; together they have a 14-year-old daughter. Rose is currently involved in individual psychotherapy.

The couple has been involved in family and couple therapy over the past three years in connection with the psychiatric hospitalization of Rose's daughter who is diagnosed as schizophrenic and still hospitalized at the time that they initiate the couple evaluation. Both feel that this therapy helped but cannot specify in what ways; both admit that their arguments and their dissatisfactions with the relationship have persisted without change. In addition, Rose felt that the therapist was on Michael's side.

They describe a pattern of chronic intense arguments—"dirty, nasty fights"—throughout their 16-year marriage. Rose describes Michael as cold, unaffectionate, and "married to his job." He sees her as insatiable, selfish, and critical and feels they are essentially incompatible. Their arguments have occasionally led to mutual and fairly contained physical aggression. In session together, they are angry and mutually accusatory. Neither can seemingly see any basis for the other's complaints and portrays him or her as seriously disturbed. There are virtually no areas of agreement. Rose expresses more dissatisfaction with the relationship but, in his individual session, Michael admits that he does not love her although he is reluctant to tell her so. They do not describe any periods of closeness, tenderness, and satisfaction alternating with this pattern of conflict.

They have already separated; Rose has initiated divorce but the process is currently "on hold." Their mistrust is expressed financially: Rose suspected that Michael would try to protect his own assets at her expense and so emptied their bank account. She believes that he is not actively pursuing divorce because he wants to avoid the financial and emotional stresses.

This couple has been engaged in an intense and extremely conflictual relationship, with no real change, over a period of 16 years. These relational patterns are not seen as inherently unworkable in therapy; they are similar to those of other couples whom I had seen benefit from couple therapy. In this case, I recommended against couple therapy with the following factors in mind:

- *the lack of resources (both in terms of any positive feelings for one another and real gratifications in the relationship, as well as their abilities to look at their own contributions and to take more flexible positions)*
- *the chronicity of the problem*
- *the degree of polarization between them*
- *the high level of mistrust between them (expressed concretely through the initiation of divorce, financial manuevers, and their physical separation, as well as verbally and interactionally in sessions)*
- *the lack of progress in previous treatment*
- *the lack of agreement between them about the nature of the problem*
- *the lack of inclination to change or compromise in either of them*
- *my own inability to imagine any kind of progress or reconciliation for them*

I saw Michael and Rose as a couple whose attachment was powerful but largely negative and self-defeating, both driven and restricted by painful relational wounds from the past and fears involving intimacy. It seemed that there was not enough common ground between what she needed and what he could provide. Furthermore, given their polarization and mistrust and how far they had already moved toward ending the relationship, it seemed extremely unlikely that they would benefit from couple therapy. None of these factors alone would have been sufficient for this prognostic judgement, but together I felt they were definitive. They had all but accepted the end of the relationship and were now, at the brink of divorce, experiencing ambivalence and doubts.

In the final session, I told them that I thought it was very unlikely that couple therapy would contribute to any significant and lasting change in their relationship and, for this reason, did not recommend it. I made clear that I recognized a powerful bond between the two of them but that I did not expect this bond to translate into any greater satisfaction in the relationship than it had for the last 16 years. I discussed the discouraging factors described above. I described their central impasse—her need for more and his sense of being unable to satisfy her—and related it to each of their individual issues and to their initial attraction.

I did not recommend that they pursue divorce; I did tell them that

I did not think the relationship would improve, whether they pursued couple therapy or not. If they accepted this assessment, they would make their own personal decisions about whether to remain in the relationship. I encouraged each to pursue in individual therapy whatever individual themes had surfaced during the evaluation, and conveyed my sense of greater optimism in the possibility of their making progress in that context rather than in couple therapy.

Contraindications

You should not recommend against couple therapy if you feel there is any possibility that treatment might prove helpful, and "helpful" does not necessarily mean "helpful in keeping the relationship together." You are concerned with the interests of both individuals as well as those of the relationship. If you feel that they may be helped individually by participating in couple therapy, then recommending this approach is perfectly appropriate. The couple sessions can provide an opportunity for each partner to better understand what drew them to the other and how they each contributed to problematic patterns, even if they later decide to end the relationship. However, both partners should be clear about the goals of these sessions. With other couples, you might feel strongly that the relationship will not improve but the partners may have difficulty accepting this conclusion. A brief series of couple sessions may help them come to terms with what seems an inevitable conclusion.

Recommending against couple therapy is also contraindicated when you sense that this recommendation poses a potential danger to one or both clients. You should *always* try to *anticipate the effects* of such a recommendation on the clients. The recommendation of no treatment is most likely to be helpful to a couple having difficulty ending a relationship that is characterized by chronic conflict and dissatisfaction, with little positive attachment and gratification, a history of treatment failures, no indications of new leverage or resources for change, and two relatively stable individuals who seem likely to be able to handle the transition to independence and new relationships.

One would *not* present such a recommendation to a couple in which one partner were desperately focused on the relationship, seriously depressed, and possibly suicidal. In these cases, concerns include self-injury and decompensation; whether the fears are for physical or emotional injury, the appropriate therapeutic response is identical. If the individual is not already involved in treatment of any kind and is willing to participate, you should recommend couple therapy and/or individual psychotherapy in an effort to create the most secure "holding" context possible. You should try to make sure that the individual is well-connected to a relationship or system outside the couple relationship that can provide support and monitoring of potential risks while the partners clarify the future of their relationship. There is every reason to soften the prognostic impressions conveyed to clients when one or both seem especially emotionally fragile, and to support them through the continuing definition of the relationship and its future.

In summary, recommending against couple therapy is contraindicated when you feel there is some possibility of benefit from such an approach to treatment and when you fear that the recommendation poses a potential threat of serious physical or emotional injury to one or both partners.

Considerations and Guidelines

Some of the most important considerations involved in recommending against couple therapy have already been raised. The first is: When in doubt, test. The second involves trying to anticipate the effects of this recommendation on both of the individuals involved. A third consideration involves whether or not you should address questions of separation and divorce in these cases. If you recommend against couple therapy, you need not and *should not* recommend for or against separation and divorce. Your mandate as a consultant to the couple has involved assessing whether couple therapy is likely to be helpful and, if so, with what approach, what goals, and within what frame. If your professional opinion is that it will not, it is entirely up to the *couple* to decide what this means to them and what choices it will lead them to make.

It is inappropriate for you to express opinions about whether or not they should continue in the relationship. You should not spontaneously offer such recommendations and should decline to respond when clients inquire directly about your opinion on this question. This is an important existential decision for each partner, in which they have the opportunity—and the burden—to define themselves in their lives. It is neither appropriate nor helpful for you to relieve them of this burden (and of the rewards that accrue from the struggle to resolve it). You can, however, respond to these requests by offering a brief, time-limited series of sessions intended to help them to answer this question for themselves.

Another consideration when recommending against couple therapy involves the question of referral. When both partners express distress of some kind and a wish for help in changing some aspect of their lives, a referral should be offered to a more promising form of treatment (individual therapy, group treatment, Al-Anon, etc.). If, on the other hand, the couple's request is solely focused on whether they could be helped by couple therapy and they express no interest in any other form of therapy, you need not offer other treatment recommendations.

If one partner wants nothing to do with treatment and the other is distressed and wants help, you should respond to the needs of that partner with a recommendation for individual sessions. These sessions can help the individual better understand the forces that maintain the current problems and clarify what he or she might do about them. You might offer to conduct these sessions yourself or to make a referral to another practitioner. (This treatment recommendation is discussed in greater detail below, under Recommending Treatment for One Partner.)

While clients are often upset by a recommendation against couple therapy, one or both may also be grateful. They may express this at the time or, more often, some time later in a letter or phone call. Frequently, they will later ask for individual sessions. These sessions can be extremely productive, especially in helping them better understand why they stayed in the relationship as long as they did and how they might avoid the same problems in future relationships.

Recommending Treatment For One Partner

Recommending treatment for one or both individuals instead of, or in addition to, couple therapy often constitutes a "grey area" in treatment recommendations. In some cases, the decision is relatively clear-cut; in others, it may be confusing and unclear. The following are common situations in which a recommendation of treatment for one partner might be indicated.

Sue and Barry, an unmarried couple, present with multiple relational difficulties. During the evaluation, it becomes clear that Barry is seriously and biologically depressed. He acknowledges suicidal thoughts and formulated plans but denies intent. The therapist wants to have him evaluated by a psychiatrist who is knowledgeable about depression and who can prescribe antidepressant medication if necessary.

Kimberly and Frank present with the complaint of frequent arguments. It turns out that almost all of these arguments occur when Kimberly has been drinking. Evaluation reveals a serious pattern of alcoholism on her part, with frequent binges, blackouts, and marked belligerence; she strenuously denies any problem with drinking and blames the arguments on her husband's nagging. There may well be a systemic problem that contributes to Kimberly's drinking but the chances are that, unless she can acknowledge and gain control of her drinking, little progress will be made in couple therapy. The therapist recommends evaluation and treatment for the drinking, which may require an inpatient stay for detoxification.

Arlene and Harold present with Arlene's having "fallen out of love." Harold makes clear his strong desire to begin couple therapy. Arlene, however, is intensely ambivalent and unable either to commit to a trial of couple therapy or to make any moves toward leaving the relationship. Finding it impossible to take a position, she asks for a referral to meet with a therapist individually in order to try to sort out her feelings and come to a decision.

A middle-aged couple, Cindy and Lou, present with complaints of increased arguing and Cindy's decreased interest in their sexual relationship. The evaluation reveals that her mother has developed Alzheimer's syndrome and that she is overwhelmed by stresses associated with this. The couple has had a good relationship for many years but it is currently strained by this development. The therapist recommends couple therapy; he meets Cindy's urgent request for help in coping with her mother by referring her to a support group in the community for family members of Alzheimer's patients.

Jenn and Matt come in with a primary complaint of Matt's lack of sexual desire. Evaluation reveals a long-standing history of deviant sexual arousal involving rape fantasies. He appears not to have acted on these fantasies but reports that they are growing stronger. The therapist refers the man to a clinician who is knowledgeable about paraphilia.

In some of these cases, the therapist might recommend concurrent couple therapy; in others, couple therapy might be deferred until a later time or not recommended at all. Just as individuals can be helped through couple therapy, couple relationships can be helped through individual treatment for one partner. Understanding this can help therapists be flexible in deciding which treatment approaches promise to be most helpful to clients in each particular case.

The following discussion is not based on a particular form of individual treatment. Instead, it covers a range of situations in which the therapist feels that some specialized form of treatment for one or both partners is likely to prove helpful and is either warranted in the light of particular problems and symptoms or necessary if any progress is to be made in couple therapy. Treatment for an individual may mean individual psychotherapy but this is not always the case; the therapist might recommend a group for incest survivors or participation in AA or an evaluation for psychotropic medication.

Clinical Indications

A recommendation of treatment for one partner is indicated when

- an individual symptom or difficulty requires specialized treatment
- the client's level of anguish or distress in relation to symptomatology is so high that to overlook it would constitute a serious failure of alliance-building
- a particular problem blocks productive couple therapy
- one partner is unmotivated for couple therapy and the other requests help of some kind
- a variety of factors contribute to the therapist's feeling that the very intense and often conflicting needs of a particular couple are "too much" for one therapist

In any particular case, one or more of these factors may be present.

When an Individual Symptom Requires Specialized Treatment. Several examples of this scenario have already been given. Other situations that might call for this recommendation include anxiety disorders (including panic attacks, agoraphobia, OCD, or PTSD), bipolar affective disorder, dissociative disorders, coercive paraphilias (Money, 1986; Wincze, 1989), alcoholism and other substance abuse, psychosis, or a serious eating disorder.

If you hear about symptoms that might indicate a neurological disorder, you should refer the client to a neurologist or neuropsychologist for evaluation. If you are uncertain about what kind of medical specialist is indicated, you should contact a physician with whom you have a working relationship and ask how to direct the client to appropriate medical services. These conditions represent so serious a risk, either to the client or to others, that you have an ethical responsibility to direct the client as quickly as possible to those services most likely to alleviate or relieve symptomatology.

When the Client's Level of Anguish Calls for Specialized Treatment. In some cases, you may not feel that the client's difficulties require specialized treatment but the client will make clear that he or she feels differently. Should you respect the client's feelings and make the referral or discourage it and try to address his or her concerns within the context of couple therapy? This decision, like many in the area of treatment recommendations, involves trade-offs.

The risks of accepting the request for specialized treatment involve the potential dilution of therapeutic influence, the danger of the client's receiving competing advice from different therapists (in the case of concurrent treatment), and its possible function as a means to avoid issues in the couple's relationship. The risks of *not* immediately accepting this request and instead encouraging the client to look to couple therapy for relief involve the client's feeling unheard, the breakdown of treatment alliances, and the possibility that the distress will not resolve in couple's work, which will lead to an exacerbation of symptomatology and an undermining of confidence in you.

These questions can only be answered on a case-by-case basis but the following factors can help you make the best decisions: How severe is the level of symptomatology? How intense is the client's distress? Does the partner welcome the notion of specialized treatment for the distressed partner or does he or she view it as an act of avoidance or abandonment? How do you imagine the client will respond to the suggestion not to pursue specialized treatment—with cautious confidence and a willingness to try out your recommendation or with an outpouring of grief and anger at having been once again "not taken seriously" in his or her life? Is there transferential significance to the request? Is it a test of some kind for the therapist of which the client may be totally unaware? If so, how should you respond to this test? The answers to these questions can help you decide whether to recommend specialized treatment for one partner and, if so, how you should present your decision to the couple.

When a Particular Problem Blocks Productive Couple Therapy. Problems in this category overlap considerably with those discussed above as problems that *require* specialized treatment. The concern here, however, is not the danger they pose but the fact that they are likely to interfere with productive couple therapy. Typical examples include a woman who is so depressed that she cannot listen to her husband's dissatisfactions with their relationship without feeling utterly worthless, hopeless, and suicidal; a veteran whose untreated symptoms of PTSD contribute to explosive rage, depression, and alcoholism; or a man who is so terrified and preoccupied by several recent panic attacks that he literally cannot concentrate or address his wife's concerns about their relationship. Each of these situations is almost certain to impede productive work in couple therapy.

Another situation that can preclude couple therapy involves the partner who is so ambivalent about the relationship that he or she cannot emotionally invest in an effort aimed at clearer definition or change. Faced with the question of whether to engage in treatment or to separate, the ambivalent partner is unable to move in either direction. In this case, you may need to recommend that this partner meet with you individually in order to resolve the ambivalence enough so that an initial move can be made in one direction or the other.

When One Partner is Unmotivated for Couple Therapy and the Other is Distressed and Requests Help. When a partner makes it clear that he or she will not participate in treatment, whether expressed clearly or disguised by logistical difficulties, the message to the other partner is, "You're on your own." This partner is usually distressed and often implicitly or explicitly asks the therapist, "What do I do now?" In these cases, individual sessions can help the person sort out his or her feelings and decide how to respond to the partner's unwillingness to participate in treatment.

When the Couple is "Too Much" for One Therapist. This category is partly derived from your assessment of the couple's needs and partly from your subjective experience with them. Some couples are especially likely to make you feel confused and overwhelmed. These couples are usually described as "difficult" or "multiproblem" couples; their problematic relationship may be one of many in a multiproblem family. They may present in crisis. Typically, a number of intense and dramatic problems are presented simultaneously. The clients' distress is acute and their needs seem urgent. You feel like a fireman who has three different alarms going off at once or, in an image more evocative of the dynamics of such cases, like a mother who awakens to find two or more children screaming piteously in the night.

These couples are distinguished from others in which multiple problems are presented by the *intensity* of affect associated with their complaints (urgency, anguish, and rage) and the fact that this intensity *does not diminish*. Some couples present with multiple problems and complaints but respond to the therapist's directive to prioritize these difficulties and are able to deal with problems sequentially in treatment. The couples being discussed here will not. Their intense, urgent neediness will persist and, if not met, may even escalate. One or both partners may fit the criteria for borderline or narcissistic personality disorder.

If you feel confident that you can manage these needs within the context of couple therapy, this is certainly the simplest and most straightforward treatment recommendation. However, if you feel overwhelmed by such a couple and in danger of losing clinical distance, the sensible thing may be to call for reinforcements. Consultation with another therapist may be all that is necessary for you to regain perspective and clinical distance. If it is not, however, you may want to recommend individual treatment for one or both partners. If possible, this should be with clinicians with whom you have good working relationships, since ongoing discussion between professionals treating these couples will probably be helpful for the clients as well as for the therapists involved. Such concurrent therapies increase the likelihood of "splitting" (Cashdan, 1988; Phillips, 1988; Scharff & Scharff, 1991; Seinfeld, 1990) into "good" and "bad" therapists but these risks may be justified by the advantages of the arrangement. Individual psychotherapies can increase the partners' sense of secure "holding" (Scharff & Scharff, 1991; Winnicott, 1971) and respond to their distress over individual symptoms and problems, which hopefully will enable you to work on the complexity of their relationship with more stable and less volatile clients.

Contraindications

Be very careful about recommending treatment for one partner when the request for treatment comes not from the individual but from the other partner. One partner's preoccupation with the other's "pathology" constitutes a common pattern in couple relationships. Partners sometimes avoid or deny their own difficulties by "playing therapist" to the other, detailing his or her pathology, hypothesizing about its origins, and urging treatment for the difficulties specified. If you give your blessing to this view of things, the individual may feel that he or she can now relax in the comfort of being the "healthy one" while the "sick one" gets the treatment he or she supposedly needs.

You should hesitate to recommend specialized treatment if the individual is reluctant to pursue such treatment, and especially if the individual's difficulties do not seem to require treatment or to interfere with productive couple therapy. However, if the individual's difficulties do seem to merit specialized treatment, his or her partner's concern may be appropriate as would be your referral for other treatment.

Considerations and Guidelines

Should Specialized Treatment be Concurrent with Couple Therapy? When you recommend specialized treatment for one partner, should this treatment be *in lieu of* couple therapy or *concurrent* with it? Several factors inform this decision. One involves the needs and wishes of the partner for whom the treatment is recommended. Does this person *want* to be involved in couple therapy along with specialized treatment (for example, when she is anxious about the survival of the relationship or the welfare of her partner)? Does this person *not* want to be involved in concurrent couple therapy (for example, when he feels so overwhelmed with his own difficulties that he finds it impossible to focus on the needs of his partner or the state of the relationship at that point in time)?

A second factor involves the needs and wishes of the other partner. Is she simply relieved to have helped secure appropriate treatment for her partner and feeling no need to pursue couple therapy or is she worried about the welfare of the relationship and/or angry about having to put her needs "on hold" while her partner pursues individual treatment?

You should also consider whether there are significant difficulties in the couple's relationship. If you feel that there are but the partners do not, there is little advantage in pressing this point. However, if the partners are confused and unsure, your conviction about the relevance of relational factors for individual symptomatology and about the probable utility of couple therapy may help them with decisions about treatment. Even if you feel that the presenting complaint is not the result of relational patterns, you might recommend concurrent couple therapy if it will have psychoeducational value for the partner and may help both partners join their efforts to cope with the problems at hand.

If you feel that there are significant problems in the couple's relationship, you must still ask yourself whether or not progress seems possible in couple therapy at this time. For example, in a case involving one partner's paralyzing ambivalence, you may feel that no movement can occur until the ambivalence is resolved to some degree; a recommendation for individual treatment would be indicated with couple therapy possibly following later.

Lastly, the therapist and the clients should consider the resources required by treatment—money, time, and psychological energy. Participation in any form of therapy will involve all of these; multiple therapies will involve even more of them. The clients need to consider and you need to know whether they can afford the financial, temporal, and emotional costs of treatment.

The answers to these "questions" may or may not converge. When they do, your job is an easier one—when they do not, it is more difficult. One partner may desperately want to pursue couple therapy while the other feels unable or unwilling to do so. Both partners may express a desire to pursue concurrent treatments but feel they cannot afford them. There is no simple solution to these dilemmas. You can make recommendations and explain the reasons for them but, as always, it is ultimately the clients' responsibility to decide which paths they will pursue.

Should Specialized Treatment be Referred to Another Clinician? When treatment for one partner is recommended, should you conduct this treatment yourself or refer to another clinician? There are advantages and disadvantages to both scenarios. Many couples will be reassured to know that they can address their multiple concerns with one clinician, especially if they have formed a good alliance during the course of the evaluation. Others will be disturbed by the implicit imbalance when the therapist agrees to meet individually with one partner, either before couple therapy begins or concurrently with it.

The following factors inform this decision: Do you feel that you have the particular expertise required for such treatment? Does the work involved *seem* to be relatively circumscribed and short-term or more extensive and long-term? Does it seem likely that both partners could tolerate the potential imbalance inherent in holding individual sessions with one partner, either before initiating or concurrent with couple sessions? Do you feel that you can maintain balanced siding in this context? Once again, the answers to these questions may converge or they may not.

If the couple has come to you requesting couple therapy, referral to another clinician for specialized treatment is the safest course of action given potential complications, especially for beginning therapists. If you feel confident that you can conduct both forms of treatment, be sure to clarify with both partners the ground rules required by the treatment plan. For example, in the case of concurrent individual and couple sessions, it is useful to suggest that complaints about the partner or the relationship be raised only in couple sessions. Let the partners know that they are free to discuss any and all aspects of any session with one another, but that you will not "report" on individual sessions to the other partner.

What Impact Will Specialized Treatment Have on the Couple Relationship? One final consideration when deciding on treatment for one partner involves the impact of the recommendation on the couple relationship. Especially in those cases where there are struggles over the definition and location of the presenting problem, such a recommendation may be read as an endorsement of one view of their difficulties. If you recommend treatment for one partner's depression, alcoholism, or symptoms of PTSD, the recommendation must be framed so that it does not suggest that this individual is "the sick one" or that all of the couple's difficulties are his or her "fault." This impression can be mitigated by an emphasis on both partners' contributions to relational difficulties and by acknowledging both of their efforts at coping.

Sex Therapy

Sex therapy with couples* focuses directly on the couple's sexual relationship, with the express purpose of changing the aspect of that relationship they have defined as problematic. The couple works together with a therapist (or, in some cases, with a male-female cotherapy team). Treatment utilizes structured exercises that involve physical intimacy and sensual and sexual contact. These exercises are designed to minimize anxiety and other negative experiences and to maximize sexual arousal, safety, and communication. The particular exercises chosen depend on the nature of the sexual difficulties involved. The partners engage in the exercises at home and report on their experiences to the therapist in conjoint treatment sessions, providing a verbal description of what actually went on during the exercise and what each was thinking and feeling during it.

On a behavioral level, the exercises are designed to reduce anxiety and to allow natural sexual excitement to emerge in the couple's encounters. The detailed focus may help identify areas in which one partner is not receiving adequate stimulation. They may also surface deeper obstacles to intimacy and sexual satisfaction such as feelings of guilt and shame related to childhood sexual abuse, negative messages about sex received in the family of origin, fear of pleasure and spontaneity, fear of dependency, or feelings of anger or mistrust in the couple's relationship. The therapist tries to identify these sources of difficulty and to help the partners work through (or around) them in order to achieve a greater level of satisfaction in their sexual relationship.

The boundary between couple therapy and sex therapy is a blurred one. Therapists who conduct couple therapy will often be led to a dis-

*Sex therapy can also be conducted with individual clients and in groups for individuals (LoPiccolo & Miller, 1978; McCarthy, 1992; Schneidman & McGuire, 1978; Williams, 1978; Wincze & Carey, 1991).

cussion of issues in the couple's sexual relationship because it is so central to intimacy and satisfaction in couple relationships and because sexual difficulties are so often either an expression of or a contributing factor to other relational problems. Similarly, sex therapists often find that they must explore and understand broader and deeper aspects of the couple's relationship in order to have an impact on the intractability of sexual patterns. In spite of this ambiguity, the distinction between these two forms of treatment remains a useful one and the question facing therapists who evaluate couples is when to recommend one over the other.

Indications

The primary indications for sex therapy are

- a presenting problem that clearly involves the couple's sexual relationship
- a good-enough working relationship between the partners
- an ability on the part of both partners to tolerate the vulnerability and confrontation involved in working directly with a therapist on these sensitive and usually private aspects of their relationship

The first clinical indicator is self-explanatory. However, therapists must be certain to evaluate for possible *physical causes* of sexual difficulties before assuming that emotional and relational factors are responsible for them (see Chapter 15 for greater discussion of this issue).

The quality of the couple's relationship is also an important indicator for sex therapy, which can be more challenging for clients than couple therapy, at least initially. Clients who seek couple therapy must be willing and able to talk with one another and to respond to the therapist's questions. Couple therapy may, but need not, impose tasks or homework assignments at the start of treatment. In sex therapy, on the other hand, the partners will most likely be agreeing to engage in regular and clearly specified physical interactions with each other between therapy sessions and to describe these interactions to the therapist. The exercises, although designed to be less anxiety-provoking at the start and gradually more challenging, immerse the clients in their area of greatest difficulty—their face-to-face physical interaction—right from the start.

The exercises also call for a high degree of cooperation. One partner may be asked to provide a certain kind of sexual stimulation for the other partner or to engage in intercourse in a particular position or a particular way (such as stopping periodically to allow the other partner's excitement to diminish). These directives create situations in which their needs may be aroused but deferred, in which they are likely to feel quite vulnerable, and in which caring attention to the other's needs is essential. For this reason, there must be a reasonable degree of trust and goodwill between the partners in order for them to make progress in treatment. This is especially true given that the exercises often surface negative feelings related to sex and intimacy, such as anxiety, fear, and shame.

This leads to the last clinical indicator for sex therapy: Both partners must be able to personally tolerate the confrontation, the intimacy, and the exposure involved in working with a therapist on the details of their sexual relationship. This requires a certain degree of ego-strength and flexibility as well as an ability to become relatively comfortable discussing intimate details of their sexual relationship with a professional.

Contraindications

The major contraindications for sex therapy are

- conflict and mistrust between the partners that is so severe as to make cooperation on the sexual exercises impossible
- individual factors that make one partner, or both, unable to participate in the process of treatment.

When conflict and mistrust are the primary obstacles to sex therapy, couple therapy may be preferable at the outset. This will hopefully enable the partners to reduce conflict and build trust, creating a foundation that increases the chances that sex therapy will be possible and helpful later in treatment.

There are a variety of individual factors that can impede sex therapy. These include feelings of shame, self-consciousness, exposure, and vulnerability so great as to make it impossible for the client to engage in the sexual exercises and to discuss them with his or her partner and/or the therapist. One partner may also be experiencing symptomatology of some kind that interferes with his or her ability to fully participate in treatment. In these cases, a recommendation for individual treatment for the symptomatic partner is indicated. Concurrent couple sessions may also be recommended if the therapist feels that the relationship is at risk or that the partners can benefit from this in spite of the individual's symptoms. Sex therapy should be deferred until this partner is more able to participate actively in treatment.

Considerations and Guidelines

One important treatment consideration has already been discussed in detail—the need for a thorough examination by a physician whenever it appears that medical factors may be contributing to sexual difficulties. A second consideration is whether the therapist who evaluates the couple will conduct sex therapy if it is indicated. This hinges on the therapist's expertise and comfort with sexual issues and sex therapy. If the therapist feels competent and comfortable in this area, there is no reason for him or her not to conduct treatment; if the therapist opts not to, he or she should be aware of professionals in the community to whom couples can be referred for sex therapy. (Therapists wishing to learn more about the practice of sex therapy will find a list of references and professional organizations in Chapter 15.)

Family Therapy

The relationship between couple therapy and family therapy is an ambiguous and contested one. Most, but not all, authorities consider couple therapy to be "a variant or subtype of family therapy" (Jacobson & Gurman, 1986, p. 2) in view of the systemic formulations and goals that organize both forms of treatment. Haley argues that a focus on the couple obscures "the structure in which the dyad functions" (1984, p. 8) while Nichols asserts that "most family therapy eventually becomes marital therapy, either in an informal, implicit sense or in a formal, explicit manner" (1988, p. 5). Child-focused problems often stem from difficulties in the parents' relationship. Some couples request couple therapy but the therapist identifies difficulties that involve children in one way or another, and may then want to recommend family therapy.

Indications

You should consider recommending family therapy when you become aware of problematic patterns not only in the couple relationship but also in relationships involving children. Such patterns might involve intense conflict between a parent and child or a "rigid triangle" (Minuchin, 1974) involving three family members (typically both parents, or parent and stepparent, and one child). You might observe extremely weak boundaries around the couple's relationship so that children are pulled into their difficulties in problematic ways—as displaced targets in the parents' conflict, as allies for one parent against the other, or merely as witnesses to frightening stormy battles.

Indications that one or more children are extremely enmeshed with a parent or that the family as a whole is so enmeshed that the children are discouraged from seeking friends outside the family would alert you to the need for involvement with the whole family. Obviously, patterns of physical or sexual abuse or neglect of children would require not only family therapy but, in most states, a mandated report to social services.

If you become aware of symptomatology in a child who is not receiving treatment, consider recommending family therapy, although in some cases, you might recommend individual treatment for the child instead. (This decision will depend largely on the experience and therapeutic convictions of the clinician involved; this is discussed below, under Considerations and Guidelines.) Such symptomatology might include signs of depression or dysphoria, extreme rebelliousness and delinquency, psychosomatic disorders, enuresis or encopresis, eating disorders, and social isolation, among others.

Contraindications

While not strictly a contraindication of family therapy, intense and uncontrollable conflict between the parents is a contraindication for *conjoint sessions* that involve parents and children together. There is nothing healing about a child watching his or her parents treat one another with hatred and contempt; nor does it inspire confidence in the therapist if he or she is unable to control such interactions. In cases such as this, if family therapy is indicated, you should probably meet with children *apart* from the parents, but only until the couple's conflict is sufficiently under control to ensure more productive family sessions.

Considerations and Guidelines

If you observe symptomatology in a child, one consideration involves whether to recommend family therapy or individual therapy for the child. As suggested earlier, this decision largely depends on the therapeutic convictions of the clinician. The case can and has been made for *both* family and individual therapy as the treatment of choice for a range of child-identified problems. Any treatment that involves a child should *always* include the parents in some manner. All problems involving children should be approached with an understanding of developmental processes, a willingness to consider the impact of family patterns, and a sense of ethical responsibility on your part to all members of the family who are significantly affected by your interventions.

If you recommend family therapy to a couple who requested couple therapy, you should make clear that the partners will not be expected to discuss intimate aspects of their relationship in the children's presence. Sessions with the couple *apart* from the children should either be included as part of the treatment package or, if necessary, deferred temporarily while more pressing child-focused problems are addressed in family sessions. A final consideration involves the fact that partners in a couple relationship are also the children of parents. Problematic triangles and intense conflicts may exist with parents as well as with children. In these cases, family sessions that include one or more parents, or siblings, of the partners may prove helpful to all involved.

Having developed a formulation of the couple's difficulties and decided on the form of treatment you will recommend, you are ready to consider how to present this material to your clients. The following chapter will discuss considerations and guidelines for designing the response that you will present to the couple in the final session of the evaluation.

⫷ 10 ⫸

DESIGNING THE
THERAPIST'S RESPONSE

THE THERAPIST'S RESPONSE to the couple weaves together observations, impressions, intuitions, and hunches into a narrative of the couple's experiences as he or she understands them. It organizes the information they have shared during the evaluation by highlighting certain themes and patterns, and suggests factors that have contributed to and maintain the difficulties they have identified. In most cases it also includes recommendations for treatment.

The response to the couple is based on the therapist's formulation but is not necessarily identical to it. The response is shaped by an effort to commmunicate the formulation in a way that is most likely to be *accessible* and *helpful* to the couple; this involves thinking about *what* to say (and what not to say) and *how* to say it. Designing the response means thinking about the themes and "frames" to be highlighted and the specific recommendations to be made. It may mean

205

omitting some parts of the formulation and emphasizing others. In short, the response is designed to tailor the formulation and recommendations to a particular couple. This chapter suggests guidelines for designing the therapist's response, and concludes with two case examples that illustrate these suggestions.

How the Response Works

The response is designed to *utilize* resources, to *harness* them to a credible view of the couple's difficulties and, in doing so, to *direct* the couple toward a means of alleviating those difficulties. These resources include the partners' *distress* or *pain* (which spurs them to action), their *optimism* or *hope* that their relationship can be changed and their *motivation* to do so, their *self-respect* (which makes them feel entitled to benefit from treatment) and their *trust* in the therapist's competence and his or her genuine wish to be of help to them. These resources are mobilized by a positive therapeutic alliance and by the therapist's formulation of their difficulties. The response is like a parabolic dish that gathers diffuse light rays and focuses them into a beam, which is more concentrated and powerful than the separate and unfocused rays.

The therapist hopes to present a view of the couple's problem(s) that is *credible* and *compelling*, that *enlists their cooperation*, and that *sets promising directions* for treatment. In other words, the response is designed to maximize therapeutic influence, to elicit cooperation, and to "set the trajectory of treatment." To do this, it should be respectful, hopeful (to the extent this is justified), empathic, and accessible to the individuals involved.

Increasing Credibility and Therapeutic Influence

The extent to which your response can contribute to individual and systemic change is directly related to how *plausible* and *convincing* it is to the clients; unless it *makes an impression* on the clients, its correctness is academic and its clinical utility nil. Whatever your theoretical orientation, whatever your particular conclusions and recommendations, in order to be clinically effective, your response must in some way capture the imagination of the clients (E. Strauss, personal communication). This is more likely to occur if you have listened closely and understood the partners' descriptions of their own experience (and been able to communicate this understanding to them); tried to utilize (or at least consider) their values, world view, use of language, definition of the problem, and goals for treatment; used clear, vivid language and metaphors; and conveyed your impressions and recommendations with conviction.

Securing Cooperation

You want your views of the couple's problems and your ideas about addressing them to be not only credible to the partners but acceptable as well. You hope that the response will encourage them to cooperate with the steps you are recommending. This spirit of cooperation is enhanced by an ongoing attitude of respect for the couple and an effort to balance your sympathies to both partners. Your ability to secure their cooperation also depends on the partners' confidence in your competence or expertise and their sense of your trustworthiness.

Setting the Trajectory of Treatment

Two different kinds of obstacles or pitfalls should be avoided: (1) unfortunate *decisions* about the directions treatment should take—namely, directions that disregard and clash with what you have learned about these particular clients, and (2) *conditions imposed by clients* which seem likely to be countertherapeutic. Examples of counterproductive decisions are

- applying direct pressure in ways that have failed repeatedly and therefore would be almost certain to do so again
- attempting to resolve a couple's most difficult and deeply polarized area of conflict at the very start of treatment—a time when this would be virtually certain to fail
- utilizing experiential techniques that are intolerably public for one or both partners
- recommending straightforward behavioral approaches for a couple who make clear that for them a good therapist must appreciate the deep psychoanalytic intricacy of their problems

This is not to say that you can never suggest such presumably unacceptable approaches to clients. If you recognize the difficulties these create with particular clients and can elicit their acceptance by addressing their discomfort in a convincing and reassuring way, so much the better. However, if you suggest these directions simply because you think they are *usually* helpful, *without considering* what the clients have already communicated about their particularity, the effort is more likely to fail.

Clients may try to impose conditions on treatment that would make failure more likely. They may have good intentions but be unaware of the negative impact of these conditions. In some cases, this may represent an effort to sabotage treatment. Such conditions might involve conducting couple therapy while one partner is actively involved in an extramarital affair, sharing secret information with the therapist and insisting that it not be revealed, or meeting so infrequently as to dilute any possible effectiveness of treatment. Be aware of these potential pitfalls and try to steer a course for treatment that avoids them.

Ann requested couple therapy for herself and her husband, Brian. She described a pattern of polite emotional estrangement for at least seven of the twenty years they had been married. There was simmering anger on Brian's part over Ann's long hours at work, and on Ann's part in relation to what she described as Brian's depression and pessimism about life. Brian had multiple sclerosis and had been treated with antidepressant medication over the previous five years. Ann admitted that she stayed late at work, saying that she avoided coming home because Brian was so withdrawn and negative. Brian admitted being pessimistic and depressed but pointed out how much he did in spite of this around the house and with the children as a way of helping Ann. He seemed to be asking to be spared demands for intimacy and a positive outlook on life but indicating his willingness to do things for Ann, even if this meant spending some more time together and talking more. Usually soft-spoken and polite, Brian seemed angrily defiant whenever Ann brought up his negative outlook on life. He made sarcastic comments about "positive thinking" and "feel-good" therapies.

I felt that I simply could not follow Ann's wishes that I somehow get Brian to change his outlook on life. It seemed clear that this would be met with internal contempt and active resistance and that I would be immediately discredited as another naive do-gooder. I did recommend couple therapy but strongly recommended against focusing on Brian's outlook on life. Instead, I suggested that we focus on what Brian could do for Ann since he indicated a willingness to discuss this. I emphasized that Brian needed and deserved to be completely in charge of what he did or didn't do about his outlook on life. Both partners accepted these terms. As it turned out, the couple made sig-

nificant progress in six sessions of couple therapy, with Brian demon-
strating that he was willing to be more available and active with Ann
and she was willing to come home earlier from work. Both were
encouraged by the willingness of the other to respond to their wishes.

Guidelines for Designing the Response

The following guidelines for designing the therapist's response can
help minimize or avoid obstacles and accomplish the goals outlined
above.

Respect

The therapist's response *must* convey an attitude of respect for both
partners. It is professionally unethical and contrary to the fundamental
premises of clinical work, as well as a form of abuse, to knowingly
treat clients with disrespect or contempt. Your comments should not
be delivered "from on high," that is, from a position of moral superiority. Ideally, you should conduct yourself, during the course of the evaluation and in your response to the couple, in such a way as to communicate a recognition that you are made of the same stuff they are.
Hopefully, you recognize some of your own imperfections and realize
that trying to appear "perfect" to the couple will only shame or alienate
them. Your behavior communicates that, starting from a position of
healthy self-respect, it is easy to extend respect to them.

Resources

This attitude of respect can be conveyed in part by being explicit about
the strengths or resources you recognize in each of the partners and in
their relationship. This does not require a long list of every positive
attribute you have noticed, but instead some effort to make them
aware that you see some of "what they have going for them." You may
focus on what they present as their most important strengths, identify
a resource that has previously been "invisible" to them, or reframe a
problem in a more positive way. By doing so, you make clear that you
have not allowed their difficulties to obscure their strengths, that you
do not see them as bereft of good qualities, and that you are not invested in feeling superior to them. *Some reference to personal or rela-*
tional resources should be included in the therapist's response to ev-
ery couple at the conclusion of the evaluation.

Empathy and Balance

The couple should feel that you can—or at least want to—empathize with them. They should have the sense that you understand how they feel about what is important to them or, if not, that you are dedicated to trying to do so. The therapist's response represents an important opportunity for you to convey this empathy.

As discussed earlier in the book, it is important to maintain balanced siding with both partners throughout the evaluation, and this is especially important in the response to the couple as its conclusion. The partners will be highly attuned to signals about how you see them, how you feel about them, and whether or not you blame one or both of them for the difficulties they have presented. The balance of sympathies that has hopefully characterized your interactions with them throughout the evaluation should be preserved at its conclusion.

Remember to express sympathy for the dilemmas or painful situations in which the partners find themselves. If you point to a specific way in which one partner contributes to their problematic interactions, try to balance this—either by noting a contribution of the other partner's as well or by sympathizing with the first partner's experience in some way. In contextual terms, this means trying to hold both partners accountable for their actions and to acknowledge their entitlement as well.* By the end of the response, both partners should feel that you have tried to hear and understand them and extended a sympathetic interest to both of them.

Accessibility

Unless specifically contraindicated in a particular case, therapists should strive to use language that is clear, direct, and conversational rather than obscure, jargon-filled, and esoteric. For example, when I talk to couples about their relational profiles and unconscious object choice, I rarely use these terms. I'll talk instead about "mix-ups," explaining that I think there is some confusion about what's going on

---

*This does *not*, however, imply that the therapist must convey neatly balanced views in all cases; an exception would be when domestic violence has occurred. If one partner has hit or abused the other, the abusive partner *must* be held accountable by the therapist for his actions. You might nonetheless express sympathy for his suffering—for example, if he was beaten as a child— but you would not condone or excuse his own use of violence. Similarly, you would not dilute his accountability with "systemic" interpretations that suggest that the other partner shares responsibility for her abuse.

within each of them and what's going on *between* them. The term "mix-ups" refers to the complexities of transference and projective identification in a simple and accessible way and becomes a useful shorthand for the remainder of the evaluation. I may refer to the partners' particular vulnerabilities and defenses in their relationship as "allergies," as in, "I think you have an 'emotional allergy' for being left alone." Your response to the couple should be couched in language they can understand.

Utilization

Whenever possible, utilize the partners' goals for treatment, their values and worldview, and their definition of the problem. Direct your response to what is most important and most pressing to them. The closer you can remain to their experience, the more likely that they will be able to assimilate and accept your impressions and recommendations. These efforts harness their concerns to the explanation(s) and recommendation(s) you offer, making the response more accessible and, hopefully, acceptable to them.

Specificity

To be credible and compelling, your response needs to be more than just an assemblage of vague assertions and global theoretical concepts. You should be able to refer to information shared during the course of the evaluation in order to buttress the conclusions you present to the couple. Specificity bolsters credibility.

Present Problem-Focus/Solution-Focus

Your response to the couple should focus on the specific current problems *they* identify. This is respectful and it helps to secure cooperation. Remember that the couple is ultimately looking for "results"—for relief, change, less conflict, more intimacy, or a clearer definition of the relationship. If you believe that their current problems are significantly influenced by less immediate factors, such as difficulties in early attachment, lack of differentiation of self, or gender politics (and if you deem it helpful to discuss this with them), you must help them see the relevance of these constructs to their difficulties and, hopefully, to potential solutions. The most complex and sophisticated theory is of little use unless it suggests possible solutions to their problems. A focus on present problems and their solutions grounds your response to the couple's immediate concerns and goals.

Brevity

Try not to overwhelm the couple with so many observations, hunches, formulations, and dynamics that they have difficulty processing the response and lose focus on its major points. Here, as earlier during the evaluation, you must edit. You must *select* the most important and compelling points and omit others, at least for the time being. Remembering the major goals of the response will help with this editing process. What do you need to say in order to present a compelling rationale for the recommendations you are making? If the partners are highly motivated, the problems fairly obvious, and the views of the therapist and couple essentially in synch, there may be very little that needs to be said beyond reiterating the shared definition of the problem, commenting on resources evident in the relationship, recommending couple therapy, and raising some thoughts about where to start or how to sequence the work. When there are sharper differences, either between the couple and the therapist or between the partners themselves, in the definition of the problem, goals or treatment preferences, the therapist's response will necessarily be more elaborate. However, the effort to edit in order to highlight major points is still worthwhile.

Vivid and Resonant Imagery

If possible, use language and imagery that is vivid and resonant. If your empathic connection with the partners is strong, the images you choose will have deeper emotional meaning for them. This will increase their sense of having been understood and strengthen therapeutic alliances. The individuals' responses to these images or phrases may be a deeply felt sense of "rightness" or a shock of recognition.

Lisa and Glen described repeated conflicts in which Lisa's desperate attempts to elicit closeness triggered Glen's exasperated criticism and infuriated withdrawal. Lisa had been emotionally shut out as a child by her mother, so much so that her mother refused to speak a word to her for one full year when she was eleven years old. This was a punishment for her siding with her sister when the latter had an argument with mother. Glen had been devastated by his first wife's infidelity and subsequent contempt during and after their divorce. In my response to the couple, I used the image of an abandoned child, who more than anything needed to be held, and a man with second-degree burns over most of his body.

Joyce complained bitterly at what she experienced as her husband's neglect of her in social situations and in relation to his children from his first marriage. She also saw him as competitive with her. She said at one point, "When we're together, he gets strokes and I don't." While I could see some justification for these feelings, they seemed to be greatly exaggerated. Her family of origin included an older brother of whom she said, "He always got strokes, and I got nothing." Her mother adored the brother and, in her experience, largely took her for granted. This discrepancy was compounded in her family by traditional gender roles; it was assumed that her brother would go through college but no finances for college were set aside for her, even though she was extremely bright and later received a doctorate and became a full professor. In thinking about this couple, and this woman in particular, I found myself coming back again and again to the phrases, "a Nobody" and "a Somebody." In my response to the couple, I used these phrases to express my sense of Joyce's experience. She seemed shocked and cried, with what felt like gratitude, revealing that as a young girl, Emily Dickinson's poem, "I'm Nobody" had been the touchstone of her sense of self.

Optimism and Realism

The enterprise of therapy, whether for individuals, couples, or families, is meaningless without hope. Clients come for treatment because they are troubled by their current situation and hope for a better one. You owe it to them to be aware of these hopes and, whenever possible, to foster and encourage them. Ideally, you can convey optimism in relation to their goals for treatment. Even when this is impossible—for example, when one partner wants to improve their relationship but the other is determined to leave it—you should try to identify what they *can* be hopeful about, for example, the possibility of understanding what went wrong in this relationship through individual therapy or a better relationship with a different partner. You owe it to clients to focus on optimism wherever it is justified; to do otherwise is to rob them of hope.

At the same time, your response should be realistic. It should not encourage extravagant hopes in the absence of any evidence that they are merited. Many couples present therapists with relationships in which both partners' hopes *cannot* be met—a sad but important fact about couple therapy. Most of the time, clients appreciate realism in a therapist, as long as it is expressed with compassion.

"Can't Say" and "Must Say" Considerations

In order to design a response that will most likely be acceptable to the couple, secure their cooperation, and set promising directions for treatment, two questions should be considered: What *can* I say to them? and What *must* I say to them? If you present your formulation and treatment recommendations in, as it were, unvarnished form— *without* considering what the clients have communicated to you about their needs, anxieties, defenses, and expectations regarding treatment—you run the risk of "missing" or even alienating them.

What Can I Say? This question derives from the recognition that what you think is going on is not always going to be acceptable and therefore helpful to every couple. Either explicitly or by implication, one or both partners may have communicated to you during the course of the evaluation that certain ways of looking at the problem will be forcefully rejected by them. Therapy is only helpful when clients give the therapist *permission*—permission to see and to point out what they don't see, permission to challenge cherished but unhelpful notions, permission to recommend changes in how they relate to one another. Throughout the evaluation and especially at its conclusion, you must consider not only what *you think* but what *they can hear*. You establish trust (and, with it, permission) by respecting what clients reveal to you about what they can and cannot accept at that moment in time. This may involve specific recommendations or highly emotionally charged topics within the relationship, or both.

⟍   *Rosemary and Vic requested evaluation on referral from a former couple therapist. They had seen that therapist for just under one year; all three felt that they had not made progress. Their presenting problems included intractable arguments and very little intimacy. Their arguments were frequent and intense, with no real repair, punctuated by periods by uneasy truce and very rare times of mutual enjoyment. Both stated that their sessions with the former therapist were unhelpful, saying that, if anything, they may have made things worse. It was clear from them and from conversations with the therapist that he had tried to build trust by encouraging them to curtail destructive and demeaning behavior and to listen to one another's complaints and feelings. Their experience of this, as presented to me in the first meeting, was that he was "telling us to fake it, to be nice to each other." The tone in which this assessment was delivered left no doubt that this was seen as naive and simplistic.*
    I felt that to suggest a compliance-based approach to this couple would lead them to dismiss and reject this treatment as they had the prior one. I decided to emphasize "deeper forces" in their relationship as the primary obstacles to intimacy and to utilize a defiance-based

approach to treatment (see Chapter 9 for discussion of defiance-based approaches).

In some cases, you have virtually no choice but to address these "off limits" issues in spite of the risks. For example, when there are indications of possible physical or sexual abuse of children, you *must* take action to protect the children regardless of how this affects therapeutic alliances with the couple. With a couple in which one partner is clearly alcoholic and in denial, you may not be able to address their situation without raising the issue of drinking. In other cases, however, what seems likely to be unacceptable to client(s) may not be a "make-or-break" issue; in these cases, you would be wise not to address this focus directly in your response to the couple. You can, however, still take it into consideration and make decisions that are informed by it.

What Must I Say? The second question turns your attention to the major issues the clients have raised. It provides a way to show them you have heard and understood what is most important to them. This might involve a husband's fears that you will, like a former therapist, recommend medication and nothing more. It may relate to a couple's primary question of whether or not they should stay together. In your response to the couple, you must indicate that you recognize the urgency of these concerns for them. You needn't have something brilliant to say about them and, if they involve problems or dilemmas, you needn't try to solve them. You *do* need to let the clients know that you have heard them and, if treatment is to follow, will continue to be mindful of them.

One case involved a woman's strenuous insistence on PMS as the major factor in her irritability toward her husband. I felt that there were significant unresolved conflicts between the spouses as well as unidentified anger on her part stemming from problematic relationships in her family of origin. However, it was important to address her concern as part of the response, indicating that it had been heard and was being taken seriously; I encouraged her to consult her physician and to let both her husband and myself know what had been discussed as soon as possible.

A couple presented with an eight-year history of explosive arguments and impulsive separations. Both agreed, however, that as one of them said, "This is the longest and the best relationship I've ever had and I don't want to lose it." For a therapist to respond only to the level of pathology in this case without indicating that he or she has heard how valuable the relationship is to both of them would be a serious error.

One case in which "can't say" and "must say" considerations clashed involved a husband, Tony, whose long-term intensive individual therapy was strongly criticized by his wife, Eve. She complained of its cost, the lack of results she saw (especially in their relationship), the frequency with which he avoided family or marital activities claiming exhaustion or upset related to what he was working through in treatment and, most importantly, the ways in which she felt totally shut out from this treatment. Tony, meanwhile, was deeply committed to the treatment and defended it as a lifeline and an arena in which he felt proud of his struggle and growth. To ally with the husband, I had to endorse the individual therapy; however, if I left it at that, I would almost certainly lose the wife. Avoiding the issue altogether would be pointless since one of them would certainly have demanded to know the therapist's position.

I chose to address the issue and to test whether they could tolerate my balancing of sympathies. It seemed to me, I said, that Tony had been moving in the right directions in his treatment, that it had taken courage and commitment to persevere with it and, using examples he had given, that there had already been progress. I added, however, that I thought Eve's view of the therapy was in some ways correct. It may have helped him but it seemed to have done so at some cost to the marriage, given how totally it absorbed his energies. I offered to look for ways in which couple therapy might serve as a bridge, to apply the insights derived from his therapy toward positive change in their relationship. This stance obviously didn't satisfy either partner totally but it communicated to both that I had heard their sides of the issue, and it reassured by its effort to represent the interests of the relationship. If, in a sense, it glossed over the conflict with the lulling but vague notion of couple therapy as a bridge, they were nevertheless sufficiently mollified and reassured, and found this acceptable.

A Final Note: Ambiguity and Certainty

As noted in the previous chapter, you cannot be expected to be omniscient. A good-enough couple evaluation does not require you to understand everything about a couple's difficulties or to feel certain about what to do about them. There is nothing wrong with acknowledging puzzlement when this is what you experience at the conclusion of the evaluation. (In some cases, your puzzlement may reflect important omissions in what they have presented to you and your expression of puzzlement may prompt subsequent disclosure.) As suggested earlier, even when you are puzzled or uncertain, your observations may catalyze new insights and your response may be helpful if it asks the right questions—even if it cannot answer them.

Two Cases

In order to illustrate some of the considerations discussed above, two cases are presented here, including summaries of the response provided at the end of each evaluation. One illustrates a relatively straightforward case, with a recommendation for couple therapy. The second calls for more complicated efforts to "set the trajectory" of treatment.*

Lori and Neal are both in their late 30s. They have been married for 15 years and have a seven-year-old son named Mark. Over the telephone, Lori says that they have "drifted apart" and "want to figure out how to be connected in a better way." In the initial couple session, Lori explains that they always disagree about how to do things and that she doesn't feel they have much in common anymore. Neal agrees, saying that he feels distant from Lori and that they have different interests. They see very little of each other because their work schedules are so different. Lori runs her own small travel business; Neal works nights as a lab tech in a local hospital. When they first met in the 1960s, both identified with the counterculture; they have retained the style, and many of the values, of that social group. Lori is outwardly more emotional; Neal is reserved but surprisingly comfortable expressing feelings.

They married soon after graduating college. They were planning to move in together without marrying but Lori's parents were so opposed to this that they agreed to "make it official." In retrospect, they both feel that it was a mistake to marry before they really felt ready. However, neither indicate that they regret choosing the other for a partner. They had a major argument on their honeymoon and both took off their wedding rings. They have kept them but neither has worn theirs

---

*This second case originally appeared in Karpel, 1986. Reprinted by permission of The Guilford Press.

since that time (this detail, while noteworthy, is somewhat less meaningful than it might otherwise be for a more traditional couple).

They trace their current conflicts to the birth of their son, agreeing that the period after his birth was "horrendous." They describe some fights before then but say that these never seemed as serious. Mark was born prematurely; there were medical complications which required frequent visits to the pediatrician and constant attention at home. He was colicky and both partners were seriously sleep-deprived for the first year after his birth. They fought often over responsibilities for Mark's care and for household chores as well.

Their conflicts have a predictable pattern. Lori complains about not getting enough help from Neal who becomes angry and either withdraws or justifies his actions. Lori becomes angry and, in her words, "verbally abusive." The conflict escalates verbally until Lori breaks contact by leaving the room. At these times, she feels that she needs to be left alone "to cool off" but Neal pursues her and winds up pushing her to greater anger. There is no history of physical violence between them. Neal also admits that he sometimes "teases" Lori which always makes her angry. "Blow outs" such as these would be followed by their making up with one another. Lori notes that more recently, the conflict ends in a kind of "uneasy truce" but is not followed by emotional repair. This change has worried both of them and—together with the fact that Lori found herself seriously thinking of leaving Neal—prompted their request for treatment.

Their sexual relationship has suffered, with Lori often feeling uninterested in sex. Neal feels that he has to "jump hurdles" for them to have sex, although both agree that, while initiation and frequency are problematic, when they do have sex, they enjoy themselves. Asked about the best parts of their relationship, Neal says, "She's changed me a lot, and for the better. I'm less quiet and more assertive. We don't do much together anymore but I enjoy doing things with her." Lori says, "He's fun. I like his sense of humor and, when we had more interests in common, I liked doing things with him." Neal says that Lori is "dependable," and that this is very important to him. Lori agrees that Neal is as well. Asked about their goals for treatment, both express a desire to feel closer to each other and to be better able to negotiate differences without their characteristic patterns of conflict.

In Lori's individual session, I learn that she is the oldest of four children. Her father is a "very difficult" man who was unsuccessful in business and suffered major depressions during her childhood. He became increasingly alcoholic and was at times violent with her, her siblings, and her mother. Her mother was "also probably depressed" and overwhelmed by her husband's difficulties and the demands of caring for four children. Lori did not feel close to her mother and couldn't talk to her about personal problems. If anything, she felt a need to protect her mother from her father's anger and the children's demands. Lori was given responsibility for her younger siblings and for a significant amount of housework. Her worst feeling, growing up, was "knowing that I had to do everything by myself, with no support from anyone else." Asked how she feels toward Neal, she says, "I think I love him but I'm all confused. I feel like we're so dysfunctional, and it's always my job to be the 'whistle-blower.'" Her sexual feelings toward Neal "come and go."

In Neal's individual session, he describes his parents' marriage as "terrible," characterized by either "verbal abuse or a total cutoff." Both of his parents are living. He describes his mother as quiet and "fragile." He says that he loves her and knows that she loves him. While he remembers idolizing his father when he was quite young, he grew to be afraid of him and then deeply angry at him. His father, he says, was extremely negative and critical of him. He had a bad temper and was a very strict disciplinarian. Their relationship settled into "a constant battle," which included physical abuse on his father's part. Neal adopted a defiant position with his father; unlike the other children (he has two older siblings), he would not "back down" in confrontations with him. He is aware that at times he provoked his father and wonders if this was to "get back at him." Otherwise, he describes himself as a shy and quiet boy with lots of friends who loved the outdoors. Asked about feelings toward Lori, he says, "I love her although I often don't like her." He says he is angry at her some but not all of the time and is still sexually attracted to her.

Before the final session of the evaluation, I spoke with a therapist who had provided child therapy for Mark and had seen the couple in this context about one year before they contacted me. In summarizing his work with them, he described the couple as "very responsive" as clients; he felt that they listened to what he had to say and consistently took action based on their joint discussions.

The following is a summary of the response I delivered to Lori and Neal in the final session of the evaluation.

"Let me share some of my impressions and thoughts about what you've presented to me over the last three meetings. The first thing I want to comment on are the resources I see in this relationship. You both describe the other person as 'dependable' and you made it clear that this means a lot to you. You have a shared sense of humor, in spite of your difficulties, which provides an enjoyable connection for both of you. It feels pretty good to sit together with the two of you, and this is not always the case. You are able to express positive feel-ings for each other, along with negative ones, and you both have positive feelings for the other's family as well. So, I want to start by emphasizing that, compared to many couples I've seen, this relation-ship has a lot going for it. Also, Mark's therapist tells me that he feels you made excellent use of that treatment, so we have a promising indicator about whether this treatment might be of help for you." **[This begins the response with a resource focus in order to convey respect and appreciation for their strengths and to build optimism for treatment.]**

"But that doesn't mean that I don't see the seriousness of the prob-lems you've discussed. I understand that both of you feel very distant and, often, disconnected from each other and that the conflicts you've described are bruising and exhausting. Neither of you feel that you get much credit for the things you do." **[Moves the response to a present problem focus in order to balance the emphasis on resources. I want to be sure that they understand that I am not looking at the relation-ship "through rose-colored glasses" and missing how painful it is to them.]**

"So, what kinds of factors are involved in causing and continuing the problems you've described? First, we need to consider some of the facts that have shaped the relationship. The fact that you got married when you did to placate Lori's parents pushed you together sooner and more profoundly than you were ready for at the time. I don't think that this is a major factor but it may have made both of you feel less wholehearted about the relationship than if the circumstances had been different. In any case, it's clear that problems became seri-ous with Mark's birth. The birth of the first child is always stressful for couples but, in your case, it was much more so because of the various medical complications you've described to me. This imposed enormous stresses on your relationship. It's at this time that the two of you become locked in an ongoing power struggle." **[Acknowledges the actual predictable and unpredictable stresses they have faced, thus normalizing their difficulties and emphasizing a framework of active coping rather than static pathology. It begins to address the central impasse of the relationship by referring to it as a power struggle.]**

"I think that the frustrations and resentments associated with this power struggle have led both of you to become more disengaged from one another. This is a common progression for couples. The fact that your arguments more recently don't lead to some form of repair is and should be worrisome. It is a warning sign that, unless you make changes in the relationship now, you may become more profoundly alienated from one another." **[Attempts to build motivation for treat-ment by highlighting the risks of ignoring current difficulties.]**

"However, I don't think that this struggle is simply a response to stress. I think it has a lot to do with what I'll call 'emotional allergies,' which each of you brought into this relationship and which make closeness and shared problem-solving difficult. For you, Neal, I think of it as an allergy to criticism, which has everything to do with your relationship with your father. The feeling you had with him was that you 'can't do anything right.' When Lori is critical or complaining, I think it triggers the same feelings you had when you were locked in conflict with your father. The response you developed to those situations is exactly the one that comes out with Lori—defiance. You resist, and, just as with your father, you even provoke anger. You do this when you pursue Lori when she is angry with you and, I think, when you tease her which, as you say, you know she hates.

"Lori, I think your allergy is to feeling taken for granted and overlooked. It's the feeling you described in your own family with the phrase, 'I have to do everything.' It means that you get no support and no help, that there isn't even anyone who realizes that you're trying to take care of everyone else, and no one's taking care of you. It makes you feel hopeless and angry at the same time. It makes it more likely that instead of asking Neal for what you want and hoping that you might get it, you won't even bother to ask but will feel your resentment build and at some point, to use your phrase, act 'abusive' to him.

"It's not hard to see how each of these allergies triggers the other. The more taken-for-granted you feel, Lori, the more likely you'll criticize Neal. The more you feel that you 'can't do anything right,' Neal, the more likely you'll resist Lori, making her feel even more angry and hopeless about getting her needs met." [**Identifies the ingredients of the central impasse and defines the problem as interactional. This part starts with sympathy for each partner's experiences in their families of origins and identifies these experiences as, in a sense, the "culprits" in their current difficulties. It suggests that the unconscious operation of these relational experiences is responsible for their inability to coordinate coping, to get their needs met and to feel intimate with one another.**]

"I think things have been made worse recently by both of you, in a sense, giving yourselves 'license' to act in ways that are harmful to the relationship: Lori, by what you call 'verbal abuse' and, Neal, by 'teasing.' It's also striking how little the two of you see of each other given your work schedules. I think you both know that you can't starve a relationship and still expect it to be healthy." [**After sympathizing with each partner's experience, I try to also hold them accountable for how they treat one another.**]

"In order to change this, one or both of you would have to be able to change your part of this interactional sequence. At the risk of oversimplification, I'd say that, Lori, you need to try to be more clear about what you need from Neal and to ask for it, not by criticizing but by appealing to his caring for you and his investment in the relationship. Understanding Neal's allergy to criticism, you need to help him see that you are not his father. Neal, you need to decide which requests of Lori's you feel are reasonable and follow through on them. If you feel that they are not reasonable or possible, you need to discuss this with Lori and to appeal to her caring about you. Understanding her allergy, you need to help her see that you do not want to take her for granted and ignore her needs." *[Identifies alternatives to the couple's problematic patterns in an effort to increase optimism that change is possible, to direct them to the changes that seem most likely to yield positive results, and to highlight the importance of individual responsibility for change, both in and outside of therapy.]*

"So, I would recommend that you continue in couple therapy. I'd suggest that we meet for six sessions and, at the end of that time, discuss whether we feel that the sessions are helping. If we feel that they are, we can continue with further sessions at that point." *[The proposal of a time-limited trial period for treatment underscores an emphasis on results and allows them to make a limited commitment to treatment rather than an open-ended one.]*

"We'd focus on what goes on between the two of you and, particularly, on whether it's possible to change these patterns in the directions I've just indicated. This gives us a way to test whether each of you is willing to try to improve things. If you are, I think you can side-step the allergies that have made your interactions so unsatisfying and rebuild trust at the same time." *[Indicates that treatment will be solution-focused, emphasizes the notion of testing resources, and alludes to the connections between action and trust.]*

"To whatever extent it is possible, I'd encourage you both to forego the license you've given yourselves to act destructively with each other; stopping behaviors that you know hurt or anger the other is a powerful way to demonstrate that you are interested in responding to their feelings and willing to do something about it." *[Encourages immediate action in order to begin restoring trust but does so in a qualified way—"to whatever extent it is possible"—recognizing the difficulty they may encounter in this effort and minimizing the danger that they will feel that they are "failing" treatment if they cannot do so at this point.]*

"I'd recommend that you at least think about when you can spend some time together, even if it's just 15 minutes on a weekday when you're both home at the same time or some other block of time on a weekend. You don't need to actually do anything about it at this point

*but at least think about it." [**Again, this directs them to immediate
actions they can take to restore closeness and trust without implying
that they should and must be able to do so at this point.**]*

"I'd also recommend that you think about your wedding rings, specifically about what you could do with them at this point that would
feel right if the relationship was more satisfying. Again, I'm not suggesting that you do anything about this at this point, just that you think
about it a bit." [**This last comment utilizes the ambiguous status of their
wedding rings as a means of concretizing, or metaphorically representing, their commitment to one another and their feelings about the relationship. It introduces the possibility of using the rings to represent
positive change in the relationship. If this occurs, it will constitute a
kind of ritual that can both symbolize and further positive change.
Again, there is encouragement without immediate pressure.**]*

Both partners said they felt understood and encouraged by this
response. They were able to use the remainder of the final session to
work out an arrangement in which Neal agreed to bring Mark to
skiing lessons on weekends, which had formerly been Lori's responsibility, in order to give her a few hours to herself. Neal emphasized
that he didn't mind doing this and that what made a real difference
for him was that Lori was asking him instead of complaining and
criticizing. This small exchange put into action most of the ingredients I had identified earlier, in my response to the couple, as desirable
in an effort to avoid power struggles and restore trust. It represented a
first step in the effort to establish trust and closeness in their relationship.

A couple in their late 30s request couple therapy. The presenting problem is their failure to conceive a child. Rachel became
pregnant one year earlier but the child was stillborn. Since then they
had been unable to conceive. There are no diagnosed medical problems; Rachel feels however that the tension in their relationship and
Walter's subsequent avoidance of sexual relations clearly make things
more difficult.

Although Walter complains about Rachel being unrealistically romantic, both partners agree that Walter is the problem. They present
themselves as a conventional, old-fashioned couple. Walter is the
boss; he does little around the house, although both work full-time.
He is critical of Rachel, frequently irritable, and occasionally demeaning in his frustrated outbursts. Rachel resents this treatment but
has great difficulty standing up for herself. She feels that she doesn't
know how to fight back and usually withdraws instead when she is

angry with him. Although she makes her unhappiness known, she also makes clear that she would not consider leaving Walter. She tries to get him to help out more, to take her less for granted, all with no sign of success. Walter freely admits that "the biggest problem is my inability to show affection," along with his automatic resistance to doing anything she asks of him. In discussing goals, both wish that he could be more affectionate and more cooperative but convey their pessimism about this really changing.

What this description fails to convey is my immediate impression of two likable, lively, playful, caring people. They had found one another, relatively late in life, she after years of living alone and he after his first wife left him. I felt that, in spite of his inability to show it, Walter was deeply attached to Rachel. Clearly, both had been traumatized by the loss of their child; Walter said that he wanted a child but was terrified that, if Rachel lost another, she would completely fall apart. He also admitted that his first wife's infidelity had devastated him and had made him more mistrustful. An only child, Walter saw his mother as critical, domineering, and "degrading" toward his father who "just took it," staying with her "out of duty." His mother was also agoraphobic and on occasion would develop somatic symptoms, apparently to avoid uncomfortable social situations.

In meeting with this couple, I was struck by how resistant Walter was to any request from Rachel and how blithely he admitted that he was the problem. For a different couple, this might have indicated that he was indifferent to his partner and unmotivated for change. However, Walter seemed to genuinely care for Rachel and very much wanted to stay married to her. The unfairness of give-and-take between them seemed to be more related to Walter's determination not to be abused and controlled (as he felt his father had been), Rachel's difficulty standing up for herself, and unexamined gender roles in their relationship. Their mutual caring and commitment to the relationship constituted resources that made me feel guardedly optimistic about the prospects for change.

However, I anticipated that Walter's reflexive resistance would constitute a significant obstacle in treatment. The complete lack of success of Rachel's efforts to encourage Walter to change and his blithe admission of his problems suggested that my trying to get him to change in therapy would probably be equally unsuccessful. Walter clearly expected that I would join Rachel in exhorting him to try harder to change; this would allow him to resist as casually as he had in the past while resting comfortably in the reassurance that not one but two other parties were now struggling to make the marriage work. Instead, I felt that therapy had to create a context in which direct pressure could be transformed into indirect pressure. This would be accomplished by challenging *Walter with a defiance-based approach* and separately coaching *Rachel to be more assertive and to apply indirect pressure at home*. At the end of the evaluation, I shared my response:

"You've both specified the changes you would like to see in Walter but you have both expressed pessimism about any of these changes happening. I think you are right. These changes will not happen. Not because Walter is selfish or anything like that. He doesn't mean for it to be like this or want it to be like this but there isn't a damn thing he can do about it. It seems to me that Walter has learned two very powerful lessons in his life, more powerful even than what you mean to him, Rachel. First, he's learned what a woman can do to a man if he lets her take control. He learned this mostly from his parents and then had it reinforced in his first marriage. The lesson is that if you give in to them, in any way—with your feelings, by helping around the house, whatever—they'll take over. When you've learned a lesson like that, you can't separate a woman's reasonable, harmless requests from DISAS-TER. I think I know what you are both feeling. How unfair it seems that a lesson learned so long ago should be carried into this relationship and cause so much conflict. But that's how it is and there is nothing we can do about it. Some people spend their whole lives living out these lessons. It's clearly not Walter's fault that he learned this lesson, but there it is, nevertheless." **[Instead of trying to get Walter to change, I am telling him that I don't think he can. In doing so, I am challenging him and hoping that he will prove me wrong. Explanations of why he can't change are included to dilute any sense of criticism or blame and to provide a plausible explanation for this "condition."]**

"I said there were two lessons. The second, which I think he learned from his mother, is: Avoid what you fear. That's what she did. She avoided the outside world, which she feared. Walter avoids what he fears, which is women. Not women per se, not a one-night stand or a casual relationship, but real closeness with a woman, because of Lesson One. So, as much as he can when he's married, he avoids this closeness. And, again, there is nothing he can do about this. Rachel, you asked if you were expecting too much. From Walter, yes, much too much." **[This adds further indirect pressure by comparing Walter to his mother, a comparison that appears to be merited but which I expect him to want to prove wrong.]**

"So what's to be done? The first and hardest lesson for you, Rachel, is to recognize that you can do nothing about changing Walter. You have to give up totally on being able to change him. But it is not all hopeless. Sometimes just facing these things can help and you could *use some help in learning how to accept Walter as he is."* **[I encourage Rachel to give up on trying to change Walter through direct pressure because this clearly does not work. This sets the stage for coaching her on how to apply indirect pressure. My work with Rachel is framed as "learning to live with Walter as he is." In fact, it will encourage her to act more effectively in her own interests. Rachel's unwillingness to leave the relationship allows us to address these goals without having to give Walter an ultimatum.]**

I recommended that Rachel come in by herself weekly with this goal in mind, and that Walter come in once a month, not to change anything, but just to "get an update" and "keep in touch." Walter was warned that he might not like Rachel's really giving up on him but he'd just have to accept it anyway. **[Separate sessions will make it much easier to pursue these different modes of treatment with each of the partners individually. Walter is encouraged to return but his sessions are not framed as therapy (why would I recommend treatment for someone who "can't change"?). In fact, these sessions will allow me to continue utilizing a defiance-based approach. The warning that he may not like Rachel giving up on him signals that not changing may not be as comfortable as he had imagined it.]** Walter was, as I had hoped, taken aback by my description of his hopeless condition and expressed reservations about whether he agreed to that extent. When given a choice of two appointment times for his first individual session, he chose the earlier of the two, indicating greater engagement in the process.

In Rachel's first individual session, I encouraged her not to ask anything of Walter and not to fight about his behavior but to refuse to be treated disrespectfully and to "transform requests into regrets." So, for example, instead of nagging Walter to pick his clothes up off the floor, she would say, "For a moment there I was going to nag you about your clothes on the floor but then I remembered what the therapist said and I know I can't change you." These statements would be delivered with an air of sadness and stoical emotional resignation. She later noted a couple of instances in which she had applied this approach: When Walter, whose one household responsibility was to do dishes, blithely left them for her, she deliberately did not make him a lunch for work as was usual. When he angrily demanded to know why, she said, "I don't make lunches for guys who don't do dishes." When Walter's aggressive and dangerous driving (about which Rachel had complained for years) upset her one day, she quietly asked him to pull to the side of the road. She got out without a word and walked the rest of the way home, ignoring his demands and then pleas for her to return to the car. If he had been behaving badly *and later asked what was wrong, she'd say, "You know and I know and there's nothing we can do about it."*

It should be noted that there wasn't an explicit alliance between Rachel and myself to try to change Walter. This might well have diminished the impact of my response to the couple and endangered their effectiveness if Walter realized this. Rachel seemed to sense that I was "up to something" other than resignation on her part but she did not press this and I at no time indicated that our goal was any different than the one on which we had agreed.

I saw the partners separately for a total of 12 sessions following the evaluation. Six weeks after the end of the evaluation, Rachel reported that she was pregnant. Walter was now cooking and washing; his critical behavior was all but gone and, when it occurred, he apologized spontaneously. Both described pleasure at the changes in their relationship.

This case illustrates the importance of "setting the trajectory of treatment." Efforts to proceed in a straightforward way, with compliance-based couple therapy, would almost certainly have failed. Walter would most likely have resisted a therapist's efforts to change his behavior as he resisted those of his wife. Instead, a direction was chosen which side-stepped his resistance. In effect, this established a therapy that moved forward on two tracks: compliance-based treatment for Rachel and defiance-based treatment for Walter. Separate individual sessions maximized what could be accomplished on these two tracks.

It is important to note that this approach could only succeed in the context of significant resources and particular conditions. Rachel made clear that she had no intention of leaving Walter, which gave us the freedom to work on "accepting Walter as he is." She had enough healthy self-respect that she could implement an approach that involved setting limits on Walter. And, perhaps most importantly, Walter clearly loved and needed Rachel. When it became clear that she would no longer accept his poor treatment and continue to struggle to make the relationship work, he was able to change his own behavior and become a more considerate and loving partner.

By this point in the evaluation, you have not only developed your formulation and decided on treatment recommendations; you have also shaped and edited these conclusions into a response that you hope will be persuasive and acceptable to the partners and will enlist their cooperation for treatment. You are ready to turn your attention to the conduct of the final session itself.

☞ 11 ☜

CONDUCTING THE
FINAL SESSION

IN THE FINAL SESSION, the therapist responds to what has transpired over the course of the evaluation. This brings together information gathered from the couple (and from collateral contacts), observations, impressions, and intuitions, and the knowledge derived from his or her own professional experience. Together, these are shaped into a response to the couple that meets and addresses their concerns. This is where the therapist most actively fulfills the role of consultant to the couple on the nature of their difficulties and the most promising directions for treatment. Guidelines for conducting this session begin with a consideration of what the therapist and the couple hope to accomplish in it.

Agendas for the Final Session

The therapist's agenda for the final session is:

1. *Preserve* the sense of *safety* and *trust* that have been established up to this point.
2. Summarize impressions and recommendations for the couple.
3. Help the couple experience a sense of *closure* to the evaluation.
4. Facilitate a smooth *transition* to treatment (if treatment is recommended).

Preserve Safety and Trust

The final session of the evaluation marks a significant departure from those that have preceded it. Up to this point, you have largely been observing and eliciting information; in this session, you actively share your views of the couple's difficulties and of their relationship as a whole. This is also the end of the evaluation. The contract established between you and the couple up to this point "expires" at the conclusion of this session; the question on everyone's mind is: Now what? Both factors pose potential threats to the sense of safety that has been established up to this point.

Even though the couple's contact with you has been brief, the final session is still a termination of sorts. They may wonder whether or not you will continue to work with them. If you are referring them to another practitioner, they may question whether they will feel safe and benefit from treatment with this individual. Clients who have felt "well held" throughout the evaluation may now feel "dropped," especially if this transition is mishandled.

This danger is compounded by the fact that you are finally ready to "show your hand"—to talk about how you see the couple and how you understand their difficulties. The "rules of the game" have changed. You are not just soliciting their thoughts but more actively expressing your own. Even when you have been careful to avoid blaming, there is a danger that one or both partners will feel hurt or blamed or misunderstood. You hope that by balancing your sympathies, by focusing on the stresses or difficulties they face, by acknowledging their resources, and by emphasizing coping rather than pathology, you can elicit their cooperation without alienating them. This is where the effort you have put into designing the response hopefully pays off, but there is no guarantee of this. These shifts, to *your* response and to the *end* of the evaluation, can threaten whatever safety and trust have been established up to this point. You must be aware of this danger and try to prevent it.

Summarize Your Impressions and Recommendations

Your response consists of observations, impressions, intuitions, and hunches, which together form a narrative of the couple's experiences as you understand them. It organizes the information they have shared during the evaluation in a way that highlights certain themes and patterns in their lives, and conveys your hypothesis about the factors that have contributed to and maintain the difficulties they have identified. It also includes recommendations for treatment or more specific recommendations concerning the structure, goals, and sequencing of treatment.

As discussed in detail in the previous chapter, the response should

- be credible and compelling
- be respectful
- identify resources in the individuals and in their relationship
- balance sympathy for both partners
- be concise and as specific as possible
- focus on the couple's present concerns—address other factors (such as childhood experiences, previous adult relationships, or broad cultural forces) only to the extent that they illuminate and suggest solutions to these concerns
- use language that is accessible and, when appropriate, vivid
- take into account those issues you *must* address and those you *cannot* for the time being.

Provide Closure

Clients need a sense of closure at the end of a session, and especially at the end of the evaluation. They want to feel that their efforts have come to a satisfactory conclusion, that "loose ends" have been tied up, questions answered, and promising directions set. This may not always be possible but you should do whatever you can toward this end. The word "satisfactory" bears comment here. I once heard the author of a book for children being interviewed on the radio. Apparently her book had a sad ending. The interviewer asked, "Don't children need a happy ending?" The author responded, "What children need is not a happy ending, but a satisfying one." The same is true for adults.

Clients may hope for a happy ending—a sense of optimism, trust, and direction—and this may be possible. In some cases, however, it may not be, and these clients are no less entitled to your best efforts to help them experience a satisfying ending. This is most likely to occur if the couple's major concerns and questions have been heard, appreciated, and addressed in your response, if the safety and trustworthiness of the therapeutic context have been preserved, and if the partners feel that their efforts have been matched by those of a therapist who is genuinely interested in helping them with the difficulties they face.

Facilitate the Transition to Treatment

You need to facilitate the transition from the evaluation to whatever form(s) of treatment are being recommended. This involves setting clear directions for treatment, explaining the rationale for these recommendations, and preserving or enhancing the couple's motivation for treatment and their confidence in you.

Setting clear directions for treatment must be understood in relative terms. There are some cases in which directions need to be set more tentatively due to ambiguity or confusion in certain areas. However, you should avoid *unnecessary* ambiguity in your recommendations. By the time the couple comes to the final session, they are looking for direction and you must try your best to provide it.

The couple cannot be expected to accept these recommendations on faith, even if their trust in you is high. You need to offer a credible and compelling rationale for the directions you recommend. The couple's transition to treatment is facilitated when your response enhances their optimism and motivation for treatment and their confidence in you. If you are referring the couple to another practitioner, agency, or service, or if you are recommending concurrent treatment by another provider along with couple therapy, try to effect a "transfer of trust" to that provider by expressing your own confidence in his or her competence and trustworthiness.

The Clients' Agendas

The clients have agendas and questions of their own for this session. These may be specific questions, such as whether one partner should move out temporarily as planned or whether a depressed partner should consider medication. More general agendas and questions are also present in the final session. The clients hope to derive some clear benefit from the time, energy, and money they have invested in the evaluation. They will be asking themselves: Does the therapist understand our problems? Does she really know how to help us with them? Does she see us *as we want to be seen* or through a lens of her own that distorts or disrespects our view of ourselves? Does she like us? Does she understand what is important to us, even if it might seem unimportant to her? Each partner is also asking more personal questions. Does she understand *me*? Does she like me? Does she blame me for our problems? Will she agree with my view of our problems? Do I trust her? These questions are always present; you should be aware of them even when they are not expressed overtly.

Opening the Session

Even when all four parts of the evaluation are conducted in one sitting, it's a good idea to begin the final session by asking if there is anything either partner wishes to add. They may remember something they had forgotten to mention earlier or they may have a delayed reaction to something that was said in one of the earlier sessions. Starting this way is respectful of the clients and it invites their active participation in this portion of the evaluation. It also allows you to assess whether they feel ready to focus on your comments or whether they are too distracted or troubled to do so. Finally, if they do have something more to share, it may represent an important addition to the impressions you have already formed.

If the final session takes place at a later date than previous ones, you should begin by inquiring about any significant developments since the last session and by getting some sense of the emotional state of the partners. Here again, you hope that they are feeling ready for this final discussion and receptive to your response, but they may not be if they are distracted or preoccupied by something else. If something important has transpired or if one or both partners are upset about a particular issue, you need to focus on this before moving into your conclusions.

If something important has transpired, you should know about it before you begin presenting your response. You'll want to know about important developments external to the evaluation and about "fallout" from earlier sessions. For example, there may have been an injury or a worrisome diagnosis for a close family member, the loss of a job, or a financial reversal. One partner may have impulsively decided to separate or disclosed a previously secret affair. One couple I evaluated had been involved in treatment for infertility; the onset of menstruation right before the final session meant that a hoped-for pregnancy had not occurred. They needed time to express their intense disappointment before I could proceed to my conclusions.

One or both partners may have reactions to something that occurred during earlier sessions. One partner may have been stunned at something the other one said during the initial session. They may both have negative reactions to something you said earlier. You should know about these developments and be prepared to handle them with sensitivity. (Keep in mind that you may be able to incorporate the new information into your response to the couple.) Usually, a brief discussion will suffice to demonstrate concern and sympathy on your part and for all of you to feel that your are now "on the same wavelength" and ready to conclude the evaluation.

However, in some cases, it may be necessary to defer your response to a subsequent session in order to devote sufficient time and attention to the material they have presented. This might be indicated when the intervening events are traumatic, when reactions to earlier sessions are especially intense, and when these reactions are congruent with the directions you consider most promising for the couple. For example, if a husband who has consistently denied his wife's suspicions about drug use suddenly discloses details of extensive and dangerous drug use in the final session, you would not want to squelch this positive development. If the response is deferred, be sure to explain this shift to both partners in order to give them clear signals about what to expect and permission to depart from the normal sequence of events. If no such material is presented at the beginning of the final session or if you have discussed it to the couple's satisfaction, you can now begin to share your impressions and recommendations for treatment.

Delivering the Therapist's Response

It is helpful to signal the transition to that part of the session in which the therapist shares impressions and recommendations. I usually say something along the following lines: "We had agreed that today it would be my job to talk a little bit about my understanding of your situation. If there's nothing else we need to discuss right now, I'll get started." Or, more simply: "At this point, it's my job to talk a bit. Shall I go ahead?"

It's worth thinking about the tone in which you deliver your response since *the tone can be as important as the content* in contributing to positive outcomes of the evaluation. The response should be delivered with a tone of *respect* for the clients. The therapist's mandate is: First of all, do no harm. The tone of the response should never be condescending, contemptuous, flippant, or otherwise disrespectful. In addition to conveying respect, the response should convey *sympathy*. People who seek out a therapist want, at the minimum, a person who is sympathetically interested in them. A therapist who is clearly intel- ligent but so detached as to seem mechanical and unsympathetic is not likely to inspire confidence and connection.

Keep in mind that your tone conveys information about how you see yourself. Ideally, it should convey a mixture of self-respect and humility. By this I mean that you convey the sense that you think well of yourself, with neither excessive self-deprecation, arrogance, nor self-congratulatory preening. Your tone suggests that you see yourself and the clients as equals. You may be defined as the expert in this context but you do not therefore see yourself as better than them. Whether or not you choose to disclose aspects of your own personal life when they are relevant to your observations about the couple (and both choices are legitimate), you communicate by your tone that your are "in the soup" of life along with them. You have something worth saying and hopefully worth their hearing but you are neither perfect nor all-knowing.

The response should be delivered with *conviction*. If, by your tone, you suggest that you're uncertain about your conclusions, it's more likely that the clients will be as well. This does not mean that you can never reveal uncertainty in the summary. You should feel comfortable indicating the parts you feel fairly sure of and those you don't.

Uncertainty can be used strategically in the response in one of two ways. You may wish to soften an observation on which you expect forceful resistance. Instead of saying, "Your children's needs are being neglected by the intensity of conflict between the two of you," you might qualify this with a gentler "I wonder whether sometimes the children's needs and feelings are overlooked when the two of you are fighting so intensely."

Uncertainty can also be used to actually underscore certain points by highlighting their elusive or mysterious nature. The therapist poses a sort of puzzle that he or she hopes will engage one or both partners' curiosity. For example, "I am convinced that Ken doesn't want to be so irritable with Ellen. But no matter how many times he swears to acts differently, it just keeps happening. I don't understand the reasons for this at this point but I think it's important. It may have something to do with Ken's description of his anger at teachers, officers (in the Army), and his father." While occasional and deliberate uncertainty may be helpful, unintended and pervasive uncertainty undermines the credibility of the summary.

When you are about to begin sharing your response, invite both partners to interrupt at any time, either for questions if they are confused by something or to add whatever comments or reactions they may wish to make. Whether or not they choose to act on this invitation, it preserves the collaborative nature of the evaluation and reduces the likelihood that they will feel like students who are passively auditing a lecture. Be sure to leave more than enough time for the couple to react. The response will probably take about 10 to 15 minutes to deliver.

Discussing the Couple's Reactions

While the formal *structure* of the four-part evaluation is coming to a close at this point, the *process* of evaluation is not yet over, especially if the partners will be continuing with you in couple therapy. Their reactions to your response add to the impressions you have already formed; in some cases, they may be especially illuminating. Precisely because you are sharing your impressions based on fairly limited knowledge of the individuals (approximately 2½ to 3 hours of contact with them), it is not unusual to be surprised at their reactions to some aspect of the response. These reactions add to or amend your first impressions; they may even indicate that changes are necessary in your treatment recommendations. While an infinite range of reactions are possible, responses to the summary tend to fall into three or four clusters: positive or negative reactions, questions, and clarifications. Rarely, clients may show no reaction.

Positive Reactions

When the partners' reactions to the summary are essentially positive, your job is greatly simplified. This is usually a sign that you have understood them fairly well on their own terms and shared something about them that they recognize to be true. Positive reactions to the summary indicate that all three parties are roughly "on the same wavelength" and can proceed to the next step, whether that be structuring and beginning treatment or clarifying other recommendations and terminating the evaluation. Some couples may seem to react positively in the session but the therapist finds out later that one or both felt angered, upset, stung, or humiliated by some part of the response.

This intense delayed (or censored) reaction may foreshadow a volatile treatment.

Negative Reactions

The partners may have a variety of negative reactions to the therapist's response; these reactions can mean very different things. First and foremost, you should consider the possibility that, despite your best efforts, you have missed or misunderstood something important about the couple. When negative reactions seem to be related to an error on your part, the best course of action is to straightforwardly acknowledge the error and apologize for it. You may lose a bit of credibility by doing so but probably not nearly as much as if instead you dogmatically defend a mistake. You may well gain credibility by admitting the error since this suggests an ability to *hear* what they are saying and to maintain self-respect without having to be "right" about everything. These are, not coincidentally, qualities that help reduce conflict and pain in couple relationships as well.

Negative reactions to the response are not always related to errors on the therapist's part. They may indicate the *accuracy* of the response. Hopefully, this means that a client's initial reaction of shock, denial, or anger will soon give way to greater acceptance and flexibility. If this does not occur, you may have misjudged what the partner or the couple were able to hear at that moment in time. The point to remember is that negative reactions are not always negative events in the evaluation or the treatment that may follow.

Questions

The partners may have questions they wish to ask during or after your response. This is usually a good sign since it bespeaks emotional engagement in the process and the ability to be assertive. It suggests that the partners are actively participating in the clinical interaction. The particular questions asked are worth noting. Questions may simply signal areas of confusion, possibly caused by the therapist's lack of clarity; however, questions may also identify important issues in the couple's relationship.

Jake seemed puzzled as to why I recommended intensive out-patient psychotherapy, and possibly hospitalization, for his wife whose dissociative symptomatology had led to episodes of disorientation and near-injury. It was as though he had been absent from the couple session in which these experiences, and many others, had been described. He was extremely preoccupied with his own symptoms of anxiety and had relied on his wife as a care-giver. He seemed to need to see nothing seriously wrong with her and consequently had no idea why I was recommending such a clear response to her condition.

If the question reveals concerns that have not previously surfaced in the evaluation, respond as you would to any potentially important issue: with respect and sympathetic curiosity. If you see no contraindications to answering a question, you can simply do so. However, you needn't feel that you must have answers to all questions that might be raised. There is no harm — and there may be some benefit — to admitting that you do not.

Clarifications

One or both partners may respond to the summary by suggesting a correction of some kind. The therapist may have misunderstood something; the clients may not have expressed themselves clearly, or one may have clarified his or her feelings since the earlier sessions. The clarification may require a course correction for treatment recommendations. For example, Corinne reacted to the summary by revealing a previously undisclosed history of child abuse. She asked for one or two individual sessions to explore this, which her husband supported wholeheartedly. The recommendation for couple therapy stood but was amended to include the individual sessions, which later led to a referral for individual psychotherapy concurrent with couple sessions.

Little or No Reaction

A more disconcerting scenario involves couples who appear to have no response to the summary. They don't react especially negatively or positively and they ask no questions. This may be due to one of several reasons.

1. They may feel insecure and uneasy expressing themselves; if this is the case, it will probably have been amply demonstrated earlier in the evaluation.
2. They may be uncomfortable challenging someone identified as an expert. Since, in this case, their lack of response may signify disagreement or discomfort with some aspect of your

response, you should try to encourage them, in whatever way you can, to share their reactions.

3. It may indicate a significant level of depression, although if this is the case, it would likely have been identified earlier in the evaluation.

4. The couple may be keeping a secret which is paralyzing them so that they are unable to either share it or ignore it.

5. There may be patterns of intimidation within the relationship, with the woman afraid to speak openly and the man enforcing her silence with implicit threats of violence. If you suspect this, you should suggest separate individual discussions within the final session to explore this possibility more fully. (See Chapter 16 for specific recommendations involving cases in which the therapist suspects domestic violence.)

Regardless of which patterns shape it, the couple's lack of response is always diagnostically significant. It suggests that treatment may be more difficult since these couples are having great difficulty participating actively in the session. They will probably need more gentle and persistent coaxing. In some cases, this nonresponse may indicate such an impenetrable boundary around the couple that the likelihood of their dropping out of treatment is high.

The partners' reactions to the therapist's response may diverge significantly, which may lead to combinations of the reactions discussed above. As always, differences are in themselves meaningful.

One couple's central impasse involved the man's sense of always being nagged by his wife and her feeling that her needs always came last. Hillary and Dennis had described similar feelings in earlier relationships and in their families of origin but, as is often the case, they had difficulty seeing that these patterns were not unique to this relationship; this was especially true of Hillary. I was careful in my response to sympathize with both partners' distress in this interactional knot and to indicate the changes on both of their parts that might allow them to move past it.

Dennis felt satisfied with my response, reasonably well understood, and optimistic about the prosect of continuing therapy. However, in spite of the effort I put into balancing my comments, the wife told me in the next session that she had been thrown into despair since she heard me saying that she would have to, once again, put her needs on hold in deference to her husband's difficulties in his family of origin. In this case, I was quite clear that I had said nothing like this since I had clearly emphasized the changes he would have to make in response to her needs. This dramatically illustrated her powerful tendency to perceive that her needs would have to be put on hold.

Wrapping Up

By this point in the evaluation, you have inquired about and discussed recent events or reactions to earlier sessions, presented your response, and discussed the partners' reactions to it. If the time allotted for the final session has expired, all three parties can now move toward wrapping up the evaluation. There may be some details left to be worked out and this is a good time to do it, whether the partners are continuing with you in couple therapy or accepting a referral for treatment elsewhere. If they will be continuing with you, they will need to work out the scheduling of sessions—how soon, how often, for how much time, etc. They will need to agree on exactly when the next session will be held. They may also need to discuss financial details such as insurance and fees. If they are accepting a referral for treatment elsewhere, they may have questions about the referral that you can answer.

If the partners are continuing with you in couple therapy and if the details have been satisfactorily worked out with a good deal of time remaining, the most natural next step is to move directly into treatment. Usually this flows easily from the couple's reactions to the therapist's response. You can simply allow this to proceed, thereby effecting a natural transition to treatment. In some cases, you may want to signal this more clearly, especially if the partners seem unsure about what to do next. You might make specific suggestions concerning the immediate focus of discussion. For example, "We have a fair amount of time left today. I think it might be useful to talk some about the dilemma you're facing in relation to this possible relocation. I don't think we'll resolve this today but let's get started." You may have to intervene actively if a highly conflictual couple begins battling over an issue which, in the summary, you suggested should only be addressed much later in treatment. You would need to interrupt the discussion, remind the partners of your earlier recommendations, and suggest what you hope will be a more useful focus for discussion.

You should *not* make a transition to treatment at this point if the amount of time is limited, the level of conflict high, and the issues explosive. It is more important to preserve safe "holding" (Scharff & Scharff, 1991) than to jeopardize it for a small amount of progress at the very end of the evaluation. In cases such as these, if the partners have accepted the response, this is progress enough for now. If the partners are not continuing with you in couple therapy—if they are being referred for treatment elsewhere or if the evaluation has led to a decision against treatment—you should *not* open up discussion of issues that you will be unable to follow with them. In these cases, you can entertain any questions they have concerning your response and, when this discussion seems finished, move toward ending the session. If the couple is continuing with you, they now have some idea of where they are headed and when they are to reconvene. If they are not, the evaluation has been satisfactorily brought to a close and they should know where they are headed next.

— 12 —

MODIFICATIONS OF
THE COUPLE EVALUATION
FORMAT IN OTHER
CLINICAL CONTEXTS

T HE FORMAT DESCRIBED in the preceding chapters presumes that
the evaluation takes place in a particular clinical context—a couple calling and requesting couple therapy. However, evaluating couples can be valuable in other clinical contexts as well. Particular circumstances may call for modifications in the standard format. The
advantages of evaluating couples in various clinical contexts are described below, as are some of the most common of these circumstances and the modifications of the format that typically accompany
them.

241

Advantages of Couple Evaluation in
Other Clinical Contexts

Evaluating couples in other clinical contexts has several advantages; it aids the therapist in:

1. assessing the "culture" of individual symptomatology
2. gaining a fuller picture of the client and his or her relational context
3. identifying resources for treatment
4. securing an ally for treatment
5. identifying a partner who may be in need of services
6. guarding against the development of symptomatology in the other partner when the symptomatic partner improves

Assessing the "Culture" of Individual Symptomatology

When individual problems are presented for assessment and treatment and when there is an ongoing couple relationship, that relationship constitutes a significant aspect of the "culture" in which the problem exists. For example, individuals in conflictual and unhappy marriages appear to be 25 times more likely to be depressed than persons in satisfying marriages (Weissman, 1987). The realization that symptoms are embedded in relational systems lies at the heart of systems theory.

This has implications not only for etiology but for recovery as well. Studies of "expressed emotion" have indicated that the relationships of psychiatrically hospitalized patients significantly influence relapse and relapse-prevention. For example, Hooley, Orley, and Teasdale (1986) and Vaughn and Leff (1976) found that spousal criticism in an inhospital interview was a better predictor of relapse after discharge than was the initial severity of the patient's symptoms. Evaluating the couple may help the clinician understand the origins of the presenting problem and identify aspects of the relational system, which if altered can facilitate positive change.

Gaining a Fuller Picture of the Individual

In addition, evaluating the couple expands the information and impressions that the clinician can utilize in formulating the case. The partner of an individual seeking treatment may have information that can help the therapist better understand the origins and persistence of the individual's problem. Even partners who may think that they have no relevant information may be able to enlighten the therapist through answers they provide to specific questions. In other words, people sometimes know more than they realize they know.

The partner's contribution may not be a matter of providing new information. Simply meeting the partner and observing the couple together may stimulate the therapist's intuition, giving him a better "feel" for the client and the marriage, or help to solidify his conviction that an impression he has formed does seem to be accurate. Meeting with couples provides not only information but also greater richness and color to the therapist's impressions. To meet the individual is one thing; to meet the partner, to sit together with the two of them, and to watch and listen to them interact is, as couple therapists know, quite another.

Identifying Resources for Treatment

The clinician may also want to meet with the couple in order to assess potential resources within the relationship. If the relationship is a culture, it can contribute not only to symptomatology but to coping and recovery as well. Does the husband of a rape victim genuinely care about his wife? Does his caring override whatever difficulties he may have with the idiosyncratic psychological meaning of rape for him? If his responses to his wife have been well-meant but hurtful and counterproductive, can he learn to respond differently? Can he manage his own needs so as to be able to provide safety and reassurance in their sexual relationship? A husband who has these resources can be an important asset to treatment. This leads us to the fourth rationale for evaluating couples.

Securing an Ally for Treatment

Even when individual therapy seems to be the treatment of choice, a face-to-face meeting between the therapist and the client's partner can elicit a powerful ally for treatment and prevent the creation of a possible opponent. When a partner sees that the therapist will extend sympathy and consideration to him or her and when the purposes and goals of treatment are explained, he or she is more likely to actively support it. The treatment may impinge on the partner's resources and interests, in light of its financial costs, the time required and inconvenience created by appointments, and the possible emotional changes experienced by the client (such as withdrawal, irritability, or unfamiliar assertiveness). The partner is more likely to be willing and able to tolerate these burdens if he or she understands why the client is in treatment and how it may benefit both of them. He or she is more likely to support the treatment if they trust that the therapist is considering his or her interests as well as those of the client.

Identifying a Partner Who May be in Need of Services

Another rationale for evaluating couples when an individual presents for treatment involves the possibility that the partner may be experiencing distress as well. Because it is not only individuals but also relational systems that experience stress, when one partner is experiencing symptomatology there is a reasonable chance that the other partner is also experiencing stress of some kind. A dysphoric woman who presents for treatment may be reacting to a husband who is seriously depressed. A man who comes in complaining about his sexual relationship with his wife may be unaware that she has an untreated history of child sexual abuse. A woman who seeks treatment after the death of a child may be married to a man who will not seek treatment for himself but is quite seriously suicidal.

In each of these cases, the therapist's effort to meet, even if just once, with the client's partner may enable him or her to identify someone who might significantly benefit from treatment. It does not guarantee that the partner will in fact ask for or receive treatment, but if the initial contact is made the chances of this occurring improve. Furthermore, if the partner improves, the relational culture is likely to be healthier for the client and, if more serious deterioration can be prevented, the client will have less stress with which to cope.

Guarding Against the Development of Symptomatology in the Other Partner When the Symptomatic Partner Improves

Therapists have observed for decades that improvement in one partner can contribute to the development of symptomatology in the other. This is one of the common clinical anomalies that spurred the development of systems theory and family therapy. The wife who complains of inhibited orgasm is cured only to have her husband develop erectile dysfunction. The alcoholic husband attains sobriety followed swiftly by his wife's onset of serious depression. The agoraphobic wife experiences a significant decrease in symptomatology only to have her husband develop panic attacks.

Unless individuals are truly isolated socially, any change they undergo—for worse *or better*—will have some impact on those who are closest to them. Most often, this impact can be absorbed by the adaptability of the relational system without serious detriment to anyone. But in some cases, when the client improves, the partner may develop symptomatology of his or her own. If the clinician has met with the partner, he or she may be better able to anticipate this. Even when this cannot be anticipated, a positive early contact between therapist and partner increases the chances that this will be brought to the therapist's attention.

For all the reasons cited above, it is advantageous for clinicians to evaluate couples in a variety of treatment contexts. The discussion that follows highlights some of the clinical contexts in which this is most likely to prove helpful and the modifications of the evaluation format that may be called for by them.

Modifications for Specific Treatment Contexts

Domestic Violence

If you suspect or know that domestic violence is involved when a couple requests treatment, be certain to inquire about violence by meeting with them *separately* during the initial contact. This allows the woman* to describe what has occurred *without* endangering herself by doing so in front of her partner. This is the most important modification of the evaluation format when domestic violence is suspected or confirmed. Other modifications are discussed in detail in Chapter 16.

Sex Therapy

When the couple is being evaluated in the context of sex therapy, you would conduct a detailed evaluation of the couple's sexual relationship as well as broader aspects of the relationship in which sexual difficulties may be embedded. The format described in preceding chapters translates well into the context of sex therapy. The method of framing the evaluation—as time-limited with the therapist's summary and recommendations delivered at the conclusion—is completely applicable. Probe questions and other assessment techniques described earlier can help you put the couple's sexual difficulties into the broader context of their relationship as a whole and to assess commitment to the relationship and motivation for treatment.

---

*Victims of domestic violence are disproportionately women and children (Browne, 1987; Dobash & Dobash, 1979).

However, when the request is specifically for sex therapy rather than couple therapy, there are two primary modifications of the evaluation format. The exploration of the presenting problem necessarily involves a far more detailed examination of the couple's sexual relationship. This particularity of focus carries over into the individual sessions as well. It is imperative to obtain a detailed sexual history for each partner; this reorganizes your priorities for information to be gathered during the individual sessions, and it makes these sessions less discretionary—given the importance of individual sexual histories for developing an accurate diagnosis of the couple's sexual difficulties.

Second, when couples present with complaints about their sexual relationship, you should recommend physical examination by medical professionals unless these have already been conducted and conveyed to you. Finally, there are questionnaires relevant to sexual functioning that can be used for more economical and more thorough assessment. References for these assessment tools can be found in Chapter 15.

Family Therapy

In families, difficulties between the parents can easily spread to include or affect children, who may express them in a disguised and symptomatic fashion. For this reason, many family therapists routinely meet with parents apart from children (when both parents are living in the home and available for treatment) as part of the initial evaluation. These sessions allow the therapist to explore aspects of parenting and family life as well as the couple's relationship itself in greater depth.

One modification called for when couples are evaluated in the context of family therapy is the shift from exploring the (usually child-focused) presenting problem to exploring the couple's relationship. A second modification involves the sequence of sessions. In general, the couple session should *not* be your first contact with the family. If they are seeking treatment for what they define as a family problem, you should meet with the whole family (or as many members as possible) for the initial contact and then meet separately with the parents. This should be mentioned in the initial telephone contact, during which you arrange the family evaluation, and presented as a routine part of the family evaluation (Karpel & Strauss, 1983).

In terms of the shift from child-focus to a focus on the couple's relationship, several points should be considered. First, this refers to a shift in the focus of *assessment*, not formulation or treatment. Not all child-focused problems are symptoms of a troubled marriage. You want to explore the couple's relationship in order to assess *possible* connections, not to foist an ideological conviction on the family. The relative ease in making this transition will depend on what emerges spontaneously from the material presented to you and on the degree of latitude the family, and especially the couple, are able to extend to you.

In the ideal scenario, the exploration of the couple's relationship emerges naturally from the material presented in the initial full-family session and the parents are relatively willing to go along with this inquiry. One advantage of meeting with the whole family is that other family members may call attention to difficulties in the parents' relationship. However, while you can follow these comments when they are offered, you should try *not* to violate boundaries by soliciting information about presumably private aspects of the marriage in the presence of the children. The detailed exploration of the couple's relationship should be conducted without the children present.

If the material presented does not, on its own, lead to the couple's relationship, you can signal the transition in the separate couple session by indicating the importance of trying to understand as much as possible about all relationships in the family. You can begin with the most benign, or "everyday," questions and proceed to what may be more provocative ones. Remember that the couple has not requested treatment for their relationship and they may be offended by your attempts to explore it. You gradually test their openness as you inquire about their relationship. In some cases, you may meet a wall of resistance to any questions about the relationship or even to the suggestion that you meet separately with them. In these cases, you have to decide whether to accept this limitation for the time being, to confront it, or to try to explore it.

Another modification of the evaluation format in the context of family therapy involves the need to abbreviate the exploration of the couple's relationship given the wider priorities of the family evaluation. Unless it becomes clear that there is a serious couple problem that supercedes the initial focus, less time will be devoted to exploration of the couple's relationship. You are also less likely to request separate individual sessions with each parent. Given the initial child-focus and the need to explore a more complicated relational system, it is less practical to devote the extra time required to these sessions.

Individual Therapy for Children or Adolescents

Those who conduct individual therapy with children and adolescents vary in their use of separate sessions with the parents, some routinely doing so, others rarely doing so, and still others, in the traditional format for child therapy, assigning this task to a second therapist. The modifications called for when a child or adolescent is being evaluated for individual treatment are comparable to those in the context of family therapy.

The shift to a focus on the couple's relationship is both easier and more complicated for the following reasons. Many child therapists routinely meet with parents initially to gather family history and information about the presenting problem. In these cases, the separate session requires no special preparation or rationale. However, when parents come to a child therapist, there is even less of an implicit supposition that they might themselves be part of the problem than there is when they attend a full family evaluation with their children. For this reason, in some cases, the shift to inquiring about the parents' relationship should be more delicate.

Regardless of these subtleties, it is always useful for those who treat children and adolescents individually to meet initially with the parents or parent-substitutes. The therapist can use these sessions to form alliances, to investigate the parents' views of the presenting problem, to gather history, and to try to assess the couple's relationship.

Individual Treatment for an Adult

It is often helpful to evaluate couples when the presenting complaint is defined by the client or referring professional as an individual problem, and when the request or referral is for individual treatment of some kind. This is true for a wide range of what are traditionally considered individual problems, especially those that have been shown to be correlated with relational difficulties (such as depression; see Chapter 18) and those that are often embedded in a characteristic relational structure (such as alcoholism; see Chapter 17). Even when the presenting complaint seems unrelated to couple difficulties, meeting with the partner can help both you and the client if the partner is willing to support the client's treatment. It can also clarify any confusion you may have regarding material presented by the individual client.

Identification of previously unrecognized factors in the couple relationship that contribute to symptomatology or impede coping may lead to a series of couple sessions designed to bolster individual treatment. Even if no serious relational difficulties are identified, you may utilize a variant of what Hafner, Badenoch, Fisher, and Swift (1983) refer to as "spouse-aided therapy," in which individual treatment is strengthened by the inclusion of the partner.

Couple evaluation should be a routine part of initial evaluation whenever an individual is admitted for inpatient or residential treatment. In these cases, the severity of the individual's difficulties make it especially important that you assess their effects on other family members. Furthermore, the quality of relationships in the home may have a significant effect on relapse-prevention (Hooley et al., 1986; Vaughn & Leff, 1976). Finally, you may want to meet with a partner in the context of an impasse in individual treatment.

The pragmatics of arranging a couple evaluation when a caller requests individual treatment—that is, before you have met with either partner—were already discussed in Chapter 5. If you have already met with one partner, you should discuss the rationale and ground rules for a couple session with that individual. It is helpful to meet with both partners together as well as individually with the client's partner. This can easily be done in one sitting by dividing one session into two parts, although in some cases more sessions may be indicated.

Explain to the partner that the session is exploratory. The rationale involves one or more of the advantages presented at the beginning of this chapter: assessing the culture of individual symptomatology, gaining a fuller picture of the client and the presenting problem, identifying resources for treatment and extending one's concern to the partner as well. Let your client know if you simply want one session with the partner as part of the evaluation; if you are not yet certain whether further involvement by the partner is indicated, this should also be mentioned.

Clearly discuss the ground rules for communication. The recommendation made earlier—that the partners are free to discuss any and all aspects of their individual sessions with one another but that you will not discuss them with the other partner—is useful in this context as well. Unlike the standard couple evaluation, secrets pose fewer dangers in this context; you can therefore assure the client that you will not discuss secret information with the partner. If couple therapy is later recommended, you can propose modifications of this agreement if they appear to be necessary (see Chapter 7 for discussion on managing secrets).

The original client may be disinclined to include the partner; he may want to have the therapy relationship "to himself." If the client feels strongly about this, the potential advantages of including the partner are outweighed by the damage done to the therapeutic relationship by insisting that the partner be included. You may want to reserve the option of raising the idea again later in treatment or you may recognize that this simply will not be acceptable.

If the session with the partner does take place, you would first meet with both partners together, and then alone with the client's partner.

Seeing the partners together enables you to see the relationship more clearly, to observe interactions between them, and to feel what it is like to sit together with both of them.

The couple portion of the session focuses at first on the original client's presenting complaints. Then, if the material presented — either in this discussion or earlier in the client's initial individual session — allows for a relatively smooth shift to an exploration of the couple's relationship, this joint portion of the session can also be used to conduct a mini couple evaluation. The portion of the session in which you meet with the partner separately can be used to build an alliance, gather observations and hunches about the presenting problem, deepen understanding of the partner and what he or she brings to the relationship, and to assess his or her feelings toward the client and level of commitment to the relationship. In essence, you are modifying the sequence of sessions but still meeting with both partners together and with each individually.

In some cases, this session may lead all three parties to opt for couple therapy or at least a series of couple sessions. In others, you can simply thank the partner for attending and set up the next individual session for the client. In the latter case, you may want to ask both partners' permission to invite the partner back again should it be indicated at a later time.

Mediation

When couples seek, or are referred for, divorce mediation, several modifications of the couple evaluation format may be necessary. Most importantly, the individuals may no longer think of themselves as a couple and the intensity of conflict between them may be so great that an initial couple session could be disastrous.* It may be necessary to begin with individual sessions before attempting to bring them together. If the mediation involves children, try to meet individually with all of them, given the certain impact of their parents' situation on them. Mediation is, by definition, task and goal focused; you may need to be even more active than you would in the context of couple therapy.

You must be knowledgeable about nuances of domestic law in the context of separation, divorce, and custody, and you must be in communication with any attorneys involved with the couple (it is highly unlikely that mediation will be helpful if either attorney opposes it).

---

*Many of the points in this section are based on a discussion with Eva Brown, Ph.D.

You can afford to be less careful about becoming aware of secrets, even when you are unable to discuss them with both partners. The partners' emotional interests have diverged (even if their investments in successful coparenting have not). As they separate the spheres of their lives, the degree of honesty they owe one another is modified.

Investigations for Foster and Adoptive Placement and Custody

The context in which these services are delivered is considerably different from that of couple therapy. The clinician is essentially the advocate of the child, and of the birth parents, rather than that of the couple wanting to provide foster or adoptive care. Often in cases of foster care and adoption, in a perfect reversal of the clinical paradigm, the couple is in effect saying, "We have a solution; you have a problem."* These contextual differences call for modifications of the evaluation format.

Evaluations for foster and adoptive placement require investigative procedures that are starkly different from those required for couple therapy: a home visit to check the safety of the environment for a child, a check of medical records (since serious medical conditions might make it impossible for an individual to provide continuity of care), letters of reference from individuals who can vouch for the prospective parents, verification of employment, and a check of criminal and financial records. Individual sessions are routinely used. However, in this context, the clinician wants to be aware of any secrets since the best interests of the child outweigh the need to preserve the therapist's trustworthiness. This is particularly true because the clinician who is evaluating the couple will, in most settings, not conduct couple therapy if this is deemed necessary but will instead refer elsewhere for such services.

The clinician has, if anything, even more license to investigate any area of the relationship, if he or she feels that it bears on the couple's ability to provide adequate care for a child. The focus of the initial couple session involves why they want to provide foster care or to adopt, rather than a particular presenting problem. Important areas of inquiry include attitudes toward and methods of discipline, how they have handled issues of separation and loss in their own lives and how they would likely handle them in the child, and attitudes they might have to the child's past, especially whether they seem able to incorporate this history into their own lives. Finally, clients may be encour-

*Many of the points in this section are based on a discussion with Joan Kagan, LICSW.

aged to be more actively involved in evaluations for foster and adoptive placement. For example, they may be asked to provide written autobiographies and to read and sign the clinician's conclusions at the end of the evaluation.

Crisis and Emergency Services

Couple evaluation is extremely helpful in the context of crisis or psychiatric emergencies. Typically, these cases present in the emergency rooms of hospitals or contact emergency services for assistance. The partner of the individual in crisis may be able to provide a wealth of information and perspective for the professionals involved. If the individual in crisis is unable to reliably describe his or her situation, either because of extreme emotional upset, confusion, or psychosis, the partner may be a more reliable informant who is familiar with the current situation as well as the history of the individual. Meeting with the partner and seeing the couple together will help the clinician understand the resources and liabilities of the individual's primary relational context. The partner may also be able to help carry out various aspects of the treatment plan.

Modifications of the evaluation format include a much more compressed time frame for assessment, more time spent separately with the partner gathering information, a primary effort to help the partners cope with the immediate crisis, possible utilization of other family members in this effort, and deferral of detailed exploration of the couple's relationship until the immediate crisis is resolved (in many cases, this will be unnecessary if the couple is not seeking treatment for relational difficulties).

Investigations of Abuse or Neglect of Children

In investigations of possible physical, sexual, or emotional abuse or neglect of children, couple evaluation may be useful but it plays a decidedly secondary role. Although many different formats may be used for evaluating these cases, the preferred format for professionals investigating charges involves meeting first with the ostensibly nonabusing parent, then with the child individually, and then with the ostensibly abusing parent. The abuse should never be investigated with both the child and the ostensibly abusing parent in the room together, although in some cases interviewing the child with the ostensibly nonabusing parent in the room may be preferable. If other professionals become involved in the case, the same sequence should be followed, although these professionals will probably want to speak first with those who have already investigated the charges.

In these cases, if a couple session seems useful, it will follow these earlier sessions as it does in other cases of crisis intervention. Other modifications include inquiry into personal histories of having being abused or witnessing abuse for each partner, inquiry into abuse of alcohol or other substances, and assessing for indications of untreated trauma for either partner (Gelinas, 1983).

Medical Illness

Couple evaluation can also be helpful in a medical context. When one partner has a serious illness or injury, the partner's responses and degree of support may be critical to the patient's course of treatment. Baird and Doherty (1986), Doherty and Baird (1983), and McDaniel, Hepworth, and Doherty (1992) have described guidelines and procedures for therapists treating clients coping with serious illness. Modifications of the evaluation format in these cases include extensive discussion of medical problems (including symptomatology, history, past and current treatment, prognosis, and the meanings of the illness for both partners), collaboration with health professionals treating the partner who is ill, and greater emphasis on patterns and meanings of illness in both partner's families of origin. (For a more detailed discussion of evaluation when one partner has a serious illness, see Chapter 20.)

~ 13 ~

OTHER FORMATS FOR
EVALUATING COUPLES

W HILE THERE IS AN ample literature on treating couples, relatively little has been written about evaluation. There are chapters in a few books on couple therapy; a handful of articles; one edited volume, which discusses the cognitive social learning perspective (O'Leary, 1987); and one book, which describes the large number of paper-and-pencil instruments that can be used in evaluating couples (L'Abate & Bagarozzi, 1993). This chapter surveys the literature on evaluation, starting with those works that most resemble the format described in this volume—the multisession clinical interview—and ending with a brief look at some of the most popular instruments used for evaluating couples.

Couple Evaluation Formats

A number of authors have discussed couple evaluation via the clinical interview format.* While others have certainly mentioned assessment anecdotally in their descriptions of couple therapy, these authors have discussed the process and the pragmatics of evaluating couples at greater length. Differences are evident among them in theoretical approach and in the format utilized for evaluation. These differences include the length and number of sessions, whether or not individual sessions are held, and the focus of evaluative sessions (e.g., a preference for "objective" versus "subjective" information, a focus on the present and/or the past), the felt need to begin or postpone intervention, and differing views of the most important goals of the evaluation.

Berman (1982) describes a four-session format similar to the one presented in this volume. She recommends 1½ hours for the initial couple session, followed by one-hour individual sessions with each partner and a final couple session. She stresses the advantages of the individual sessions, citing alliance building, freer history taking, seeing how the individual appears away from the partner, evaluating psychiatric symptoms, and assessing commitment.

Berman's approach to evaluating couples is influenced by her long association with the Marriage Council of Philadelphia, which has produced a significant body of work on couple therapy. Under the rubric of the Intersystems Model, which encourages simultaneous consideration of individual, interactional, and intergenerational systems, several other authors have also addressed couple evaluation. Hollander-Goldfein (1989) uses a similar four-part format. She is willing to see one partner individually in the first session if need be and will use individual sessions with the other "to catch up" in order to attain balanced alliances. She suggests that if the other partner is not seen within the first three or four sessions, couple therapy will not be effective.

Hof and Treat (1989) suggest the need to focus on five areas for assessment: "(1) psychometric indicators of marital adjustment; (2) individual development and personality styles; (3) assessment of the current relationship style of the couple; (4) identification and assessment of the original and current marital contract; and (5) exploration of the

---

*(Bader & Pearson, 1988; Baucom & Epstein, 1990; Beavers, 1985; Berman, 1982; Guerin et al., 1987; Hof & Treat, 1989; Hollander-Goldfein, 1989; Jacobson & Margolin, 1979; L'Abate & Bagarozzi, 1993; Napier, 1987; Nichols, 1988; O'Leary & Arias, 1987; Scharff & Scharff, 1991; Weeks & Treat, 1992).

extended family/multigenerational context" (p. 4). For psychometric instruments, they utilize the Locke-Wallace Dyadic Adjustment Scale and the Marital Satisfaction Inventory. They note that an effective evaluation can be accomplished in two to four sessions.

Weeks and Treat (1992) emphasize common mistakes that are often made during the evaluation phase with couples: taking sides, intervening too quickly, proceeding without having clarified problems and goals, discussing problems abstractly, allowing differences to escalate, assuming that the partners perceive the problem in the same way, making premature interpretations, attempting to answer questions too soon, getting hooked in the past, and allowing the couple to take charge of the session. They describe a form used to help trainees develop a formulation in couple cases; the form includes demographic data, information related to the presenting problem, the therapist's initial impressions and reactions to the couple, assessment of each of the three major systems (individual, interactional, and intergenerational), hypotheses, treatment plan and prognosis, and the trainee's assessment of his or her own strengths and weaknesses in dealing with these particular clients. (For further information, see Weeks & Treat, 1992, pp. 8–18.) Finally, the authors stress the importance of orienting the couple to therapy, by exploring any expectations they have about treatment and by educating them about specific boundary issues (such as lateness, missed appointments, and telephone contact) and ground rules related to treatment.

Napier (1987) allows two to three sessions for the evaluation, with the first running about two hours. He tries to meet initially with the entire family, refuses to hold individual meetings, and insists that the couple agree to at least suspend any concurrent individual psychotherapy. Napier emphasizes the importance of understanding "the 'transferential knot,' that critical interface of transference issues in which each partner's struggle exacerbates the other's transference issues" (p. 29). Napier stresses the need to identify an important area of conflict and to make "a bilateral interpretation that attempts to explain some of the 'extra voltage' in their encounter" (p. 29), suggesting that unless this is accomplished, they may not return for more sessions.*

---

*While the therapist does need to inspire some degree of confidence and hope in the couple during the first session, Napier's format may be especially vulnerable to clients' dropping out since he does not appear to structure the evaluation prior to or at the beginning of the first session. This danger can be minimized with the format described in this volume by alerting couples before the first session to the fact that they will receive a summary of the therapist's impressions and recommendations at the *conclusion* of the evaluation.

Beavers (1985) recommends a primary focus on the present rather than on the past in the first session, with efforts to explore the history of the relationship and the partners' families of origin in later sessions. He tries to identify the couple's idiosyncratic "spin-out," "a stereotyped dance, choreographed with precision and performed with misery. A particular defensive pattern in her will trigger a particular response in him which produces a greater amount of her typical pattern, which leads to . . . and so on" (p. 100). For Beavers, identifying this pattern and helping the couple to become aware of it constitute major goals of couple therapy. He notes that efforts on the therapist's part to interpret this current, visible interactional pattern are less risky at the start of treatment than are more abstract interpretations regarding family of origin, projection, and repetition.

Guerin et al. (1987) do not specify the length of their evaluations. They do, however, recommend that each partner be seen "at least once" individually during the evaluation. The focus of their inquiry includes multigenerational patterns in both partners' families of origin, each of the partners as individuals, and surrounding triangles. The inquiry is also directed toward identifying the couple's stage of marital conflict, a central organizing principle of their approach to treatment.

Nichols (1988) pays particular attention to the initial telephone call, during which the evaluation is arranged, describing this as in essence "the first interview"; he urges therapists to assess attachment, commitment, relationship problems, and strengths in the initial couple session. Nichols does not discuss any subsequent evaluative sessions, either conjoint or individual, and appears to wrap up the evaluation in the first couple session.

Scharff and Scharff (1991) describe an approach to evaluating couples that is derived from object relations theory. The format involves about five sessions, including one or two sessions with the couple, one or more individual sessions with each partner, and a final feedback session. However, in their conceptualization of couple relationships and couple therapy, the Scharffs differ significantly from many other practitioners.

Their work with couples emphasizes the importance of affect, unconscious communication, transference and countertransference, and the couple's sexual relationship. "We are interested in affective moments because these provide access to the unconscious areas from which the feeling has emerged. These moments bring us a living history of the relationships in the families of origin" (p. 82). This proves more helpful, they suggest, than a "formally obtained social history or genogram" (p. 82).

Because they assume that unconscious representations within each

partner are centrally implicated in the difficulties many couples experience, gaining access to these representations is a major focus of evaluation and treatment. Scharff and Scharff attend to unconscious communication by working with dream and fantasy material, by observing
nonverbal language, by noting themes emerging from verbal associa-
tions, and by exploring the couple's sexual relationship.

Probably the most unique aspect of their work, in relation to most
other couple and family therapists, is the emphasis on utilizing the
therapist's countertransference as a means of understanding the partners' unconscious representations and conflicts.

> At times the countertransference . . . obtrudes as a feeling of discom-
> fort, a fantasy or a dream and then we can take hold of it and get to
> work. Through tolerating and then analyzing our countertransfer-
> ence we can experience inside ourselves the couple's transference
> based on unconscious object relations. (p. 83)

The Scharffs also stress what they refer to as "negative capability,"
which involves the capacity to tolerate uncertainty and confusion
without forcing cognitive closure. "We try to be free of the need to get
information and to make sense of things. As we listen, we let our
senses be impinged on, we hold the experience inside, and then we
allow meaning to emerge from within" (pp. 82–83). This stance, in
keeping with their emphasis on unconscious processes, is notably at
variance with practitioners who stress the need to intervene actively
in the very first evaluative session.

An innovative method for conducting the initial interview with
couples has been described by Chasin, Roth, and Bograd (1989). The
procedure, which utilizes techniques derived from psychodrama, is
designed to activate the partners' strengths, to deemphasize their focus
on current problems, and to utilize experiential methods in the service
of rapid change. The authors indicate that this format may be useful
with all couples (except those in crisis) and that they are likely to use
it in a first interview with couples who have been unsuccessful in prior
treatment, as an intervention when their own couple cases seem to
be at an impasse in treatment, and as a format for consultation with
the stuck cases of colleagues. The session is expected to last 1½ to 2½
hours.

The therapist begins by obtaining explicit agreement on rules for
the session; these include "safe and voluntary participation" (p. 123)
and emphasize both partners' rights to refuse to answer any question
or carry out any suggested activity. If they choose to do so, they needn't
explain why and can simply indicate their unwillingness by saying

"Pass." The partners are also asked to agree to temporarily postpone statements related to their presenting problems until later in the session. Next, they are each asked to describe their personal strengths and their goals for the relationship.

They are then encouraged to enact a scene that represents a concretization of these goals for each partner. In these scenes, the therapist helps the partners show each other exactly how they wish the other would respond to them in a particular situation of their choosing. So, for example, the husband selects a situation in which he is worried about developments at work. He directs his wife to role-play him while he role-plays her responding in the way he wants. The roles are then reversed, with her role-playing herself in the situation and trying to respond in exactly the way he has demonstrated. If need be, they continue to switch roles until he feels that the response fits his image. The partners then repeat the same procedure based, this time, on her desires.

Chasin et al. describe several rationales for this procedure: problematic areas in which reactivity is high and flexibility and empathy are low are bypassed, proactive stances ("I want") rather than reactive ones ("I hate") are encouraged, greater understanding of the partner's dreams is developed, wishful longing is stimulated, fears are desensitized, cognitive perspectives are multiplied, a pattern of changed behavior is rehearsed, and the experience of being gratified by the partner is actualized. (Another byproduct of this procedure may be increased trust as one partner sees the other actively participate in the effort to gratify his or her wishes.)

The therapist then directs the couple to enact a scene related to painful experiences in each partner's past. The partner will be used to reform the past by enacting an effort to give the individual the help which he or she needed but didn't receive at the time. Each partner is encouraged to imagine a painful scene that took place "long before the two of you got together" and to enact it. For example, the woman remembers being told that her parents were going to separate. Roles are switched, with the man enacting the woman's role in the scene and the woman enacting someone helping her in the way that she would have wished for. Then, roles are switched again, with the woman enacting herself and the man, this time, following her lead in enacting the role of the healing person. If the scene requires a neglectful or hurtful person, Chasin et al. stress that the *therapist*, and not the partner, should take this role. (They assert that, in their experience, this does not have a detrimental effect on the therapeutic relationship.) The exercise is conducted for both partners' memories of painful past events.

The authors indicate that these scenes are chosen because of the thematic connection that often exists between these early painful experiences and the couple's current difficulties. They also feel that this exercise increases empathy for the partner by breaking "fixed images" (p. 130) and allowing him or her to see the other in a different light, gives the partner "an experience of effectiveness not usually available to him or her" (p. 130), and utilizes the very person who has been seen as hurtful or neglectful in the present to heal the wounds of the past, with "reverberating effects within the couple" (p. 130). Finally, the partners are encouraged to provide "succinct statements" about their current problems before the session closes. The authors describe the uses and limitations of the method, as well as variations on it based on idiosyncratic factors such as inadequate commitment, high levels of denial or misrepresentation, and the unwillingness of one or both partners to enact certain scenes.

Chasin, Roth, and Bograd have contributed a novel and provocative approach for interviewing couples in evaluation or consultation. It is noteworthy, however, that the authors describe using this method most often with couples who are either currently or previously in couple therapy. If we imagine instead a couple coming in for a first appointment, the danger of this format becomes more clear—the therapist begins intervening with very little information about the partners and gives only minor attention to their major complaints. In this context, the method constitutes a gamble. The partners may be grateful for the therapist's forceful interruption of their negative interactions and for his or her redirection to their strengths and longings; or they may feel constrained from discussing what they came to discuss— their problems—as well as uncomfortably exposed. The therapist may also overlook important symptoms and problems, such as domestic violence or serious depression, that may call for prompt and careful attention.

Jacobson and Margolin (1979) have described a format for couple evaluation that derives from a behavioral, or social learning, framework. The format involves an initial couple session which is followed by the partners' completion of instruments at home. A second couple session is used to evaluate their communicational patterns by observing interaction between them, this session also being followed by information gathering via instruments at home. The evaluation concludes with a final feedback session with both partners in which the therapist discusses his or her impressions and recommendations.

The authors note that the purpose of assessment from a behavioral standpoint is to provide information that allows the therapist to (1) describe problems in the relationship, (2) identify variables that control problem behaviors, (3) select appropriate therapeutic interventions, and (4) recognize when the intervention has been effective. They also identify four questions that are central to their inquiry: "(1) What are the beliefs that each spouse holds about the relationship? (2) What is the nature of the day-to-day interaction of the couple? (3) What factors contribute to the central relationship problem? and (4) How do the spouses attempt to bring about change in the relationship?" (p. 69).

Noteworthy features of their approach include their avoidance of a problem-focus in the initial couple session (similar to that of Chasin et al.), their primary reliance on instruments for gathering information about the presenting problem, and their avoidance of individual sessions. Jacobson and Margolin feel that the primary goals of the initial contact should include "extinguishing feelings of hopelessness, generating positive expectancies, and inducing some positive interaction between the couple" (p. 53). They assert that "when the couple leaves the office after the initial interview, they should view their relationship in a more positive way than when they walked in" (p. 55). They also feel that "the interview is not a particularly efficient way of conducting a functional analysis of a distressed relationship. . . . there is no evidence that the interview provides [reliable, valid, and useful] information" (p. 52). For these reasons, they strongly suggest that the first couple session not include a detailed exploration of the presenting problem.

> To begin therapist contact with a thorough delineation of the problem areas might serve to magnify these feelings of despair and hopelessness, and the couple is likely to leave the office feeling worse than when they entered. . . . there is no need to focus on these problem areas in the first place, since the formal assessment procedures will accomplish that end at less risk to the initial formation of a relationship. (p. 53)*

---

*Many therapists—myself included—would disagree with these assumptions. If the exploration of the presenting problem is framed by the therapist as one important part of the evaluation and balanced with attention to the resources, or strengths, of the relationship, few couples will be unnecessarily discouraged by this process. Furthermore, it is inappropriate for a therapist to assume that all couples should feel more optimistic about their relationship without having assessed that relationship. Some couples cannot be helped by couple therapy. The therapist hopes that the couple will feel optimistic about gaining insight into the dilemmas they face and being able to make choices which are in their best interests, but it is a mistake to confuse this with optimism about the relationship itself. Furthermore, most practicing therapists do rely primarily on interviews to understand the couple's difficulties and their overall relationship. While this may not meet the standards of behavioral research data, it is more than adequate to help couples who want treatment in most cases.

Jacobson and Margolin use the first couple session to gather a history of the relationship and to "orient the couple to the assessment process, relieve anxiety and hopelessness, and create positive expectancies" (p. 66). At the end of the first session, they discuss the projected length of treatment (eight to twelve 1½-hour sessions), the use of homework assignments, statistics on the success of their treatment approach with other couples, and explain technical matters such as the use of videotape, record-keeping, and confidentiality.

Between the first and second and between the second and final sessions the couple is asked to fill out various paper-and-pencil instruments at home which are then analyzed by the therapist. (The authors' selection and use of these instruments are discussed below.) The therapist uses the second couple session to explore any areas of ambiguity or special interest from the first session and to observe the couple interacting with one another in a structured problem-solving situation.

Jacobson and Margolin recommend against therapists meeting individually with the partners as part of the evaluation, asserting that "individual sessions militate against the notion of a relationship focus. . . . However the rationale for individual sessions is presented, the idea that secrets are permissable is necessarily fostered" (p. 130).*

In the final couple session, Jacobson and Margolin recommend having the couple sign a written contract in order to finalize their commitment to treatment. The contract specifies "the nature of the obligation on both sides. . . . [This] provides a ritual which symbolizes the commitment on the part of both partners to the process of change. If they agree in writing . . . , they are more likely to persevere in these endeavors once therapy commences" (p. 124).

The format utilized by Jacobson and Margolin provides a striking contrast to that of the Scharffs. Jacobson and Margolin are in pursuit of the most objective data possible. They encourage therapists to intervene as quickly as possible, preferably in the first session. They avoid meeting with the partners individually. The Scharffs are trying to grasp the subjective experience of the partners. They endeavor to resist the urge to intervene quickly, believing that this subjective experience will require time in order for countertransference to develop. They utilize at least one individual session with each partner.

O'Leary and Arias (1987) describe a format that is also derived from a social learning perspective. After the initial telephone call, the thera-

---

*This concern about secrets is often given as a rationale for avoiding individual sessions during the evaluation. As indicated in Chapter 7, I strongly disagree with this argument.

pist mails a battery of assessment forms to the couple, which is completed by them and returned before the first session. The initial session involves *individual* interviews with each partner. The authors feel that this allows them to form a truer picture of each partner's views on their problems, to assess for individual difficulties that may interfere with couple therapy, to explore each partner's awareness of his or her own contribution to their problems, and to hear about material the partners may be uncomfortable discussing with one another, such as lack of love for the partner, sexual fantasies, current or previous affairs. The individual sessions are followed by a couple session.

Baucom and Epstein's (1990) format for evaluation derives from a cognitive-behavioral viewpoint. They also send out a battery of assessment forms to the couple to be completed and returned before the first session. They do not utilize individual sessions. The evaluation requires two to three hours and may be held in one sitting or spread out over several sessions. The four phases of the evaluation involve obtaining a marital history, discussing current concerns and relational strengths, obtaining a sample of the couple's communication, and providing feedback to the couple. The therapist utilizes the information provided by assessment forms to guide discussion of current concerns. A sample of the couple's communication is obtained by asking them to spend about 10 minutes trying to resolve a "moderate-size problem" in their relationship.

Instruments and Inventories

Up to this point, this chapter has focused on the clinical interview as the primary form of couple evaluation. However, there are also a large number of paper-and-pencil instruments and inventories available for therapists who wish to use them. Jacobson and Margolin (1979) point out that these instruments span a variety of

- observational targets (behaviors, interactional sequences, relationship perceptions, beliefs, affective states, symptoms)
- observer sources (self, partner, significant other, trained observers)
- observational methods (interviews, questionnaires, behavioral rating forms, checklists, tracking instruments, observational coding systems)
- time intervals (one-time measurements, daily, continuous)
- settings (home, therapy session, social environment)

For example, there are many different questionnaires and checklists that can be administered to the partners to assess marital satisfaction, observation of the partner's behavior, areas of desired change, attributions of one's own and the partner's behavior, intimacy, anger, conflict, depression, and sexual patterns, to name only a few. There are behavioral coding systems for observing and quantifying aspects of the couple's interaction. However, L'Abate and Bagarozzi (1993) suggest that validity and reliability of many of these coding systems are questionable. Jacobson and Margolin (1979) assert that "outside observers are not privy to many of the behaviors that are important to intimate adult relationships" and conclude that "collecting several hours of data in couples' homes does not provide much information on how the spouses manage their exchange of major reinforcers. At this stage of our technology, gains from such observation do not warrant the high costs of sending outside observers into the home" (pp. 87–88). The therapist may also want to tailor checklists or questionnaires to assess and measure progress in treatment on idiosyncratic concerns of a particular couple (Jacobson & Margolin, 1979).

Some instruments provide a global picture of some aspect of the couple's relationship, such as overall satisfaction; others are highly specific in the areas they assess. For example, L'Abate and Bagarozzi (1993) list and describe over 25 different inventories for assessing specific aspects of a couple's sexual relationship. Many of these have an extremely narrow focus, such as the Negative Attitudes Toward Masturbation Scale (Abramson & Mosher, 1975) and the Attitudes Toward Homosexuality Scale (MacDonald, Huggins, Young, & Swenson, 1973).

Jacobson and Margolin (1979) discuss the advantages of using assessment instruments.

> For the therapist, questionnaires present a low-cost and low-effort method of gathering information. They also offer a vehicle for collecting information that can be uncomfortable and unproductive for the therapist to pursue during an interview (e.g., "Do thoughts of divorce occur to you more frequently than once per week?"). From the clients' vantage-point, questionnaires are relatively effortless, at least in comparison to other assessment procedures. Furthermore, they often elicit the types of information that spouses are eager to communicate to the therapist. Inventories that can be scored have the advantage of being used as outcome measures to assess the amount of attitudinal change over the course of therapy. These instruments should also be considered as a means of collecting follow-up data. (p. 78)

They caution, however, that in selecting particular instruments, the therapist should consider the specific abilities, such as basic literacy skills, of both partners. They also note that some assessment procedures that the therapist deems useful require a substantial commitment on the part of the couple. For this reason, they assert that "the therapist must be enthusiastic about each assessment task, stressing its utility and its intrinsic interest to the participant. The therapist must also feel confident that what is being requested of the clients is, indeed, essential to the treatment process" (p. 103).

In terms of selection of instruments, Jacobson and Margolin suggest that the assessment include instruments that sample a variety of methodologies and that provide information on the four areas of assessment that they consider most important (partners' beliefs about the relationship, nature of day-to-day interaction, factors contributing to the central relationship problem, and how the partners attempt to bring about change in the relationship). They recommend that the therapist include "formalized instruments to obtain reliable data on the basis of standardized norms, as well as tailor-made procedures to measure progress on couples' idiosyncratic concerns" and note that "the clinician's ultimate choice of which procedures to adopt hinges on the practical issues of cost and utility" (p. 100).

Finally, in light of the demands assessment instruments place on the clients, Jacobson and Margolin, unlike Baucom and Epstein and O'Leary and Arias, recommend that the couple not be asked to complete self-report questionnaires before the initial session with the therapist. They acknowledge that when the instruments are completed before the first session, the therapist will know more and need to gather less information during that session. However, they note that this requires a high degree of effort from the couple before they have even met the therapist and may be experienced by them as "demanding and unpleasant," making the first treatment experience a negative one. For these reasons, they feel that the disadvantages of requiring completion before the first session outweigh the advantages.

Some of the instruments most widely used in evaluating couples include the Locke-Wallace Marital Adjustment Test, the Spanier Dyadic Adjustment Scale, the Spouse Observation Checklist, the Areas-of-Change Questionnaire, and PREPARE-ENRICH.

The Locke-Wallace Marital Adjustment Test (MAT)

The Locke-Wallace Marital Adjustment Test (MAT) (Locke & Wallace, 1959) is one of the most widely used instruments for evaluating couples. It is composed of only 15 items and can therefore be administered and scored easily and briefly. Its test-retest reliability is high and it is sensitive to changes in couple therapy, which makes it a useful measure for assessing progress in treatment. O'Leary and Arias (1987) note, "Almost all measures of outcome in marital therapy such as commitment, positive feelings about the spouse, sexual satisfaction, and observational measures of problem-solving skills correlate with the MAT" (p. 294). However, as L'Abate and Bagarrozi (1993) point out, Locke and Wallace stressed that the scale was best suited for use with middle-class couples.*

The Spanier Dyadic Adjustment Scale (DAS)

The Spanier Dyadic Adjustment Scale (DAS) (Spanier, 1976) is a self-report inventory that is used to provide an overall indicator of marital adjustment. DAS scores correlate highly with those of the MAT. It consists of 32 items, which yield four factors: dyadic consensus, dyadic cohesion, dyadic satisfaction, and affectional expression. The therapist can use the summary score as a measure of adjustment or use specific item responses to identify areas of disagreement in particular content areas, such as religion, amount of time spent together, and career decisions.

The Spouse Observation Checklist (SOC)

The Spouse Observation Checklist (SOC) (Weiss, Hops, & Patterson, 1973) is one of several instruments developed at the University of Oregon and Oregon Research Institute; it is designed to assess specific current behaviors in a couple's relationship. It describes over 400 behaviors that might occur in a relationship and asks both partners to select an agreed-upon 24-hour period and, at the end of it, to check the behaviors that occurred during that time. Each partner reports about the behavior of the partner and of him- or herself. The items are grouped into 12 content areas such as affection, communication, child care and parenting, financial decision making, among others. The individual indicates that a behavior occurred by placing it into either a "pleasing" or "displeasing" category.

As Baucom and Epstein point out, the therapist cannot assume that the SOC provides an accurate report of which behaviors actually occurred since many might be unnoticed or differently interpreted by the observing partner. However, discrepancies that arise from these differences can alert the therapist to "significant cognitive factors which may be filtering the spouses' experience of their encounters"

---

*The MAT is included in its entirety with instructions for scoring in the Appendix to O'Leary, 1987.

(1990, p. 141). He or she can also be alert for behaviors expected to be important for most couples but which the partners do not report as having occurred. Finally, the therapist can examine the average frequency of overall pleasures and displeasures that occur during a given day.

The Areas-of-Change Questionnaire (A-C)

The Areas-of-Change Questionnaire (A-C) (Weiss et al., 1973) has two parts, each consisting of 34 items. In the first part, the individual addresses his or her own behavior; in the second, that of his or her partner. In Part I, the individual—let's assume a man—uses a six-point rating scale to indicate how much he does or does not want his partner to change her behavior in a particular area, such as "participating in decisions about spending money." Other areas include communication, relatives, friends, sex, work habits, leisure time, and so on. In Part II, he uses the same six-point scale to record how much he thinks his partner wants him to change his behavior in these same areas.

The summary score provides a global index of the amount of change desired by each partner. Responses on particular items can direct the therapist to areas in which the desire for change is especially great. Responses also allow the therapist to identify areas which seem to be working well in the relationship. Finally, comparisons of Part I of one partner's responses with Part II of the other's yields information about whether the latter understands what the partner wants from him or her. Summary scores of the A-C correlate with global measures of marital adjustment and are sensitive to changes in behavioral marital therapy.

PREPARE, PREPARE-MC, and ENRICH (PREPARE-ENRICH)

Olson and his colleagues (Fowers & Olson, 1986, 1989, 1992; Larsen & Olson, 1989; Olson, Fournier, & Druckman, 1986) have developed a technologically sophisticated set of inventories for evaluating couples, referred to as PREPARE, PREPARE-MC, and ENRICH (PREPARE-ENRICH). Each inventory consists of 125 questions, which the individual scores on a five-point scale. The questions are designed to assess 14 areas, including communication, conflict resolution, sexual relationship, equalitarian roles, realistic expectations, financial management, among others. They also include global measurements of marital satisfaction and realistic expectations, as well as a validity scale, which corrects for a respondent's tendency to respond in a socially desirable but not necessarily accurate manner.

PREPARE is used with premarital couples; ENRICH, with married couples or couples cohabiting for two years or more; and PREPARE-MC, with premarital couples who have children. Norms are based on either 100,000 or 300,000 couples, depending on the inventory used. Reliability and validity are high. Olson et al. claim, based on several studies, that the inventories can predict divorce with between 80% and 90% accuracy.

The authors encourage therapists to instruct couples to complete the questionnaire forms after an initial interview, separately from each other, and in the therapist's office rather than at home. The therapist sends the completed questionnaires to a central office where they are scored by computer. This generates an 11-page computer report that compares the partners' scores on each scale, identifying it as either a "relationship strength" (both partners are very satisfied with this area and agree on most issues) or "possible strength" (somewhat satisfied and agree on many issues) or "possible growth area" (dissatisfied and disagree on some issues) or a "growth area" (generally dissatisfied and disagree on several issues). The report also provides specific responses on particular items in order to facilitate more detailed analysis of the content of responses. Finally, using the conceptual frame of the Circumplex Model (Olson, Russell & Sprenkle, 1989), the report for ENRICH describes the type of relationship each partner feels they have and the type they would like to have (reports for PREPARE describe the family of origin of each partner). The therapist spends about $100 for the materials required to administer and interpret the inventories; Olson et al. suggest that the costs for each couple's computer report ($25) be passed along to the clients.

PREPARE-ENRICH is more time-consuming to complete and more costly, both for the therapist and the couple. However, these disadvantages are balanced by the wealth, organization, and specificity of information provided and the time saved by having the computer rather than the therapist score the couple's responses.*

Therapists who use assessment instruments must consider which to use, when to administer them, and how to weigh the trade-offs they involve—the value of the information obtained against the time, cost, and effort required from both the couple and the therapist. Some therapists, such as Jacobson and Margolin (1979), rely on these instruments as the primary form of assessment of current problems in the relation-

*To inquire about or purchase PREPARE-ENRICH, write to: PREPARE-ENRICH, P.O. Box 190, Minneapolis, MN 55440–0190, or call 1-800-331-1661.

ship. Others, such as Hof and Treat (1989), rely on clinical interviews but also administer one or two of the most commonly used instruments. Most therapists who treat couples probably use instruments only rarely if at all.

The case against using instruments rests on the conviction that much, if not all, of the information gleened from them can be obtained via clinical interviews, making the use of instruments unnecessarily time-consuming, costly and potentially alienating for clients. In the evaluating format described in this volume, the use of individual sessions and probe questions assess information comparable to that obtained by many paper-and-pencil instruments. Further limitations of instruments involve the rigidity of fixed categories, the unsuitability for populations other than those for whom the instrument was developed, the "atomism" or extreme specificity of information obtained, and the loss of understanding of the personal meaning of what is being assessed for the respondent.

If therapists do choose to utilize assessment instruments, the risks described above can be minimized in the following ways:

1. Inform the couple about instruments to be used—and explain the reasons for their use—when the evaluation is being arranged.
2. Meet with the couple in person before giving them instruments to complete.
3. Use information obtained from instruments as a springboard for further inquiry during interviews; this makes it more likely that you will come to understand the idiosyncratic meanings associated with responses for the particular clients involved.

Readers who wish to learn more about a wide range of evaluative instruments, including self-report questionnaires relevant to couple relationships, observer checklists, and observer scoring systems, should consult Baucom and Epstein (1990), L'Abate and Bagarozzi (1993), and O'Leary (1987).

⌐ 14 ⌐

CRITERIA OF A
"GOOD-ENOUGH"
COUPLE EVALUATION

THE DISTINCTION BETWEEN good-enough and its implicit alternative—perfection—is a liberating one for clients and it should be for therapists as well. Like all craftspeople, therapists study and learn from the masters. However, the image of the Actualized Master can easily turn from useful guide into oppressive and unreachable ideal. Idealized and unrealistic images can undermine a therapist's confidence in his or her own knowledge and skills. Therapists need to know what constitutes a good-enough evaluation and good-enough treatment. This can help them feel less intimidated by the tyranny of the ideal, more confident about the services they provide and, when results are not positive, more able to distinguish their own responsibility from the clients'.

What is a good-enough couple evaluation? What is the minimum that therapists should try to accomplish in order to fulfill their responsibilities to the couple, to themselves and, when this is relevant, to others involved (such as children)? The answers to these questions begin with a recognition of the collaborative nature of couple evaluation.

The Couple Evaluation as a Collaborative Process

Couple evaluation, like all clinical work, is a fundamentally collaborative enterprise. There is virtually no facet of the evaluation in which we can justifiably say, "The therapist must accomplish X." With few exceptions, we need to say instead, "The therapist *attempts* to X" or "The therapist *endeavors* to Y." Like all relationships, the evaluation is like a tennis game and the results depend on the participation of all parties. One party hits the ball over the net; what does the other person do with it? Does he hit it back? Does he fumble it? Does he stand with arms folded or walk off the court? If he hits the ball back, what does the first person do next?

The purposes of the evaluation can only be accomplished if the therapist and the couple collaborate in the process. The therapist's job is to structure the evaluation so that it is most likely to meet its goals, to join with both partners so as to facilitate this process, to know what to ask and observe (and how to ask and observe) in order to understand the couple's difficulties, and to make sensible and, hopefully, helpful recommendations. The couple must be able to extend some measure of trust to the therapist and to respond as honestly as possible to his or her questions. In other words, a portion of the responsibility for the success of the evaluation rests with the therapist; a portion rests with the couple. Each of the participants has the power to thwart the purposes of the evaluation by not fulfilling his or her part of the collaboration.

The concept of a good-enough evaluation, joined with an appreciation for its collaborative underpinnings, can help therapists in several ways: first, by liberating them from the tyranny of the ideal; second, by underscoring the baseline of what they do need to accomplish; and finally, by reminding them that they cannot accomplish anything alone. With this understanding, they can "hold up their end of the bargain" and not punish themselves if one or both partners do not hold up theirs. The criteria of a good-enough evaluation involve the following five areas: (1) building alliances, (2) conducting the inquiry, (3) managing the process and direction of the evaluation, (4) upholding ethical standards, and (5) providing feedback.

Building Alliances

Building alliances is the most important component of the evaluation since, without positive alliances, the collaborative process breaks down and little else can be accomplished. Try to convey to both partners that you are sympathetic to their welfare and genuinely interested in how they experience the relationship. Try to make clear that you will look out for both parties' interests in your discussions. In other words, you are, from the start, *predisposed to be sympathetic* to both of them. You will not side with one partner against the other, judging or dismissing either as "unworthy," "sick," or "bad" (although you will hold both accountable for how they treat each other).

Treat them with respect and convey self-respect as well. Try to demonstrate that you are trustworthy as well as professionally competent. You have no personal axes to grind, at least none which will enter into their work with you. In a good-enough evaluation, you needn't be loved or revered by the clients; they needn't feel that you are the most sympathetic or competent or brilliant professional they have encountered. They simply need to feel enough safety and trust that they can talk honestly about themselves, and allow you to form some understanding of their difficulties in order to recommend steps that might help them.

Remember that some alliances simply cannot be made, due to the resistance of one or both clients or to idiosyncratic factors (e.g., a husband who refuses to believe that a female therapist can be competent). Your part is only half of the game; this aspect of a good-enough evaluation has been fulfilled when you have made the best effort possible to secure and merit the trust of both partners.

Conducting the Inquiry

Information must be gathered, and although this book discusses many different facets of couple relationships and many different areas to assess, no therapist needs to explore all of them in any particular case. For a good-enough evaluation, you must try to understand the nature of the presenting problem within its context, and the forces that maintain it. Try to be aware of the meaning of the couple's difficulties to the individuals involved and the aspects of their situation that are most pressing or painful to them. This aspect of a good-enough evaluation has been fulfilled when you have seriously endeavored to assess the presenting problem in its context, along with the forces that maintain it, and attempted to understand the needs, values, and agendas of the clients in relation to treatment recommendations.

Managing the Process and Direction of the Evaluation

To understand where the partners want the evaluation to lead and what conditions are necessary to accomplish this requires an effort on your part to understand their goals and agendas for the evaluation (both overt and covert). The couple who wishes to decide whether to continue working on a relationship that has been dissatisfying for years or to finally end it have a very different agenda for the evaluation than does the couple who would never think of separation and wants advice on how to reduce their level of conflict.

You might do an excellent job of forming alliances, achieve a good understanding of a couple's presenting problems, and develop what appear to be sensible recommendations for treatment; however, if you fail to see that the husband is trying to "hand off" his wife—to help her secure an ally so that he can leave her with less guilt, all of you will be working at cross purposes from one another. A good-enough evaluation requires that you try to understand both partners' goals and agendas for the evaluation and, in some way, to address them.

Endeavor to manage the evaluation so that something constructive can be accomplished. For example, with a couple whose conflict is so intense and unremitting that it is virtually impossible to gather information, you must try to contain the conflict so that the work of the evaluation can be conducted. This might involve active intervention when arguments begin or opting for separate sessions with each partner. This aspect of a good-enough evaluation has been fulfilled if you have done your best to understand where the clients want the evaluation to lead and attempted to supervise its progress in that direction.

Upholding Ethical Standards

The recognition and fulfillment of ethical responsibilities to clients constitute essential and often overlooked aspects of clinical work. While different therapists may interpret ethical responsibilities in different ways and hold themselves to differing standards, the following are the most common, and hopefully minimal, standards of ethical conduct for therapists.

Never knowingly commit—or omit—any act that will result in injury to a client. In other words, you must, as in the Hippocratic Oath, "First of all, do no harm."

Always use your position of influence and trust in the clients' interests rather than your own. This means that you must avoid dual relationships—forms of relationship, other than that of therapist and client, which are superimposed over the existing therapy relationship. These relationships (for example, sexual relationships between therapist and client) represent an exploitation of the client's trust and a violation of his or her interests.

Maintain strict confidentiality (unless the clients request that this be waived in order for you to communicate with a particular agency, practitioner, or insurance carrier). The clients' right to confidentiality is not without exception since therapists are mandated in most states to report on various types of abuse, to inform persons whom the therapist knows may be in danger from a client, and to prevent suicide attempts when this is possible. You should be well-informed about the laws governing confidentiality and privilege in the state in which you practice.

Know the limits of your own competence and do not present yourself as having expertise that you do not possess. You have a responsibility to refer clients to appropriate treatment providers when you do not possess required expertise, when you do not choose to or cannot provide treatment yourself, or when you must—for whatever reason— terminate treatment with clients who wish to continue in therapy.

Manage your own feelings toward clients when these threaten to disrupt or subvert treatment. If you are aware that your feelings toward a client are interfering with the goals of evaluation or treatment, you must either engage in a careful process of self-examination, seek consultation with another professional about these feelings, or refer the case to another practitioner.

Fulfill your legal obligations as a mandated reporter when you become aware of child abuse or abuse of the elderly, when you are aware that an individual may be in danger from a client, and when you suspect that a suicide attempt by a client is likely.

Failure to uphold these standards constitutes a violation of your ethical responsibilities to clients and others. In addition, these violations may lead to censure by professional organizations; they may also be punishable by law or provide the basis for a malpractice judgement. All therapists should familiarize themselves with the ethical standards of their professions and with legal statutes regulating practice in their states. This aspect of a good-enough evaluation is fulfilled by your being aware of these ethical responsibilities and monitoring your behavior in order to uphold them.

Providing Responses and Recommendations

A therapist must be able to do more than simply gather information during the course of the evaluation; he or she needs to comment on the information and impressions gathered in an effort to help the couple pursue some direction for ameliorating their difficulties. This may involve a recommendation for continuing in couple therapy—and perhaps more specific suggestions such as how to get started, which problems to address in what order, and how often to meet—or it may involve recommending a different approach to treatment.

Feedback can be provided as the evaluation proceeds or at its conclusion. In either case, you want to suggest interpretations and directions that you believe will be most helpful to your clients. You are not responsible for having the answer to every important question facing the couple or for being certain of your hunches when this is impossible. Asking the right questions, even when you don't have the answers, can be more helpful than trying to answer the wrong ones. You hope that your responses, impressions, intuitions, and recommendations will be helpful to them, but you cannot and should not be expected to guarantee this.

"Knowing your customers" and tailoring your responses to maximize the likelihood of their acceptance are important components of this process. This aspect of a good-enough evaluation has been fulfilled when you have considered the information gathered, made your own best judgement of what directions will prove most helpful to the clients, and presented this in a way that you hope will be congruent and acceptable to them.

If you have tried to fulfill these criteria to the best of your ability, then you have given enough to the evaluation. Hopefully, both partners will fulfill their parts in this collaboration and all three parties will feel satisfied with its progress and its outcome. However, even if the partners do not, you can feel satisfied that you have done your job in a competent and trustworthy manner.

⌁ III ⌁

SPECIAL ISSUES

THE FOLLOWING CHAPTERS examine a number of problem configurations commonly encountered by therapists who treat couples. Each introduces special considerations into the evaluation and, to varying degrees, requires special handling by the therapist. Some pose potential threats to the evaluation and to subsequent treatment. Therapists will be better prepared to meet these challenges if they are aware of basic information about these problems and widely accepted guidelines for assessment and clinical management.

Chapters 15 through 20 examine, respectively, sexual difficulties, domestic violence, alcoholism, depression, extramarital involvements, and serious illness. Each chapter includes a review of basic information (such as prevalence and characteristic patterns), a consideration of common patterns and effects in couple relationships, guidelines for assessment, principles involved in clinical management, information about common forms of treatment, and recommended readings for therapists and, in most cases, for clients as well. The material in some of these chapters is partially based on interviews with experts in the particular problem area. If an individual is cited without any publication date, this indicates that the points in question were communicated in the course of these interviews.

~ 15 ~

SEXUAL DIFFICULTIES

I T IS A TRUISM among couple therapists that conflict is likely to interfere with a couple's satisfaction in their sexual relationship. It's difficult for partners to be loving, generous, spontaneous, vulnerable, and
playful when one is furious at the other or, even worse, afraid of him
or her, or when he or she feels mistreated, neglected, or constantly
criticized. It is equally true—and important for couple therapists to
recognize—that sexual difficulties in an otherwise satisfying relationship can damage both partners' self-esteem and contribute to emotional disengagement and escalating conflict which spill into other
areas of the relationship. Relationships in which the partners are loving and happy with one another can be seriously damaged by a compar-

This chapter was prepared with assistance from Joseph LoPiccolo, Ph.D., Professor of Psychology, University of Missouri, Columbia, Missouri, and Stephen
R. Treat, D.Min., Senior Therapist, Marriage Council Incorporated of Philadelphia, Philadelphia, Pennsylvania.

atively minor and easily treatable sexual disorder, such as early ejaculation, or by significant differences in the partners' "sexual scripts" (Rosen
& Leiblum, 1988, 1992) or "lovemaps" (Money, 1986). These difficulties are often compounded by the rigid and self-defeating *meanings*
that partners attach to them.

Longings for sexual satisfaction are central to most couple relationships; they derive from cultural expectations, physiological needs and,
perhaps most importantly, deep psychological needs for attachment,
intimacy, and passionate vitality in a relationship. Because of the fundamental importance of these longings, the quality of a couple's sexual
relationship and the quality of their relationship as a whole are insepa-
rably fused. Clinicians who routinely evaluate couples need to appreciate the ways in which difficulties in one area can contribute to or
create difficulties in others.

The importance of a satisfying sexual relationship for the couple's
overall satisfaction is suggested by the term, "the pleasure bond" (Masters & Johnson, 1975). This phrase conveys a recognition that, while
partners can feel connected on many different levels, there is a unique
feeling of connection that comes from the intimacy of being sexual
partners. This bond is made up of the experience of knowing the other
person's body and his or her sexual needs and responses and being
known in the same way, the sense of accessibility to the other and
allowing oneself to be accessible, and of shared moments of passion,
playfulness, vulnerability, and satisfaction.

These feelings express the uniqueness of this intimate emotional
and physical relationship which, as the Scharffs (1991) point out, is,
alongside the mother-infant dyad, the only wholly psychosomatic
partnership. These are generally the only kinds of relationships in
which we are hugged and cuddled, fondled and played with by another
person whom we come to know at deeper and more intimate levels as
time goes on.

Sexual Dysfunctions

If the notion of the "pleasure bond" conveys the ideal of sexuality in
couple relationships, the reality is often more complicated and problematic. Masters and Johnson (1970) estimate that 50% of all American couples suffer from some type of sexual dysfunction and, in a
survey of happily married couples, Frank et al. (1978) report that 40%
of the men reported erectile or ejaculatory dysfunction and 63% of
the women reported arousal or orgasmic dysfunction. Even where no
diagnosable dysfunction exists, there may be what Lief (1991) refers to
as "sexual difficulties" (see below).

Probably the most widely used schema of human sexual response is Kaplan's (1979) triphasic model, which separates sexual response into three phases: desire, arousal, and orgasm. The model has helped organize the conceptualization, diagnosis, and treatment of sexual disorders. For example, early ejaculation in the male and inhibited orgasm in males and females are disorders of the orgasm phase. Erectile problems involve the arousal phase. An important development in the sex therapy field over the past 15 years has been a growing awareness of the prevalence of inhibited sexual desire, a desire phase disorder. An assumption generally accepted among sex therapists is that the earlier in the sequence of phases a problem is found, the more difficult it is to treat.

The more accurately the therapist can identify the specific sexual disorder(s) involved in a particular case, the less likely that time, hope, and money will be misspent on treatment directed at a misdiagnosed problem. Treatment targeted at an erectile disorder will be frustrating and unproductive if the therapist has overlooked the fact that the man has no sexual desire for his wife. Schover, Friedman, Weiler, Heiman, and LoPiccolo (1982) have proposed a multiaxial, problem-oriented diagnostic system which is more specific and inclusive than the DSM-III diagnostic categories.

Beyond the diagnosable sexual disorders, there are a variety of "sexual difficulties" (Lief, 1991) that couples present. These include disjunctions in their sexual preferences involving the frequency and timing of sexual contact (time of day or night), the setting, the time devoted to foreplay, the repertoire of sexual activities included in an encounter, coital positions, timing of penetration, afterplay, the degree of passion and affection expressed during sex, the acceptability of fantasy, and involvement with other sexual partners.

These difficulties highlight the idiosyncratic nature of each person's sexuality. While there are obviously commonalities across individuals, especially given the biologically driven and instinctual basis of sexuality, there is at the same time a striking diversity in the ways in which individual human beings express these instinctual patterns, in the wide range of objects to which they are attracted, and in the idiosyncratic matches and mismatches that occur when two particular individuals join in a sexual relationship.

Individuals may have highly idiosyncratic scripts for what kind of person or situation they find sexually exciting and for what kind of activities they need to engage in for sexual satisfaction. John Money (1986) refers to these as "lovemaps."

[A] lovemap is not present at birth. Like a native language, it differentiates within a few years thereafter. It is a developmental representation or template in your mind/brain, and is dependent on input through the special senses. It depicts your idealized lover and what, as a pair, you do together in the idealized, romantic, erotic, and sexualized relationship. A lovemap exists in mental imagery first, in dreams or fantasies, and then may be translated into action with a partner or partners. (p. xvi)

Rosen and Leiblum (1992) refer to these patterns as "sexual scripts."

Sexual scripts define the range of sexual behaviors that are acceptable, with whom, under what circumstances, and with what motives. The sexual scripts of partners in a relationship may vary considerably, and this lack of congruence frequently paves the way for the development of a sexual dysfunction or desire disorder. (p. 244)

Ideally, there is enough overlap in the partners' scripts that a mutually satisfying sexual relationship can be worked out. In many cases, however, this is problematic. For example, a woman who needs a forceful, confident partner and a high level of sexual spontaneity and variety in order to be sexually excited is paired with a gentle, romantic man whose ideal sexual relationship involves slow, gentle stimulation and a limited range of sexual positions and activities. The couple may love each other and have an otherwise satisfying relationship but continually disappoint or frustrate each other sexually.

The difficulty of integrating lovemaps is even greater when one partner's sexual script is paraphilic. Paraphilia involves "an extreme degree of investment in, or consumption by, a sexual behavior that dominates and directs a person's sexual practices. Paraphilic sexual practices are central to a person's sexual excitement. In many cases sexual excitement cannot occur without the paraphilic behavior" (Wincze, 1989, p. 383). Typical examples include voyeurism, exhibitionism, transvestitism, and pedophilia. As this very limited list suggests, paraphilias can be *coercive*, in which a person such as a child or stranger is victimized, or *noncoercive*, as when a man habitually masturbates while cross-dressing (Wincze). Money (1986) describes approximately 40 different paraphilias, organized by the different thematic content of the lovemaps involved. An undisclosed paraphilic lovemap has significance for the couple and for the therapist who evaluates them. What at first appears to be a common sexual dysfunction, such as erectile difficulty or inhibited sexual desire, may be masking an undisclosed paraphilia; in these cases treatment aimed at the apparent difficulty will almost certainly fail. Also, these couples are very likely to experience difficulties associated with the paraphilic's compulsive sexual behavior, ranging from disinterest in the partner to humiliating and expensive legal difficulties.

The therapist should also be aware of the extremely negative impact on sexuality that can occur when one partner is a survivor of child sexual abuse, whether the abuse was committed by a family member, some other trusted adult (such as a neighbor, a friend's parent, a priest or minister), or a stranger.

Finally, therapists must understand that the causes of sexual difficulties vary. Zilbergeld (1992) suggests that they may stem from sexual ignorance and a debilitating faith in common sexual myths. He also stresses the importance of the conditions in which sex takes place; the partners may be either unaware of or unable to ask for the conditions that are necessary for their sexual response systems to operate without interference. Medical problems may also cause sexual difficulties. Distress in the overall couple relationship may cause sexual problems. Humphrey (1987) points out that sexual response is often disrupted when one partner is involved in an extramarital affair.

Like any other symptom or problem, sexual difficulties may also serve systemic functions in the couple's relationship (LoPiccolo & Daiss, 1988; Zilbergeld, 1992). A couple in which the wife's orgasmic difficulty is the focus for treatment may be unconsciously protecting the husband from having to face his own sexual fears and insecurities. In an unmarried couple, the man's erectile difficulties may serve to postpone a deeper level of commitment in the relationship which would trigger his fears of entrapment. Part of the assessment of sexual difficulties involves trying to identify when such patterns are operating and what functions are being served.

Assessment

For the therapist who is evaluating couples, it is important to distinguish between those couples who are coming in with a clear sexual complaint as part of the presenting problem and those who do not identify sexual difficulties initially. Because of the central importance of the sexual relationship for the overall couple relationship, some assessment of the couple's current satisfaction with their sexual relationship should be done *in all cases of couple evaluation* (LoPiccolo & Daiss, 1988; Scharff & Scharff, 1991). The discussion that follows assumes that the couple has identified sexual problems as a reason for treatment. When procedures would differ for couples who do *not* identify sexual problems, this will be noted.

In *all* cases involving exploration of a couple's sexual relationship, it is critical that the therapist adopt a *nonjudgmental stance*. The only exception to this rule involves cases in which one partner is being coerced or sexually abused. If sexual activity is nonconsenting, your obligation to prevent injury overrides the desirability of a nonjudgmental stance. It is also important to remember that sexual problems are defined by the partner's subjective discomfort or unhappiness, not by an objective criteria of sexual performance. If the partners have extremely infrequent sex but are both satisfied with this pattern, there is *no* sexual problem. The same can be said for what would otherwise be diagnosable sexual disorders or noncoercive paraphilic patterns which they are able to incorporate into their sexual relationship. Unless one or both partners complain about the pattern, it does not constitute a sexual problem for them. Therapists must be careful to follow the *clients'* agendas for treatment without imposing their own values about sexuality.

For couples who specifically identify sexual problems, the exploration of these problems can take place early in the first couple session; the procedure is comparable to other couple cases, the only difference being that the presenting problem is sexual in nature. For couples who do not identify sexual difficulties, this area of inquiry should come much later in the initial session. In *all cases*, you should try to establish trust and rapport before exploring sexual issues.

If a particular couple identifies sexual problems but has great difficulty discussing them, you might choose to explore other areas of the relationship first as a way of helping them feel more comfortable. If you decide to do this, be sure to explain your switching tracks to the couple; not doing so may convey the impression that *you* are uncomfortable talking about sexual matters. You might say, "Most people find it difficult initially to discuss these private matters with a third person. If you don't mind, let me ask about some other aspects of your lives together, and we'll come back to the sexual difficulties in a little while." If you have "read" the clients well, there will be figurative—if not literal—sigh of relief, trust and safety will have been enhanced, and the likelihood of a productive exploration of the problem later in the session increased.

LoPiccolo and Daiss (1988) point out that the therapist should be sure to explain the nature, and limits, of professional confidentiality and privilege; this is done both for legal purposes and to allay any fears based on misconceptions about confidentiality. Schover (1989) urges that therapists be mindful of how much detailed information they put into case records, especially in settings such as hospitals or HMOs where records may circulate widely and be accessible to a large number of staff.

The therapist should signal the transition to the exploration of sexual issues; LoPiccolo and Daiss suggest that the difficulty of such discussion be acknowledged. "A good therapeutic statement is, 'I know it's a little uncomfortable to talk about something as personal as your sexual relationship. I'll try to make this as easy for you as I can, and certainly please let me know if there is anything I can do that will make you more comfortable'" (p. 188). For couples who don't identify sexual problems, the transition might be facilitated with the probe question suggested in Chapter 6: "Could you describe the evolution of your sexual relationship—how it has changed, if at all—over the course of your relationship?"

Assessing sexual problems needs to be very specific for accurate diagnosis and successful treatment. While specificity is always important, this is especially so when exploring sexual problems in light of the extreme privacy usually associated with sexuality. This heightens feelings of shame, making it more likely that important details may be omitted and contributing to a high level of sexual ignorance in the culture at large. This means that clients often come for treatment with important misconceptions about sex. A colleague once evaluated a young couple in which both partners complained of the husband's early ejaculation. Detailed questioning revealed that he generally lasted about 25 minutes before ejaculating, a pattern that many men dearly wish for but that was insufficient for this man's partner to reach orgasm. The cotherapy team helped the partners learn how the man could provide more direct stimulation for the woman, making it easier for her to come to orgasm. Tiefer and Melman (1989) provide the example of a recent immigrant to this country who complained of erectile difficulty. "Painstaking interview finally clarified that he had erectile problems only on the second or third intercourse attempt of each of these casual encounters, a pattern that he utilized because sexual opportunities were so infrequent since his emigration" (p. 212).

LoPiccolo and Daiss suggest that the therapist begin with broad questions and proceed to more specific ones. One technique that facilitates a very specific exploration of the current sexual relationship involves what some sex therapists refer to as "video with voice-over" (Goldner & Rosenheck, 1990). The therapist introduces this by pointing out that, unlike arguments over finances or in-laws, he or she cannot observe the couple's sexual relationship. For this reason, they need to provide a detailed verbal description of a typical sexual encounter, including what they actually do and what each is thinking or feeling as the encounter progresses. The therapist asks about the conditions under which sex occurs in order to ascertain whether the partners' necessary conditions for sex are being met.

The therapist also asks specific questions, with a tone of professionalism, caring, respect, and comfort with the subject matter: How do you decide when it's time to begin intercourse? What are you feeling when he's stimulating your breasts? What are you experiencing when you're thrusting? He or she hopes to identify internal or interactional factors that may be contributing to the couple's sexual difficulties. For example, a detailed inquiry reveals that, although she has never told him, his efforts to stimulate her genitally are too rough and off the mark, or that when he touches her breasts as part of foreplay she becomes tense and fearful, remembering experiences of child sexual abuse.

During this detailed inquiry, the therapist must avoid language that is extremely colloquial or, conversely, too technical, and, of course, that which is judgmental. It is preferable to talk about "difficulty with erections" or "difficulty with orgasm" rather than "impotence" or "frigidity," "when you enter" rather than "intromission."

LoPiccolo and Daiss recommend that separate individual sessions be used to explore "taboo" topics. These include sexual fantasies and masturbation practices, homosexual thoughts, fantasies, and experiences; unpleasant or traumatic sexual experiences, and deviant or nontypical sexual practices. Exploration of sexual fantasies sheds light on each partner's sexual script. A good neutral question that can elicit information about sexual trauma or deviant sexuality was suggested by Ann Burgess in a workshop at a conference I attended several years ago: "Have you ever been involved in any sexual experience that made you feel uncomfortable?"

Deviant sexual practices should be assessed since they may be implicated in more obvious sexual disorders such as inhibited sexual desire or erectile difficulties. LoPiccolo and Daiss recommend inquiring about *adolescent* masturbation, fantasies, and practices since clients may be more willing to admit deviant practices historically, especially if the question is introduced by mentioning that most adolescents experiment with a wide range of practices as they explore their sexuality. If the therapist responds supportively and nonjudgementally, the client may then disclose current fantasies and practices.

The inquiry in the individual meeting also includes "taboo areas" in the general couple relationship. "Do they find their spouse to be sexually skilled and a good lover? Does their spouse have adequate personal hygiene habits?" (LoPiccolo & Daiss, pp. 191–192). Is there anything about the partner's love-making that turns them off sexually?

A sexual history should be taken for each partner, including when the client became aware of sex, attitudes, and implicit messages about sexuality in his or her family of origin, early sex play, and first sexual experiences. Sex therapists differ on how much detail is required in this area. LoPiccolo and Daiss defer these detailed histories until after the evaluation is completed, at which point they become the first step of treatment. Outlines for history-taking in sex therapy cases are provided in Lobitz and Lobitz (1978) and LoPiccolo and Heiman (1978).

Therapists must be aware that medical factors may be contributing or causing a couple's sexual problems; a brief medical history of each partner, including illnesses, injuries, and any current medication may alert the therapist to this possibility. It is a good idea to recommend that the partners undergo a medical evaluation, if they have not already done so. The importance of medical evaluation is not simply a matter of careful assessment; the therapist needs to consider the time, money, and hope wasted if the couple diligently pursues psychologically or interactionally based treatment when there are medical obstacles to sexual functioning. And, as LoPiccolo and Daiss point out, "treating a sexual problem stemming from medical causes as a psychological problem may result in a malpractice suit" (p. 202).

Finally, sexual difficulties may serve systemic functions in a couple's relationship; as in the exploration of any presenting problem, the therapist should try to identify when this is the case and what functions might be served by the problem. LoPiccolo and Heiman (1978) recommend that the therapist end the couple interview by asking, "Is there anything else that you would like to tell me about your background that you feel bears on your sexual life?" This open-ended question invites the partners to disclose idiosyncratic factors that the therapist could not anticipate in a general screening.

There are also pencil-and-paper instruments used to assess sexual difficulties. Some of the more commonly used instruments include the Sexual History Form (Heiman & LoPiccolo, 1983; LoPiccolo, Heiman, Hogan, & Roberts, 1985), the Sexual Interaction Inventory (LoPiccolo & Steger, 1974), the Derogatis Sexual Functioning Inventory (Derogatis, 1975, 1978; Derogatis & Melisaratos, 1979) and the Sexual Opinion Survey (Fisher, 1988; Fisher, Byrne, White, & Kelley, 1988).

It is beyond the scope of this chapter to discuss the treatment of sexual disorders. Leiblum and Rosen's volume (1989), is an excellent introduction and can be supplemented by Kaplan's volumes (1974, 1979) and that of LoPiccolo and LoPiccolo (1978).

When To Refer for Sex Therapy

In an ideal world, therapists who evaluate and treat couples would all be trained and skilled in sex therapy as well. However, not all couple therapists are skilled in sex therapy and not all wish to be. Therapists who want to increase their skills in sex therapy can educate themselves by seeking training in sex therapy programs or by attending sex therapy workshops. They can explore the readings provided at the end of this chapter, join professional organizations for sex therapists, such as the American Association of Sex Educators, Counselors, and Therapists (435 North Michigan Avenue, Suite 1717, Chicago, IL 60611), and seek consultation and supervision in sex therapy cases.

Therapists who are untrained in sex therapy should appreciate the complexity of sexual problems and approach these cases with humility, and they should be especially cognizant of medical causes of sexual problems. Unless they have training or extensive experience in sex therapy, therapists should not attempt to conduct sex therapy. If they have some but not extensive experience, they might decide to provide treatment but only with close consultation or supervision by an expert in this area. Finally, if they feel uncomfortable with the idea of conducting sex therapy or have no interest in doing so, they should be aware of skilled practitioners to whom they can refer couples with sexual difficulties.

Recommended Reading for Therapists

Althof, S., & Kingsberg, S. (1992). Books helpful to patients with sexual and marital problems: A bibliography. *Journal of Sex and Marital Therapy, 18,* 70–79.

Kaplan, H. (1974). *The new sex therapy: Active treatment of sexual dysfunctions.* New York: Brunner/Mazel.

Kaplan, H. (1979). *Disorders of sexual desire and other new concepts and techniques in sex therapy.* New York: Brunner/Mazel.

Leiblum, R., & Rosen, R. (1989). *Principles and practice of sex therapy: Update for the 1990s.* New York: Guilford.

Lobitz, W., & Lobitz, G. (1978). Clinical assessment in the treatment of sexual dysfunctions. In J. LoPiccolo & L. LoPiccolo (Eds.), *Handbook of sex therapy* (pp. 85–102). New York: Plenum.

LoPiccolo, J., & Daiss, S. (1988). Assessment of sexual dysfunction. In K. O'Leary (Ed.), *Assessment of marital discord* (pp. 183–221). Hillsdale, NJ: Lawrence Erlbaum.

LoPiccolo, J., & Heiman, J. (1978). Sexual assessment and history interview. In J. LoPiccolo & L. LoPiccolo (Eds.), *Handbook of sex therapy* (pp. 103–112). New York: Plenum.

LoPiccolo, J., & LoPiccolo, L. (Eds.). (1978). *Handbook of sex therapy.* New York: Plenum.

LoPiccolo, J., & Steger, J. (1974). The sexual interaction inventory: A new instrument for assessment of sexual dysfunction. *Archives of Sexual Behavior, 3,* 585–595.

Masters, W., & Johnson, V. (1966). *Human sexual response.* Boston: Little, Brown.

Masters, W., & Johnson, V. (1970). *Human sexual inadequacy*. Boston: Little, Brown.

Money, J. (1986). *Lovemaps: Clinical concepts of sexual/erotic health and pathology, paraphilia, and gender transposition in childhood, adolescence, and maturity*. New York: Irvington.

Scharff, D., & Scharff, J. (1991). *Object relations couple therapy*. Northvale, NJ: Jason Aronson.

Schover, L., Friedman, J., Weiler, S., Heiman, J., & LoPiccolo, J. (1982). Multiaxial problem-oriented system for sexual dysfunctions: An alternative to DSM-III. *Archives of General Psychiatry, 39*, 614–619.

Wincze, J. (1989). Assessment and treatment of atypical sexual behavior. In S. Leiblum & R. Rosen (Eds.), *Principles and practice of sex therapy: Update for the 1990s* (pp. 382–404). New York: Guilford.

Wincze, J., & Carey, M. (1991). *Sexual dysfunction: A guide for assessment and treatment*. New York: Guilford.

Recommended Reading for Clients

[In the Spring, 1992 issue of the *Journal of Sex and Marital Therapy*, Althof and Kingsberg present the results of a survey of sex therapists concerning books they have found helpful for clients in various areas related to sexuality and sexual problems. The books listed below represent some of the most popular sources among sex therapists, as reflected in that survey. The reader is referred to the original article for information on a much larger range of books available.]

Barbach, L. (1975). *For yourself: The fulfillment of female sexuality*. Garden City, NY: Doubleday.

Barbach, L. (1982). *For each other: Sharing sexual intimacy*. New York: Anchor/Doubleday.

The Boston Women's Health Collective. (1985). *The new our bodies, ourselves: A book by and for women*. New York: Simon & Schuster.

Goldstein, I., & Rothstein, L. (1990). *The potent male: Facts, fiction, future*. Los Angeles: Body.

Heiman, J., & LoPiccolo, J. (1988). *Becoming orgasmic: A sexual growth program for women*. Englewood Cliffs, NJ: Prentice-Hall.

Kaplan, H. (1989). *PE: How to overcome premature ejaculation*. New York: Brunner/Mazel.

Kitzinger, S. (1983). *A woman's experience of sex*. New York: Putnam.

Levine, S. (1988). *Sex is not simple*. Columbus, OH: Ohio Publishing Co.

Zilbergeld, B. (1992). *The new male sexuality*. Bantam.

✕ 16 ✕

DOMESTIC VIOLENCE

O F THE VARIOUS TOPICS covered in Part III, there is none more destructive and potentially more dangerous than domestic violence. For this reason, clinicians who evaluate couples should be familiar with typical patterns involved in domestic violence as well as ground rules for assessment and treatment. If a therapist evaluating a couple mishandles the inquiry into serious illness, he or she may fail to understand the significance of illness in the couple's current difficulties; if he or she mishandles the inquiry into domestic violence, one partner (in the vast majority of circumstances, the woman) may be beaten, even killed, as a result.

This chapter was prepared with assistance from Richard Meth, C.I.S.W., Director, Center for Marriage and Family Therapy, Storrs, Connecticut, and Michelle Bograd, Ph.D., Faculty, Family Institute of Cambridge, Cambridge, Massachusetts.

Prevalence and Characteristic Patterns

The prevalence of domestic violence is appalling. A. Toufexis found that "[v]iolence against women by their husbands or partners occurs more often in Canada and the U.S. than all incidents of car accidents, muggings, and rape combined" (cited in Avis, 1992, p. 227). The Department of Justice estimates that between 2,000 and 4,000 women are killed each year by their current or former husbands or boyfriends (Bograd, 1992), accounting for *half* of all homicides against women (Walker, 1989). Almost one third of married couples experience violence at some point in the relationship (Straus, Gelles, & Steinmetz, 1981). "Severe, repeated violence occurs in 1 in 14 marriages (Dutton, 1988), with an average of 35 incidents before it is reported" (Avis, 1992, p. 226). Avis points out that physical abuse "always involves emotional and verbal abuse and often includes sexual abuse, such as forced intercourse after a beating, being forced to participate in undesired sexual acts, and having pain inflicted during intercourse" (pp. 227–228).

While some violence in couple relationships is committed by women against men, there is widespread agreement that domestic violence is overwhelmingly a phenomenon of male violence against women. Avis, for example, citing Browne (1987) and Dobash and Dobash (1979), asserts that 95% of marital violence is perpetrated by men (husbands or exhusbands) against women. Women may become violent in order to defend themselves or to retaliate for physical abuse; their violence is much less likely to inflict serious injury, or even death, and, as Jacobson (1993) points out, is not used to maintain a climate of fear and intimidation as is often the case for male violence.

Ganley (1981) points out that domestic violence includes not only battering but also sexual abuse, psychological abuse, and the destruction of property and pets. This is important because even therapists who are aware of battering and rape in couple relationships may overlook these other forms of violence and intimidation. Experts have long understood that domestic violence is not a phenomenon limited to lower socioeconomic groups; recently, a number of widely publicized cases have helped dispel this myth.

Jacobson (1993) differentiates between couples in which physical aggression has occurred but in which no one has been hurt and the wife is not afraid of her husband, and couples in which violence has "been consolidated as a method of subjugation and control." The distinction is analogous to families in which there is drinking and alcoholic families (see Chapter 17), except that, in the case of violence, the distinction characterizes the *husband's use of violence*—not some aspect of *the relationship* (which would dilute the man's individual responsibility for his violence). Jacobson suggests that couple therapy may prove helpful for the former couples but should not be attempted for the latter ones. However, *the therapist's operating premise should be that any and all violence in a couple relationship is unacceptable and damaging to the relationship.*

Walker (1979) first described the triphasic interactional pattern that characterizes domestic violence. The first phase involves a period of *tension building* during which a series of minor conflicts, over a period of weeks or months, raises the level of emotional intensity in the relationship. Walker (1989) suggests that the woman may be able to slow down or speed up this progression but that her influence wanes as this phase progresses. The batterer's anger then reaches a *period of inevitability* when attempts at control no longer work. At this point, phase two—the *explosion*—occurs. This phase, which involves the *acute battering incident,* is the briefest of the three but causes the greatest physical harm. Following this is the third phase, a period of *loving contrition* and reconciliation or, in some relationships, simply a period of *no tension.* The woman is often lulled into believing that the abuse will not be repeated but in these relationships, at some point, phase one will begin again, leading to another incident of battering.

Domestic violence tends to escalate over time in frequency and severity (some would say *always* escalates, e.g., see Walker, 1989). Walker (1984) found that weapons were more likely to be used in more recent attacks on women than on initial attacks. Pagelow (1981) found, in interviewing battered women, that 74% reported an increase in the severity or frequency of attacks, or both, over time. This is important for clinicians who evaluate domestic violence since a relatively less serious episode does *not* indicate that more serious attacks can be ruled out; if anything, the progressive nature of domestic violence suggests that the level of violence is likely to increase unless checked. Walker (1991) points out that the "most dangerous time for the man to actually kill the woman is at the point of separation or shortly afterward, when he realizes that she really wants to be free to live her own life" (p. 24).

There is a significant correlation between domestic violence and the use of alcohol and other drugs. Various studies suggest that between 36% and 52% of wife batterers abuse alcohol (Gelles & Cornell, 1985). Shapiro (1986) asserts that drug and alcohol abuse are involved as precipitants in at least 80% of all physical and sexual abuse. Richard Meth suggests that abusive men are likely to be obsessively possessive of their female partners, feeling that they cannot live without them. Goldner, Penn, Sheinberg, and Walker (1990) relate battering to men's socialization, which stresses the need to be different from "girls" (and later, women). They see battering as "a man's attempt to reassert gender difference and gender dominance" (p. 348) when this dominance becomes threatened in some way. This might involve the man's sudden unemployment, the wife's earning a higher wage, a sexual "failure," or a loss that induces unacceptable feelings of vulnerability. Goldner et al. suggest that the man's "dread of the collapse of gender difference" impels him to try to reassert his dominance in the most immediate way possible—by sheer physical force.

Others have related domestic violence at least partially to efforts to regulate closeness (Krugman, 1986) and the inability to negotiate and resolve conflicts (Shapiro, 1986). Whatever else it may be, domestic violence involves an effort to control another person by force and intimidation. Feminist therapists see domestic violence as an extreme expression of a much wider societal pattern of male dominance (Avis, 1992; Bograd, 1984; Walker, 1991).

A variety of explanations have been offered for why women remain in relationships in which they are battered. Some have suggested that a process similar to the "Stockholm syndrome"—in which hostages come to identify psychologically with their captors—operates in these relationships (Mathias, 1986). Others point to the real economic disadvantages of the woman as a potent obstacle to her leaving her abuser (Bograd, 1984). Walker (1989) has applied the concept of "learned helplessness" to understand why these women stay in the abusive relationship. Goldner et al. (1990) suggest that staying in the relationship represents "an affirmation of the feminine ideal: to hold connections together, to heal and care for another, no matter what the personal cost" (p. 357).

Finally, as in all couple relationships, attachment plays an important role in preserving the relationship. Partners in couple relationships form *deep attachments* to one another and often find it difficult to end the relationship, in the face of chronic dissatisfaction, persistent indifference by the partner, protracted criticism and disrespect, or even, in these cases, physical abuse. Furthermore, as suggested by observers of abused children (Green, 1980) and by primate researchers (Harlow & Harlow, 1971; Seay et al., 1964), abuse may actually *intensify* attachment (see Chapter 1).

The consequences of domestic violence extend beyond the particular incident of abuse and beyond the woman who is usually the victim. Kaufman (1992) points out that one incident of battering creates "a climate of terror" which endures in the relationship. Furthermore, approximately 80% of incidents of domestic violence against women are witnessed by their children (Jaffe, Wolfe, & Wilson, 1990; Leighton,

1989; Sinclair, 1985). Recent research on the effects of *witnessing* violence have underlined how serious this actually is. "Children who witness domestic violence often have a level of adjustment problems comparable to that of children who are physically abused themselves" (Jaffe, Wilson, & Wolfe, 1987, cited in Avis, 1992, p. 228). This is especially significant in light of research which suggests that witnessing an assault by father against mother increases a boy's likelihood of later using violence in his own home *700* times (Kalmuss, 1984; Straus et al., 1981). Seventy-five percent of men who abuse their partners observed violence between their own parents (Jaffe et al., 1987).

Basic Principles

Domestic violence challenges our view of the relationship, or the family, as a haven of safety; it also challenges our basic assumptions concerning treatment. As Moltz (1992) suggests, "In the presence of violence the very idea of treatment is called into question. . . . fundamental concepts such as the safety of the therapeutic situation, confidentiality, therapist responsibility to a client—all are thrown open to question" (p. 223). There are, however, some basic principles which can orient the therapist in this potentially dangerous terrain.

First, in the assessment and treatment of domestic violence, *safety comes first*. This means that preventing further violence is the first and most important responsibility for the clinician; *all* other considerations are secondary.

Second, *the abuser* is held *fully responsible* for his actions. This most basic point should not be diluted or obscured either by the abuser's claim that his partner "provoked" the violence, and is therefore partly responsible for it, or by abstract theoretical notions of "circularity" or other systemic formulations. Therapists must remember that domestic violence is not only a clinical problem but a criminal offense, punishable by law. Both partners may have contributed to an argument, but the *abuser alone* is responsible for the violence.

Third, *violence is violence*. Some therapists make a distinction between "mild" and "severe" violence. Bograd (1984) points out that this distinction, like that between reduction in violence and cessation of violence, is a problematic one. The primary goal of clinical intervention with domestic violence must be the complete cessation of all forms and acts of violence. Softening this stance will very likely be interpreted by the abuser as an endorsement of some forms of violence by the clinician.

These principles are especially important for family therapists whose training may contribute to confusion in this area. Theoretical constructs that emphasize the "circularity" of interactional sequences, the "needs of the system," and the "function of symptoms" may make it difficult to place the attribution of responsibility for the violence where it belongs—with the abuser. As Lamb (1991) and Bograd (1984) point out, terms such as "battering relationships" and "violent couples" blur this attribution of responsibility, thereby doing the woman a dis-service and potentially colluding with the man's violence.

Assessment

In the assessment of domestic violence, the first and most essential questions are: Is violence occurring? If so, is the victim safe and aware of potentially helpful services? (Rosenbaum & O'Leary, 1986) All of the following specific questions and recommendations are designed to answer these two questions and to respond based on the answers as quickly and safely as possible.

Therapists should inquire about domestic violence *in all cases* since many couples are unlikely to readily disclose it. This serves not only to prompt verbal disclosure if violence has occurred but to give the therapist an opportunity to observe nonverbal reactions to the ques-tions. Richard Meth recommends against the use of the word, "vio-lence" at this juncture.* The inquiry can be embedded in questions about couple conflict. Meth suggests that some of the following ques-tions may be helpful: "What happens when you get angry?" "Do either of you get really loud or is it fairly quiet?" Other questions, which become increasingly direct, include: "Has either of you ever done something in the heat of an argument that you regretted?" "In the course of your relationship, as things escalated, has it ever happened that either one of you has ever pushed or shoved the other or done anything physical in the course of an argument?"

The psychological and relational profile of typical abusers can also provide "tip-offs" that raise the therapist's index of suspicion for abuse. The abuser's profile may feature problems with alcohol or drugs (or participation in other compulsive behavior such as gambling), obses-sive attachment to the partner ("I can't live without her"), pathologic jealousy, a need to control the woman's every move and/or to isolate

---

*While avoiding the word "violence" makes practical sense at this early stage, if it becomes clear that violence has occurred, the therapist needs to be completely clear in naming and condemning it when it is both appropriate and safe to do so.

her from friends and family, a narcissistic blow of some kind such as a job loss, expression of rage but not loss, a history of violence in other relationships (either with women, or with men in brawls), a history of witnessing abuse, and possibly a history of abusing children.

If you suspect past or current domestic violence, you should *separate the partners* and pursue the inquiry individually. This can be casually presented as a standard part of the evaluation. (If you have used the format presented in this book, you will have already prepared both partners for this prospect.) This splitting into separate individual meetings is designed to protect the woman since pursuing the inquiry with both partners together encourages her to incriminate herself in front of the abuser and invites retribution after the session. In separate individual sessions, the question of whether or not abuse has occurred or is currently occurring can be explored more safely and in greater detail.

In the individual session with the woman, find out what happens when they fight. Meth suggests the following questions: "Have you ever felt that [the partner] was out of control?" "Has he ever pushed, grabbed, slapped, or hit you?" Bograd (1986) encourages questions about the circumstances and specifics of the violence: "How do the fights start?" "Where?" "When?" "Are alcohol or other drugs typically involved?" "Does he hit with an open hand or with a closed fist?" "Have you ever been bruised or cut?" "Have you ever required medical attention after a fight?" Remember to ask about sexual assault and nonphysical forms of abuse, such as psychological abuse and attacks on pets or property.

Walker (1991) provides a number of very useful suggestions for inquiring about domestic violence when meeting with the woman. She asks for details of the abuse that occurred during the *first* incident, a *typical* incident (or several in the case of a longer relationship), the *worst* (or one of the worst), and the *last* incident prior to the session itself. This allows you to get a sense of the progression—and possible escalation—of the violence. Walker stresses the importance of assessing for lethality, especially if the woman is still in the situation. Citing Browne (1987), she points out that the "presence of weapons, reports of abuse incidents that lead to choking, throwing the woman into objects, forceful shaking, head-banging, and threats to kill are the most important signs" (p. 24). She asks whether there have been times when the woman believed that she would have been killed had something not intervened.

Walker urges therapists to assess for the presence of other diagnosable disorders, such as posttraumatic stress disorder, depression, and, especially, neurological damage, noting that the latter is common in battered women, particularly if the abuse has included blows to the head. She also discusses the stance or tone of the therapist:

> Battered women often are sensitive to another person's reactions to them, which is another coping skill, and so, if the psychologist appears impatient, skeptical, horrified by the abuse details, or does not attempt to understand what she is talking about, she will probably give a sanitized version of the story. A slow, step-by-step, non-judgmental, compassionate attitude is the way to demonstrate trustworthiness, and it will encourage the woman to give accurate details. Comments that indicate empathy with her situation are helpful, but care must be taken not to make suggestible or judgmental comments about either her or his behavior as she describes it. A general statement indicating that violence is not justified under any situation except self-defense, no matter what her behavior was, along with acknowledgement of the variety of feelings experienced when living with violence is most helpful. Denigration of the man by the therapist makes it difficult for the client to seek treatment and still try to save the relationship. (1991, p. 23)

Conduct a similar inquiry with the man. Here, too, questions involve how he reacts when he is angry, whether he has ever regretted anything he has done during an argument, if he ever hit or pushed his partner, etc. If abuse has been acknowledged or alluded to in the initial couple session, pursue the details of those incidents. Ask him how he sees precipitants and typical circumstances for arguments: When and where do they typically take place? Are alcohol or other drugs involved? Are there particular actions by his partner that he feels increase the likelihood that he will be violent? This must be done *without* suggesting that you see these behaviors as a justification for violence. Be mindful of the tendency among abusers to "consistently underestimate or distort the actual physical details and . . . consequences of their violence" (Avis, 1992, p. 248).

If you become aware of domestic violence, be especially sure to evaluate—or refer for evaluation—any children who may be living in the home. As indicated earlier, they may also be abused or suffering from the effects of witnessing violence between the adults.

Immediate Responses

Figure 2 contains a decision tree for therapists confronted with domestic violence. If violence is occurring and the woman is not safe, you should assist her in securing safety for herself and, when there are

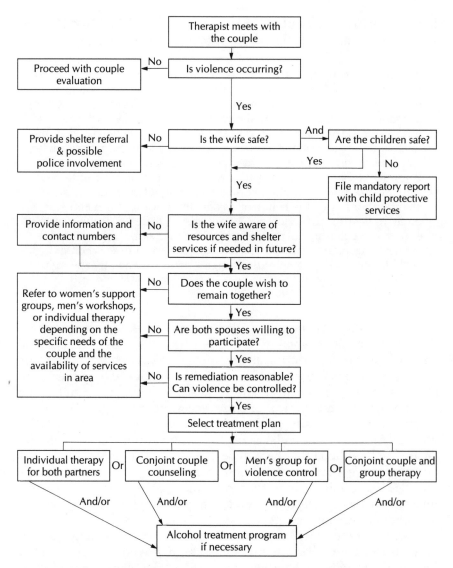

Figure 2. A decision tree for assessing domestic violence. Readers should note that this figure cannot convey all of the complexities of the process of evaluating a couple in which domestic violence is suspected; it should be used as a complement to the text. (Adapted from Rosenbaum & O'Leary, 1986, with permission)

children, for the children as well. Interventions may involve arranging for the woman to seek shelter, bringing in other family members such as grandparents in order to counter the woman's isolation (Mathias, 1986), educating the woman about her legal rights and procedures for separating, helping her to arrange for a restraining order on the abuser, or filing for child protective services when children are endangered. In some cases, it may mean arranging for a police escort from the office to a shelter.

If the woman is not safe but refuses to leave, you cannot force her to do so. You should, however, certainly try to convey your own concerns for her safety, emphasizing the details she has herself disclosed, perhaps discussing outcomes in similar situations and describing the progressive nature of domestic violence. Hopefully, this will counteract what may be a tendency on the woman's part to minimize or deny the danger of the situation. If there are children in the home and you feel that they may be in danger, in most states you are legally obligated as a mandated reporter to call in protective services. Working jointly with protective services, you can further evaluate whether the children are at risk for being abused or witnessing abuse and, if so, act to remove the abuser from the home.

Walker (1991) recommends helping the woman "design an escape plan before she leaves [the] . . . office, so that even if she does not return, she has gained some ability to keep herself safer than before" (p. 24). Such a plan might include having a second set of car keys—and a small amount of money—kept at the ready and knowing where she would go or whom to call. Safety, as Walker (1984) points out, means that the woman must leave prior to the start of the second phase, or acute battering incident. You can provide her with information about how to call for legal assistance in an emergency and the telephone numbers and addresses of shelters and other services for domestic violence. Therapists who are unfamiliar with local shelters and other services for battered women can call the National Domestic Violence Hotline (1-800-333-SAFE) to locate them.

If there is current violence but the partners are unwilling to separate, you should also speak with the man about a safety plan for him, including what he will do if he begins to feel out of control and what steps he will take to prevent violence. Finally, if there is a discrepancy between the level of violence described by the partners, with the man reporting lower levels, given the potential risks involved and the known tendency of abusers to minimize their own violence, you should operate on the assumption that the woman's description is more accurate.

Treatment Recommendations

There is a growing body of research and opinion that encourages extreme caution in the use of couple therapy in cases involving domestic violence. There is a clear consensus that *couple therapy should not be conducted if the violence is still occurring*. Coyne (1986) cites the danger of "coercive interactions, an inhibited therapist, a reticent couple and the ever-present risk of precipitating later violence" (p. 67). Rosenbaum and O'Leary (1986) caution that, if the partners have separated because of the violence, the abuser may use couple sessions to follow the woman back to a presumably secret place of residence. Bograd (1984) suggests that there will likely be an inadequate alliance with the male, the focus on violence may be diluted by attention to other relational issues, the therapy may perpetuate traditional sex roles, and the therapist may pursue the preservation of the relationship, rather than the protection of the woman, as a primary goal. Dobash and Dobash (1988) feel that couple therapy contributes to the woman's social isolation, has only short-lived results, and communicates to the abuser that there will be no serious consequences for his actions. Kaufman (1992) cautions that couple therapy may contribute to the reprivatization of violence.

Many experts suggest that the abuser be involved in a program for violent men before couple therapy even be considered; some feel that couple therapy should only be conducted after a specific period of time *without* violence has passed. Treatment programs are likely to use a combination of group meetings and education in an effort to challenge the abuser's denial, change his attitudes about violence and, most importantly, enable him to accept responsibility for past violence and for controlling violence in the future. Bograd (1992) notes that some programs do not accept the notion of "cure," and instead emphasize the concept of "recovery," which suggests that the abuser is always at risk for returning to violent behavior.

Experts also recommend that the woman be seen individually in therapy and/or participate in groups for women who have been abused by their partners. She may be able to see her own situation more clearly by seeing the lives of other women living with domestic violence; this may help break through her minimizing and denial. The group also relieves the woman's social isolation when this is a feature of the couple relationship.

If the woman's safety has been assured, and if you have her permission, you can explain to the man that couple therapy cannot be conducted because it would not be safe for the woman. Most experts agree that the man's dependency on the woman often provides therapeutic leverage at this point. The hope is that once he realizes that he cannot hold onto the relationship if he is violent and that he will not be protected from legal consequences, either by his partner or by the therapist, his need for her can help motivate him to face and try to change his patterns of violence.

However, therapists should be cautious about the results of these programs. Bograd (1992) points out that

> voluntary programs for batterers have low recruitment and high attrition (Russell, 1988) and that—on average—only 25–30% of batterers who enter treatment complete therapy. . . . One study (Edelson & Grusznski, 1989) revealed that, although batterers decreased the use of physical force following treatment, there were *no* differences between batterers who had and had not completed therapy in their subsequent use of verbal threats or psychological abuse. (p. 250)

The qualified results of these treatment programs for abusers bring us to one of the most important points in the treatment of domestic violence—the importance of legal sanctions, whether they involve restraining orders on the abuser returning to the home or the threat or actuality of arrest and punishment. As indicated earlier, domestic violence is not only a clinical problem; it is a crime. An oft-cited study undertaken by the Minneapolis Police Department compared outcomes when police intervened in domestic disputes by simply talking with the offender (or recommending counseling) and when he was arrested. They found that 35% of offenders who were only counseled by police repeated the abuse within six months, in contrast with only 19% of offenders who were arrested and spent at least one night in jail. As Bograd states:

> [T]here is growing empirical evidence that psychotherapy is not sufficient for changing or motivating batterers without the added boost of legal and social consequences which strengthen the clout of the therapeutic encounter. . . . Effective amelioration of family violence requires linkages to larger systems. (1992, pp. 249–250)

However, if the therapist does feel that couple therapy is indicated—for example, if the violence is clearly not current or if the abuser is involved in specialized treatment for battering or has recently completed such treatment—there are a number of ground rules and techniques that have been suggested to facilitate such treatment. The couple must know that you will act effectively to control violence in sessions. Both the woman and the therapist must actually feel safe if joint sessions are to be held; if either does not, the sessions must be stopped. Rosenbaum and O'Leary (1986) remind therapists to make clear that coming to sessions intoxicated is forbidden and that no weapons of any kind can be brought to therapy; they also encourage therapists to remove potential weapons from easy reach in sessions. Shapiro (1986) recommends that the abuser be given permission to leave a session if he feels he is losing control, hopefully taking some time to calm down before resuming. Betty Carter, cited by Mathias (1986), believes that, given the connection between domestic violence and alcoholism or drug abuse, couple therapy should not be conducted while the abuser is still using these substances. Both Kaufman (1992) and Walker (1991) recommend that if a male therapist is treating the couple a female therapist be included in the treatment team. Others (Cook & Frantz-Cook, 1984; Libow, Raskin, & Caust, 1982) recommend a structured separation between the partners as an essential first step in treating these couples.

Couple treatment should focus on violence-prevention techniques. These typically include efforts to identify common cues to violence so that these can be avoided or serve as warnings that violence may be imminent; "no-violence contracts," which commit both partners to trying to prevent escalations that may lead to violence; and "time-out" procedures. A time-out is an agreement between the partners that if either feels a risk of violence occurring, he or she can immediately physically separate from the other, with the other agreeing not to prevent this in any way. The no-violence contract might also include a similar agreement: if the man becomes violent, he must leave the home for a specified period of time. These techniques are especially important in light of the fact that there is often a "honeymoon" period after initiating treatment which may be simply a treatment-related instance of the third phase of the battering cycle. The therapist's emphasis on prevention challenges the naive notion that the danger of violence is now over.

The therapist may need to consult and coordinate efforts with a number of other professionals and organizations—such as those involved in treatment programs for the man and the woman and legal authorities such as lawyers and probation officers—when they become involved in particular cases. If the violence is well under control, the therapist can help the couple with related difficulties by offering techniques for reducing reactivity and resolving conflicts in nonviolent ways. However, an unequivocal stance on the therapist's part against any and all acts of violence must be maintained. Avis (1992) summarizes the imperatives of such treatment:

Therapy must carefully avoid any collusion in the abuser's denial, minimization, avoidance, or projection . . . [especially by] focusing on the behavior of his wife or daughter or mother, or anyone else in the family system. . . . the primary focus of any therapeutic effort must be on changing the violent behavior itself, and treatment must thus focus on the details of this behavior, on its impact on others, and on the belief system which supports it. . . . therapists must work in conjunction and cooperation with the police and courts in order to utilize legal sanctions and mandated treatment. (p. 229)

Finally, the therapist's notes in these cases may be used in court. Therapists should keep thorough and careful notes. They should document all collateral contacts, recommendations, and referrals made to the couple. (See Walker [1991] for further suggestions about what should be included and excluded from such notes.) The therapist should also explain to couples that while he or she is legally obligated to maintain their confidentiality, therapeutic communications are *not* necessarily "privileged" since this is decided by the courts, and neither therapist nor client can withhold information that is deemed relevant by them. Therapists should familiarize themselves with the relevant statutes in the states in which they practice.

Recommended Reading for Therapists

The July, 1992 issue of the *Journal of Marital and Family Therapy* contains a special section on domestic violence as does the May–June, 1986 issue of the *Family Therapy Networker.*

Bograd, M. (1984). Family systems approaches to wife battering: A feminist critique. *American Journal of Orthopsychiatry, 54*(4), 558–568.
Hansen, M., & Harway, M. (Eds.). (1993). *Battering and family therapy: A feminist perspective.* Newbury Park: Sage.
Schecter, S. (1982). *Women and male violence.* Boston: South End.
Walker, L. (1979). *The battered woman.* New York: Harper & Row.
Walker, L. (1984). *The battered woman syndrome.* New York: Springer.
Walker, L. (1989). Psychology and violence against women. *American Psychologist, 44,* 695–701.
Walker, L. (1991). Post-traumatic stress disorder in women: Diagnosis and treatment of battered woman syndrome. *Psychotherapy, 28,* 21–29.
Yllo, K., & Bograd, M. (Eds.). (1988). *Feminist perspectives on wife abuse.* Newbury Park: Sage.

⌒ 17 ⌒

ALCOHOLISM

A S A PRACTICING THERAPIST, I remember being stunned about 15 years ago when I began to realize just how pervasive and devastating the effects of alcohol really are. It seemed as if almost every case that presented for treatment, whether it involved an individual, a couple, or a family, had in some way been touched by the destructive effects of alcoholism. If it wasn't a problem in the current life relationships of the clients, it was nearly always involved in recent family history. The descriptions of the father, or mother, who drank and became enraged or depressed or socially embarrassing became monotonously familiar, as I expect they are for most clinicians. Along with caffeine and nicotine—the effects of which may be harmful but in no

This discussion was prepared with assistance from JoAnn Krestan, L.S.A.C., private practice, Brunswick, Maine, and Lewis Breitner, Ph.D., private practice, Westfield, Massachusetts.

way approach the nearly epidemic consequences of drinking—alcohol is America's drug of choice.

Prevalence and Effects of Alcoholism

Various surveys document the prevalence of alcoholism in the general population. Calahan (1982) reported that 13% of men and 2% of women when questioned described a drinking pattern the investigators characterized as "heavy." Results obtained by Clark and Midanik (1982) were nearly identical: 12% for men and 3% for women. Royce (1981) estimates that 4% of the total population, or about 8.8 million Americans, are alcoholic. Most experts assume that these figures are, if anything, conservative due to underreporting in surveys such as these.

Royce also points out that problem drinkers are involved in 42% of all automobile accidents and that alcohol is implicated in 67% of child abuse cases, 40% of rape cases, 51% of felonies, and 38% of suicides. A partial list of physical complications resulting from alcoholism includes hepatitis, cirrhosis, peripheral neuropathy, gastritis, and a variety of reproductive disorders. Chronic alcoholism increases the risk and severity of heart disease, pneumonia, tuberculosis, and neurological disorders. Consumed excessively during pregnancy, alcohol can lead to fetal alcohol syndrome. It contributes to depression in both men and women and the mortality rate among people with alcohol dependence is two or three times that of the general population (APA, 1987). Krestan and Bepko (1989) point out that every alcoholic directly affects the lives of at least four or five other people, suggesting that conservatively 35 to 44 million Americans are directly affected by the consequences of alcoholism.

How can alcoholism be distinguished from nonaddictive drinking? The National Council on Alcoholism defines it as follows: "The person with alcoholism cannot consistently predict on any drinking occasion the duration of the episode or the quantity that will be consumed" (1976). This highlights one central feature of all definitions of alcoholism: the drinker's inability to control the amount of alcohol consumed. The second central feature involves the continuation of consumption in spite of serious negative consequences in the individual's life.

DSM-III-R (APA, 1987) lists nine characteristic symptoms of dependence on alcohol or other psychoactive substances: (1) consuming larger amounts than intended, (2) persistent desire and one or more unsuccessful efforts to cut down or control usage, (3) significant amounts of time spent procuring or recovering from usage, (4) intoxication or withdrawal symptoms which are dangerous or interfere with important obligations, (5) withdrawal from social, occupational, or recreational activities because of usage, (6) usage continues in spite of social, psychological, or physical problems caused or exacerbated by the use of the substance, (7) increasing tolerance, (8) characteristic withdrawal symptoms, and (9) usage to relieve or avoid withdrawal symptoms. For a diagnosis of alcohol dependence by DSM-III-R standards, at least three of these symptoms must be present, with some symptoms having persisted for at least one month or having occurred repeatedly over a longer period of time. DSM-III-R differentiates between "mild," "moderate," and "severe" dependence, as well as dependence in partial or full remission.

DSM-III-R also specifies the diagnosis of alcohol abuse, rather than dependence, for those cases in which maladaptive patterns of alcohol use exist but do not meet the criteria described above. In these cases, there is continued alcohol use despite awareness of persistent problems and recurrent use in situations in which it is physically hazardous. Symptoms have persisted for at least one month, or have occurred repeatedly over a longer period of time, but do not meet the criteria specified for alcohol dependence. Alcohol abuse is much more common than alcohol dependence.

Alcoholism is seen as a progressive disorder. Drinking follows a predictable course of increasing physical tolerance, increasing consumption, and steadily increasing costs in the person's life. This is not the only pattern of drinking but it is probably the most common. The alcoholic feels and acts one way when not drinking and another way when he or she is drinking. The cyclic shifting from the "wet" mode of drinking to the "dry" mode of nondrinking is a hallmark of alcoholism (Berenson, 1976). A distinction is also usually made between "dryness," when an alcoholic is not actually drinking but still exhibits attitudes and coping strategies that are typical of alcoholism, and "sobriety," which refers to a cessation of drinking, usually in association with Alcoholics Anonymous (AA) or other forms of alcohol treatment and with a corresponding change in attitudes. While controversy exists over the classification of alcoholism as a disease, most experts in this area accept this classification.

Alcoholism and Couple Relationships

The connection between alcoholism and couple relationships is already widely recognized. The term "codependent" is used by both professionals and laymen. Experts in this area make a central distinction between relational systems* in which one partner is having difficulty with alcohol and those relationships which are, in the commonly used term, "organized around alcohol" (Steinglass, 1979). Paraphrasing the usual terminology, this chapter will distinguish between "couples with an alcoholic member" and "alcoholic couples." In the former, one partner has a drinking problem but this has not significantly changed the couple's relational patterns. In these cases, treatment of other problems—job stress, couple or family conflicts—may alleviate the drinking problem (Krestan & Bepko, 1989).

For other couples, however, the alcoholic's drinking becomes addictive. Over time, a series of accommodations by the partner to the alcoholic's drinking leads to a serious skew in the division of responsibility, relational patterns dominated by the drinker's cyclic shifts from "dryness" to "wetness" (Berenson, 1976), and the "invasion" of the "regulatory behaviors" of the relationship, including short-term problem-solving strategies, daily routines, and family rituals (Steinglass, Bennett, Wolin, & Reiss, 1987). For these couples, alcoholism becomes a way of life.

The relationship itself comes to be characterized by the alcoholic's swings from wet to dry states. Steinglass et al. (1987) provide vivid examples of families in which all members feel and act in a predictable and dramatically different way based on whether they are in a wet or dry state. In one family, for example, the sight of a half-empty liquor bottle on a Friday afternoon—the signal that father had begun a weekend binge—would initiate a dramatic series of changes in the family's life. Family members avoided interacting with one another as well as inviting friends or neighbors into the house. Meals, which in the dry state were predictable, well-prepared and whole-family affairs, became catch-as-catch-can, improvised and solitary, with each family member grabbing a bite to eat whenever they became hungry.

In another example, an alcoholic family—interviewed and videotaped when the alcoholic was dry and again when he was intoxicated—displayed remarkable, family-wide changes in interactional patterns in these two conditions. Changes in eye contact, level of animation, physical closeness, and sheer amount of interaction were observable and were replicated even when the family was simply viewing segments of videotape from these two earlier sessions.

The couple may become dependent on drinking as a means to cope

---

*Most theorists and researchers have focused on families as the relevant systems of interest. This discussion will apply their assumptions and findings to the smaller system of the couple's relationship.

with stresses and challenges in the short-term even though the long-term costs may be high. The invasion of alcoholism into important rituals can be seen in a family whose Christmas celebration is largely organized around the alcoholic's drinking: start the meal early before she's had too much to drink; have it at home so that she can excuse herself to an upstairs bedroom if she gets too drunk; hurry the children to bed before she's at her worst; don't under any circumstances let her drive.

Over time, the drinker becomes less and less responsible in his actions and his obligations to his partner or children. As his responsibility decreases, his partner "picks up the slack." The partner comes to feel overburdened and resentful but may not feel entitled to challenge this arrangement; the drinker comes to feel unworthy and peripheral. The partner becomes responsible for most if not all functional tasks and the drinker is no longer viewed as a fully responsible adult. This development of overfunctioning and underfunctioning roles is considered by most experts to be the hallmark of alcoholic systems. Both partners suffer from a "pride structure" (Bepko & Krestan, 1985) which fuels the continuation of their addictions. They are unable to change their own behavior—the alcoholic's drinking and the partner's accommodating, or "enabling," of the drinking—but equally unable to admit this. Bepko and Krestan point out that when both partners drink alcoholically, there is often a competitive struggle for the dependent role.

Finally, one of the characteristics most often associated with alcoholic systems is denial.

> [W]hat characterizes the alcoholic system at all levels is untruth—the attempt of the self to be not self or an altered self, and the participation of all the cast of characters surrounding the alcoholic in increasingly dysfunctional patterns of behavior based on distortion and confusion about self in relationship to self and self in relationship to others. (Bepko & Krestan, 1985, p. 13)

For alcoholic couples, abstinence will be a necessary but not sufficient goal of treatment. The interactional patterns that have been "invaded" by alcoholism must also be treated in order for abstinence to be maintained (Meeks & Kelly, 1970).

Assessment

Couples for whom alcohol may be a problem present for evaluation in several ways. The partners may both acknowledge that drinking is a problem, or they may both be in denial about the drinking problems of one or both. One partner may insist that the other has a drinking problem while the other denies it. They may have started out as "drinking buddies" but come for treatment when one partner "defects" from their pattern of drinking heavily together, as women sometimes do when they become mothers.

The first order of business when evaluating couples for alcohol problems is to try to answer two basic questions: Is alcohol a problem in this relationship? Is this an alcoholic relationship? The effort to answer these questions will require different approaches based on whether or not the partners acknowledge problem drinking at the start of the evaluation. If you suspect alcoholism but the partners seem reluctant to acknowledge it, you should conduct the inquiry in this area more carefully in an effort to minimize defensiveness; you should also be alert for clues or "tip-offs" that one or both partners may have a drinking problem.

Remember that not all drinkers are alcoholic. If the drinker can control his or her alcohol intake, if there have been no serious losses or consequences related to the drinking, and if neither partner is complaining about it, the likelihood is that alcohol abuse or dependence are not a part of this couple's relationship. This determination is difficult to make, however, when one partner complains about the other's drinking and the other denies it. When alcoholism is involved, denial on the part of the drinker is to be expected. You should also remember that accusations of alcoholism may be part of a larger power struggle in the relationship—for example, an effort to paint each other as "sick" or "pathological" in some way—or they may reflect unusual sensitivity to drinking due to alcoholism in the complaining partner's family of origin.

When Alcoholism is Suspected

Figure 3 presents a decision tree for therapists who suspect a drinking problem. Lewis Breitner suggests in these cases that questions about drinking be embedded in an inquiry about other medical and psychological problems. You might begin by asking about any serious medical illnesses either for the partners or their families of origin, noting without comment those that are typically alcohol-related. You can then ask about any serious psychological problems, such as depression or psychosis. This is followed by asking about a history of "problems with alcohol or any other drugs" in the family or origin, and then in the current relationship. Bepko and Krestan (1985) point out that the use of terms such as "problem" and "alcoholism" in this context also serves as an indirect probe. The more defensive the couple's response, the higher the index of suspicion that alcoholism is a problem. These

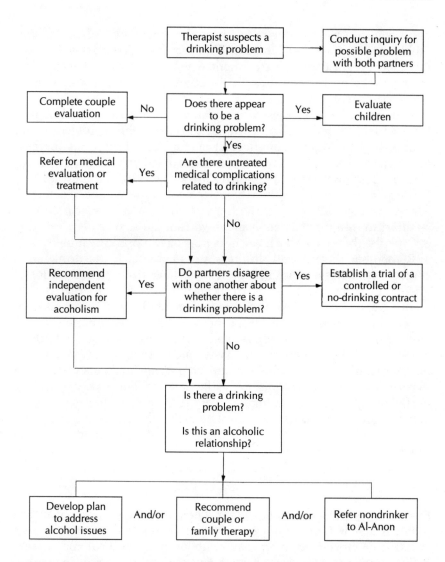

Figure 3. A decision tree for assessing a drinking problem. Readers should note that this figure cannot convey all of the complexities of the process of evaluating a couple in which alcoholism is suspected; it should be used as a complement to the text.

terms also allow you to explain exactly what you mean by "alcohol-ism" and to ask the partners to describe their views on what consti-tutes a drinking problem. Questions about drinking can be embedded in questions about the use of coffee, cigarettes, and over-the-counter medications.

Specific questions that may be useful when alcoholism is suspected but not acknowledged include: Does anyone worry about anyone's drinking? Has anyone ever argued about anyone else's drinking? What do you do to relax? Asking about daily routines and family rituals may surface concealed drinking. Bepko and Krestan (1985) encourage therapists to "make a secrecy map," asking about who does and doesn't know about the drinking and one or both partners' concerns about it. The fewer the people who know, the greater the degree to which the partners have isolated themselves socially, and the more likely that the drinking constitutes a serious problem. Also inquire about the use of other substances, especially in drinkers who are under 50 years of age, since in this group, multiple substance abuse is more common. Treadway (1987) notes that, when alcoholism is unacknowledged, the shift to inquiring about drinking in the evaluation may generate tre-mendous anxiety and lead to an intensification of the presenting problem.

Because of their common association with alcohol abuse, the fol-lowing can serve as "tip-offs" that problems with alcohol may exist: sexual affairs, depression, domestic violence (toward either the partner or children), incest, school or behavioral problems for one or more of the children, sexual dysfunction, reports of difficulties at work, other compulsive disorders such as gambling, overeating, or abuse of pre-scription drugs and, perhaps most importantly, marked imbalances in levels of responsibility between the partners. Medical problems typi-cally associated with alcoholism, descriptions of a high tolerance for alcohol in either partner, and a positive family history for alcoholism are all possible indicators. If, by introducing the subject in this way, you gain permission to ask in greater detail about drinking, the inquiry can proceed as indicated below. If you do not feel such permission has been obtained, proceed more carefully and consider the suggestions given below under Guidelines.

When Alcoholism is Acknowledged

When alcoholism is acknowledged, you can move directly to a detailed inquiry about drinking patterns. However, if *both* partners acknowl-edge that drinking is a problem for one of them, this presents a very different scenario than that in which *one* partner complains about the other's drinking and the other denies any problem. In the former case, your inquiry can be direct and straightforward. In the latter case, there are conflicting signals about how much latitude you have to explore the issue. Although one partner has put the issue on the table, you must consider the sensitivities of the alleged drinker.

The following questions can help assess the extent and seriousness of drinking: Who drinks? Is it one partner or both? When and under what circumstances do they drink? How much do they drink? What changes occur as a result of the drinking? Who is most affected—that is, troubled—by the drinking? What is the longest period of time the drinker has gone without consuming any alcohol? Has the drinking negatively affected their lives? This might involve health problems, arrests for driving while intoxicated, blackouts, legal problems, job loss, or separations. Does the drinker undergo noticeable mood changes when drinking that negatively affect the relationship? Are there incidents that indicate secrecy or lack of control, such as finishing off liqueurs that are reserved for special occasions or hiding bottles around the house? Breitner suggests asking the drinker about the benefits or gratifications of drinking as he or she sees them. This represents an effort to join with the drinker and will help you better understand what the drinker actually faces losing.

There are several short questionnaires (20 to 30 items) that are helpful in diagnosing alcoholism. These questionnaires can be used to guide your inquiry about the drinking or they can be given to the partners to fill out. Responses to particular items can serve as a jumping-off point for more detailed inquiry. These questionnaires typically provide a scoring system that allows the therapist to categorize the phase or severity of drinking. One of the most frequently used is the Michigan Alcoholism Screening Test (Selzer, 1971).

Bepko and Krestan encourage the therapist to take a detailed family history of alcoholism, recommending a genogram of at least three generations and an inquiry into how alcoholism was perceived and dealt with by the alcoholic and the family as a whole. "Experiences and attitudes of other members of the family relative to drinking will strongly influence the present family 'thinking' or 'ethic' about the problem" (1985, p. 82).

In the current relationship, what solutions have already been attempted? Has the drinker attended AA? Have there been attempts at detoxification or rehabilitation programs? Be certain to inquire about any medical problems the alcoholic may be experiencing. If the drinker acknowledges past difficulties with drinking but claims to have discontinued drinking, you should evaluate the details of his or her reported sobriety (Bepko & Krestan, 1985). When did the person—

let's assume a man—stop drinking? Has he had anything at all to drink since then? Has he attended AA meetings? If so, when did he start and how often does he attend? Does he have a sponsor and a home group? Does he continue to minimize the extent and consequences of his past drinking? Responses to these questions may help you differentiate between someone who is genuinely involved in recovery from alcoholism and someone whose efforts have been halfhearted and sporadic.

Is This an Alcoholic Relationship?

If you feel confident that a drinking problem exists, you should also try to ascertain whether or not the couple's relationship is an alcoholic system. Try to ascertain the time lapse between the onset of drinking and the time of the client's presentation for evaluation. The longer the time lapse, the more likely that the relationship has become organized by alcoholism. Steinglass et al. (1987) suggest that a mid-life couple with a long-standing alcohol problem is likely to be an alcoholic system.

Look for predictable, repetitive patterns involving *both* partners when one is drinking. Do their descriptions of their interaction indicate the systemic shifts from wet to dry states which characterizes alcoholic systems? How does the partner feel and what does he or she do when the drinker is drinking? How lopsided is the division of responsibility between the partners? You might also inquire about daily routines and family rituals. If alcoholism has invaded regulatory mechanisms, you can expect to see a prominent role played by drinking in one of two ways: The drinking may intrude into these events or the events themselves may be heavily "choreographed" in order to minimize or avoid difficulties with drinking.

Guidelines

Questions about drinking should be presented in a casual and nonjudgmental way in order to avoid triggering unnecessary defensiveness (Treadway, 1987). However, both the drinker and the partner may need to minimize or deny that the problem exists. Instead of simply accepting all statements at face value, you should feel free to inquire further and, when it seems appropriate, to express some degree of skepticism or to check responses against those of the other partner (Krestan & Bepko, 1989).

Several points relating to gender in the assessment of alcoholism are also important. Bepko and Krestan (1985) point out that, for women, the burden of shame and stigma associated with drinking is typically

greater since drinking is so widely identified as a male behavior. Krestan also points out that most scales used to measure alcoholism are
based on male drinking patterns. Women's drinking, she suggests,
tends to be more "telescoped," that is, to develop more quickly. She
recommends keeping in mind the greater shame associated with wom-
en's drinking and, in light of this, proceeding more carefully in the
initial inquiry.

Whether the drinker is male or female, you must remember to balance alliances with both partners. Detailed inquiry into one partner's
drinking can strain these alliances. Bepko and Krestan suggest that
this danger can be minimized in two ways:

> It is often effective to ask the alcoholic at this point in a gently
> humorous way about the spouse's "compulsion"—for instance, over-
> concern with housecleaning, money management, and so on. . . .
> This is actually an interventive technique that allows the clinician
> to join with the alcoholic in a way that also begins to address the
> saint/sinner organization that is predictably true of the relationship.
> . . . The therapist might [also] . . . begin to reflect out loud at this
> point on some of her own "crazy compulsions," or she might talk
> about the way her husband is "driven crazy" by some behavior of hers
> that is hard to live with. (1985, pp. 82–83)

If you feel confident that there is a significant problem with alcohol
(and especially if you feel that this is an alcoholic relationship) and if
the couple has children, you should make every effort to meet with
the children as part of the evaluation. Their impressions and observations may help confirm the diagnosis and provide extra leverage to
motivate the drinker to pursue treatment. Most importantly, however,
the children are likely to be negatively affected by the parent's drinking. You may be uniquely positioned either to provide services or to
refer to another practitioner or program such as AlaTeen.

When drinking is not the presenting problem, be certain to address
what the couple presents as their major concern. You should investigate these issues thoroughly and address them in your response at the
conclusion of the evaluation, linking any possible connections that
may exist between these problems and patterns involving drinking.
You should, as always, be thinking about systemic functions that may
be served by the drinking.

Take care not to let your inquiry into possible alcoholism damage
your efforts to join with the couple. The knowledge that a drinking
problem exists is of little use if the couple is so alienated by the evaluation that they refuse to consider or even come back for treatment

recommendations. Bepko and Krestan (1985) caution therapists to inquire more pointedly into drinking only when the clients have "begun to express confidence and trust in the clinician's ability to help them and when the clinician feels he can convince the family that no further progress can be made in working towards their goals until the issue or potential issue is addressed" (p. 91). Above all, Krestan cautions therapists *never to argue* with either partner about drinking. This will usually elicit massive defensiveness and undermine therapeutic alliances. Uncertain conclusions can be presented tentatively, as you test and confirm hunches. More definite conclusions can be presented in a more matter-of-fact and nonjudgmental tone.

Finally, be aware of how stressful it is to an alcoholic couple or family when the drinker finally begins to become sober. Treadway (1987) and Bepko and Krestan (1985) emphasize the disorienting effects of sobriety on the partner and other family members: sudden ambiguity about the roles they should play, anxiety about whether their actions may lead the alcoholic to resume drinking, and bitterness over past events associated with the drinking. These authors also note that it is during this early period of sobriety that separation and divorce are most likely to occur in alcoholic systems.

Recommendations for Treatment

Whether alcoholism is suspected or confirmed, there are several recommendations that might be made concerning further assessment and possible treatment, ranging from simply asking the drinker to keep a diary of his or her alcohol consumption over several weeks to arranging for immediate inpatient detoxification. Options in between these choices include: recommending couple therapy in which issues of drinking will continue to be explored as trust hopefully increases, suggesting an independent evaluation for alcoholism by another professional, establishing a controlled drinking—or no drinking—contract, recommending popular readings on patterns and effects of drinking, suggesting AA for the drinker and/or Al-Anon for the partner, recommending the use of Antabuse, and referring the drinker to specialized outpatient treatment for alcoholism.

If you become aware of untreated medical complications of alcoholism, you should refer for medical evaluation or, in extreme cases, inpatient treatment for detoxification. If one partner is actively drinking and you have identified alcohol abuse or dependence, stopping the drinking should be the first priority of treatment. If possible, therefore, referral for treatment that is directly targeted at alcoholism is indicated. This might involve inpatient and outpatient programs specifically designed to address chemical dependencies or AA.

Most experts in this area agree that while systemic therapy—treatment for the family or couple—is the treatment of choice for alcoholic *relationships*, it is not the treatment of choice for *alcoholism* (Bepko & Krestan, 1985; Berenson, 1976; Breitner, personal communication; Steinglass et al., 1987; Treadway, 1987). Just as treatment for alcoholism does not necessarily change relationships that have become organized around alcohol, couple or family therapy is not sufficient to arrest and change the attitudes and patterns that have contributed to alcoholism.

There is also a strong consensus that AA constitutes a powerful form of treatment for alcoholism. Lewis Breitner points out that, compared with outpatient treatment, AA is free, available 24 hours a day, and readily accessible in virtually every part of the United States. Berenson (1976) states: "During the 'wet' phase of active drinking, participation in AA and Al-Anon is the treatment of choice, with family therapy having only an ancillary role" (p. 27). When AA is indicated, the drinker can be encouraged to attend six to eight meetings before evaluating whether or not to continue. Recommending Al-Anon for the partner helps to balance alliances, provides extra support and education to the partner, and may create a new bond in the relationship as both partners become involved with their programs. If the alcoholic refuses to be involved in either AA or any other form of treatment and if the partner is upset by the drinking, you can recommend that he or she attend Al-Anon and/or individual psychotherapy. Bepko and Krestan (1985), citing Bowen, point out that it is usually easier to get an "overfunctioner" to stop overfunctioning than it is to get an "underfunctioner" to stop underfunctioning.

If there is disagreement between the partners about the extent and seriousness of one partner's drinking, there are several options to pursue. You can ask the drinker—let's assume a man—if he would be willing to keep a diary of all alcohol consumption for a period of time and to discuss it when the couple returns for their next appointment. A slightly more confrontational approach would involve a controlled drinking, or no drinking, contract. For example, Krestan asks the drinker to describe his "normal two drinks." Whatever this involves, she will then ask him to agree to drink this much but no more for several months. She will be interested in whether or not he is able to control his drinking enough to not go above this level; perhaps more importantly, this provides a context in which to explore what he experiences in the process. Does he become more tense because he can't relax? Is he desperately waiting until he can drink again the next day? If the contract involves no alcohol at all for a certain period of time, does he find that his concentration, energy, mood, or sexual functioning improve?

Treadway (1987) notes that a controlled drinking contract may not satisfy the partner. He then points out to the couple that he does not consider the level of drinking either safe or appropriate, but he encourages the partner's cooperation in an effort to put the drinker in charge of his alcohol consumption and to extract the partner from the reactive, monitoring position. He also uses the results of this contract to assess whether the drinking can be treated within the context of family therapy or needs to be explicitly labelled an illness and treated with abstinence and AA. He adds,

> Throughout, I openly discuss the possibility that the alcohol use may be a problem that cannot be controlled with will power and limit setting but in fact may need to be treated like a disease. I don't push this metaphor, but, when it becomes apparent that the drinker cannot control his behavior, I provide the benign frame that the alcoholic has not failed, but has simply been using the wrong approach. My message is, "You can't heal a broken leg by exercise and you can't cure drinking by will power." (p. 21)

One approach suggested by Breitner is that of recommending an "independent evaluation" of the drinker's alcohol use by an expert. This is especially useful when the nondrinker is concerned with or upset by the drinking, the drinker denies having a problem, and the truth is hard to establish given their discrepant responses. It provides a "breathing space" so that the therapist is not forced to take an immediate position on the issue. It helps, at least briefly if not more lastingly, to disentangle the partners' repetitive interactions about drinking. It encourages the drinker to take greater individual responsibility for his or her drinking which makes it easier to encourage the partner to focus on his or her own reactivity and overfunctioning. Finally, it allows the couple therapist to address other difficulties in the couple's relationship.

At the completion of the independent evaluation (which may involve the partner and other family members), the other professional communicates his or her impressions and recommendations to the therapist evaluating the couple and separately to the drinker. If possible, the partner attends this feedback session. The recommendations of the independent evaluator can then be integrated with those of the couple therapist into a treatment program that suits the couple's problems and needs.

Another treatment option involves the use of Antabuse—a medication that induces violent symptoms of illness when alcohol is consumed. Breitner suggests that Antabuse be used either as an "insurance policy" for individuals who are already motivated to stop drinking or as a way to "jump-start" sobriety. However, Antabuse is easy for the drinker to quit and it is unlikely to alter the attitudes and "pride structure" that maintain alcohol abuse.

Couple or family therapy may be indicated. However, experts agree that one cannot simply generalize family therapy principles to alcoholic couples or families. Treatment needs to be directive, educate the partners about the nature of alcoholism and its effects on relational systems, and provide concrete steps that can be taken by both partners to change alcoholic patterns. Literature that describes treatment models for alcoholic systems in greater detail is listed below.

Recommended Reading for Therapists

Bepko, C., & Krestan, J. (1985). *The responsibility trap: A blueprint for treating the alcoholic family*. New York: Free Press.

Brown, S. (1985). *Treating the alcoholic: A developmental model of recovery*. New York: Wiley-Interscience.

Krestan, J., & Bepko, C. (1989). Alcohol problems and the family life cycle. In B. Carter & M. McGoldrick (Eds.), *The changing family life cycle: A framework for family therapy, Second edition*. Boston: Allyn & Bacon.

Selzer, M. (1971). The Michigan Alcoholism Screening Test: The quest for a new diagnostic instrument. *American Journal of Psychiatry, 127*, 1653–1658.

Steinglass, P., Bennett, L., Wolin, S., & Reiss, D. (1987). *The Alcoholic family*. New York: Basic.

Recommended Reading for Clients

Drews, T. (1980). *Getting them sober* (Vol. 1). South Plainfield, NJ: Bridge.

Johnson, V. (1990). *I'll quit tomorrow: A practical guide to alcoholism treatment*. San Francisco: Harper.

⌐ 18 ⌐

DEPRESSION

DEPRESSION IS THE MOST common problem mentioned by people seeking psychological services (Beach, Sandeen, & O'Leary, 1990) and it is one of the most visible and widespread psychiatric problems experienced in the general population. Approximately 9% to 26% of women and 5 to 12% of men have had a major depression at one time in their lives (APA, 1987). For this reason alone, it is very likely that clinicians who work with couples will encounter depressed individuals in their practice. However, there are even more compelling reasons why therapists should be aware of and informed about the symptoms and signs of depression as well as effective treatments. One involves the significant risk of suicide for depressed individuals. Approximately 60% of completed suicides are believed to be caused by depression or

This chapter was prepared with assistance from Lewis Cohen, M.D., Director of Psychiatric Consultation, Baystate Medical Center, Springfield, Massachusetts.

depression combined with alcoholism and about 15% of depressed individuals will eventually commit suicide (Beach et al., 1990). There is also a very high correlation between depression and dissatisfaction and conflict in a couple relationship.

Depression and Couple Relationships

An individual in a "discordant"—that is, conflictual and unhappy—relationship appears to be *25 times* more likely to be depressed than a person in a nondiscordant relationship (Weissman, 1987). About 50% of relationally discordant women* are depressed (Beach, Jouriles, & O'Leary, 1985; Weissman, 1987) and about 50% of depressed women are unhappy in their primary couple relationships (Rounsaville, Weissman, Prusoff, & Herceg-Baron, 1979a, 1979b).

Studying newly married couples, researchers have found that reports of marital discord early in the relationship are highly predictive of later depressive symptomatology (Beach, Arias, & O'Leary, 1988; Markman, Duncan, Storaasli, & Howes, 1987). Hooley et al. (1986) and Vaughn and Leff (1976) found that spousal criticism during an in-hospital interview was strongly predictive of relapse after discharge. In fact, spousal criticism was a better predictor of relapse than the initial severity of the patient's symptoms. Hooley and Teasdale (1989) have shown that relational discord and perceived criticism by the partner are positively correlated with relapse following successful treatment for depression with medication.† And finally, Paykel et al. (1969) found that the most frequent event preceding the *onset* of depression was an increase in a couple's conflict. Other studies have supported this temporal connection between relational conflict and depressive symptomatology (Birchnell & Kennard, 1983; Ifeld, 1976; Paykel, 1979). Welz (1988) found that feelings of isolation in one's closest rela-

---

*Women have much higher rates of depression than do men—in fact, nearly twice as high. A variety of explanations, including sociocultural, psychological, and biological theories, have been offered to explain this discrepancy, without a definitive consensus among researchers.

†These studies form part of a growing body of research on what has been called "expressed emotion" in the relationships and families of individuals with psychiatric disorders such as depression and schizophrenia (Brown, Birley, & Wing, 1972; Brown & Rutter, 1966; Florin et al., 1992; Hooley, 1986; Hooley et al., 1986; Valone, Norton, Goldstein, & Doane, 1983; Vaughn & Leff, 1976; Vaughn et al., 1982). There is compelling evidence that family members' excessive criticism *or* excessive worry and preoccupation with the symptomatic individual contribute to increased symptomatology and relapse after successful treatment with medication or hospitalization.

tionships and little affection shown by the partner were the best factors differentiating individuals who attempted suicide from community controls. Conversely, women who had a confiding relationship with their spouses (or others) were found to be three times *less likely* to be depressed than women without such relationships facing similar life stresses (Brown & Harris, 1978).

It is generally assumed that the connections between depression and relational discord are not unidirectional. The studies cited above indicate that prolonged dissatisfaction and conflict in a couple relationship contribute significantly to the likelihood of depressive symptomatology. It is also true that prolonged depression in one partner introduces high levels of stress into a couple relationship and may have significantly negative effects on the partner and on children. Studies have shown that even brief interactions between depressed persons and strangers prompt rejection and devaluation from the stranger and, even more importantly, contribute to a negative mood in the stranger (Biglin, Rothlind, Hops, & Sherman, 1989).

Coyne, Kahn, and Gotlib (1987) found that 40% of the spouses of depressed persons had distress that was serious enough to meet standard criteria for referral for psychiatric services and that, after the depressed person recovered, only 17% of the spouses met this criteria. A number of studies have concluded that as many as 40% to 50% of the children of a depressed parent have a diagnosable psychiatric disturbance themselves (Coyne et al., 1987; Cytryn, McKnew, Bartko, Lamour, & Hamovit, 1982; Decina et al., 1980). All of these findings attest to the close connection between depression and discordant couple relationships.

It should be noted, however, that not all couples with a depressed partner necessarily have relational difficulties. Many such couples report satisfaction with their relationships and do not exhibit typical discordant interactions (Biglin, Rothlind, Hops, & Sherman, 1989; Hooley, 1986). The assumption is that, in these cases, other etiological factors, such as life stress and biological mechanisms, are more centrally involved in the development of depression. There is no evidence that couple therapy is likely to be especially helpful to these couples, although "spouse-aided" individual psychotherapy (Hafner et al., 1983) and psychoeducation for both partners may be a powerful adjunct to treatment.

Basic Information About Depression

Depression is one of several "mood disorders" described by DSM-III-R (APA, 1987), all of which are characterized by "a prolonged emotion that colors the whole psychic life." The major diagnostic distinction is between bipolar disorders and depressive disorders. Bipolar disorders involve the presence of one or more manic or hypomanic episodes and usually a history of depressive episodes as well. Depressive disorders involve the presence of one or more periods of depression without manic or hypomanic episodes.

A depressive episode involves depressed mood and loss of interest or pleasure in all, or nearly all, activities. The individual feels sad, discouraged, "helpless and hopeless." He or she feels apathetic about previously enjoyed activities and is likely to withdraw from social relationships. Associated symptoms include: fatigue and loss of energy, appetite disturbance (typically decreased appetite with accompanying weight loss but, in some cases, an increase in appetite and weight gain), sleep disturbance (usually insomnia, with difficulty falling asleep, or frequent awakening during the night, or early morning awakening, but, as with appetite, the opposite—excessive sleeping— may be seen), psychomotor agitation (pacing, hand-wringing, inability to sit still) or psychomotor retardation (slowed body movements, slowed speech, long pauses in speaking), difficulty with concentration and memory, feelings and thoughts of worthlessness and self-reproach, and thoughts about death, often including suicidal ideation.

Other commonly associated features include anxiety, tearfulness, irritability, brooding or obsessive rumination, panic attacks, phobias, and excessive concern with physical health. Some severely depressed individuals—about 10% or 15%—do not report feeling sadness. They do, however, typically describe an inability to experience pleasure or the blunting of all emotional experience, including sadness (Whybrow, Akiskal, & McKinney, 1984). If untreated, a depressive episode is likely to last up to six months or longer.

When there is a history of at least one manic episode, the diagnosis is bipolar affective disorder. There are significant differences between bipolar and depressive disorders. Bipolar disorder is much less common than depressive disorder—only 0.4% to 1.2% of the adult population (APA, 1987) experience bipolar disorder, compared with estimates of 5% to 12% of males and 9% to 26% of females for depressive disorder; the evidence of a genetic component is also much stronger for bipolar disorder. Bipolar disorder starts on the average 15 years earlier than depressive disorder and recurs more frequently with shorter individual episodes (Coyne, 1987). Bipolar disorder is typically treated with medication—specifically, lithium carbonate. There is, Coyne points out, "no evidence that psychotherapy is effective for bipolar disorder" (p. 400). Because of its much greater prevalence, the remainder of this chapter will be concerned with depressive disorder, referred to simply as depression. "Depression," as used here, does not simply describe a transient feeling of sadness, but a major psychiatric disturbance that colors every aspect of the individual's life and may lead him or her to try to end it.

There are several models for the etiology of depression. (The DSM intentionally ignores the issue of etiology, and arrives at the diagnosis by noting the phenomenology of the individual.) Biological models draw on twin and other family studies, patient response to medication, and studies of specific neurochemical and neuroendocrinal processes. Psychological models focus on cognitive distortions and negative self perceptions, and reinforcement paradigms such as "learned helplessness" (Seligman, 1975).

There is strong evidence for the importance of cognitive factors in the development and persistence of depression. For example, longitudinal research conducted by Lewisohn, Hoberman, and Rosenbaum (1988) found that cognitions typically associated with depression predicted who developed depressive symptomatology eight months later, even after controlling for initial levels of depression. Cognitive psychotherapy has repeatedly been shown to be an effective form of treatment for depression. Interpersonal and systemic models include: early psychoanalytic notions that depression involves "anger turned inward," studies that focus on the weakness or absence of social support, and models emphasizing marital discord. Finally, some theorists have drawn attention to cultural or macrosocial variables such as economic fluctuations and changes in industrial development. Most experts now assume that there is no single cause for depression, but that biological, psychological, and interpersonal factors are all possible contributants to the development of depressive symptomatology.

Medication and Other Treatments for Depression

Therapists who evaluate couples should be aware of treatments for depression, including the use of antidepressant medication. This is especially important because "turf battles" between advocates of biological, psychodynamic, and family systems approaches have contributed to strong prejudices about the strengths and weaknesses of different forms of treatment. Antidepressant medication has proven to be extremely effective in relieving depressive symptoms such as sleep and appetite disturbance, feelings of hopelessness, fatigue, and apathy. Beach et al. (1990) report, "In controlled trials, both the most recently developed as well as the older forms of antidepressants provide improvement rates of 66% to 75%, in contrast to placebos, which show improvement rates of 30% to 60%" (p. 28). Coyne (1987) suggests that between 60% and 90% of patients benefit from antidepressant medication. He notes that there is no evidence that antidepressant medication interferes with psychotherapy. Given the intense psychological pain experienced by severely depressed individuals and the significantly increased risk of suicide, the potential benefits of medication *cannot be ignored* by any group of practicing clinicians. Some biologically oriented therapists feel that *every* patient who meets the criteria for a major depression should receive a course of antidepressant medication while others are more selective in the use of medication.

However, treatment with antidepressants is not without its limitations. It is not entirely clear which individuals respond well to medication. McLean and Hakstian (1979) found that over a third of all depressed patients fail to comply with or drop out of treatment when given antidepressants. Even when patients receiving antidepressants do show positive mood changes, medication appears to have little positive effect on their close relationships (Rounsaville, Prusoff, & Weissman, 1980; Weissman & Paykel, 1974) which often remain hostile and unsatisfying. Dysthymia, a more chronic type of depression, does respond well to the new generation SSRIs, such as Prozac, Zoloft, and Paxil. Successful treatment with antidepressants does not assure that the individual will not experience subsequent episodes of depression in the future. Data do suggest that the specific antidepressant which has helped an individual in previous episodes of depression is most likely to help in subsequent episodes. Finally, many antidepressants are lethal when taken in high doses, making them potentially dangerous if large quantities are available to suicidal or substance-abusing patients.

Individual psychotherapy also constitutes a major form of treatment for depression. A recent multicenter study by NIMH (Elkin et al., 1989) indicated that interpersonal psychotherapy—an individual treatment approach that addresses abnormal grief, interpersonal deficits and disputes, role transitions, and loss—worked as well as antidepressant medication for many patients. Most authorities agree that successful psychotherapy for depression tends to be relatively brief, goal-oriented, and structured and to emphasize positive changes in cognition and behavior (Beach et al., 1990; Coyne, 1987).

Couple therapy has also been found to be particularly effective for depressed individuals. In one study of behavioral marital therapy versus individual cognitive therapy, couples in both treatments experienced a significant decrease in depressive symptomatology. Couples in marital therapy also showed significant improvement in marital adjustment. Both sets of changes were maintained on follow-up one year later (O'Leary & Beach, 1990). Studies conducted by Foley, Rounsaville, Weissman, Sholomshas, and Chevron (1987) and Weissman (1988) indicate that the inclusion of a partner in interpersonal psychotherapy for depression is at least as effective as individual therapy in alleviating symptoms of depression and more effective at improving the quality of the relationship. In a comparison of medication and marital therapy, Friedman (1975) found that marital therapy was superior to medication in terms of effects on marital and family relationships but that medication was faster and generally superior for symptom relief and clinical improvement.

ECT (electroconvulsive therapy) has also proved helpful in cases of severe depression that did not respond to other treatments. It may be especially beneficial for the elderly and other physically frail patients since its effects are actually less dangerous to these patients than are those of antidepressant medication. (For further information about ECT, see Welch, 1991.)

Assessment

Figure 4 contains a decision tree for therapists who suspect depression. If a couple reports that one partner has been depressed or if you suspect depression, you should *always* inquire *in detail* to evaluate the severity of symptoms. This can be done in the couple session, in the individual sessions, or in both. Has the person experienced a decrease in appetite? Is there an accompanying loss of weight? Has eating increased? Is there an associated weight gain? Has his sleep pattern changed? Is there difficulty falling or staying asleep? Does he wake often during the night or early in the morning, unable to fall back asleep? Is there less interest in sex or in other activities that are usually enjoyable for him? Does he feel depressed, "blue," or "down in the dumps?" Is he tired and unable to accomplish what he usually does? Is there a feeling of apathy, of "just not caring" about things? Is there difficulty with concentration or memory? Does he feel critical of himself, preoccupied with feelings of guilt or self-reproach? Does he feel discouraged, hopeless, and powerless to change his situation? When was the last time he felt happy?*

Does this partner look depressed? Does he sigh often or pause as though simply speaking is an effort? Does he appear agitated and anxious? Is there hand-wringing or pacing? Is his speech full of self-criticism and self-reproach? Does he seem hopeless? Is there a history

---

*This last question is suggested by L. Cohen, personal communication.

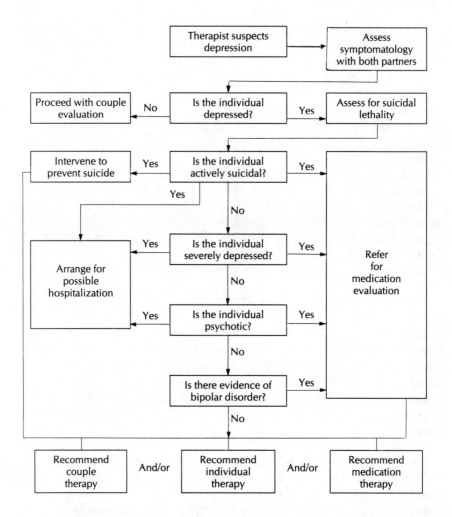

Figure 4. A decision tree for assessing depression. Readers should note that this figure cannot convey all of the complexities of the process of evaluating a couple in which depression is suspected; it should be used as a complement to the text.

of depression or bipolar affective disorder in family members? Has any family member been treated for depression? If so, with medication, ECT, or hospitalization? Has he had periods of depression earlier in life? Were they treated? If so, how and with what results?

Depression can be mistaken for a normal grief reaction (uncomplicated bereavement). However, uncomplicated bereavement is not usually accompanied by morbid preoccupations with worthlessness, prolonged impairment, psychomotor retardation, global guilt, and preoccupation with death (APA, 1987). Suicidal thoughts seem to affect less than 10% of the bereaved (Beach et al., 1990) as opposed to a much higher proportion of depressed persons.

Depressive symptoms can be generated by illness or as side-effects of medication. Depression often accompanies some forms of cancer, hyper- and hypothyroidism, lupus, diabetes, hepatitis, mononucleosis, multiple sclerosis, and stroke. It can be precipitated by a wide range of medications including, among others, antihypertensives such as reserpine, beta-blockers, anti-anxiety agents, corticosteriods, sedative-hypnotics, and oral contraceptives (Beach et al., 1990). In light of this, you should always inquire about illnesses or medications currently being taken. You should also inquire about patterns of drinking in view of the high correlation between alcohol and depression. Be aware that psychosis may accompany depressive symptoms; assess for the presence of a thought disorder.

You should *always* inquire about suicidal feelings whenever you suspect depression, even if the patient does not report them. This is especially important for therapists working with couples. Depression in the context of couple conflict is "associated with a particular proneness for suicidal ideation and behavior" (Beach et al., 1990, p. 89).

These questions can be asked in the initial couple session but should also be pursued in individual sessions. If you are unsure whether you are getting a complete picture of suicidal thoughts, feelings, and possible actions, you should *spend some part of the initial session with each partner separately and inquire about this before ending the session.* Ask about suicidal thoughts and impulses and about the individual's sense of perceived control over them. Ask her to describe them in detail: How long have these thoughts been there and how often do they come? Has she thought of how she would kill herself? In other words, has she formulated a plan? Are the means she has thought about readily available—guns and ammunition in the home, for example, or, in the case of someone thinking about an intentional car accident, an automobile? Has she taken steps of any kind toward actually fulfilling this plan—for example, taking a bottle of pills out to look at them or buying a hose for carbon monoxide poison-

ing in a closed garage? Has she ever "heard voices" telling her to commit suicide? (This last question assesses for auditory or "command
hallucinations," which would be of the highest concern since it may
indicate psychotic thought processes.)

Has she ever felt suicidal or made any kind of a suicide attempt in
the past? What did she do and what were the results? Did she require
medical attention of any kind? Has anyone in her family ever made a
suicide attempt? With what result? Positive answers to *any* of these
questions should raise concern. Answers to questions further along in
the sequence, such as a formulated plan, steps already taken, available
means, previous attempts, or a positive family history for suicide, are
especially worrisome in terms of possible lethality.

If you suspect your client is acutely suicidal, you must try to prevent the possibility of a suicide attempt. This is an ethical matter and
a legal one since, in most states, clinicians are mandated to take such
actions. In a case involving mild suicidal thoughts with no plan or
serious intent and a declared desire to live, this might mean having the
person agree to a contract of not acting on suicidal feelings in the
time between sessions and making yourself accessible for emergency
telephone calls (or, if this is impossible, directing the person to other
emergency services). It might involve notifying a partner or close relative and arranging for that person to come to the clinic or office to
take personal charge of the depressed person. (If the depressed person's
partner is already present, this task is greatly simplified.) In some
cases, it may require emergency hospitalization.

If you will be providing treatment, be sure to have the client keep
you informed about any changes in suicidal ideation or intent. Be
aware that the period of time when he or she begins to improve may
be the most dangerous time. The previously depressed person was to
some extent anergic (tired and exhausted) and apathetic. A combination of increased energy but persisting hopelessness and self-critical
ideation may lead to an increased risk that he or she will now be able
to act on suicidal thoughts. Two paper-and-pencil instruments that
help track the client's level of depressive symptomatology and lethality are the Beck Depression Inventory and Beck's Scale for Suicidal
Ideation.*

The partner of the depressed person can be of enormous assistance
both to the therapist and to the other partner. He or she can provide
important information by sharing his or her own impressions of the

---

*Addresses for ordering these instruments are provided at the conclusion of
this chapter. The reader is referred to Bongar, 1991, 1992 for further discussion of assessment and management of lethality.

individual's recent mood and behavior and whether or not this represents a significant change from previous functioning. The partner may also be valuable in assisting with the decision of whether or not a patient with suicidal ideation needs to be hospitalized. Be sure to evaluate the partner and children for depression or other difficulties in light of the high incidence of diagnosable psychiatric disturbance in the partners and children of depressed persons.

When evaluating couples in which one partner is depressed, two final caveats should be kept in mind. First: To an even greater degree than in other couple evaluations, uncontrolled negative interactions between the partners can have serious consequences. With all couples, after a very few minutes for the therapist to observe these interactions, they contribute little to the initial session. They may deepen feelings of antagonism and hopelessness and lead to diminished expectations of real help from the therapist. When one person is depressed, the risks are even greater. The partner's criticism may intensify the depressed person's sense of worthlessness as well as his or her hopelessness about improving the relationship. For this reason, you should be active and forceful in interrupting such interchanges, steering the discussion to a more neutral or positive tone and, if need be, separating the partners and continuing the evaluation with each individually.

Second, as Beach et al. (1990) point out, be prepared for "depressive venting"—intense and protracted expressions of pain and anguish experienced by the individual. While you must respond sympathetically to these feelings, you should not allow the evaluation to be dominated by them. Efforts should be made to redirect the process of the session to other areas, such as further information gathering, and again, if necessary, you may split the session and interview both partners separately. If possible, try to evaluate the kinds of areas that would normally be covered in other couple evaluations. However, especially if the individual's depression has not been previously diagnosed or treated, his or her symptoms of depression should take precedence, both in information gathering and in considerations related to treatment.

Treatment Recommendations

The three most common recommendations for couples in which one partner is depressed are: individual psychotherapy, evaluation for antidepressant medication, and couple therapy. Each case must of course be evaluated on its own merits; however, there are some guidelines for selecting one or another of these treatments.

A recommendation for medication evaluation and possible individual psychotherapy should be made in most cases when any of the following conditions are met:

- The depressed person is seriously suicidal.
- Symptoms of depression are severe (with sleep and appetite disturbance, psychomotor retardation or agitation, marked lethargy, and hopelessness).
- There is evidence of a bipolar affective disorder.
- The individual appears to be psychotic.

In these cases, the depressed person may be in so much psychic pain that involvement in couple therapy is impractical and has the additional risk of fueling his or her sense of worthlessness and self-reproach. It is imperative that you do what you can to help alleviate the intense pain of depressive symptoms as quickly as possible, for simple humanitarian reasons and in light of the risk of lethality. While several studies have demonstrated the efficacy of couple therapy for depression, none have shown it to relieve serious depressive symptomatology more quickly than medication or problem-focused, cognitive psychotherapy.

The best indicators of a probable positive response to medication include an acute onset of depressive symptoms with "melancholic features," depression in the context of a bipolar affective disorder, and successful treatment in the past with antidepressant medication (Baldessarini, 1988). In these cases, couple sessions may still be useful as an adjunctive or second phase of treatment, presumably after the depressed partner has responded positively to medication or individual psychotherapy. When there are clear relational difficulties, they can be addressed in these sessions once the individual's symptoms are in remission.*

When the couple seems to have a satisfactory relationship, the partner's involvement in couple sessions may be used to support the depressed person's individual treatment and to provide psychoeducation about depression to both partners. As indicated earlier, traditional couple therapy is neither necessary nor helpful for couples who are satisfied with their relationship.

Decisions involving treatment often depend on idiosyncratic factors. For example, for an individual who was extremely uncomfortable

---

*See Beach, Sandeen, and O'Leary (1990) for a detailed description of the phases and techniques of treatment that they have found most helpful for couples with a depressed partner.

sharing personal feelings with his or her partner even before becoming depressed and who seems horrified at the prosect of couple sessions, individual psychotherapy is probably the most sensible first step. For a couple in which the depressed person very much wants his or her partner's support in treatment, couple sessions as an adjunct to individual treatment may be preferable. A client who is frightened by the prospect of psychotherapy and insists that he or she only wants symptom relief would welcome referral for medication evaluation, with decisions concerning possible couple therapy to follow.

Beach et al. (1990) summarize these and others considerations in the following way.

> We believe that marital therapy as a primary or solitary intervention modality is appropriate when the following considerations have been satisfied: (1) the risk of suicide has been carefully assessed and risk of precipitous suicidal gestures has been determined to be low; (2) the depressed patient has received a thorough diagnostic assessment and has been accurately diagnosed as nonbipolar . . . , and neither psychotic features nor organic mood disorders are present; (3) the presence of marital discord has been clearly established; (4) marital discord appears to play an etiological or maintaining role in the depression; (5) both spouses have been seen individually and assessed for hidden agendas, desire for immediate divorce, low level of commitment to work on improving the marriage, and presence of extramarital sexual activity, and the therapist has some confidence that both spouses are interested in working at improving their marital relationship. (p. 89)

In summary, couple relationships have not only been found to be implicated in the etiology and onset of depression, but also in its remission and in the prevention of subsequent episodes.

Recommended Reading for Therapists

Beach, S., Sandeen, E., & O'Leary, K. (1990). *Depression in marriage: A Model for etiology and treatment.* New York: Guilford.

Bongar, B. (1991). *The suicidal patient: Clinical and legal standards of care.* Washington: American Psychological Association.

Bongar, B. (1992). *The assessment, management, and treatment of suicide: Guidelines for practice.* Oxford: Oxford University Press.

Cameron, O. (1987). *Presentations of depression: Depressive symptoms in medical and other psychiatric disorders.* New York: Wiley.

Cassem, N. (1991). Depression. In N. Cassem (Ed.), *Massachusetts General Hospital handbook of general hospital psychiatry* (3rd ed.). St. Louis: Mosby Year Book.

Coyne, J. (1987). Depression, biology, marriage and marital therapy. *Journal of Marital and Family Therapy, 13,* 393–408.

Maltzberger, J., & Buie, D. (1980). The devices of suicide: Revenge, riddance, and rebirth. *International Review of Psycho-analysis, 7,* 61–72.

Welch, C. (1991). Electroconvulsive therapy in the general hospital. In N. Cassem (Ed.), *Massachusetts General Hospital handbook of general hospital psychiatry* (3rd ed.). St. Louis: Mosby Year Book.

Instruments

The Beck Depression Inventory can be ordered from: Psychological Corporation, Order Service Center, P.O. Box 839954, San Antonio, TX 78283–9954.

Beck's Scale for Suicidal Ideation can be ordered from: Center for Cognitive Therapy, Room 602, 133 South 36 Street, Philadelphia, PA 19104.

Recommended Reading for Clients

A short pamphlet on depression is available and can be obtained from the National Institute of Mental Health: *Depression: What you need to know.* To order, write to: D/ART/Public Inquiries. National Institute of Mental Health, Room 15-C-05, 5600 Fishers Lane, Rockville, MD 20857.

Cammer, L. (1969). *Up from depression.* New York: Pocketbooks.

DePaulo, J., & Ablow, K. (1989). *How to cope with depression: A complete guide for you and your family.* New York: Ballantine.

Fieve, R. (1980). *Moodswing* (rev. ed.). New York: Morrow.

Papolos, D., & Papolos, J. (1992). *Overcoming depression* (rev. ed.). New York: HarperCollins.

Organizational Support for Clients

National Depression and Manic-Depression Association; 730 North Franklin Street, Suite 501; Chicago, IL 60610; phone (312) 642-0049; fax (312) 642-7243

─ 19 ─

EXTRAMARITAL
INVOLVEMENTS

O NE OF THE MOST common precipitants for couples seeking treatment is the disclosure or discovery of one partner's romantic/
sexual relationship outside the primary couple relationship. The prevalence of these relationships is high in the general population (and even
higher among couples seeking treatment) and their effects on the primary couple relationship are dramatic and often destructive.

The definitions and terminology used in this area are important
because of the heterogeneity of relational patterns often subsumed
under the simple heading of "affairs" and the implicit—and sometimes
explicit—value judgments that therapists hold in this area. None of

This chapter was prepared with assistance from Eric S. Strauss, Ph.D., private
practice, West Springfield, MA.

the terms commonly used to describe these relationships encompasses the full range of relevant patterns. The term "extramarital sex" is problematic because not all couples are married and not all problematic outside relationships are sexual. "Affair" usually denotes an ongoing sexual or romantic attachment; not all outside sexual activity has the continuity this term implies. "Infidelity," as Westfall (1989) points out, is a moral/religious term; "adultery," a legal one.

Many therapists feel that the critical aspects of these relationships are the *secrecy* that is often involved and the *potential threat* to the primary couple relationship. Pittman addresses this deftly when he suggests, "The infidelity is not in the sex . . . but in the secrecy. It isn't whom you lie with. It's whom you lie to" (1989, p. 53). There are many couples who experience the whole range of characteristic patterns and reactions to such relationships even when there has been little or no actual sexual activity. For these reasons, although no term fits all of the potential patterns perfectly, the discussion that follows will use the term "extramarital involvement" (EMI). It refers to *significant emotional attachments and/or sexual activity which occurs outside a committed couple relationship, whether the primary couple is married or not.* The three parties will be referred to as the involved partner, the uninvolved partner, and the outside partner.

Prevalence and Characteristic Patterns

A range of figures have been cited for the prevalence of EMIs. Most surveys have specifically inquired about *sexual* relationships occurring outside *marriage*. Kinsey and his associates (1948, 1953) found that 50% of the married men they surveyed reported having had extramarital sexual relationships as did 26% of married women surveyed. More recently, the Kinsey Institute New Report on Sex (Reinisch, 1990) reviewed six studies to find rates of 37% for husbands and 29% for wives. The Janus Report on Sexual Behavior (Janus & Janus, 1993) found very similar figures: 35% of married men and 26% of married women reported having had at least one incident of extramarital sex.

Prevalence rates among clients in couple or family therapy appear to be even higher. In their survey of marital and family therapists, Humphrey and Strong (1976) found that about 46% of all couples presenting for treatment were concerned with one or both partners' EMIs. When the study was replicated in 1984, similar or even higher rates were found (Humphrey, 1985). These rates indicate that, in terms of prevalence alone, therapists who evaluate couples should be informed about typical patterns involved in EMIs. If we look at the *effects* of EMIs, the need for therapist awareness in this area becomes even clearer. Humphrey's survey (1985) found that a separation resulted for 45% of those couples in which the husband had an EMI, and for 31% of the couples in which the wife did. This led to divorce for 10% of the couples when the husband's EMI was involved and 17% of the couples when the EMI was the wife's. Humphrey notes that these figures were lower than those in the original 1976 study, suggesting somewhat higher tolerance for EMIs a decade later.

EMIs have been differentiated in terms of the motives for the EMI, the circumstances or context in the primary relationship, the meanings they hold for the partners, the particular patterns which develop, and the consequences they have for the primary relationship. While a wide range of causal factors have been suggested for the prevalence of EMI, most experts agree that they are most often symptomatic of difficulties in the primary couple relationship, usually involving intimacy and/or sexuality. A variety of more specific formulations have been offered by different theorists on the functions of EMIs for the parties involved. Many, such as Moultrop, see the EMI as "an emotional solution to an emotional dilemma" (1990, p. 8) in the primary couple relationship. More specifically, it is suggested that the EMI provides a way for one—or both or all three—of the partners involved to regulate distance in their relationships. This formulation fits neatly into the Bowenian notion of triangles serving to diffuse and rechannel anxiety and tension in dyadic relationships (Bowen, 1978). There is widespread agreement that ongoing EMIs only rarely reflect purely sexual needs and are likely to involve more complicated emotional attachments.

Pittman (1989) describes four characteristic patterns of EMIs: accidental infidelities, marital arrangements, philandering, and romantic affairs. Accidental affairs tend to be unplanned and unexpected. The involved partner is not necessarily dissatisfied with his or her marriage and the EMI is less likely to involve strong feelings of attachment and an ongoing relationship. Marital arrangements do not involve romantic love between the involved spouse and the outside partner but they supplement or balance the emotional/sexual needs of one—or two or all three—of the individuals involved. Philanderers require "a steady change of sexual partners" (p. 156) which protects them from becoming emotionally committed to any one partner. In romantic affairs, the involved partner feels strongly attracted and attached to the outside partner. The relationship is more likely to persist over time and to involve extensive secrecy. These EMIs are usually the most disruptive and threatening to the primary couple relationship. Most EMIs I have seen clinically fall into this category; my guess is that this is also true for most other practitioners.

Pittman suggests that the choice of partner for an EMI "seems based on the other person's *difference* from the spouse rather than *superiority* to the spouse. The point of difference may diagnose a problem for which the affair is seen as a cure. . . . More often, people are not seeking an alternative to their marriage, but a supplement to it" (1989, pp. 42–43). Moultrop notes that the involved partner's differing relationships with the uninvolved partner and the outside partner become "an external metaphor or representation of the internal split in the involved spouse" (1990, pp. 142–143). The nature of the EMI provides an unspoken commentary on the involved partner's experience of the *limitations* which have evolved in the primary couple relationship. An EMI can represent an act of revenge against a partner for what the involved partner sees as neglect or injurious actions in the past. Revenge is particularly likely to be a motive when the outside partner is closely related to the uninvolved partner, for example, as a best friend, a sibling, or, often most humiliating socially, a coworker, employer, or employee.

EMIs have dramatic and often destructive effects on couple relationships. Negative effects typically involve some if not all of the following: the negative feelings of the uninvolved partner, including shock, a sense of betrayal, damaged trust and security in the relationship, anger, anxiety, and depression, and intrusive thoughts and images about the EMI; the negative feelings of the involved partner, including anxiety, shame, and guilt, and intense ambivalence; and the damage to the trustworthiness and security of the primary relationship. EMIs frequently lead to separation and divorce.

While the awareness that one's partner is emotionally or sexually involved with another person is distressing enough for most people, the destructive effects of EMIs are compounded by the secrecy and deception that often accompany them. This intensifies their feelings of betrayal and humiliation and damages their sense of fairness, trust, and safety in the relationship. Pittman relates this deception to another important negative effect of EMIs—namely, confusion. "Infidelity may not be the worst thing that one marriage partner can do to another, but it may be the most confusing and disorienting and therefore the most likely to destroy the marriage—not necessarily because of the sex, but because of the secrecy and the lies" (1989, p. 22). The damage is compounded when others—such as friends, relatives, and even children—are made aware of the EMI and thus drawn into the deception of the unaware partner.

An EMI can irrevocably contaminate a couple's sexual relationship and destroy the possibility of intimacy between them. It can trigger a series of escalating retaliations, leading to the breakup of the relationship. When EMIs involve sexual activity, they may lead to the uninvolved partner's infection with sexually transmitted diseases, with serious—and in the case of HIV and AIDS—potentially lethal consequences. When the primary couple has children, the negative effects of the EMI are often—and sometimes devastatingly—felt by them. At the very least, both parents are likely to have less energy to devote to children while they are coping with the crisis created by the EMI; at the worst, the marriage may continue, having been permanently damaged by the EMI, or end in divorce.

Not all of the effects of EMIs are negative. My own clinical experience and some surveys suggest that EMIs can, in fact, have positive effects on the primary couple relationship. In one survey, 26% of couples in which the husband had an EMI and 21% of couples in which the wife had the EMI were seen by their therapist as having an improved marital relationship by the end of therapy (Humphrey, 1987). I have seen couples use the crisis precipitated by the EMI to recommit to their relationship and to revitalize it. However, this seems to happen in a minority of cases. Using an EMI to revitalize a marriage is rather like using explosives to warn boaters away from dangerous reefs. The negative effects of the "cure" are more than likely to outweigh the damage done by the original danger.

Some of the variables most relevant to the meaning, the consequences, and the resolution of EMIs include the following:

- frequency and duration of the EMI
- degree of emotional connection between the involved partner and the outside partner
- degree of emotional connection and commitment in the primary couple relationship
- degree of secrecy surrounding the EMI
- level of—and physical location of—sexual activity
- genders of the three parties (is the primary couple heterosexual or homosexual? Is the EMI the same or different?)
- prior relationship of the outside partner and the uninvolved partner (strangers, relatives, neighbors, etc.)
- prior relationship between the involved partner and the outside partner (coworkers, congregants in same church, neighbors, etc.)

- continuing proximity and contact with the outside partner due to life circumstances (neighbors, relatives, etc.)
- number of EMIs
- unilateral or bilateral EMIs
- whether the EMI was disclosed by the involved partner or discovered by the uninvolved partner
- degree of acceptance of and consent for EMIs in the primary couple relationship
- family history of EMIs—especially with negative consequences—for either primary partner
- tolerance of EMIs within the partner's ethnic or social community
- coincidence of EMI with other couple or family stressors
- existence of children in the primary couple relationship*

These variables mediate the extent of the damage done in the primary couple relationship and the likelihood and difficulty of healing. For example, although a "one-night stand" with a stranger when the partners have had to temporarily live in different geographical areas for work may be extremely distressing to the uninvolved partner, it will probably have less destructive effects than a long-term EMI with a close friend of the uninvolved partner, when the involved partner feels he or she is "in love" with the outside partner, when sexual activity has taken place in the couple's home, and when many other people have known about the relationship and participated in the deception of the uninvolved partner.

Assessment

For purposes of assessment, the most important questions involve who does or does not know about the EMI and whether or not it has ended. These factors yield several common scenarios. In one, the therapist suspects an EMI even though none has been reported. In another, one partner reveals a secret EMI to you in an individual session. In other cases, the couple presents for evaluation reporting an EMI which is described as having ended. Or, the couple may report that one partner is currently involved in an ongoing EMI. The focus and the course of

*This list of variables represents my own clinical observations as well as factors identified by Humphrey (1987) and Westfall (1989).

the evaluation differs in each of these scenarios although there are also large areas of overlap.

In all of these cases, the couple evaluation format described in this book is ideally suited to exploring the presenting problem and its wider relational context, and setting directions for treatment. The use of individual interviews with both partners and the therapist's suggestion to hold off on any major relational changes until the completion of the evaluation are especially helpful in the context of possible or actual EMIs.

The therapist should be clear about his or her feelings on the question of responsibility for EMIs. As with alcoholism and substance abuse, there is often real confusion about this issue. The position held by most experts is that the involved partner must be held responsible for starting the EMI even if there are identifiable weaknesses or problems in the primary couple relationship that may have contributed to it. Both partners may have been responsible for the problems in their relationship that made the EMI more likely, but the uninvolved partner cannot be held responsible for the EMI actually occurring. In Frank Pittman's words, "The one being betrayed can't make affairs happen, can't make the betrayer stop, and can only make him- or herself available for solving whatever problems there might be in the marriage" (1989, p. 47).

The Therapist Suspects an EMI

The possibility of an undisclosed EMI may be brought to your attention by the suspicions of the uninvolved partner, or you may find yourself reacting to the involved partner's descriptions, omissions, or incongruities. The most obvious clues typically involve persistent evasiveness or vehement but unexplained insistence on or objections to certain plans and arrangements.

A less obvious indicator in some cases involves intense triangulation between the primary partners over a third party, such as a close friend of one partner. The primary partners may argue over how much time one partner spends with this friend or over whether or not he or she is a "good influence" on the partner. In several of these cases, I later discovered that there had in fact been an EMI for one partner. However, the outside partner was *not* the friend who was the original focus of conflict. For these couples, it seems as if the patterns that might be enacted if the secret EMI were disclosed are instead systemically channelled into a different triangle. The likelihood of this "detouring" is, of course, increased if the friend knows about the EMI and has agreed to be used as a "cover" for contact between the involved and the outside partners.

In these cases, you may be faced with dilemmas involving secrets, especially in the discussion that takes place in the individual session with the suspected involved partner. Therapists must define their own positions on the issue of secrets in couple evaluation and treatment. My own are presented in Chapter 7 (see also Karpel, 1980); to recap these guidelines, you would discuss the importance of both partners' sharing all relevant information, but point out the dangers and difficulties that develop when a therapist agrees to keep information secret from one partner in couple therapy. You would add that you do not unilaterally disclose secret information, but offer to help the individual plan when and how to disclose if this seems necessary. Having done this, you would allow the individual to choose how he or she wanted to proceed.

If it seems clear that there is no EMI or if the individual continues to deny one despite your suspicions, proceed with the evaluation on the basis of the information that has been provided. Hunches and recommendations may be influenced by your suspicions, depending on how strong they are, but they cannot be definitively shaped by them without confirmation.

The Therapist Learns of a Secret EMI

If you have used the guidelines for managing secrets presented in Chapter 7, unwanted disclosure of a secret EMI is unlikely but certainly still possible. Remember that an agreement to keep information secret that is relevant to the other partner and to the difficulties they are experiencing creates a number of potentially very serious problems. You have entered into a secret alliance with one partner which may compromise your efforts at balanced siding. You are now contributing to the mystification of the other partner and, should the EMI later be revealed, seriously compromising your own trustworthiness for that partner who may feel betrayed by your collusion in the secret. Furthermore, if couple therapy does follow, the therapy is vulnerable to the same negative effects that secrets engender in any relational system: confusion, distortion, and mystification at an informational level; anxiety, constriction, shame, and guilt at an emotional level; diminished relational resources and the threat of further negative consequences accompanying inadvertent discovery or disclosure.

For example, imagine a couple who presents with the husband's "erectile disorder" as the primary complaint. You learn that the husband is involved in an EMI without any sexual difficulties. Consider proceeding with sex therapy which this couple has requested, without the EMI being disclosed. This highlights the practical complications, the ethical dubiousness, and the sheer wrongheadedness of such an enterprise. For these reasons, in most cases I would discourage therapists from simply agreeing to keep secret a current EMI* and trying to conduct couple therapy under these circumstances (see Karpel, 1980; Imber-Black, 1993).

You can explain these complications to the involved partner and offer to help him or her disclose the EMI in a way that minimizes destructive consequences. In some cases, you may feel that the EMI should not be disclosed immediately, for example, if there is a preexisting crisis or if the uninvolved partner is seriously depressed. In these situations, as long as the involved partner agrees that disclosure might be necessary at a later point in treatment, you can offer to proceed. If the involved partner refuses to disclose the EMI under any circumstances, my own feeling is that you should not recommend couple therapy. You can conduct and conclude the full evaluation, offering whatever insight and guidance is possible under the circumstances to both partners. You may in some cases recommend individual treatment for one or both partners.

The Couple Presents with an Already Disclosed EMI

If the couple reports an EMI at the beginning of the evaluation, the conduct of the evaluation is more straightforward. The central question involves whether the EMI is over or continuing in the present. However, in either case the partners are likely to go through a predictable series of initial reactions. The disclosure creates a crisis that often precipitates the request for couple therapy. It is, however, also the time when they are least likely to be able to explore the origins and meanings of the EMI. They, and the therapist they consult, will need to deal with the immediate consequences of the disclosure; a temporary stabilization has to be achieved before they can reflect on the significance of the EMI. Westfall stresses that "the emotional and cognitive disequilibrium they experience is a normal response to the crisis and . . . is likely to continue to a lesser degree for several months" (1989, p. 170).

---

*EMIs that are secret but have already ended present a more ambiguous picture; they typically do not pose the same level of threat to the couple relationship nor does knowledge of them compromise the therapist's siding as profoundly. Here too, therapists must clarify their own values as to whether these relationships can and should be treated differently from current EMIs. They should consider the relevance of the past EMI for the couple's present difficulties, the likely negative consequences of disclosure, and the threat to the therapist's trustworthiness if the EMI is later discovered.

The uninvolved partner typically feels hurt, humiliated, angry, and betrayed and, in rare instances, may precipitously decide to end the relationship. More often, however, this partner becomes intensely focused on keeping the relationship together. I have repeatedly heard men, for example, say essentially the following: "I always *knew* that if I found out she was having an affair, I'd divorce her. Just like that. But that's not how I feel now, and I just want to make it work out." The involved partner usually feels guilty and ashamed of the violation of their original contract and of the deception involved in the EMI. If the EMI has ended, he or she may experience grief over the loss of the relationship with the outside partner. Unlike situations that involve grief for a spouse, friend, or family member, there is much less social support for grief over an EMI but the experience can be just as painful. If the EMI is continuing, the involved partner is likely to be subject to intense ambivalence over how to resolve his or her relational dilemma.

The primary couple may experience a "honeymoon" (Scharff, 1978) in the aftermath of the disclosure. They may have long, searching conversations and report that they haven't talked so much with each other in years. A bland sexual relationship may be revitalized. In other cases, however, the relationship is characterized by intense conflict and their sexual relationship may be disrupted or terminated altogether. When this occurs, it may be at the instigation of either primary partner—by the uninvolved partner because of his or her sense of deep betrayal and rejection and/or because of "contamination" of the sexual relationship by thoughts and images of the EMI, or by the involved partner who may have struggled with a facade of sexual interest for years and now feels that he or she can abandon any pretense of desire for the uninvolved partner.

When the EMI is known to both primary partners and reported to the therapist, there are several guidelines for assessment, whether the EMI is current or ended:

1. Be prepared, as you would in any case involving an acute crisis, to schedule extra sessions in order to support and stabilize both partners and to respond to the urgency of their concerns.

2. Encourage the couple to avoid precipitous decisions, suggesting instead that decisions be informed by a careful examination of factors which led up to the EMI and each partner's sense of his or her best interests.

3. Remember to evaluate for psychological and/or physical symptomatology in both partners. The stress that accompanies the crisis of disclosure or the period of time leading up to it may

have negatively affected one or both partners. Westfall notes that higher rates of depression have been found in couples presenting with EMIs, pointing out that it is often the *involved partner* who is more depressed. Although relatively uncommon, suicide attempts following discovery of an EMI do occur.

4. Listen for possible negative effects on children. If these are reported or suspected, either bring the children in for evaluation or refer them to another practitioner who can do so.

The Couple Reports an Ended EMI

If the EMI has ended, the partners will now have to deal with the fallout and crisis precipitated by it. Later, they will need to examine the factors in their relationship that may have contributed to it. These cases are more likely to result in ongoing couple therapy aimed at preserving the primary couple relationship.

In some cases, the involved partner may report that the EMI has ended but the uninvolved partner and/or the therapist doubt it. This scenario involves, therefore, a mixture of features associated with other scenarios already described. The EMI has already been disclosed and presumably precipitated characteristic negative effects. If individual sessions are held, the same guidelines for managing secrets are in order. The therapist's hunches inform treatment recommendations in the same way they would in the first scenario discussed.

The Couple Reports a Continuing EMI

If the EMI is continuing, the challenges for the partners and for the therapist are greater. They will have to deal with the crisis precipitated by the EMI and with feelings and questions associated with its continuation, especially the choices which each of them face in relation to it. Typically, while the uninvolved partner pursues the involved partner, questioning his or her feelings about the outside partner and pleading or insisting that he or she give up the relationship, the involved partner experiences intense ambivalence regarding the two relationships. He or she is usually torn between the familiarity, the shared history, and the security of the primary couple relationship—with an added emotional pull when there are children—and the excitement, gratification, and attachment to the outside partner.

A variety of outcomes are possible. The involved partner may choose the primary relationship and end the EMI; he or she may instead choose the outside partner. He or she may physically separate in order to "get some space"; these separations often represent a conscious or unconscious desire to pursue the EMI. In some cases, the involved partner simply cannot choose; instead he or she is paralyzed until either the uninvolved partner or the outside partner finally makes a move to end the impasse. Confusion and uncertainty may continue for months.

It is especially important to recognize that the partners' individual interests may or may not converge in areas fundamentally important to their relationship. For example, the overriding goal of the uninvolved partner—the continuation of the primary relationship—may constitute a kind of spiritual "death sentence" for the involved partner. Even if their interests continue to converge on the welfare of their children and the benefits of an amicable relationship, this fundamental divergence of interests may inevitably lead to the end of the relationship.

Therapists have taken differing positions on the question of whether to conduct couple therapy when there is an ongoing EMI. Many argue that the therapist should not attempt to do so under these circumstances. Others, such as Humphrey (1987) and Moultrop (1990) take the opposite position, citing the potential for deceit when the therapist insists that the EMI end as a condition for treatment and the difficulty of actually monitoring this. They also point out the danger of intensified resistance from the involved partner and a greater risk of one or both partners dropping out of treatment.

There are, however, sound reasons for assuming that in many cases productive couple therapy is unlikely if one partner has a continuing EMI and is ambivalent about his or her commitment to the primary relationship. Proceeding with couple therapy in these cases can be a frustrating and disappointing experience for all involved. However, this does not necessarily mean that the couple cannot benefit from couple evaluation or from a somewhat extended series of sessions designed to help them come to some resolution of their dilemma.

It is important to frame the goals of these sessions as being to help each partner cope with the stresses of the situation, to clarify feelings about where his or her interests lie and, if possible, to make choices that support these interests while considering those of the partner and children. These sessions are dominated by the "crisis of commitment" which is precipitated by the EMI. Make clear that they are not intended to "patch up" the couple relationship since both partners are not fully committed to this goal. Individual sessions are especially useful; they may be extended into a short series of parallel individual sessions or interspersed with couple sessions.

If the sessions lead to a decision by the involved partner to recommit to the primary couple relationship and if the uninvolved partner accepts this, the couple can, if they choose, continue in couple therapy. If instead there is a decision by one or both partners to separate, they may want assistance with some aspect of this process. In some cases, it may be impossible to come to any decision. If you feel that the sessions are neither helping to resolve the impasse nor providing much relief for either partner, a recommendation of individual treatment—for whichever partner is interested—may be in order. You can offer to reconvene couple sessions if a change in the stalemate makes this seem more likely to be helpful. As in other cases that involve a recommendation against couple therapy, you should evaluate the wisdom of this recommendation with each particular couple (see Chapter 9).

The reader may notice that, in this discussion of clinical management, the outside partner is nowhere to be seen. Humphrey (1987) notes that in his surveys, the numbers of therapists who reported bringing outside partners into sessions was "infinitesimal." Westfall (1989), on the other hand, suggests that the therapist might invite the outside partner into couple therapy to break a deadlock in treatment; she adds that the mere suggestion of doing so may serve the same function. Moultrop (1990) discusses including the outside partner in treatment under certain conditions, for example, in a couple session with the involved partner when that partner wishes to terminate the EMI or when the outside partner requests inclusion. My own feeling is that the complications and disadvantages of inclusion generally outweigh its potential advantages; whether in evaluation or treatment of the couple, inclusion of the outside partner will probably create many more problems than it resolves. If the outside partner were to contact the therapist, a referral to another practitioner is probably the most helpful response.

EMIs are common and powerful in their effects on the primary couple relationship. While in some cases, they may contribute to the revitalization of a troubled or stagnant relationship, in most others their effects are negative and long-lasting. As Humphrey (1987) concludes,

an [EMI] strikes at the very existence of the continuation of the marriage, and even for those that survive, clinical evidence suggests that recovery for the marital pair must be anticipated to take months or years before trust, comfort, and stability have fully returned. Some clients report they never completely recover from the aftereffects of the [EMI]. These marriages may appear stable, but much of the joy and happiness in them is permanently lost. Sometimes the [EMI], seemingly forgotten, emerges as a contributor to marital friction or divorce years later. (p. 162)

Recommended Reading for Therapists

Humphrey, F. (1987). Treating extramarital relationships in sex and couples therapy. In G. Weeks, & L. Hof (Eds.), *Integrating sex and marital therapy: A clinical guide.* New York: Brunner/Mazel.

Moultrop, D. (1990). *Husbands, wives, and lovers: The emotional system of the extramarital affair.* New York: Guilford.

Pittman, F. (1989). *Private lies: Infidelity and the betrayal of intimacy.* New York: Norton.

Westfall, A. (1989). Extramarital sex: The treatment of the couple. In G. Weeks (Ed.), *Treating couples: The intersystem model of the Marriage Council of Philadelphia.* New York: Brunner/Mazel.

~ 20 ~

Serious Illness

ILLNESS AND INJURY constitute one of several "hidden areas" in clinical evaluation, especially in couple and family evaluation.* It's not
that therapists are unaware that illness exists or that they don't appreciate the fact that it can seriously affect a couple's relationship. It's
that it simply doesn't occur to most to bring this understanding into
the enterprise of evaluation in a serious and rigorous way. Because of
the far-reaching effects of acute and chronic illness on the individuals
who experience them and on those individuals' primary relationships,
therapists need to inquire about illness with every couple they evaluate. In this sense, illness is like domestic violence, child abuse, sub-

This chapter was prepared with Susan McDaniel, Ph.D., Associate Professor of
Psychiatry and Family Medicine, University of Rochester School of Medicine
and Dentistry, Rochester, NY.
*In the discussion that follows, the term "illness" refers to both illness and
  serious injury.

stance abuse, and sexual dysfunction. These difficulties are so common, so relevant to emotional and interactional patterns in couple's relationships, and so likely to be either concealed or overlooked, that the therapist must be aware of and inquire directly about them.

The Impact of Illness In Couple Relationships

For therapists who are evaluating couples, the importance of this issue lies in the power of illness and loss, in Susan McDaniel's words, to "drive the emotional and family dynamics" of the system. This is comparable to the effects of death on a relational system, since the issue of loss is paramount in serious illness, whether in the ultimate sense of death or in less extreme (but no less stressful) losses. These involve the loss of good health and, in different cases, might include losses associated with functioning, work, recreation, physical attractiveness, the sense of physical integrity, and, ultimately, hope.

The discovery of a serious illness can affect relational systems like "an emotional shock wave," in much the same way that death affects families (Bowen, 1978). This is true for couples and whole families. It is common to find what appear to be unrelated symptomatic expressions in a relational system that has recently experienced stresses and losses associated with illness and death. These might include: the development of psychological or somatic symptoms in the patient's partner, increased conflict between family members, accidents involving other family members, or acting out by adolescents and younger children. These developments may not be consciously associated with the illness or death by family members, unlike cases in which a partner might be well aware that he is drinking more because of stresses associated with his wife's illness.

When feelings of terror, shock, anger, and chronic anxiety are not expressed and cannot be discussed by the couple, the potential for these disturbing and disruptive emotions to be expressed in other ways, such as emotional withdrawal, psychiatric symptomatology, and escalating conflict, increases dramatically. Partners cannot "detour" around issues of life and death without seriously distorting the emotional life of the relationship.

The sudden onset of acute and chronic illness constitute significant stresses on couples. These stresses disrupt established patterns in the relationship, transform the balance of entitlements and obligations (and thus the terms of trustworthiness), and require active coping by both partners. Recalling the ABCX Model presented in Chapter 2, the therapist can assess the resources the partners mobilize in their efforts to cope and how they "define" the stressor—in this case, the illness. This last factor, typically referred to as the *meaning* of the illness for each partner (Wynne, Shields, & Sirkin, 1992), is especially important. The following case illustrates the importance of both the partners' personal and family histories of illness and the idiosyncratic meanings that illness holds for them.

Tony is 56 years old; Liz is 45. They have been married for five years, a second marriage for both of them. They have no children together, although Tony has three grown children from his first marriage. They present for evaluation with a primary complaint involving erectile difficulties.

Their medical histories are highly significant. Liz was diagnosed with uterine cancer three years earlier. This led to surgery, followed by chemotherapy. Her personal and family history of illness is equally significant. Her mother was also diagnosed with uterine cancer; after a five-year struggle with the illness, she died. This was four weeks before Liz's own cancer was diagnosed.

Tony was diagnosed with prostate cancer within a few weeks of Liz's surgery. The cancer was confined to the prostate and treated with excision and radiation. His personal and family history of illness is also significant. Tony describes himself as a "sickly" child who "did not eat." He describes his mother as "always sick," although there is no evidence of diagnosed medical conditions. He sees his mother as having been bitter and discontented in life and constantly hypochondriacal. Tony's first wife developed lupus eight years after they were married. Although deeply discontented, he stayed in the marriage for another 15 years.

These histories combine with both partners' different personality styles to shape the meanings of illness for them. Liz is terrified by her illness and the example of her mother's death—an easily understandable reaction. She feels that "time is running out," and this urgency and dread colors and intensifies any other problems and discontents in her life. Tony is just the opposite. Perhaps as a reaction to his mother's misery and preoccupation with her health throughout her life, he maintains a cheery, optimistic denial around his own cancer. He sees it as "an inconvenience; I had a plumbing problem. They fixed it." Unfortunately, this buoyant attitude leads him to neglect his own follow-up care. Unless Liz badgers him, he is "too busy" for regular check-ups and ignores medical advice about diet and exercise. This is deeply upsetting to Liz who absorbs full responsibility for worrying about and dealing with both of their illnesses. This further impairs

her own health—she has many somatic symptoms of stress—and con-
tributes to intense conflict between them over these differing coping
styles.

Finally, these issues are deeply connected to the presenting prob-
lem of Tony's erectile disorder. The problem began almost exactly at
the time of the diagnosis of Liz's cancer. Tony had also experienced
erectile difficulties with his first wife some years after her illness was
diagnosed. One can speculate about whether the erectile problem is
simply a response to the massive stress imposed by multiple illnesses
(and exacerbated by the partners' very different responses to them), a
reaction to changes in their patterns of love-making following Liz's
surgery, a symptomatic way of saying "No" to another seriously ill
partner after 22 years of unhappy marriage caring for his first wife, or
a reactivation of negative feelings toward his bitter and "always sick"
mother. The point is, however, that whether one or more of these
hunches are accurate, no therapist can understand the problems this
couple present without understanding the illnesses they are experi-
encing, their personal and family histories of illness, and the mean-
ings the illnesses hold for them.

This is the most important point for therapists who routinely evaluate couples—that the couple's experience of serious illness may contribute significantly to the difficulties they present on evaluation.
Stresses and losses associated with illness can also affect the partners
psychologically, contributing to depression and/or anxiety and, in
some cases (for example, those involving serious injury or extensive
surgery), posttraumatic stress disorder.

Assessment

You should inquire about illness in *all couple evaluations*. For cases in
which illness is not part of the presenting problem, the question can
be put simply: "Does either of you have an acute or chronic illness or
has either of you suffered a serious injury?" This can be asked when
you are gathering identifying data and inquiring about other facts of
life, such as work, living arrangements, children, and financial status.
For cases in which illness is a significant factor in the couple's request
for treatment, this inquiry might take place as part of the exploration
of the presenting problem.

Whenever illness is identified in the initial inquiry, you should take
the time to gather information in several areas. First, solicit what

McDaniel refers to as the "illness story." This involves the individual's description of the course of the illness up to that point, including when it began or was first diagnosed. Ask how it has affected the person physically and psychologically, as well as how it affects his or her life functioning. What has his or her *experience* of the illness—and of the health care delivery system—been? What treatments (such as chemotherapy, radiation, surgery, or physical therapy) has he or she undergone? Does he or she take any medication? Are there any side effects of either the medication or other treatments?

You should also inquire about the individual's understanding of the nature, the course and the prognosis of the illness. Again, the question can be put simply: "I'd be interested in your telling me about your understanding of this illness." Try not to intentionally, or inadvertently, pierce what may be the individual's denial in relation to the illness. You might ask the person, "Tell me what your physician has told you about the illness."

McDaniel stresses that therapists should also be willing to be honest about the extent or limits of their familiarity with the illness and should not be afraid to admit ignorance. This allows the client to be the expert and represents an effort on your part to begin a process of self-education about the particular illness. Request permission to speak with medical providers involved in the person's treatment and then contact those providers and ask for their understanding of the illness and its effects on this particular person. Ask if the provider can direct you to a general review article on the illness to bolster your understanding of it. Because of the prevalence of denial and, sometimes, secrecy when illness is present, you should also ask the *partner* about his or her understanding of the illness and its effects. It may be especially useful to conduct this inquiry in the partner's separate individual session.

Gather a family history of significant medical illness, injury, and deaths, ideally with the use of a genogram. McDaniel stresses the importance of "losses and reorganizations related to health events" in the individual's and family's history. This is especially important in shaping the *meanings* of the illness to the individual. You should also gather a family and life history in relation to illness for the *partner*. As for the individual who is ill, this history significantly affects the *meanings* of the present illness for the partner.

Ask the partners how they feel the illness has effected their relationship. Ask explicitly about the couple's resources for coping with the illness, for example, "What characteristics of each of you as individuals and of your relationship do you think have helped you cope with this illness?" You will want to consider which resources are currently being mobilized in coping (such as an active effort to learn more about the illness, or spiritual beliefs) and which appear to be untapped.

Treatment

When couple therapy is recommended, consider the following guidelines. If the person who is ill has an extensive history of medical treatment and no history of psychotherapy, you should spend some time initially clarifying the differences between medical treatment and psychotherapy or couple therapy. You should, above all, not promise that therapy will *cure* the illness.

When the referral for couple therapy involves a serious illness, your goals will include:

- supporting the couple's efforts at coping with the illness
- helping to "put the illness in its place" (Gonzales, Steinglass, & Reiss, 1989)
- normalizing negative feelings
- encouraging communication between the partners about their fears, doubts and anger in relation to the illness
- supporting the relationship between the couple and the physician or other medical providers

By emphasizing a framework of active coping, you support the empowerment of the partners who are adopting an active, rather than a victim, stance in relation to the illness. This can also serve to reduce blaming between the partners since the emphasis is placed on the external challenges they mutually face. Apropos of this, McDaniel recommends that the therapist work to "externalize the symptom," a technique discussed in other treatment contexts by White and Epston (1990). This helps counteract a tendency for the illness to dominate the person's sense of identity. The individual may come to experience him- or herself first and foremost as "a cancer patient" or "a paraplegic." Externalizing the illness helps the individual reclaim a sense of identity which emphasizes the *person* rather than the illness.

"Putting the illness in its place" represents the relational equivalent of this process. One common response pattern when couples experience a serious illness is for the illness to become the major consideration in virtually all areas of the relationship. Decisions are made with the illness as the central or only consideration and other priorities and agendas are forgotten or overlooked. This may be highly adaptive in the acute phase of coping but it becomes maladaptive over the longer haul. You can help the couple *balance* the claims, or requirements, of the illness with other legitimate and important claims in the relationship, such as the partner's needs for "time off" and replenishment, the ill person's need to have an identity and a way to participate in the relationship as more than an invalid, and the children's and other family members' needs. This enhances shared coping as well as a more positive sense of self in the person who is ill. The therapist's efforts to help the partners talk about their feelings in relation to the illness minimizes the likelihood that these feelings would remain unexpressed and taboo in the relationship and find symptomatic expression in distancing and withdrawal, increased conflict, and either somatic or psychological symptomatology.

Try to actively support the partners' relationship with their physician or medical treatment team. This is vitally important for the couple's process of coping with the illness. If there are difficulties in this relationship, you may be able to facilitate their resolution. Maintain regular communication with medical providers. You may want to arrange a meeting that includes the couple, the physician, and yourself to discuss areas of confusion or conflict.

Finally, remember that if the referral for evaluation is related to one partner's illness, treatment should focus on the illness, not on "systemic" interpretations which can be interpreted as blaming the partner. There may well be problematic interactional patterns that can be identified. However, when couples are dealing with a serious illness in one partner, the *factual reality* of this stress should remain a central feature of your formulation and interventions.

Recommended Reading for Therapists

Gonzales, S., Steinglass, P., & Reiss, D. (1989). Putting the illness in its place: Discussion groups for families with chronic medical illnesses. *Family Process, 28,* 69–87.

McDaniel, S., & Campbell, T. (1986) Physicians and family therapists: The risks of collaboration. *Family Systems Medicine, 4,* 4–8.

McDaniel, S., Hepworth, J., & Doherty, W. (1992). *Medical family therapy: Psychosocial treatment for families with health problems.* New York: Basic.

Schover, L. (1989). Sexual problems in chronic illness. In S. Leiblum & R. Rosen (Eds.), *Principles and practice of sex therapy: Update for the 1990s.* New York: Guilford.

Seaburn, D., Lorenz, A., & Kaplan, D. (in press). The transgenerational development of chronic illness meanings. *Family Systems Medicine.*

Wynne, L., Shields, C., & Sirkin, M. (1992). Illness, family theory and family therapy. *Family Process, 31,* 3–18.

Recommended Reading for Clients

Strong, M. (1988). *Mainstay: For the well spouse of the chronically ill.* New York: Penguin.

[This book also contains an extensive list of other readings that might be helpful to partners of the chronically ill.]

REFERENCES

Abrams, W. (1977). Intimacy and differentiation: Developmental stages in the early years of marriage. *Dissertation Abstracts International, 38,* 1881A. (University microfilms No. 77-21, 628)

Abramson, P., & Mosher, D. (1975). Development of a measure of negative attitudes toward masturbation. *Journal of Consulting and Clinical Psychology, 43,* 485–490.

Ahrons, C., & Rodgers, R. (1987). *Divorced families: A multidisciplinary developmental view.* New York: Norton.

Ainsworth, M., Blehar, M., Waters, E., & Wall, S. (1978). *Patterns of attachment: Assessed in the strange situation and at home.* Hillsdale, NJ: Lawrence Erlbaum.

Albee, E. (1962). *Who's afraid of Virginia Woolf?* New York: Atheneum.

Althof, S., & Kingsberg, S. (1992). Books helpful to patients with sexual and marital problems: A bibliography. *Journal of Sex and Marital Therapy, 18,* 70–79.

American Psychiatric Association. (1987). *Diagnostic and statistical manual of mental disorders* (3rd ed.-rev.). Washington, DC: Author.

Anderson, C., & Holder, D. (1988, October). *Marriage at mid-life.* Workshop

355

presented at the 46th Annual Conference of the American Association for Marriage and Family Therapy, New Orleans, LA.

Avis, J. (1992). Where are all the family therapists? Abuse and violence within families and family therapy's response. *Journal of Marital and Family Therapy, 18*, 225-232.

Bach, G., & Wyden, P. (1968). *The intimate enemy: How to fight fair in love and marriage.* New York: William Morrow.

Bader, E., & Pearson, P. (1988). *In quest of the mythical mate: A developmental approach to diagnosis and treatment in couples therapy.* New York: Brunner/Mazel.

Baird, M., & Doherty, W. (1986). Family resources in coping with serious illness. In M. Karpel (Ed.), *Family resources: The hidden partner in family therapy.* New York: Guilford.

Baldessarini, R. J. (1988). Update on recent advances in antidepressant pharmacology and pharmacotherapy. In F. Flach (Ed.), *Psychobiology and psychopharmacology* (pp. 90-108). New York: Norton.

Barlow, D., & Cerny, J. (1988). *Psychological treatment of panic.* New York: Guilford.

Baucom, D., & Epstein, N. (1990). *Cognitive-behavioral marital therapy.* New York: Brunner/Mazel.

Beach, S., Arias, I., & O'Leary, K. (1988, August). *Life events, marital discord, and depressive symptomatology: Longitudinal relationships.* Paper presented at the 96th annual meeting of the American Psychological Association, Atlanta, GA.

Beach, S., Jouriles, E., & O'Leary, K. (1985). Extramarital sex: Impact on depression and commitment in couples seeking marital therapy. *Journal of Sex and Marital Therapy, 11*, 99-108.

Beach, S., Sandeen, E., & O'Leary, K. (1990). *Depression in marriage: A Model for etiology and treatment.* New York: Guilford.

Beavers, W. R. (1985). *Successful marriage: A family systems approach to couples therapy.* New York: Norton.

Bepko, C., & Krestan, J. (1985). *The responsibility trap: A blueprint for treating the alcoholic family.* New York: Free Press.

Berenson, D. (1976). Alcohol and the family system. In P. Guerin (Ed.), *Family therapy: Theory and practice.* New York: Gardner.

Berheide, C. (1984). Women's work in the home: Seems like old times. *Marriage and Family Review, 7*, 37-50.

Berman, E. (1982). The individual interview as a treatment technique in conjoint therapy. *American Journal of Family Therapy, 10*, 27-37.

Biglin, A., Rothlind, J., Hops, H., & Sherman, L. (1989). Impact of distressed and aggressive behavior. *Journal of Abnormal Psychology, 98*, 218-228.

Birchnell, J., & Kennard, J. (1983). Does marital maladjustment lead to mental illness? *Social Psychiatry, 18*, 79-88.

Blanck, C., & Blanck, R. (1968). *Marriage and personal development.* New York: Columbia University Press.

Bograd, M. (1984). Family systems approaches to wife battering: A feminist critique. *American Journal of Orthopsychiatry, 54*, 558-568.

Bograd, M. (1986). Holding the line: Confronting the abusive partner. *Family Therapy Networker, 10*, 44-47.

Bograd, M. (1992). Values in conflict: Challenges to family therapists' thinking. *Journal of Marital and Family Therapy, 18*, 245-256.

Bongar, B. (1991). *The suicidal patient: Clinical and legal standards of care.* Washington: American Psychological Association.

Bongar, B. (1992). *The assessment, management, and treatment of suicide: Guidelines for practice.* Oxford: Oxford University Press.

Boszormenyi-Nagy, I. (1965). A theory of relationships: Experience and transaction. In I. Boszormenyi-Nagy & J. Framo (Eds.), *Intensive family therapy.* New York: Harper & Row.

Boszormenyi-Nagy, I. (1979). Therapeutic leverages in mobilizing trust. Report 2 UNIT IV: *The American family.* Philadelphia: The Continuing Education Service of Smith, Kline & French laboratores. (Reprinted in R. Green & J. Framo [Eds.], *Family therapy: Major contributions* [pp. 393–416]. New York: International Universities Press, 1981)

Boszormenyi-Nagy, I. (1987). *Foundations of contextual therapy: Collected papers of Ivan Boszormenyi-Nagy.* New York: Brunner/Mazel.

Boszormenyi-Nagy, I., & Krasner, B. (1986). *Between give and take: A clinical guide to contextual therapy.* New York: Brunner/Mazel.

Boszormenyi-Nagy, I., & Spark, G. (1973). *Invisible loyalties: Reciprocity in intergenerational family therapy.* New York: Harper & Row.

Boszormenyi-Nagy, I., & Ulrich, D. (1981). Contextual family therapy. In A. Gurman & D. Kniskren (Eds.), *Handbook of family therapy.* New York: Brunner/Mazel.

Bowen, M. (1978). *Family therapy in clinical practice.* New York: Jason Aronson.

Bowlby, J. (1969). *Attachment and loss: Vol. 1.* New York: Basic.

Bowlby, J. (1973). *Attachment and loss: Vol. 2.* New York: Basic.

Bowlby, J. (1980). *Attachment and loss: Vol. 3.* New York: Basic.

Bowlby, J. (1988). *A secure base: Parent-child attachment and healthy human development.* New York: Basic.

Brown, G., Birley, J., & Wing, J. (1972). Influence of family life on the course of schizophrenic disorders: A replication. *British Journal of Psychiatry, 121,* 241–258.

Brown, G., & Harris, T. (Eds.). (1978). *Social origins of depression: A study of psychiatric disorder in women.* New York: Free Press.

Brown, G., & Rutter, M. (1966). The measurement of family activities and relationships: A methodological study. *Human Relations, 19,* 241–263.

Browne, A. (1987). *When battered women kill.* New York: Free Press.

Calahan, D. (1982). Alcohol use in American life. In E. Gomberg, H. White, & J. Carpenter (Eds.), *Alcohol, science and society revisited.* Ann Arbor: University of Michigan Press.

Campbell, S. (1980). *The couple's journey: Intimacy as a path to wholeness.* San Luis Obispo, CA: Impact.

Carter, E., & McGoldrick, M. (1980). *The family life cycle: A framework for family therapy.* New York: Gardner Press.

Carter, E., & McGoldrick, M. (Eds.). (1989a). *The changing family life cycle: A framework for family therapy* (2nd ed.). Needham Heights, MA: Allyn & Bacon.

Carter, E., & McGoldrick, M. (1989b). Overview—The changing family life cycle: A framework for family therapy. In E. Carter & M. McGoldrick (Eds.), *The changing family life cycle: A framework for family therapy* (2nd ed.). Needham Heights, MA: Allyn & Bacon.

Cashdan, S. (1988). *Object relations therapy: Using the relationship.* New York: Norton.

Census: Money Key to Stability. (1993, January 15). *Daily Hampshire Gazette*, p. 5.

Chasin, R., Roth, S., & Bograd, M. (1989). Action methods in systemic therapy: Dramatizing ideal futures and reformed pasts with couples. *Family Process, 28*, 121–136.

Clark, W., & Midanik, L. (1982). Alcohol use and alcohol problems among U.S. adults. In National Institute on Alcohol Abuse and Alcoholism, *Alcoholic consumption and related problems* (Alcohol and Health Monograph No. 1). Rockville, MD: Author.

Cook, D., & Frantz-Cook, A. (1984). A systemic treatment approach to wife battering. *Journal of Marriage and Family Therapy, 10*, 83–93.

Cousins, N. (1979). *Anatomy of an illness as perceived by the patient: Reflections on healing and regeneration*. New York: Norton.

Coyne, J. (1986). Confronting the conventional wisdom. *Family Therapy Networker, 10*, 67–68.

Coyne, J. (1987). Depression, biology, marriage and marital therapy. *Journal of Marital and Family Therapy, 13*, 393–408.

Coyne, J., Kahn, J., & Gotlib, I. (1987). Depression. In T. Jacobs (Ed.), *Family interaction and psychotherapy*. New York: Plenum.

Cytryn, L., McKnew, D., Bartko, J., Lamour, M., & Hamovit, J. (1982). Offspring of patients with affective disorders II. *Journal of Consulting and Clinical Psychology, 55*, 347–352.

DeCasper, A., & Fifer, W. (1980). Of human bonding: Newborns prefer their mothers' voices. *Science, 208*, 1174–1176.

Decina, P., Kestenbaum, C., Farber, S., Kron, L., Gargan, M., Sackeim, H., & Fieve, R. (1980). Clinical and psychological assessment of children of bipolar probands. *American Journal of Psychiatry, 140*, 548–553.

Derogatis, L. (1975). *Derogatis sexual functioning inventory*. Baltimore. Clinical Psychometrics Research.

Derogatis, L. (1978). *Derogatis sexual functioning inventory*. Baltimore. Clinical Psychometric Research.

Derogatis, L., & Melisaratos, N. (1979). The DSFI: A multidimensional measure of sexual functioning. *Journal of Sex and Marital Therapy, 2*, 85–105.

De Shazer, S. (1985). *Keys to solution in brief therapy*. New York: Norton.

De Shazer, S. (1988). *Clues: Investigating solutions in brief therapy*. New York: Norton.

Diamond, D., & Doane, J. (1990). *The transgenerational transmission of patterns of attachment and affective style*. Paper presented at the 98th Annual Convention of the American Psychological Association, Boston, MA.

Dicks, H. (1967). *Marital tensions: Clinical studies towards a psychological theory of interaction*. London: Routledge & Kegan Paul.

Doane, J., Hill, W., & Diamond, D. (1991). A developmental view of therapeutic bonding in the family: Treatment of the disconnected family. *Family Process, 30*, 155–175.

Dobash, R., & Dobash, R. (1979). *Violence against wives: A case against the patriarchy*. New York: Free Press.

Dobash, R., & Dobash, R. (1988). Research as social action: The struggle for battered women. In K. Yllo & M. Bograd (Eds.), *Feminist perspectives on wife abuse*. Newbury Park, CA: Sage.

Doherty, W., & Baird, M. (1983). *Family therapy and family medicine: Toward the primary care of families*. New York: Guilford.

Dunne, H. (1991). *One question that can save your marriage.* New York: Putnam/Perigee.

Dutton, D. (1988). *The domestic assault of women: Psychological and criminal justice perspectives.* Toronto: Allyn & Bacon.

Edelson, J., & Grusznski, R. (1989). Treating men who batter: Four years of outcome data from the domestic abuse project. *Journal of Social Service Research, 12,* 3–22.

Elkin, I., Shea, M., Watkins, J., Imber, S., Sotsky, S., Collins, J., Glass, D., Pilkonis, P., Leber, W., Docherty, J., Fiester, S., & Parloff, M. (1989). National Institute of Mental Health Treatment of Depression Collaborative Research Program: General effectiveness of treatments. *Archives of General Psychiatry, 46,* 971–982.

Erikson, E. (1959). *Identity and the life cycle.* New York: International Universities Press.

Erickson, M. (1960). The utilization of patient behavior in the hypnotherapy of obesity: Three case reports. *American Journal of Clinical Hypnotherapy, 3,* 112–116.

Erickson, M. (1965). The use of symptoms as an integral part of hypnotherapy. *American Journal of Clinical Hypnotherapy, 8,* 57–65.

Fairbairn, W. (1952). *Psychoanalytic studies of the personality.* London: Tavistock.

Fisher, L., Anderson, A., & Jones, J. (1981). Types of paradoxical intervention and indications/contraindications for use in clinical practice. *Family Process, 20,* 25–35.

Fisher, W. (1988). The sexual opinion survey. In C. Davis, W. Yarber, & S. Davis (Eds.), *Sexually-related measures: A compendium.* Lake Mills, IA: Graphic.

Fisher, W., Byrne, D., White, L., & Kelley, K. (1988). Erotophobia-erotophilia as a dimension of personality. *Journal of Sex Research, 25,* 123–151.

Florin, I., Nostadt, A., Reck, C., Franzen, U., & Jenkins, M. (1992). Expressed emotion in depressed patients and their partners. *Family Process, 31,* 163–172.

Foley, S., Rounsaville, B., Weissman, M., Sholomshas, D., & Chevron, E. (1987, May). *Individual vs. conjoint interpersonal psychotherapy for depressed patients with marital disputes.* Paper presented at the annual meeting of the American Psychiatric Association, Chicago, IL.

Fowers, B., & Olson, D. (1986). Predicting marital success with PREPARE: A predictive validity study. *Journal of Marital and Family Therapy, 12,* 403–413.

Fowers, B., & Olson, D. (1989). ENRICH marital inventory: A discriminant validity study. *Journal of Marital and Family Therapy, 15,* 65–79.

Fowers, B., & Olson, D. (1992). Four types of premarital couples: An empirical typology based on PREPARE. *Journal of Family Psychology, 6,* 10–12.

Framo, J. (1981). The integration of marital therapy with sessions with family of origin. In A. Gurman & D. Kniskren (Eds.), *Handbook of family therapy.* New York: Brunner/Mazel.

Frank, E., Anderson, C., & Rubinstein, D. (1978). Frequency of sexual dysfunction in 'normal' couples. *New England Journal of Medicine, 299,* 111–115.

Friedman, A. (1975). Interaction of drug therapy with marital therapy in depressive patients. *Archives of General Psychiatry, 32,* 619–537.

Ganley, A. (1981). Counseling programs for men who batter: Elements of effective programs. *Response, 4*, 3-4.

Gans, M. (1976). Separation-individuation derivatives and closeness in adult love relationships (Doctoral dissertation, California School of Professional Psychology, 1975). *Dissertation Abstracts International, 36*, 3600B.

Gelinas, D. (1983). The Persisting negative effects of incest. *Psychiatry, 46*, 312-332.

Gelles, R., & Cornell, C. (1985). *Intimate violence in families*. Beverly Hills, CA: Sage.

Goldberg, J. (1992) What's sex got to do with it? *Family Therapy News, 23*, 1-12.

Goldner, V. (1985). Feminism and famiy therapy. *Family Process, 24*, 31-47.

Goldner, V. (1989). Generation and gender: Normative and covert hierarchies. In M. McGoldrick, C. M. Anderson, & F. Walsh (Eds.), *Women in families: A framework for family therapy* (pp. 42-60). New York: Norton.

Goldner, V., Penn, P., Sheinberg, M., & Walker, G. (1990). Love and violence: Gender paradoxes in volatile attachments. *Family Process, 29*, 343-364.

Goldner, V., & Rosenheck, S. (1990, April). *Systemic sex therapy with difficult couples*. Workshop at the Ackerman Institute, New York, NY.

Gonzales, S., Steinglass, P., & Reiss, D. (1989). Putting the illness in its place: Discussion groups for families with chronic medical illnesses. *Family Process, 28*, 69-87.

Goodrich, T., Rampage, C., Ellman, B., & Halstead, K. (1988). *Feminist family therapy: A casebook*. New York: Norton.

Green, A. (1980). *Child maltreatment*. New York: Aronson.

Guerin, P., Fay, F., Burden, S., & Kautto, J. (1987). *The evaluation and treatment of marital conflict: A four-stage approach*. New York: Basic.

Haffey, M. (1986). *Couple development: An exploratory study of the developmental process in marital relationships*. Unpublished doctoral dissertation, Boston University School of Education.

Hafner, R., Badenoch, A., Fisher, J., & Swift, H. (1983). Spouse-aided versus individual therapy in persisting psychiatric disorders: A systemic comparison. *Family Process, 22*, 385-399.

Haley, J. (1963). *Strategies of psychotherapy*. New York: Grune & Stratton.

Haley, J. (1976). *Problem-solving therapy: New strategies for effective family therapy*. New York: Harper & Row.

Haley, J. (1984). Marriage or family therapy? *American Journal of Family Therapy, 12*, 3-14.

Hare-Mustin, R. (1978). A feminist approach to family therapy. *Family Process, 17*, 181-194.

Harlow, H., & Harlow, M. (1971). Psychopathology in monkeys. In H. Kimmel (Ed.), *Experimental Psychopathology*. New York: Academic Press.

Hazan, C., & Shaver, P. (1987). Romantic love conceptualised as an attachment process. *Journal of Personality and Social Psychology, 52*, 511-524.

Heiman, J., & LoPiccolo, J. (1983). Clinical outcome of sex therapy: Effects of daily v. weekly treatment. *Archives of General Psychiatry, 40*, 443-449.

Hendrix, H. (1988). *Getting the love you want: A guide for couples*. New York: Harper & Row.

Henry, J. (1965). *Pathways to madness*. New York: Random House.

Hicks, S., & Anderson, C. M. (1989). Women on their own. In M. McGoldrick,

C. N. Anderson, & F. Walsh (Eds.), *Women in families: A framework for family therapy* (pp. 308–334). New York: Norton.

Hill, R. (1958). Generic features of families under stress. *Social casework, 49,* 139–150.

Hochschild, A. (1989). *The second shift.* New York: Avon.

Hof, L., & Treat, S. (1989). Marital assessment: Providing a framework for dyadic therapy. In G. Weeks (Ed.), *Treating couples: The intersystem model of the marriage council of Philadelphia.* New York: Brunner/Mazel.

Hoffman, L. (1980). The family life cycle and discontinuous change. In E. Carter & M. McGoldrick (Eds.), *The family life cycle: A framework for family therapy.* New York: Gardner Press.

Hoffman, L. (1981). *Foundations of family therapy: A conceptual framework for systems change.* New York: Basic.

Hollander-Goldfein, B. (1989). Basic principles: Structural elements of the Intersystem approach. In G. Weeks (Ed.), *Treating couples: The intersystem model of the marriage council of Philadelphia.* New York: Brunner/Mazel.

Hooley, J. (1986). Expressed emotion and depression: Interactions between patients and high versus low EE spouses. *Journal of Abnormal Psychology, 95,* 237–246.

Hooley, J., Orley, J., & Teasdale, J. (1986). Levels of expressed emotion and relapse in depressive patients. *British Journal of Psychiatry, 148,* 642–647.

Hooley, J., & Teasdale, J. (1989). Predictors of relapse in unipolar depressives: Expressed emotion, marital distress, and perceived criticism. *Journal of Abnormal Psychology, 98,* 229–235.

Humphrey, F. (1985, October). *Extramarital affairs and their treatment by AAMFT therapists.* Paper presented at American Association of Marriage and Family Therapy, New York.

Humphrey, F. (1987). Treating extramarital relationships in sex and couples therapy. In G. Weeks & L. Hof (Eds.), *Integrating sex and marital therapy: A clinical guide.* New York: Brunner/Mazel.

Humphrey, F., & Strong, F. (1976). *Treatment of extramarital sexual relationships as reported by clinical members of AAMFC.* Paper presented at Northeastern American Association of Marriage and Family Counselors, Hartford, CT, May 22, 1976.

Ifeld, F. (1976). Methodological issues in relating psychiatric symptoms to social stressors. *Psychological Reports, 39,* 1251–1258.

Imber-Black, E. (1993). *Secrets in families and family therapy.* New York: Norton.

Izard, C. (Ed.). (1982). *Measuring emotions in infants and children.* Cambridge: Cambridge University Press.

Jacobson, N. (1983). Beyond empiricism: The politics of marital therapy. *American Journal of Family Therapy, 11,* 11–24.

Jacobson, N. (1993, October). *Domestic violence: What are the marriages like?* Presentation at the 51st Annual Conference of the American Association for Marriage and Family Therapy, Anaheim, CA.

Jacobson, N., & Gurman, A. (1986). *Clinical handbook of marital therapy.* New York: Guilford.

Jacobson, N., Holtzwoth-Munroe, A., & Schmaling, K. (1989). Marital therapy and spouse involvement in the treatment of depression, agoraphobia, and alcoholism. *Journal of Consulting and Clinical Psychology, 57,* 5–10.

Jacobson, N., & Margolin, G. (1979). *Marital therapy*. New York: Brunner/ Mazel.

Jaffe, P., Wilson, S., & Wolfe, D. (1987). Children of battered women. *Ontario Medical Review, 54*, 383–386.

Jaffe, P., Wolfe, D., & Wilson, S. (1990). *Children of battered women*. Newbury Park, CA: Sage.

Janus, S., & Janus, C. (1993). *The Janus report on sexual behavior*. New York: John Wiley.

Jellinek, E. (1960). *The disease concept of alcoholism*. New Haven, CT: College & University Press.

Kalmuss, D. (1984). The intergenerational transmission of marital aggression. *Journal of Marriage and the Family, 46*, 11–19.

Kantor, D. (1980). Critical identity image: A concept linking individual, couple, and family development. In J. Pearce & L. Friedman (Eds.), *Family therapy: Combining psychodynamic and family systems approaches.* New York: Grune & Stratton.

Kaplan, H. (1974). *The new sex therapy: Active treatment of sexual dysfunctions*. New York: Brunner/Mazel.

Kaplan, H. (1979). *Disorders of sexual desire and other new concepts and techniques in sex therapy*. New York: Brunner/Mazel.

Karpel, M. (1976). Individuation: From fusion to dialogue. *Family Process, 5*, 65–82.

Karpel, M. (1980). Family secrets: I. Conceptual and ethical issues in the relational context. II. Ethical and practical considerations in therapeutic management. *Family Process, 19*, 295–306.

Karpel, M. (Ed.). (1986). *Family resources: The hidden partner in family therapy*. New York: Guilford.

Karpel, M. (1993, October). *Wounded hearts: Restoring trust in couples therapy*. Workshop presented at the 51st Annual Conference of the American Association for Marriage and Family Therapy, Anaheim, CA.

Karpel, M., & Strauss, E. (1983). *Family evaluation*. Needham Heights, MA: Allyn & Bacon.

Katz, A. (1978). *Intimacy: The role of awareness in young adult couples*. Unpublished doctoral dissertation, Boston University.

Kaufman, G. (1992). The mysterious disappearance of battered women in family therapists' offices: Male privilege colluding with male violence. *Journal of Marital and Family Therapy, 18*, 233–244.

Kierkegaard, S. (1938). *The journals of Soren Kierkegaard* (A. Dru, Ed. and Trans.). London: Oxford University Press.

Kinsey, A., Pomeroy, W., & Martin, C. (1948). *Sexual behavior in the human male*. Philadelphia: Saunders.

Kinsey, A., Pomeroy, W., Martin, C., & Gebhard, P. (1953). *Sexual behavior in the human female*. Philadelphia: Saunders.

Kleiman, J. (1981). Optimal and normal family functioning. *American Journal of Family Therapy, 9*, 37–44.

Krasner, B. (1986). Trustworthiness: The primal family resource. In M. Karpel (Ed.), *Family resources: The hidden partner in family therapy*. New York: Guilford.

Krestan, J., & Bepko, C. (1989). Alcohol problems and the family life cycle. In B. Carter & M. McGoldrick (Eds.), *The changing family life cycle: A framework for family therapy* (2nd ed.). Boston: Allyn & Bacon.

Krugman, S. (1986). Challenging the tradition. *Family Therapy Networker, 10,* 41–43.

L'Abate, L., & Bagarozzi, D. (1993). *Sourcebook of marriage and family evaluation.* New York: Brunner/Mazel.

Laing, R. (1969). *The politics of the family and other essays.* New York: Pantheon.

Lamb, S. (1991). Acts without agents: An analysis of linguistic avoidance in journal articles of men who batter women. *American Journal of Orthopsychiatry, 61,* 250–257.

Larson, A., & Olson, D. (1989). Predicting marital satisfaction using PRE-PARE: A replication study. *Journal of Marital and Family Therapy, 15,* 311–322.

Leiblum, S., & Rosen, R. (Eds.). (1989). *Principles and practice of sex therapy: Update for the 1990s.* New York: Guilford.

Leiblum, S., & Rosen, R. (1992). Couples therapy for erectile disorders: Observations, obstacles, and outcomes. In R. Rosen & S. Leiblum (Eds.), *Erectile disorders: Assessment and treatment.* New York: Guilford.

Leighton, B. (1989). *Spousal abuse in metropolitan Toronto: Research report on the response of the criminal justice system* (Report No. 1989-02). Ottowa: Solicitor General of Canada.

Lerner, H. (1985). *The dance of anger: A women's guide to changing the patterns of intimate relationships.* New York: Harper & Row.

Lerner, H. (1989). *The dance of intimacy.* New York: Harper & Row.

Levant, R. (1982). Developmental process in marriage. *Medical Aspects of Human Sexuality, 16,* 83–95.

Levinson, D. (1978). *The seasons of a man's life.* New York: Knopf.

Lewis, J., Beavers, W., Gosset, J. & Philips, V. (Eds). (1976). *No single thread: Psychological health in family systems.* New York: Brunner/Mazel.

Lewisohn, P., Hoberman, H., & Rosenbaum, M. (1988). A prospective study of risk factors for unipolar depression. *Journal of Abnormal Psychology, 97,* 251–264.

Libow, J., Raskin, P, & Caust, B. (1982). Feminist and family systems therapy: Are they irreconcilable? *American Journal of Family Therapy, 10,* 3–12.

Lief, H. (1991, October). Integrating sexual and couples therapy. Presentation at the conference, "Treating Couples and their Families," Harvard Medical School, Department of Continuing Education, Boston, MA.

Lobitz, W. & Lobitz, G. (1978). Clinical assessment in the treatment of sexual dysfunctions. In J. LoPiccolo & L. LoPiccolo (Eds.), *Handbook of sex therapy* (pp. 85–102). New York: Plenum.

Locke, H., & Wallace, K. (1959). Short marital-adjustment and prediction tests: Their reliability and validity. *Marriage and Family Living, 21,* 251–255.

LoPiccolo, J. (1985). Guidelines for assessment and treatment of sexual deviance. Distributed by J. LoPiccolo.

LoPiccolo, J., & Daiss, S. (1988). The assessment of sexual dysfunction. In K. O'Leary (Ed.), *Assessment of marital conflict* (pp. 183–221). Hillsdale, NJ: Lawrence Erlbaum.

LoPiccolo, J., & Heiman, J. (1978). Sexual assessment and history interview. In J. LoPiccolo & L. LoPiccolo (Eds.), *Handbook of sex therapy* (pp. 103–112). New York: Plenum.

LoPiccolo, J., Heiman, J., Hogan, D., & Roberts, C. (1985). Effectiveness of single therapists versus co-therapy teams in sex therapy. *Journal of Consulting and Clinical Psychology, 53,* 287–294.

LoPiccolo, J., & LoPiccolo, L. (Eds.). (1978). *Handbook of sex therapy.* New York: Plenum.

LoPiccolo, J. & Miller, V. (1978). A program for enhancing the sexual relationship of normal couples. In J. LoPiccolo & L. LoPiccolo (Eds.), *Handbook of sex therapy* (pp. 451–458). New York: Plenum.

LoPiccolo, J., & Steger, J. (1974). The sexual interaction inventory: A new instrument for assessment of sexual dysfunction. *Archives of Sexual Behavior, 3,* 585–595.

Luepnitz, D. (1988). *The family interpreted.* New York: Basic.

MacDonald, A., Huggins, J., Young, S., & Swenson, R. (1973). Attitudes toward homosexuality: Preservation of sex morality or the double standard? *Journal of Consulting and Clinical Psychology, 40,* 161.

Madanes, C. (1981). *Strategic family therapy.* San Francisco: Jossey-Bass.

Madanes C. (1984). *Behind the one-way mirror: Advances in the practice of strategic therapy.* San Francisco: Jossey-Bass.

Main, M., & Cassidy, J. (1988). Categories of response with the parent at age six: Predicted from infant attachment classifications and stable over a one month period. *Developmental Psychology, 21,* 407–412.

Main, M., Kaplan, N., & Cassidy, J. (1985). Security in infancy, childhood, and adulthood: A move to the level of representation. In I. Bretherton & E. Waters (Eds.), *Growing points in attachments: Theory and research in child development. Monographs of the Society for Research in Child Development, 209,* 66–104.

Markman, H., Duncan, W., Storaasli, R., & Howes, P. (1987). The prediction and prevention of marital distress: A longitudinal investigation. In K. Hahweg & M. Goldstein (Eds.), *Understanding major mental disorder: The contribution family interactional research.* New York: Family Process.

Masters, W., & Johnson, V. (1970). *Human sexual inadequacy.* Boston: Little, Brown.

Masters, W., & Johnson, V. (1975). *The pleasure bond.* Boston: Little, Brown.

Matas, L, Arend, R., & Sroufe, L. (1978). Continuity of adaptation in the second year of life: The relationship between quality of attachment and later competence. *Child Development, 49,* 547–556.

Mathias, B. (1986). Lifting the shade on family violence. *Family Therapy Networker, 10,* 20–29.

McCarthy, B. (1992). Treatment of erectile dysfunction with single men. In Rosen, R. & Leiblum, S. (Eds.), *Erectile disorders: Assessment and treatment* (pp. 313–340). New York: Guilford.

McCubbin, H., Boss, P., Wilson, L., & Lester, G. (1980). Developing family invulnerability to stress: Coping patterns and strategies wives employ in managing family separations. In J. Trost (Ed.), *The family in change.* Vasters, Sweden: International Library.

McCubbin, H., Cauble, E., & Patterson, J. (1982). *Family stress, coping and social support.* Springfield, IL: Charles C. Thomas.

McCubbin, H., & Patterson, J. (1981). *Systematic assessment of family stress, resources, and coping: Tools for research, education and clinical intervention.* St. Paul, MN: Family Social Science.

McCubbin, H., & Patterson, J. (1982). Family adaptation to crisis. In H.

McCubbin, E. Cauble, & J. Patterson (Eds.), *Family stress, coping and social support*. Springfield, IL: Charles C. Thomas.

McCubbin, H., & Patterson, J. (1983a). Family transitions: Adaptation to stress. In H. McCubbin & C. Figley (Eds.), *Stress and the family* (Vol. 1). New York: Brunner/Mazel.

McCubbin, H., & Patterson, J. (1983b). The family stress process: A double ABCX model of adjustment and adaptation. In H. McCubbin, M. Sussman, & J. Patterson (Eds.), *Advances and developments in family stress theory and research*. New York: Hawthorn Press.

McDaniel, S., Hepworth, J., & Doherty, W. (1992). *Medical family therapy: Psychosocial treatment for families with health problems*. New York: Basic.

McGoldrick, M. (1989). Women through the family life cycle. In M. McGoldrick, C. M. Anderson, & F. Walsh (Eds.), *Women in families: A framework for family therapy* (pp. 200–226). New York: Norton.

McGoldrick, M., Anderson, C. M., & Walsh, F. (Eds.). (1989a). *Women in families: A framework for family therapy*. New York: Norton.

McGoldrick, M., Anderson, C. M., & Walsh, F. (1989b). Women in families and in family therapy. In M. McGoldrick, C. Anderson, & F. Walsh (Eds.), *Women in families: A framework for family therapy* (pp. 3–15). New York: Norton.

McGoldrick, M., & Gerson, R. (1985). *Genograms in family assessment*. New York: Norton.

McGoldrick, M., Pearce, J., & Giordano, J. (Eds.). (1982). *Ethnicity and family therapy*. New York: Guilford.

McGoldrick, M., & Preto, N. (1984). Ethnic intermarriage: Implications for therapy. *Family Process, 23*, 347–364.

McLean, P., & Hakstian, A. (1979). Clinical depression: Comparative efficacy of outpatient treatment. *Journal of Consulting and Clinical Psychology, 47*, 818–836.

Meeks, D., & Kelly, C. (1970). Family therapy with the families of recovering alcoholics. *Quarterly Journal of Studies on Alcohol, 31*, 399–413.

Minuchin, S. (1974). *Families and family therapy*. Cambridge, MA: Harvard University Press.

Moltz, D. (1992). Abuse and violence: The dark side of the family. An introduction. *Journal of Marital and Family Therapy, 18*, 223.

Money, J. (1986). *Lovemaps: Clinical concepts of sexual/erotic health and pathology, paraphilia, and gender transposition in childhood, adolescence, and maturity*. New York: Irvington.

Moultrop, D. (1990). *Husbands, wives, and lovers: The emotional system of the extramarital affair*. New York: Guilford.

Napier, A. (1987). Early stages in experiential marital therapy. *Contemporary Family Therapy, 9*, 23–41.

National Council on Alcoholism. (1976). Definition of alcoholism. *Annals of Internal Medicine, 85*, 764.

Nichols, W. (1988). *Marital therapy: An Integrative approach*. New York: Guilford.

O'Hanlon Hudson, P., & Hudson O'Hanlon, W. (1991). *Rewriting love stories: Brief marital therapy*. New York: Norton.

O'Hanlon, W., & Weiner-Davis, M. (1989). *In Search of Solutions: A new direction in psychotherapy*. New York: Norton.

O'Leary, K. (Ed.). (1987). *Assessment of marital discord.* Hillsdale, NJ: Lawrence Erlbaum.

O'Leary, K., & Arias, L. (1987). Marital assessment in clinical practice. In K. O'Leary (Ed.), *Assessment of marital discord.* Hillsdale, NJ: Lawrence Erlbaum.

O'Leary, K., & Beach, S. (1990). Marital therapy: A viable treatment for depression and marital discord. *American Journal of Psychiatry, 147,* 183–186.

Olson, D., Fournier, D., & Druckman, J. (1986). *PREPARE/ENRICH inventories: Counselor's manual* (rev. ed.). Minneapolis, MN: PREPARE/ENRICH, Inc.

Olson, D., Russell, C., & Sprenkle, D. (1989). *Circumplex model: Systemic assessment and treatment of families.* New York: Hawthorne.

O'Rand, A., & Henretta, J. (1982). Women at middle age: Developmental transitions. *The Annals of the American Academy of Political and Social Science, 404,* 57–64.

Pagelow, M. (1981). *Woman-battering: Victims and their experience.* Beverly Hills: Sage.

Papp, P. (1977). *Full length case studies.* New York: Gardner.

Papp, P. (1980). The Greek chorus and other techniques of paradoxical therapy. *Family Process, 19,* 45–47.

Paykel, E. (1979). Recent life events in the development of the depressive disorders. In R. Depue (Ed.), *The psychobiology of depressive disorders: Implications for the effects of stress.* New York: Academic.

Paykel, E., Myers, J., Dienelt, M., Klerman, G., Lindenthal, J., & Pepper, M. (1969). Life events and depression: A controlled study. *Archives of General Psychiatry, 21,* 753–760.

Phillips, A. (1988). *Winnicott.* Cambridge, MA: Harvard.

Pinderhughes, E. (1991, October). *Understanding race, ethnicity, and power in couples treatment.* Presentation at the conference, "Treating Couples and their Families," Harvard Medical School, Department of Continuing Education, Boston, MA.

Pittman, F. (1989). *Private lies: Infidelity and the betrayal of intimacy.* New York: Norton.

Prochoska, J. (1992). In search of how people change: Applications to addictive behaviors. *American Psychologist, 47,* 1102–1114.

Ravich, R. (1974). *Predictable pairing: The structures of human atoms.* New York: Peter H. Wyden.

Reinisch, J. (1990). *The Kinsey Institute new report on sex: What you must know to be sexually literate.* New York: St. Martin's.

Rohrbaugh, M., Tennen, H., Press, S., & White, L. (1981) Compliance, defiance, and therapeutic paradox: Guidelines for strategic use of paradoxical interventions. *American Journal of Orthopsychiatry, 51,* 454–467.

Rose, P. (1983). *Parallel lives: Five victorian marriages.* New York: Alfred A. Knopf.

Rosen, R., & Leiblum, S. (1988). A sexual scripting approach to problems of desire. In S. Leiblum & R. Rosen (Eds.), *Sexual desire disorders.* New York: Guilford.

Rosen, R., & Leiblum, S. (Eds.). (1992). *Erectile disorders: Assessment and treatment.* New York: Guilford.

Rosenbaum, A., & O'Leary, K. (1986). The Treatment of marital violence. In

N. Jacobson & A. Gurman (Eds.), *The clinical handbook of marital therapy*. New York: Guilford.

Rounsaville, B., Prusoff, B., & Weissman, M. (1980). The course of marital disputes in depressed women: A 48-month follow-up study. *Comprehensive Psychiatry, 21,* 111–118.

Rounsaville, B., Weissman, M., Prusoff, B., & Herceg-Baron, R. (1979a). Marital disputes and treatment outcome in depressed women. *Comprehensive Psychiatry, 20,* 483–490.

Rounsaville, B., Weissman, M., Prusoff, B., & Herceg-Baron, R. (1979b). Process of psychotherapy among depressed women with marital disputes. *American Journal of Orthopsychiatry, 49,* 505–510.

Royce, J. (1981). *Alcohol problems and alcoholism*. New York: Free Press.

Russell, M. (1988). Wife assault theory, research, and treatment: A literature review. *Journal of Family Violence, 3,* 193–236.

Sackett, G. (1965). Effects of rearing conditions on the behavior of the rhesus monkey. *Child Development, 36,* 855–868.

Sackett, G. (1972). Isolation rearing in monkeys: Diffuse and specific effects on late behavior. *Colloquia Internationaux du CNRS, No. 198, Models Animaux du Comportement Humain*. Paris: Editions du Centre National de la Recherche Scientifique, 61–110.

Sackett, G., Griffin, G., Pratt, C., et al. (1967). Mother-infant and adult female choice behavior in rhesus monkeys after various rearing practices. *Journal of Comprehensive Physiological Psychology, 63,* 376–381.

Sager, C. (1976). The role of sex therapy in marital therapy. *American Journal of Psychiatry, 133,* 555–558.

Sager, C. (1981). Couples therapy and marriage contracts. In A. Gurman & D. Kniskren (Eds.), *Handbook of family therapy*. New York: Brunner/Mazel.

Scharff, D. (1978). Truth and consequences in sex and marital therapy: The revelation of secrets in the therapeutic setting. *Journal of Sex and Marital Therapy, 4,* 35–49.

Scharff, D., & Scharff, J. (1991). *Object relations couple therapy*. Northvale, NJ: Jason Aronson.

Schneidman, B., & McGuire, L. (1978). Group treatment for nonorgasmic women: Two age levels. In J. LoPiccolo & L. LoPiccolo (Eds.), *Handbook of sex therapy*. New York: Plenum.

Schover, L. (1989). Sexual problems in chronic illness. In S. Leiblum & R. Rosen (Eds.), *Principles and practice of sex therapy: Update for the 1990s*. New York: Guilford.

Schover, L., Friedman, J., Weiler, S., Heiman, J., & LoPiccolo, J. (1982). Multiaxial problem-oriented system for sexual dysfunctions: An alternative to DSM-III. *Archives of General Psychiatry, 39,* 614–619.

Searles, H. (1965). *Collected papers on schizophrenia and related subjects*. New York: International Universities Press.

Searles, H. (1973). Concerning therapeutic symbiosis. *The Annual of Psychoanalysis, 1,* 247–262.

Seay, B., Alexander, B., & Harlow, H. (1964). Maternal behavior of socially deprived rhesus monkeys. *Journal of Abnormal and Social Psychology, 69,* 345–354.

Seinfeld, J. (1990). *The bad object: Handling the negative therapeutic reaction in psychotherapy*. Northvale, NJ: Aronson.

Seligman, M. (1975). *Helplessness: On depression, development, and death.* San Franciso: Freeman.

Seltzer, L. (1986). *Paradoxical strategies in psychotherapy: A comprehensive overview and guidebook.* New York: Wiley.

Selvini Palazzoli, M., Boscolo, L., Cecchin, G., & Prata, G. (1978). *Paradox sand counter-paradox: A new model in the therapy of the family in schizophrenic transaction.* New York: Aronson.

Selvini Palazzoli, M., Boscolo, L., Cecchin, G., & Prata, G. (1980). Hypothesizing—circularity—neutrality: Three guidelines for the conductor of the session. *Family Process, 19,* 3–12.

Selzer, M. (1971). The Michigan Alcoholism Screening Test: The quest for a new diagnostic instrument. *American Journal of Psychiatry, 127,* 1653–1658.

Shapiro, R. (1986). Passing the buck: Too often therapists steer clear of violent cases. *Family Therapy Networker, 10,* 64–66.

Sheinberg, M. (1988). Obsessions/counter-obsessions: A construction/reconstruction of meaning. *Family Process, 27,* 305–316.

Sinclair, D. (1985). *Understanding wife assault: A training manual for counselors and advocates.* Toronto: Ontario Government Bookstore.

Spanier, G. (1976). Measuring dyadic adjustment: New scales for assessing the quality of marriage and similar dyads. *Journal of Marriage and the Family, 38,* 15–28.

Spitz, R. (1945). Hospitalism: An inquiry into the genesis of psychiatric conditions in early childhood. *Psychoanalytic Study of the Child, 1,* 53–74.

Spitz, R. (1965). *The first year of life.* New York: International Universities Press.

Sroufe, L. (1983). Infant-caregiver attachment and patterns of adaptation in pre-school: The roots of maladaptation and competence. In M. Perlmutter (Ed.), *Minnesota Symposium in Child Psychology, 16,* 41–81.

Steinglass, P. (1979). Family therapy with alcoholics: A review. In E. Kaufman & P. Kaufman (Eds.), *Family therapy of drug and alcohol abuse.* New York: Gardner.

Steinglass, P., Bennett, L., Wolin, S., & Reiss, D. (1987). *The alcoholic family.* New York: Basic.

Stern, D. (1985). *The interpersonal world of the infant: A view from psychoanalysis and developmental psychology.* New York: Basic.

Straus, M., Gelles, R., & Steinmetz, S. (1980). *Behind closed doors: Violence in the American family.* New York: Doubleday.

Stroufe, L. (1983). Infant-caregiver attachment and patterns of adaptation in pre-school: The roots of maladaptation and competence. In M. Perlmutter (Ed.), *Minnesota Symposium in Child Psychology, 16,* 41–81. Minneapolis: University of Minnesota Press.

Stuart, R. (1980). *Helping couples change: A social learning approach to marital therapy.* New York: Guilford.

Tannen, D. (1990). *You just don't understand: Women and men in conversation.* New York: William Morrow.

Tarasoff v. Regents of University of California, 551, P.2d, 334 (1976).

Tiefer, L., & Melman, A. (1989). Comprehensive evaluation of erectile dysfunction and medical treatments. In S. Leiblum & R. Rosen (Eds.), *Principles and practice of sex therapy: Update for the 1990s.* New York: Guilford.

Tomashiro, R. (1978). Developmental stages in the conceptualization of marriage. *The Family Coordinator, 27*, 237–244.

Toufexis, A. (1987, December). Home is where the hurt is: Wife beating among the well-to-do is no longer a secret. *Time,* p. 68.

Treadway, D. (1987). The ties that bind. *Family Therapy Networker, 11*, 17–23.

Tronick, E. (1989). Emotions and emotional communication in infants. *American Psychologist, 44*, 112–119.

Valone, K., Norton, J., Goldstein, M., & Doane, J. (1983). Parental expressed emotion and affective style in an adolescent sample at risk for schizophrenia spectrum disorders. *Journal of Abnormal Psychology, 92*, 399–407.

van der Kolk, B. (1987). *Psychological trauma.* Washington, DC: American Psychiatric Press.

Vaughn, C., & Leff, J. (1976). The influence of family and social factors on the course of psychiatric illness. *British Journal of Psychiatry, 129*, 125–137.

Vaughn, C., Snyder, K., Freeman, W., Jones, S., Falloon, I., & Liberman, R. (1982). Family factors in schizophrenia relapse: A replication. *Schizophrenia Bulletin, 8*, 425–426.

Ventura, M. (1988). In the marriage zone. *Family Therapy Networker, 12*, 30–41.

Walker, L. (1979). *The battered woman.* New York: Harper & Row.

Walker, L. (1984). *The battered woman syndrome.* New York: Springer.

Walker, L. (1989). Psychology and violence against women. *American Psychologist, 44*, 695–701.

Walker, L. (1991). Post-traumatic stress disorder in women: Diagnosis and treatment of battered woman syndrome. *Psychotherapy, 28*, 21–29.

Walsh, F. (1989). Reconsidering gender in the marital quid pro quo. In M. McGoldrick, C. M. Anderson, & F. Walsh (Eds.), *Women in families: A framework for family therapy* (pp. 267–285). New York: Norton.

Walsh, F., & Scheinkman, M. (1989). (Fe)male: The hidden gender dimension in models of family therapy. In M. McGoldrick, C. M. Anderson, & F. Walsh (Eds.), *Women in families: A framework for family therapy* (pp. 16–41). New York: Norton.

Walters, M., Carter, B., Papp, P., & Silverstien, O. (1988). *The invisible web: Gender patterns in family relationships.* New York: Guilford.

Wartner, U. (1986). *Attachment in infancy and at age six, and children's self-concept: A follow-up of a German longitudinal study.* Unpublished doctoral dissertation, University of Virginia.

Watzlawick, P., Beavin, J., & Jackson, D. (1967). *Pragmatics of human communication.* New York: Norton.

Weeks, G. (Ed.). (1989). *Treating couples: The intersystem model of the Marriage Council of Philadelphia.* New York: Brunner/Mazel.

Weeks, G., & Hof, L. (1987). *Integrating sex and marital therapy.* New York: Brunner/Mazel.

Weeks, G., & Treat, S. (1992). *Couples in treatment: Techniques and approaches for effective practice.* New York: Brunner/Mazel.

Weiss, R. (1979). *Going it alone: The family and social situation of the single parent.* New York: Basic.

Weiss, R., Hops, H., & Patterson, G. (1973). A framework for conceptualizing marital conflict, a technology for altering it, some data for evaluating it. In L. Hamerlynck, L. Handy, & E. Mash (Eds.), *Behavior change: Methodology, concepts and practice.* Champlain, IL: Research Press.

Weissman, M. (1987). Advances in psychiatric epidemiology: Rates and risks for major depression. *American Journal of Public Health, 77,* 445–451.

Weissman, M. (1988, November). *Conjoint versus individual interpersonal psychotherapy for depressed patients with marital disputes.* Paper presented at the 22nd annual meeting of the Association for Advancement of Behavior Therapy, New York, NY.

Weissman, M., & Paykel, E. (1974). *The depressed woman: A study of social relationships.* Chicago: University of Chicago Press.

Weitzman, L. (1985). *The divorce revolution.* New York: Free Press.

Welch, C. (1991). Electroconvulsive therapy in the general hospital. In N. Cassem (Ed.), *Massachusetts General Hospital handbook of general hospital psychiatry* (3rd ed.). St. Louis: Mosby Year Book.

Welz, R. (1988). Live events, current social stressors, and risk of attempted suicide. In H. J. Moller, A. Schmidtke, & R. Welz (Eds.), *Current issues of suicidology.* New York: Springer-Verlag.

Westfall, A. (1989). Extramarital sex: The treatment of the couple. In G. Weeks (Ed.), *Treating couples: The intersystem model of the Marriage Council of Philadelphia.* New York: Brunner/Mazel.

Wetzel, J. (1987). *American youth: A statistical report.* Report commissioned by the William T. Grant Foundation Commission on Work, Family and Citizenship.

Whitaker, C., & Keith, D. (1981). Symbolic-experiential family therapy. In A. Gurman & D. Kniskren (Eds.), *Handbook of family therapy.* New York: Brunner/Mazel.

White, M., & Epston, D. (1990). *Narrative means to therapeutic ends.* New York: Norton.

Williams, M. (1978). Individual sex therapy. In LoPiccolo, J. & LoPiccolo, L. (Eds.), *Handbook of sex therapy* (pp. 477–484). New York: Plenum.

Wilson, R. (1986). *Don't panic: Taking control of anxiety attacks.* New York: Harper & Row.

Wincze, J. (1989). Assessment and treatment of atypical sexual behavior. In S. Leiblum & R. Rosen (Eds.), *Principles and practice of sex therapy: Update for the 1990s* (pp. 382–404). New York: Guilford.

Wincze, J., & Carey, M. (1991). *Sexual dysfunction: A Guide for assessment and treatment.* New York: Guilford.

Winnicott, D. (1958). *Collected papers: Through paediatrics to psycho-analysis.* London: Tavistock.

Winnicott, D. (1965). *The maturational processes and the facilitating environment: Studies in the theory of emotional development.* London: The Hogarth Press and the Institute of Psycho-Analysis.

Winnicott, D. (1971). *Playing and reality.* London: Tavistock.

Whybrow, P., Akiskal, H., & McKinney, W. (1984). *Mood disorder: Toward a new psychobiology.* New York: Plenum.

Wynne, L. (1984). The epigenesis of relational systems: A model for understanding family development. *Family Process, 23,* 297–318.

Wynne, L., Shields, C., & Sirkin, M. (1992). Illness, family theory and family therapy. *Family Process, 31,* 3–18.

Zilbergeld, B. (1992). *The new male sexuality.* New York: Bantam.

INDEX

371